The Biking Birder 2016 – A Green B

'An inspiration to us all! Congratulations Gary! It is good to see more Green Year-lists and Eco Bird Races taking place - Viva La Evolution'
James Walsh

'I think what you've done is absolutely splendid, with a smidgen of endearing bonkers! Kudos to you.'
Mike Blair

'I can't help but feel that this is a greater achievement than the world and ABA records being pursued at the moment because of the sheer stamina and commitment required.'
Stuart Reeves

'His enthusiasm is infectious, birding could do with a few more like him.'
Jabberwocky

'Your efforts are an inspiration to all of us Gary! More power to your pedals.'
Phil Hurrell

'This is a good yearlist let alone green yearlist. A really impressive effort.'
Paul Chapman

'Hats off to you Gary, I have enough trouble cycling up the hill to our nearest postbox half a mile away!'
Richard Prior

'Perhaps a D-Day Invasion level of planning is against the British tradition of amateurism, but personally I prefer a successful blitzkrieg to a Captain Scott disaster.'
John Dixon

'As an effort goes, comparable at least to the current global big year currently on in my opinion - the stresses, trials and tribulations as intense, although different of course and some people more suited to one type than another. And then there's looking at the ethics/higher moral ground of course …'
Dan Chaney

Best Luck. You can do it!
Ponc Feliu Latorre
(purest Green Birding European record holder)

Biking Birder 2016

The Quest for 300

by

Gary Brian Prescott

The Biking Birder

DEDICATION

To Joshua and Rebecca, my children with my love, my life and hopes.

ISBN-13:978-1979338035

ISBN-10:1979338035

Facebook – Gary Brian Prescott - https://www.facebook.com/gary.prescott.92

Facebook – Biking Birder - https://www.facebook.com/bikingbirder2015/

Twitter – gary brian prescott - https://twitter.com/bikingbirder16

email – bikingbirder2010@hotmail.com

All photographs taken throughout the year on my small bridge camera, a Canon SX50, can be found on my Flickr pages, an album for each day :

https://www.flickr.com/photos/90527016@N08/albums

Cover artwork by Samuel Perfect

Map by Sarah Jenkins - http://www.sarahjenkinsartist.net/

Incidental bird sketches by Jason John Oliver

Chapter heading artwork by Steve Cale -

http://www.smartartgalleries.com/artists/Steve-Cale

CONTENTS

Acknowledgements

To acknowledge everyone who I need to thank, since I started my Biking Birder adventures back on January 1st 2010, is an impossible task. So many hundreds of people have supported me personally, so many have donated to the charities that I have supported in that time and so many have followed my adventures, freely given advice and good wishes and offered assistance.

To start my thanks I must go back to 2004 and to an unknown teacher at Ernesford Grange School in Coventry. It was there that a teacher talked to me of his three year cycling adventure around South America. This man got me thinking and from the conversation with him the idea to cycle around the UK, visiting every RSPB and WWT nature reserve was sown.

Next my thanks goes to Marilyn Calvert, the wonderful Headteacher, now retired, of Rigby Hall Special School in Bromsgrove, Worcestershire back in 2009, who gave me permission to have a one year sabbatical from my teaching post in 2010. Without that first year who knows when I would have started and how it would have changed my life? To other staff at that wonderful school, my thanks and love goes to Kath Cooper, Helen Bastin, Danielle Walker, Louise Giles, Maggie Rafiqi and Tracy Smith. Here I can't forget the caretaker there back when together he and I created an Eco School of excellence, Gerald 'Bob Carolgees' Crumpton and his wife, Judy not forgetting Leah!

Visiting all of the RSPB reserves and the Wildfowl & Wetlands Trust centres in 2010 and again in 2015 gave me the opportunity to meet so many incredibly dedicated people and I thank them all. From 2016 there are some RSPB staff though whom I would especially like to thank. Mark Thomas and Tim Jones, Paul Fisher and everyone at Insh Marshes RSPB reserve.

To have such a famous bird observatory as North Ronaldsay in Orkney, UK become an annual place of birding pilgrimage is due to the close friendships that have grown between me and so many who work there. My thanks to the observatory warden, Alison Woodbridge and her husband Kevin. Also to Bryony Baker, Larissa Simulik, Gavin and Heather Woodbridge and Ellen Somerwill and especially to the three SpokesFolks team members, Erin Taylor, George Gay and Samuel Perfect. The friendliest of bird observatories on an island who's remoteness gives birders the ultimate challenge of finding their own rarity. Unbounded thanks to all.

A birder has a patch, a birdwatching place local to his or her home where one spends so many hours on so many days in so many years. Here one gets to know the birds present, the birds transient and the once in a lifetime birds that thrill one and provide conversation points in hides for eternity. My own patch, Upton Warren nature reserve, a Worcestershire

Wildlife Trust flagship reserve, with its briny scrapes and freshwater pools, has been my patch for many decades. I may on occasions have moved away but it is the place that I feel is my birding home. There was only one place to start each of the three Biking Birder years, Upton Warren and each time close friends were there to see me leave on January the first, maybe with the same intention as those music lovers towards Eugene Quills in Peter Sellers' Balham sketch. Yet those same friends would be there on my return at the end of the each year. So many thanks to Gert Corfield, Tim and Mary, Bill Box, Peter Evans, Andy Pitt, Dave Walker, Mike Wakeman, Mike Wheeler, Sue and Dave Wilkes, Phil Wood,Vern Wright and especially to John Belsey. Friendships formed through the mutual love of a small nature reserve, its wildlife and the work shared to maintain its habitats.

Thanks to my patient friends, who proof read the text. My brother Paul has always been there for me when needed. The site manager of Rainham Marshes RSPB reserve Howard Vaughan has been a friend since that first day when I arrived at Rainham Marsh RSPB reserve in 2010 covered in sleet and grit. Then there is 'The Oracle,' Phil Andrews, more on him later. I thank you all.

Then there are The Birding Clams. A group of birding friends who transcend companionship and fraternity and have become that rare thing in one's life, true friends. To Jason Oliver, Tony Barter, Ian Crutchley, Steve Allcott, Martyn Smith, Adam Archer and Rob Gilbert I give my thanks. The first named four were students of mine at a Secondary school in Wolverhampton, UK called Coppice High School back in the 1980s. So wonderful to see and hear of their birding exploits after so many years.

The kindness of strangers, so many over the months and years and some that have become close friends. After a night sleeping in a bird hide, something I love to do as I am surrounded by the sounds at night and the sights immediately first thing, I met a birder who invited me to his home to meet his wife and seven year old child. Inspirational family immersed in love for each other, The Craigs, Mya-Rose, Helena and Chris, my love and thanks to you. Kerry Reynolds and Dominik, met at a RSPB campaign opening rally, Stepping Up For Nature, in London in 2011, a mother and son combination, who's love for each other and for nature is all pervading, my love and thanks to you. The Forsyths; Alastair, Louise, Ellen and Mollie, who shared their home with a complete stranger, my love and thanks to you. Doug and Sue Hilton with our shared love of Sir Peter Scott, thanks so much for the most incredible diversion away from my path taken last year.

All you need is love.

Thanks to everyone who donated to one of the charities I supported last year through the pages on Just Giving : Sam V, Garth, Paul Herrieven, Nicky & Amelie, Dominik Rigby, Mike Grundman, John Pritchard, Judy, Sally W, Nick Carter, Rita L, Monica, Alan, Matthew Capper, Wino's Wendy's Wildlife World, Steve Collett, Cath Mendez, Emma Oldfield, Neal Chard, Pauline & Mark of Mad Hatters B & B, Hayle, Paul Smith, Ceinwyn, Mike, Rachel, Leslie, Ben, Linda, Jan of Castleneuk B & B in Castleside, Durham, Mary, Betty, Martin of Tophill Nature Reserve, Anne, Richard, Gareth, Ian, Jess, Chris, Daisy-May, Phil & Linda, Fiona, Ian, Steve & Jannette, Pat & Geoff, Trudy, Robert, John, Chris, Graham, David, Nick & Helga, Barbara and David from Halstead, Sue & Pete and the staff at Minsmere RSPB reserve, Barry, Geoff and Carol, Dougal, Malcolm, Dave and Paul, Terry, Tracy, Lesley, Darren and Lynn, William & Caroline, the Oompa Lumpas of Hunstanton, Mark & Helen, Zoe, Ethan, Ruth, Maya and Dana, Bob & Ros, Lyz, Janet, Stuart, Andrew, Nick, Monica, Heather & Keith, David & Peter, Shirley and Geoff, Jane & Ian & Lynne, Barbara, Diane, Tony & Monique, Rebecca, George, Charlie, Conrad, Elizabeth, Zac & Mark, Margaret, Peter and Mark, and the Gibbin family, Tracie & Wayne of Sidegate Guest House in Ipswich, Dave Lovatt, June, Les and Kevin in the cafe at Old Moor RSPB reserve, Jane and Linda, Jethro, Moira and Ron, Chris and Jayne from Clitheroe, Yvonne, Jocyln (Smugglers YH), Duncan and Tricia, Jasper, Donna, Susan, John, Clare & Eleanor, Ryan & Vicky, Henry, Jules, Moira & Ron, Jane & Lynda, Mary and Anna from Durham, The Royal Mackintosh Hotel, Dunbar, who gave the cost of my stay as a donation! Also to Jonathan who gave a donation when I showed some Waxwings I had just found to him. Also to Ivan, Viv Chadwick, Michael Davis, Mark Ballamy, Sheila Barnett, Chris Lamsdell, Dan, Lee Gregory, Stuart Griffiths, Lewis & Carol, Judie, Robert Morris, Marie, Chris Thomas, Mark, Ian Sutton, Anne Beckett, Mark L, Kirstie Ross, Richard & Lyn Ebbs, Peter Carr, Mike and Mike, P & H, Paul Lewis, Lisa Hillier, Jake, Pauline & Paul, Steve Dewsnapp, Brian Minshull, Julie, Trudy & Geoff from Bromsgrove, John Humble, Mary, David Spencer, Chris Greenwood, Vaughan Evans, Graham Wykes, Gareth Jones, Shirley Scott, Amy Lawes, Yoav Periman, Amanda, Jennie Brimmell and Kareen.

Thanks and love to my family, my brother Paul and niece Maya, my sister Donna and her husband Charlie and nieces Natasha and Emily and nephews Ben and Tim but most of all thanks to Mum and Dad. They have been the ones to suffer a child who collected dead animal skins, feathers, bones and fossils, who endured the occasional room full of huge Bluebottles and booming, loud progressive Rock music. Finally thanks and much love to my children, Rebecca and Joshua. They have an unusual father who loves them and I am so proud of them both. Thanks to you all.

Foreword

Chris Boardman, Chris Hoy, Jason Kenny, Chris Froome, Laura Trott, Bradley Wiggins .... in 2016 one Gary Prescott attempted to add his name to this long line of illustrious British cycling champions. At sixty years old, asthmatic and (by his own admission) slightly over-weight, Gary - often simply referred to as the Biking Birder - cut a slightly surprising figure as a potential cycling record holder but what he may have lacked in physical prowess he more than compensated for in sheer will and determination and in 2016 he reached for the stars in attempting to set a new European Green Birding record for the most bird species seen in one calendar year.

Gary, a retired special needs teacher from Worcestershire, had always been a keen birder, cyclist and promoter of environmental causes so the world of Green Birding, not incurring a carbon footprint in the pursuit of the birds - a growing movement particularly in North America - came naturally to him. 2016 was the culmination of six years of preparation as Gary attempted to set a European Green Birding record, trying to surpass the 304 species seen by Ponc Fileu Latorre of Catalonia in 2014. This book follows his progress throughout the course of the year from the very tip of Cornwall to the far reaches of the Northern Isles and virtually everywhere else in between.

The Green Birding challenge was for Gary far more than just ticking off birds and it engaged him in a personal crusade to make this planet a better place for current and future generations. Gary fundraised for four charities close to his heart - Royal Society for the Protection of Birds, Wildfowl & Wetland Trust, Asthma UK and the Chaskawasi-Manu Rainforest children project in Peru - raising many thousands of pounds in donations. He also delivered lectures and presentations on both his adventures and environmental issues around the country during the course of his journey, including several guest slots at regional bird fairs and a feature on *Springwatch*. However he was probably happiest in undertaking direct action to clear up the thoughtless waste produced by the human species.

However this account is far, far more than simply tales of "twitching" and ticking off new birds as beloved by the British tabloid newspapers. As well as the highs and the lows of a year out on the road on a bike - the physical pain, accidents, injuries, dejection of missing new birds by a few minutes, the swings of motivation and despair - what is really inspiring and heart warming is the people he met over the course of the year. Whether this be the renewing of lifelong friendships, momentary random acts of kindness from complete strangers or immersing himself in close-knit island communities, Gary's infectious personality and zest for life shine through in an inspiring and uplifting manner.

My small role in this incident filled year was acting as "The Oracle", relaying up-to-date information of the rarer, more difficult-to-connect-with bird species so Gary could plan his route accordingly, all from the comfort of my sofa. There was just a tiny element of *schadenfreude* as a brief text message from me could send Gary in unbinding faith of a wild goose chase (literally on occasions!) up mountain and down dale, often in adverse weather conditions. I could only admire from a distance the perseverance, dedication and overall *joie de vivre* that Gary managed to maintain for (the majority of) the year.

So immerse yourself in Gary's twelve months of adventure; at some point along his journey across the length and breadth of Britain even the most ardent cynic will not help but smile to themselves as to the absurdities, triumphs or simple pleasures that this undertaking generated.

The Oracle, Phil Andrews.

WHY GREEN BIRDING?

Green birding has developed as a way to bird that does not have a negative impact on the environment. Even when talk of global climate change was fairly new to most of us, some birders realized that the extreme driving and flying that a few birders undertake for big years and big lists, is detrimental to the environment. If a person really cares about birds, it seems inconsistent to be driving and flying thousands of miles to pursue birds (with the extreme carbon footprint of such efforts). The BIGBY movement that developed in Quebec was an effort to bird in a more environmentally responsible way and to encourage birding in one's local patch. This also fosters the study all of nature in the birder's local area, not just birds. It leads to a deeper appreciation of your local area and, hopefully, even preservation and restoration efforts there. In this way, green birding often leads to green naturalism and nature activism.

There are birding advantages to green birding. On a bike or on foot, birders can see and hear birds all the time, not just at stops or for fleeting moments through the windows of a speeding car. Green birders are able to stop at any time to see and study birds found en route, not just at pullouts. Consequently, more species are seen in less distance and green birding big day species totals are approaching the totals once only recorded on big days in cars, even though the distance covered in a day by bike is far less.

Green Birding also still satisfies the competitive urge possessed by some birders. The sport of birding can be done responsibly. The Big Green Big Year, "BIGBY," was soon followed by all sorts of variations on big green years for counties, states and countries. Birders started green big days, green big hours, county green lists, walking big days and big years. The Big Sit, which originated independently of this movement, was now seen also as a way to green bird. Birders could satisfy their urge to compete at various levels in a way that was not bad for the environment and which fostered a greater appreciation of birds and all nature in their local area. This has been further promoted by eBird, the online bird database developed by National Audubon and Cornell, with its local patch challenge. With eBird, birders are not only encouraged to bird locally, but to note nesting and seasonality of birds, important data for the study of birds and the effects of climate and habitat change.

Green birding has a physical challenge not present in motorized big days and big years. Top big days often involve over 100 miles of cycling over varied terrain, and big years can involve thousands of miles of pedaling. This additional challenge heightens the satisfaction of a successful big day or big year. It usually pushes those participants, who are able, to new levels of fitness. For those who are not physically able, there is the big

foot hour and the Big Sit. A wheelchair category in the green birding records is certainly open for any of the green birding categories.
Last, there is a more spiritual side to green birding which becomes more evident on long bike rides. The birder on the road for a big day, and especially for multiple days, experiences the terrain, the weather, the sounds of the wind, birds, cars, and sees the effects of man on the terrain more intimately than those speeding by in a car. The birder starts to feel more like a slow bird moving from one location to another. The green birder is apart from the people speeding by and, like a bird, is also vulnerable to those cars and the weather. Days on the road aren't boring; the birder gets into into a groove after a few days where the sixty to a hundred miles (or more) on the bike feels routine. The bicycle birder achieves a different and satisfying mental state on the road. In the quest for birds the green birder becomes like a bird - totally in the moment.

Jim Royer, California, USA

Author of the excellent World of Green Birding Records blog.

Route taken in 2016

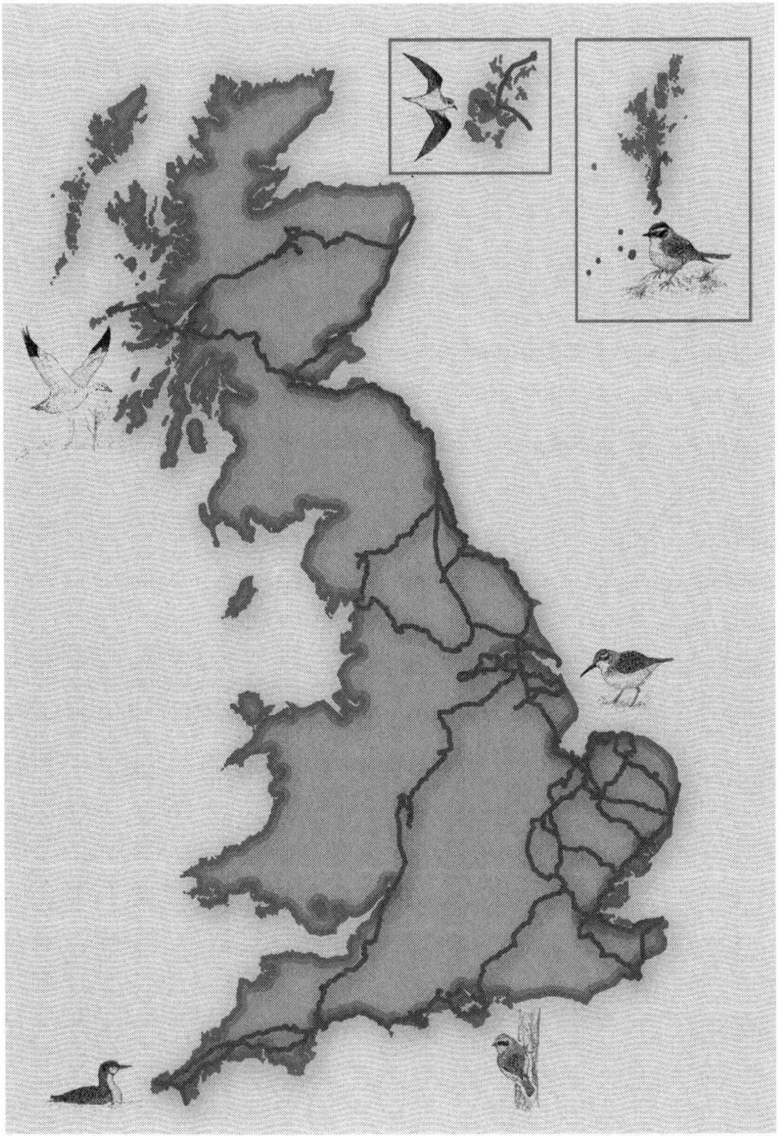

1

JANUARY 2016

Make the boy love natural history, if you can.

Robert Falcon Scott

Friday 1st January **light SE**

Frost, high cloud.

A New Year, 2016 and a fresh determination to see **300** different bird species this year. It has to be this year as it will be the last year that my ageing legs will stand up to a whole year of day after day cycling. After all I will be celebrating my sixtieth birthday this year. My third year of cycling for birds begins.

It is 5:30 a.m. and a frosty, calm morning sees me awaking from cold slumber in a hide at Upton Warren, a Worcestershire Wildlife Trust Reserve, off the A38 south of Bromsgrove. I feel excited about the coming year. There is a thrill that every bird sound at this time of the morning is a new bird for the year. The Green Year list begins, a BIGBY, a Big Green Big Year looms once more. **Canada Geese** are the first birds to make a sound, not the most attractive noise but music to my ears? Hardly. The various honks are closely followed by **Coot, Mallard** and **Moorhen**.

I am sitting in my Arctic quality sleeping bag in the Arthur Jacobs's hide when I think I hear a **Tawny Owl**. I hear it again, definitely. This is a very rare bird at Upton Warren and despite the early hour I text a couple of Upton birders the news excitedly. They'll kill me!

Walking along a sloppy, muddy path along the Salwarpe brook in the dark, with the only light coming from the orange neon lights of the adjacent A34, I stop and try to record the haunting hooting. A single hoot and I press the video button on my camera. At thirty two seconds the owl hoots, just a few twoo-its and the essential evidence is mine. I make three furrows in the mud by the pathway to show other birders where the bird is sitting. It seems to be quite deep in the Education Reserve Woodland, an out of bounds area of now blackened trees and bushes, between The Moors and the sailing pool.

I squelch back along the muddy track sliding on some frost, back to the hide and await the first sunrise of the New Year. A **Water Rail** squeals in the reed bed that I know is in front of me.

An hour or so later the dim dawn light allows some silhouetted birding, always a magic time. The first views of birds on a New Year morning. So begins the real thing. The muted murk of the early morning is gradually brightening. A **Robin** sits on a small hawthorn to the left by some bird feeders. **Lapwings** can be seen standing still on an island on the other side of the large Moors Pool.

7:30 a.m. a pink wash over the eastern clouds and more birds call in the semi light; **Carrion Crow, Teal, Cetti's Warbler, Dunnock** and **Wren.** The Cetti's does its Mozart call and the Dunnock sings a more pleasant, softer phrase.

Across The Moors Pool I can make out the birds with white plumage; **Black-headed Gull** and **Mute Swan.**

7:50 a.m. and it is light enough to start really watching birds. A **Blackbird** comes into the hawthorn next to the feeders. Now I am listening hard; adding **Blue, Coal** and **Great tit, Bullfinch, Reed Bunting, Greenfinch** and **Wood Pigeon** in very quick succession. Out on the water there are good numbers of **Tufted Duck, Pochard** and **Shoveler** with a single **Great-crested Grebe.** The bird of the day arrives, a **Great White Egret** and it proudly parades along the far reed bed edge. Two **Little Grebes** come close and dive in the nearest channel searching for small Rudd. A couple of **Herring Gulls** fly over with skeins of **Lesser Black-backeds.** These gulls are on their way to the rubbish tips further south, having spent the night at Bartley Reservoir on the edge of Birmingham. Bartley was Bill Oddie's birding patch until he too discovered the route to Upton Warren. Sightings of Bill at The Warren are as rare as an American Wader now-a-days. Respect and love for such a famous birder is still felt here.

Birders are arriving and I decide to walk around the reserve. A group of **Curlew** fly in, announcing their arrival with echoing calls. A few **Redwings, Jackdaws** and then a couple of **Magpies** fly over also; two for joy. Fourteen **Cormorant** are wing-drying on the provided platforms, a **Mistle Thrush** is on the telegraph wires and a large female **Sparrowhawk** disturbs all the duck before she circles the pool and relaxes by roosting in a tree nearby. A flock of small birds are atop some alders included both **Lesser Redpolls** and **Siskins**, both birds that were very scarce in the winter months early last year.

Into a packed East Hide, the Great White Egret is an obvious start of the year draw for the local Brummie birders. There are more birds to add to the growing day list. A flock of seven **Goldfinches** charm their way over the water to some nearby teasel heads. A **Redshank** is strutting around an island, a **Grey Wagtail** lands on another.

Walking back along the trail, a **Song Thrush** pops out and at the back of a waterlogged North Moors a few **Chaffinch** are in amongst the hawthorns.

I cycle down to the other area of the nature reserve to the south, The Flashes. These are a series of three large brackish pools behind a large sailing pool. There I meet up with John Belsey, the undisputed 'King of The Warren' and together we go to the hides that overlook the brackish pools. Upton Warren has shallow pools that contain briny water. Salt laid down millions of years ago, left over from a long gone ocean, percolates upward to create saltmarsh-like conditions in this centre of England county. It is because of this that Avocets breed here, despite the nearest coastline being over one hundred miles away.

A **Buzzard** is feeding on a rabbit perched up on a post of the fox-proof fence. That makes the fiftieth bird species seen today. The Warren's fence is about ten feet high and has been instrumental in allowing breeding waders, especially Avocets to have a high productivity per pair. Eleven pairs of Avocet last year fledged twenty nine young; a phenomenal number per pair.

More birds for the list are seen, **Stock Dove, Great-spotted Woodpecker, Pied Wagtail, Common Snipe** and **Grey Heron.**

Out on the short grass a vivid **Green Woodpecker** is feeding and over the nearby tall radio masts a pair of **Ravens** are cronking. The Snipe need surveying and so John and myself, joined by Dave Jackson, another Upton Warren regular birder, go out onto the marsh to see how many there are. Six Common and four **Jack Snipe** are flushed. The latter soon landing not far away in their usual fashion. A **Kestrel** is hovering nearby, a windhover whose name comes from the French word for a noisy bell! **Linnets** fly over. Another task is to check the fox-proof fence and so we walk the perimeter happy to find that no holes have appeared that would allow the crafty predator to enter the sanctuary.

How this area has changed over the decades that I have been birding here. Back in the 1970s there were no phragmites, no reeds, just a wader-rich, muddy shoreline with a short ditch between the second and third flash. Now there is too much reed bed, rewilding maybe but unless control happens the famous flash will be just a reed-surrounded pool.

Leaving The Flashes I return to The Moors where a small flock of **Long-tailed Tits** are moving along the hawthorn hedgerow. Out on the water the only new bird for the day is a male **Gadwall.**

Time to leave, the cycle back to my Mum and Dad's house is mostly uphill. Mum and Dad live in Romsley, a village in North Worcestershire that enjoys wonderful views from it's elevated position. Six birds join the year list on the way there; **Fieldfare, Starling, Collared Dove, House Sparrow, Goldcrest** and **Jay.**

So it is the end of the first day. The Green Year list stands at **sixty four**, eleven better than the first day total last year. A great start with a few birds that I didn't get until much later in the year last year; Lesser Redpoll and Jack Snipe for instance.

11.86 miles **1042 feet elevation up** **372 feet down**

Saturday 2nd January **Fresh E to W**

Drizzle or light rain all day.

Two sessions of cricket are on the TV, the South Africa versus England Test match in the morning. Watching my favourite sport with Dad, means that I am late leaving for the Hoopoe reported near to Wolverhampton. This is the same bird I saw near the end of last year; a superb over-wintering bird.

From the back window overlooking a large oak woodland I add **Nuthatch** and **Treecreeper** to the list before setting off.

I cycle past the places of my early childhood; two of our family homes having been in Stourbridge. Past the pathway where I got stung by a bumblebee as I poked the nest with a stick, when around seven years old, blinding me with severe swelling. Past the road that Mum claimed she took the Christmas presents for Santa to collect and check before Christmas Day. So many memories. Down the High Street in order to see my old school, King Edward's Grammar School, Stourbridge. It is as magnificent a set of buildings as I remember. Memories of my teachers, Daisy Druller, Fanny Wicks, Fluff and Wack! Strange how the male teachers have nicknames only. I have no recollection of their real names. The ladies, Fanny and Daisy were wonderful, old to me back then, kind teachers who loved to share their stories of the war with the boys only classes, of the air raid shelters in the playground. Fluff was a vicious, uninterested bore of a French teacher with no real interest in teaching at all. He used to put his feet up onto his desk and press the button for the tape. "Ecoutez et Repetez!" First day initiation, First Year boys crammed into the outside toilet area to be chosen one by one to have their head flushed down the loo! This was allowed by the staff for a couple of days before the Head announced that enough was enough. I never did get flushed, luckily.

I cycle onto the ring road and head for Wall Heath, cycling past the pub where many years ago my second wife, Jane and I had our wedding reception many years ago. Happy day.

The special bird is not on view when I arrive and two birders haven't been able to find it despite searching for a couple of hours. I try to locate it in a scrubby area on the far side of the quarry. It flics up from dense vegetation into a tree and stays unseen amongst the ivy on the tree trunk for an hour or so. **Hoopoe** goes onto the Green Year list. What a fabulous bird to have so early in the year.

Eventually the crested exotic does return to the same spot and gives everyone now present great, close views. Three new birds for the year list takes it to **sixty seven**.

19.19 miles **115 elevation up** **1376 feet down**

Sunday 3rd January **Fresh SW - S**

Heavy rain all day

Another late start due to the cricket, watching Ben Stokes and Johnny Bairstow's incredible record breaking stand before lunch. The former gets 200, the latter gets to 100 after lunch and records of all sorts tumble.

Outside the rain is heavy and the wind is in my face. The cycle is not too pleasant! The route today is from Wolverhampton to Worcester, all along the busy A449. There are practically no birds. In all the time cycling I see only one Jay, one Magpie, a few Rooks and a Pheasant. There are a lot of almost bare fields devoted to winter wheat and it is these that cause the three floods I have to cycle through. Each stretch of foot deep water rushing off the wheat fields is the colour of rancid orange juice and must be carrying a tremendous amount of sand and silt. Soil erosion will deplete the ability of these fields to produce food in the future.

Just after the round-a-bout where I need to take the road towards Worcester centre, a lady has stopped her car and calls me over. On hearing that I am doing a cycle ride for charity, Kim gives a donation and a banana; both are very much appreciated. What a fantastic lady, Kim tells me that she is a triathlete from Bewdley, Worcestershire. Wonderful.

The **Rooks** I see are new for the year list and so is a single **Pheasant** that is crossing a field just north of Worcester. In the city itself the River Severn is a foot away from bursting its banks and the fifty or so Mute Swans are on an area that has flooded over riverside pathways down towards the cathedral.

The Green Year list now stands at **sixty nine**.

29.46 miles **1104 feet elevation up** **1646 feet down**

Monday 4th January **Light SW**

Occasional heavy shower

The cycle route is once again an easy one, the main A38 to Tewkesbury from Worcester, then the same road goes to Gloucester and along to Slimbridge and the home of The Wildfowl and Wetland Trust, The W.W.T.

All sounds simple and the trip goes smoothly and steadily enough despite a light, in the face wind and occasional heavy showers. The mild weather from last year is continuing and I should count my blessings and do.

A few **Skylark**s in a field near Kempsey are the first bird to add to the year list. Otherwise the fields are bare and the hedgerows decimated, slashed square.

Common Gull and **Shelduck** are in a field just before Slimbridge. Both are year ticks. These make the list stand at seventy two.

Reaching Slimbridge at 3:00 p.m. I rush down the Zeiss Hide. Six people in there haven't seen the reported **Grey Phalarope** but luckily I find it and try to point it out to the other birders present.

On Rare Bird Alert and Birdguides the bird is reported as being elusive. It is easy to see why. It is amongst thick, dark green sedges on our side of the pool along the far end of the viewable field. This makes it easy for the rare, very white looking wader to disappear and it quickly does just that.

Luckily a Buzzard comes low over the area after about fifteen minutes and all the Teal and Lapwing take off. The Phalarope does likewise, taking off and landing on an area of exposed mud. A lady from Cheslyn Hay, Staffordshire named Sheila has a telescope and I put her onto what is a lifer for her. She is so pleased she gives me a kiss on my cheek!

Now that the main bird is safely UTB, under the belt, a twitcher's term, I can look for other year list birds and enjoy the massed flocks of Lapwings and **Golden Plover** nervous due to the presence of a **Peregrine**. **Dunlin** also fly both in front of us and out over the expansive Severn Estuary. A **Little Egret** heads upstream while on the nearby lake there are **Wigeon** and **Pintail** amongst the masses of teal.

Out on The Dumbles there are a few **Great Black Backed Gulls** as well as around a hundred Barnacle Geese. I don't know whether these are genuine wild birds and don't add them to the list. **Greylag** are present as well and I do add them.

Off to the nearby Wild Goose Hostel for the night as Slimbridge closes. There I meet two superb workers for the W.W.T., Kane and Ed. Ed's eyes sparkle as he describes his job of monitoring Common Scoter in Scotland. Kane later asks if he can both donate some money to the WWT on my behalf and sponsor me also! My eyes sparkle!
The Green Year list now stands at **eighty one**.

41.87 miles 994 feet elevation up 1014 feet down

Tuesday 5th January very light SW

Sunny intervals, mild 9C.

A great friend, Mark Simkins, arrives on his large Honda motorbike at 10:30 a.m. and so the day's birding begins at Slimbridge, Gloucestershire, the H.Q. of the Wildfowl & Wetland Trust.

After a quick chat with the effervescent Ellie, the fund-raising officer for the W.W.T., it is to the Rushy Pen hide we go and we find the two female **Scaup** amongst the masses of Tufted Duck. There are also a few **Bewick Swans** to add to the year list. These please me as last year, incredibly, I only saw one! Decades ago hundreds used to arrive and stay the winter at Slimbridge, each one could be named by Sir Peter and possibly my favourite pair of Bewicks were Morecambe and Wise! It was seen that each Bewick Swan had a different pattern of yellow and black on their bills. A chart in a long bird hide showed a painting of each bird seen and named. Now-a-days, due to climate change, there are much fewer.

Mark and I head out to the Holden Tower to look over The Dumbles towards the River Severn. There are masses of birds with very large flocks of Lapwing and Golden Plover. Dunlin are mixed in amongst them and there are small numbers of a few duck species. There is also still the flock of Barnacle Geese but I am unsure about their origin. Category C I am later told, but I feel the same way about these as I did the Snow Geese on Coll last year and I don't count them.

On Tack Piece, a flooded field within the sea wall, there are a huge number of Teal. The W.W.T. Website recent sightings page reports that there were over 23,000 there yesterday and a search through them doesn't give me a Green-winged Teal. I have to look after what happened last year at RSPB Loch Leven. Whilst visiting that reserve I managed to find a Green-winged Teal by using the telescopes in the café of the visitor's centre. This was only after initiating the rescue of an upside down cow from a pond!

There are a few, relative to what numbers there used to be here in the past, **White-fronted Geese,** the first year tick of the day. Now-a-days the geese stay over in the Netherlands. There is also a flock of around one hundred **Black-tailed Godwits**, another year tick. A large female Sparrowhawk is hunting along the hedgerow and a buzzard is sitting on a post with its wings in a strange relaxed pose. With a view over towards the Zeiss hide I find the Grey Phalarope again.

The rest of the day is spent alternating brief wild bird watching moments with prolonged travel experience chats; Mark having been to Patagonia recently as well as having trekked up both Mount Kenya and Kilimanjaro last year.

Once Mark leaves I return to the hides overlooking Tack Piece and find **Ruff**, the final year tick of the day.

Back at the excellent and very quiet Wild Goose Lodge nearby I have an early night, falling asleep early to the sound of a hooting Tawny Owl.

The Green Year list now stands at **eighty six**.

An evening email from The Oracle details available birds:-

Cattle Egret - Steart and Mudgley
Glossy Ibis Shapwick
Dusky W - Meare Heath
Am Wigeon - Bowling Green Marsh
Hud Whimbrel - Marazion
Pacific Diver - Marazion
Bonaparte's Gull - Teignmouth
Yb Warbler - Hayle
Spoonbill - Hayle
Firecrest - Hayle
Ross' Gull - Lizard
Ring-billed Gull - Mount's Bay
GW Teal - Wadebridge
GG Shrike - East Budleigh

I am heading that way. I wonder how many of these will stick around?

Wednesday 6th January **Light SW**

Sunny Intervals

Back to Slimbridge to meet up with Matt Neale, the WWT's fundraising officer. He is delayed and so I rush down to the Holden Tower, the high tower hide that looks over to the River Severn, to search for Little Stint. A group of four birdwatchers new to the sport of birding have new telescopes so I wangle myself a scan through one of the scopes over The Dumbles grassland. Finding two **Little Stints** is not as hard as one might think and I show the telescope owner the diminutive waders. The telescope also makes it easy to spot some distant **Avocets**. Celebrating the two year ticks, including a bird, Little Stint, that I only saw once last year, I turn to leave and see the face of a quiet birder in the corner of the hide. It is Phil, a birding friend from my home patch of Upton Warren. Greeting a friend from home, I ask him why didn't he say hello? We bird together for the next hour and chat about Upton matters.

Matt Neale is now available and so I head back to the Trust HQ to discuss how I can raise as much as I can for this wonderful charity. Ideas are exchanged, emails also and so I am off to search for the reported Black Redstart at reasonably nearby Sheerness Harbour. I reach there after taking a wrong turn, finding myself looking over the water to the harbour from the wrong side. A van is parked here in a lay-by and I ask the driver for directions. The driver turns out t have been a WWT reserve warden in the past, the warden of the wonderful Caerlaverock WWT reserve in Scotland. Strangely enough we chat about birds.

On the correct side of the harbour it doesn't take long to find the male **Black Redstart**, yet he is soon off chasing a female through some nearby trees.

The rest of my day is spent cycling to Bristol, mostly along the main A38 road, which is mostly downhill for the last ten miles into the city. Very busy roads with lots of noisy traffic, I look forward to days ahead when it is mostly quiet and empty country lanes.

A night ahead of me at Bristol Youth Hostel, my evening is spent with a great friend, Cath Mendez. We had met when I was on Fair Isle last year and she was enjoying a birding holiday whilst staying at the superb Fair Isle Bird Observatory. We went out for a meal and enjoyed talking about the Fairest of Isles.

The Green Year list now stands at **eighty nine**.

33.26 miles 1135 feet elevation up 1129 feet down

Thursday 7th January Strong W-NW

Cool, sunny intervals.

After saying goodbye to Cath Mendez, I cycle through the city of Bristol with light rain falling. I head for Chew Valley Lake. The push up and over Dundry Hill is tough but the downhill cycle afterwards is exhilarating. The contrast of views from the top was striking; urban sprawl with its confusion of buildings and lines to the north, Bristol. To the south fifty shades of green and brown, where the stained fields have surrounding skeletons of winter trees and hedges naked from their springtime foliage.

An American Lesser Scaup has been reported at Chew Valley Reservoir, residing in Sutton Wick Bay and I reach there finding the fabulous birder and friend Chris Craig in the hide. Chris has just returned from the Craig family's latest birding adventure. He talks of Chile, Tierra del Fuego, Antarctica and The Falklands. Chris has a World list nearing 5,000 and his famous birding daughter, Mya-Rose, known as Birdgirl, is not far behind. Mya-Rose has almost the same British list as mine, around 460, has seen 4,300 or thereabouts in the World and is only thirteen! Her blog received the runners up award in the prestigious Birdwatch Blog of the Year Award last year.

http://birdgirluk.blogspot.co.uk/

The wind is very strong and blowing across the lake straight at us, making the views of the duck sporadic in the waves. **Goldeneye** are seen with good numbers of Tufted Duck and Pochard. A female **Goosander** flies past.

After a while it is obvious that the Lesser Scaup isn't here. Chris says that he will drive around to the sheltered west side and search there. If he finds it he will phone me.

A phone call has me cycling around to the Moreton Hide. A **Green Sandpiper** is beside a pool created by the recent rain as I approach the hide. As soon as I enter a gentleman with a telescope insists that I see the male **Lesser Scaup** and I quickly do, just as it takes off and flies out of view. Another new bird for the year is also in front of the hide, a duck, actually a blue-billed drake, we cannot name! (I later heard it was shot the next day.) Birders will know of which species I am talking about and why it can't be named. Sadly now-a-days a bird of this species, if found, is whispered about carefully. In no way should one discuss such through social media circles.

A **Kingfisher** calls and lands on a small crack willow briefly before the brilliant blurring blue departs.

A wonderful evening is spent with the Craig family, who kindly put me up for the night. Talking of her trip to Antarctica, Mya-Rose talks about what it was like to sleep out under the stars in a pit dug deeply into the snow!

The Green Year list now stands at **ninety five**, ten birds more than at this stage last year.

18.85 miles 1602 feet elevation up 1237 feet down

Friday 8th January light S

Very sunny, warm, 9C

Chris Craig and I stand on their patio as I prepare to leave and a **Marsh Tit** comes down to their peanut feeder; another first for the year for me.

After the big push up onto The Mendips, another bird is soon added when I see three **Stonechats** before plunging the heavy laden bike down the steep, bendy road through Cheddar Gorge.

On flatter ground with drains and dykes, two Green Sandpipers fly over me and a completely white Pheasant is alone in a muddy field. This is the only Pheasant I have seen since leaving Worcestershire.

I reach the spot where a Cattle Egret has been reported recently on Rare Bird Alert and Birdguides and there is indeed a herd of a dozen large cows.

There isn't a Cattle Egret with them though, just four Little Egrets poking around the cow pats. I cycle further down the narrow country lane and a very close Buzzard poses on a dead tree stump.

A cyclist passes who is having a problem keeping his handlebars straight. In fact they are twisting around in his hands and how he doesn't go flying into an adjacent ditch is beyond me. I call out and he stops and a quick use of my alum keys secures the handlebars tightly.

I return to the cows and wait. One of them nearby keeps up a cow's favourite pastime of shoving her long tongue into her nostrils. Charming!

Lunch consists of two three day old doughnuts and some orange squash. Live it up Son.

After waiting about forty-five minutes, walking up and down the small side country lane, the **Cattle Egret** suddenly flies over and lands in a field away from the cows beside a small ditch. It just sits there and preens. Another good to see rare bird goes onto the list. To Shapwick National Nature Reserve and Ham Wall R.S.P.B. Reserves next to meet Pete Dommett, a freelance writer for a photo shoot. Pete has written an article about Green Birding for youngsters to go into the Wildlife Trust Magazine, Watch and he wants to include a short piece about my exploits. If you want to know more about Pete or commission him then email him at :-

dommett@blueyonder.co.uk

Pete is a friendly companion for the afternoon and is also into nature in a big way. We walk down to try and see the Dusky Warbler, seemingly my bogey bird, which has been seen in bushes beside the path through the extensive R.S.P.B. reserve. Last year unknown to me at the time, a Dusky Warbler was beneath me on a cliff of Tyneside Geo on Fair Isle. A Red-flanked Bluetail had captured my attention and by the time a birder told me of the Dusky, it had gone. Never did get to see one last year. I want to see this one and I have time to do so.

Marsh Harriers, bird number **99**, are making the ducks nervous as we negotiate the mud. Reaching the Dusky Warbler area we meet a couple who I last saw at Mid Yell, Shetland last year. They have just seen the rare bird and my confidence is high that we will do likewise. The weather is lovely and so warm. There is even a hawthorn bush with blossom and leaves. That bush is in for a shock when Winter arrives, if it ever does? It has been what one used to consider exceptionally mild so far.

Two hours later all confidence has dissipated. No Dusky Warbler. Pete decides to take a few photographs of me instead and a **Chiff Chaff** lands on a twig beside his head. Bird number **100**!

Back at the car park, made much larger last year due to the large number of visitors that come here at this time of year to see what I would imagine is the largest Starling murmuration and roost in Britain, Pete and I continue past quite a number of people gathered along the long path through Shapwick Heath. Masses of Starlings go overhead, tens of thousands of them. The sunset on this beautiful warm, windless day is quite lovely with flock after flock of the fascinating birds going past.

I go to a hide after Pete leaves for home and make myself comfortable for the night. Great White Egrets come into roost, seven of them, but there is no sign of the reported Glossy Ibis.

Two dips of important birds; if I am going to get the 300 then I need birds of the quality of Dusky Warbler and Glossy Ibis. Not too disappointed, this just means I will have to bird the reserves again tomorrow instead of moving on.

26.60 miles 1045 feet elevation up 1473 feet down

The following is a set of questions and answers sent by Pete. I hope that this may answer some of the questions you may have about my cycling, Biking Birding, travels before 2016.

Interview questions for Gary Prescott – aka 'The Biking Birder' for 'Wingbeat' (the RSPB members' magazine for teenagers) . . . . Pete.

Your 2015 trip:

Q1**. What gave you the idea for your 2015 trip?**

I had cycled around every R.S.P.B. and W.W.T. Nature Reserve in Britain in 2010. Then, I had a relaxed attitude to Green Bird listing and although I knew that a Norfolk birder named Chris Mills had set a Green Year list record of 251, I thought that I would easily beat it. During that year I visited cathedrals, museums, ancient history sites such as Callinish on Lewis and I gave talks to schools and colleges about being Green and Climate Change. I also climbed the five highest peaks of Great Britain; Snowdon, Scarfell Pike, Slieve Donard, Ben Nevis and, on the Isle of Man, Snaefell. At the end of the year I had a list of 253.

Reviewing the list I took off Sooty Shearwater as I wasn't happy that I had seen it properly. Then near the end of 2011 the British Birds & Rarities Committee, The B.B.R.C., published their report on rare birds of 2010. These eminent birders decided that the Red-breasted Goose, that I had seen on the Exeminster Marshes RSPB reserve, was an escaped bird and therefore uncountable. I was back to 251, level with Chris Mills.

Near the end of 2011, at Cley in Norfolk, an extremely rare bird turned up and American Western Sandpiper. With a group of birding friends known as The Birding Clams (Clear Lunacy & Madness Society) I went to see it. We arrived about an hour before daylight and the bird hide nearest to where the bird had been seen the previous day was already filling up with birders. In the dark I sat on one of the benches and two Belgian birders, who had travelled over to see the bird, sat next to me and started chatting. As the dawn progressed and daylight grew, they looked at me and said "are you Gary Prescott?" It turned out that their friend was, according to them doing a Big Green Year in Belgium to try and beat my record. I had never thought of it as a European one before, but obviously Laurent Raty had and wanted to beat it.

I never did find out whether Laurent did beat me that year but in 2013 a young Spaniard named Ponc Feliu Latorre did a Big Green Year, cycling around Spain birding and broke my record. In fact he took it past the 300 mark to 304!

Not wanting to be second or possibly third to Laurent, I planned to repeat my 2010 trip in 2015. I would visit all of the R.S.P.B. and W.W.T. Nature Reserves again, trying to raise as much as I could for each of my three chosen charities, those two mentioned and Asthma UK and change the route to give me a chance of beating Ponc's European record.
During 2014 though I went out to Peru twice and met some amazing indigenous children of the Machiguenka Community, who live in the Manu Rainforest. The project that supports these children in their quest for an education became the fourth charity that I chose to support in 2015, Chaskawasi-Manu.

Q2. **Can you explain what the 'Green Year List' is exactly?**

It's the most species seen in a year, January 1st to December 31st, by means of sustainable transport with the lowest carbon footprint. That is by bicycle, canoe or kayak, or walking. For a 'pure' BIGBY, the American term for such a venture which stands for Big Green Big Year, one shouldn't use any form of carbon transport. I had to use ferries to get to some of the many islands I visited during 2015 and so on the official Green Bird list I have an 'F' after my name.

A Californian Green Birder, Jim Royer, maintains a superb blog that lists the Green Records of the World. This can be found at

http://greenbirdingworld.blogspot.co.uk

Q3. **How many species did you see during your 2015 trip?**

290. The European record was missed by 16 yet I had so many near misses. A cat ate a Dusky Warbler for instance ten minutes before I got to the garden where it had been seen and a Baird's Sandpiper was frightened away by a dog running by it and was never seen again as I went to look at it through someone's telescope.

Q4. **How many reserves did you visit?**

242 (232 RSPB + 10 WWT). I also visited nature reserves belonging to various Wildlife Trusts, such as Cley and Holme which are Norfolk Wildlife Trusts reserves, and National Nature reserves, such as Shapwick. I also visited bird observatories such as Dungeness, Flamborough, Spurn, North Ronaldsay and Fair Isle.

Q5. **How many miles did you cover on your bike?**

Over 9,000 miles. I haven't completed every day's mileage chart yet.

Q6. **Which was your favourite reserve and why?**

Leighton Moss RSPB Reserve has everything; wonderful habitats and birds, very diverse wildlife including extremely rare orchids and butterflies, moths and bats. Then there are the staff who are the friendliest and welcoming people. The centre with its shop and café is superb and the whole set up is excellent with great viewing hides and even a very high elevated platform that looks over a very large reedbed, one of the largest reedbeds in Britain. The views are so beautiful and the surrounding landscapes are incredible for nature. Red Deer come out late in the afternoon and there is always the chance of seeing otters. I also love urban RSPB reserves such as Rainham Marshes. Brilliant place. Rathlin Island in Northern Ireland is so spectacular and it is a wonderful adventure just getting there. Ynhs-Hir in Wales is fabulously diverse and Bempton Cliffs in Yorkshire are amazing. With so many incredible reserves the experience of visiting all of them twice has been thrilling. Then there are the WWT reserves. Slimbridge is of course absolutely fantastic and other reserves such as London – Barnes, Welney, Arundel, Llanelli, Caerlaverock, Washington and Castle Espie are brilliant for how they engage so many people with nature in superb surroundings. So difficult to pick out just one. I love them all!

Q7. **Which was your favourite bird and why? Where did you spot it?**

Favourite bird of the 2015 trip: Citril Finch at Holkham, Norfolk. A phone call from Phil Andrews, a Midland birder who texts me news constantly, could only mean a mega rare bird was somewhere nearby. On hearing that a Citril Finch, a bird more usually found in the high Alpine trees of Switzerland or the Pyrenees and only seen in Britain once before was at Holkham, fifty eight miles away from where I was that morning, I cycled those miles in five hours. Screaming 'get out the way' laughingly as I cycled down the bridlepath for the last mile or so as crowds of birders came towards me, they having already seen the bird, found the crowd, jumped off the bike and rushed towards a friend whom I could see amongst the throng. Two of The Birding Clams were there, Steve Allcott and Tony Barter, having come all the way from Wolverhampton and I spent the next hour talking with them and enjoying watching the Citril Finch. There were so many birding friends there that day from all over Britain including another one from the Midlands, Eric Phillips. Eric was a Green Birder and had been for decades. Sadly Eric died suddenly and unexpectedly a few weeks after seeing the Citril Finch; I had a carbon day to go to his funeral, and therefore the Citril Finch gained a new poignancy. Eric was a lovely man, very much respected and loved by the Midland birding community and very much missed. A Beautiful small green and yellow finch of such rarity seen with very close friends . . . perfect.

Actual favourite bird: a Swift. Aerodynamically shaped, a Swift is speedy, agile and sleek. They migrate to Southern Africa and, to me, herald the warm days of Summer far more than the Cuckoo or Swallow. A young Swift doesn't land for three years, spending all of that time on the wing, even sleeping whilst flying.

Q8. **What was the rarest bird you saw on this trip?**

The Citril Finch was the second for Britain yet the rarest was a Chestnut Bunting, found by a birder, who kindly gave me a bed for the night back in 2010, Julian Branscombe. Thrilled that Julian found such an amazing rare bird. On the 29th of October 2015 I saw this on Papa Westray in Orkney after taking three days to get there from Fair Isle. It hasn't been accepted yet by the British Birds & Rarities Committee; we have to wait for the BBRC report to come out sometime this year, but birders feel that this will happen making it the first accepted record of this far Eastern bird. Here's a summary of it from Birdguides:-

Chestnut Bunting currently sits on Category E of the British List with a number of previous records, from both spring and autumn, presently considered as escapes from captivity. However, there are nine accepted Western Palearctic records, all occurring between late September and mid-November. Recent occurrences include birds in Finland in September–October 2002, Norway in October 2010, Hungary in September 2011 and France in October 2009 and October 2014. These illustrate enough of a pattern to suggest that birds are occurring in an apparently wild state in Northern and Western

Europe in autumn, in a similar manner to other Far Eastern species such as Chestnut-eared, Black-faced and Yellow-browed Buntings.

The Papa Westray bird fits perfectly in to the established pattern of accepted Chestnut Bunting records in the Western Palearctic, and there is no reason to suspect it is anything other than a wild bird. It therefore potentially represents the first record of this species for Britain. I was the last person to see this bird and birders jokingly checked the soles of my boots in case I had trodden on it, it was that tame.

Q9. **Which bird was the trickiest to find?**

One's I didn't see! (joking) Radde's Warbler on Fair Isle was difficult because it kept hiding in vegetation. It took a couple of hours to get good views. The mega rare Siberian Rubythroat was seen after chasing around Fair Isle for almost two miles. It led us a merry dance as it went from dyke to dyke, stone wall to stone wall.

Q10. **Are there any funny or memorable anecdotes from your '15 trip?**

In 2010 I arrived on the Isle of Harris in the Outer Hebrides. Harris is very mountainous and after pushing the bike up a particularly steep road to get to a mountain pass, I came to a picnic bench with a fabulous view over the landscape of sea lochs and mountains. I stopped for some lunch and was joined by a family from Sheffield. As we sat there three coaches of German tourists stopped in the same lay-by and surrounded me asking about the bike and about what I was doing. Many of them didn't like their packed lunches and so I ended up with a pannier full of sandwiches, boiled eggs and chocolate bars.

Later that day I arrived at an ambition place, Callanish. I had always wanted to visit this extremely wonderful and famous ancient monument and whilst walking around one of the amazing stone circles there a huge blind pig came up to me knocking my legs. In my excitement over being at Callanish I was on the phone to my Mum at the time and I told her that someone wanted to say 'hello'. The pig grunted and snuffled to her and to show my appreciation for his conversation after Mum had gone I shared some of the sandwiches I had been given by the German tourists. I only realised later that I had given the pig ham sandwiches!

In 2015, I cycled from Bridgewater, Somerset to Bristol one day in early March. On reaching Ashton Gate I couldn't find the cycle path to the city centre. I went up to a couple who were out walking a dog. I asked for directions and they asked about what I was up to and why. On hearing of my trip to every RSPB and WWT reserve etc., the gentleman said that he had met someone like me a few years ago and that that cycling birder had slept in a Disabled toilets one night. That was me! It turned out that I had met this man back in 2010 when he repaired my bike. He lived in Ipswich at the time and had since moved to Bristol, I couldn't get over the coincidence of the meeting.

In 2010 one day I was lost. I was trying to find the way to the beautiful cable-stay bridge over the River Dee from near to Flint. There were three small houses in a line along one road and I knocked on the door of one of them to ask for directions. A man opened the door, screamed "you're the man with a Robin on your bike!" He rushed out and saw the bike and explained that he had been searching for images of Ospreys only the night before and had seen about my adventures. Here I was now at his door. We have been great friends ever since, Steve Dewsnapp.

I camp a lot and in Summer I like to leave the flap open so that I can see the stars. One morning in the Lake District I opened my eyes to find the ugliest shaved sheep in my tent with me. It's face was next to mine and my scream frightened it off!

Q11 **What were the trip highlights?**

Arriving on Fair Isle is always a highlight. The boat, the Good Shepherd, is a bobbing vomit bucket of a boat and when the immense cliffs of Fair Isle and Sheep Rock come into view the relief is just as immense. The excitement of being on Britain's best place for rare migrating birds, the place with so many amazing friends whom are such a privilege to know and a place of such incredible scenery is intense.

Sleeping in a prehistoric stone tomb on Orkney as heavy rain fell outside was a highlight. Look up the Dwarfie Stone on Hoy.

Sitting on a cliff edge at Flamborough with Puffins sitting next to me was wonderful.

Climbing the Cairngorms and having a baby Snow Bunting sit within a few feet from me and have its mother come regularly to feed it whilst I sat there; that was a great moment. It would be fed and immediately fall asleep sheltering behind a small grass tussock awaiting the next feed.

Walking down the centre of Fair Isle as the glow from the Northern Lights lit up the sky. Seeing groups of Orcas pass Fair Isle.

Meeting Phil Jupitus after pushing the bike along a marshy waterlogged path. Reaching a tarmac road again after a lovely OAP couple had told me I must take the cycle path, I pushed the bike along near to a railway station and saw a bloke sitting on a bench. I asked him the way to Southend and suddenly realised it was Phil Jupitus. He turned out to be very interested in what I was doing and we had a chat for twenty minutes or so, especially about when he was the lead singer for The Bonzo Dog Doo Dah Band a few years ago, in place for the long deceased Viv Stanshall, during a nostalgia tour with Adrian Edmundsen. I had seen him on that tour at The Civic Hall in Wolverhampton. Most people will know him better for his television appearances on Never Mind The Buzzcocks. Later in the evening I received a good luck message from him on Facebook, appreciated. Such a lovely man.

Having the privilege of being a main guest on Springwatch both for the early morning show with Brett Westwood and later in the evening with Chris Packham. The Craigs were all there that day as well and during the early evening break between rehearsals, it is all carefully rehearsed, and the actual evening show Birdgirl Mya-Rose and I chatted with Chris. Brett and I both grew up in Stourbridge, Worcestershire and knew each other before the show.

Q12 **How much money did you raise?**

I would love to have raised so much more and I am still trying to do so. Last year the total was around **£3500**

Q13 **How did you feel when you broke the British record?**

Actually I didn't realise I had but when I did I was over the Moon, texting friends and posting on Facebook etc.

Q14 **Which bird did you see to break the record?**

Sooty Shearwater whilst on North Ronaldsay, Orkney, staying at the wonderful North Ronaldsay Bird Observatory. They have a superb hostel attached to the observatory and the staff there must include, as well as the wonderful warden Alison and her husband Kevin, the best bunch of young, enthusiastic bird fanatics anywhere.

Your 2016 trip:

Q1. **What's your challenge this year?**

To break the European Green Year List which stands at 304 birds. Currently it is held by Ponc Feliu Latorre from Spain. The main aim is, though, to see 300 birds by cycling. This number is an iconic number in British birding. Back in 1980 Richard Millington published a book about getting 300 birds by carbon means, Carbon Twitching. The book was called A Twitcher's Diary and changed the way bird listing was perceived. Since then many birders have seen 300 as being a target for a Big Year. I want to be the first to do it by Green means. When I get the 300 and I am confident I will, then Ponc's record of 304 is the next target to beat.

Q2. **What's your planned route?**

January – down to the SW, turn around at Land's End and start the trip across the south coast.
February & March - the south and east coast to Yorkshire
April & May – East coast concentrating on East Anglia.
June & July – England SE corner and south coast to Dorset.
August – from Oxford (Blenheim Palace – Countryfile Live.) I have been invited to take part) to the east coast to get to Aberdeen asap.
September & October – Shetland and Fair Isle
November – Down East Coast
December – Most likely East Anglia (Norfolk) and then back to Worcestershire to finish at Upton Warren WWT nature reserve, where it all started on January 1st.

Q3. **What's the bird you'd most like to see this year?**

The 300th. I would like to see a Terek Sandpiper or a Siberian Thrush.

Q4. **Who are you raising money for this time?**

Same four charities as last year; Asthma UK, the RSPB and Wildfowl & Wetland Trust (WWT) and Chaskawasi-Manu.

Q5. **What was this year's first bird? 100th bird?**

First bird was a Canada Goose at Upton Warren nature reserve, Worcestershire. The 100th bird was a Meadow Pipit at Ham Wall RSPB reserve followed by a rare Siberian bird, a Dusky Warbler, the bird that I missed when one got eaten by a cat last year, remember?

Q6. **What are you looking forward to next on your '16 trip?**

The exhilaration of seeing some fantastic birds, meeting some incredible people and seeing new places and ones that I have loved before. The Paradise that is Fair Isle!

General questions:

Q1. **How did you get into birding? At what age did you start?**

Walking home from Primary school around the age of eight, masses of starlings on their way to Birmingham centre used to fly over me, thousands of them. I was fascinated. I didn't really get into birding until college when I met other students who were interested in birds. We used to go exploring the Dee Estuary together. I had always had a deep love of nature but unfocussed. Until College I used to go off for the day exploring the fields, hedges, woody culverts and streams local to my home. Parenting then was saying goodbye as I went out the door. Gone at eight in the morning or before, I wouldn't be home until dark.

After college I started a birding club at the Secondary school where I was employed as a science teacher and the kids' enthusiasm pulled me deeper into the world of birding.

Q2. **How did you get into birding on your bike?**

I had had phases when I cycled before during my life but it was only when I started commuting to work by cycling and trains that I got the idea of doing more birding by bike. From cycling to nature reserves local to my home at the time, Warwick, in the early 2000s I started to dream of a year long challenge. The idea of being a Biking Birder grew and I started planning routes, itineraries and where certain bird species would be at certain times of the year.

When I was a Special Needs teacher in Bromsgrove, starting in 2005, I had the job of organising Eco Schools in the school. Eco Schools is a superb platform run by the Keep Britain Tidy group, that gives children of all ages experience of all Green Issues. This gave me an insight into the effects of climate change and I started to Green Bird more often in order to do 'my bit' to cut my carbon footprint. The passion for Green Birding increased and now the only list I have is my Green list, both my life Green list and the year list.

Q3. **Describe yourself as a teenager in 3 words...**

solitary, bullied, different

Q4. **What's your background? (e.g. where did you grow up, what jobs have you done etc..)**

Born in Birmingham, family moved to Stourbridge, West Midlands when I was five. At the age of eleven we moved to Redditch where I lived until college. Free time was spent walking alone around the fields and woods around Redditch before it became a New Town.

Jobs:-

Two Secondary Science teaching posts for twelve years. One year of teaching Infants children. Seven years as a Junior school teacher with responsibility for music. Ran an internet selling business from home for four years. Special Needs teacher for eight years including MLD/SLD (Mild and Severe Learning Difficulties), autistic, deaf and ESBD (Emotional, Social & Behavioural Difficulties)

Q5. **Who inspired/inspires your love of birds / nature?**

Sir Peter Scott, the founder of The Wildfowl & Wetland Trust. I wrote him a letter when I was a ten year old and he sent back a letter that has inspired me ever since. It detailed his life and told me to study and never lose my love of nature. The fact that such a famous man would write to a young schoolboy still amazes me. It must have been a class project but what I do remember is that I received a wonderful, handwritten reply from him. The letter on small sheets of Basildon Bond paper, detailing his life and what I must do to become a naturalist. That letter remains to this day a very special, inspirational and motivational letter to me. I only wish I still had it but sadly it has been lost. If I close my eyes I can still see it though. Nowadays what I see myself inspires me and motivates me to see more.

Q6. **What motivates you to keep going day after day?**

The next place to visit, the next person I am going to meet, the next natural thing I am going to see be that an orchid, a butterfly, a mammal or a bird, a habitat or biome. The next bird I need to see for the Year list.

Q7. **Where do you sleep? What's the strangest place you've slept on one of your trips?**

All sorts of places, bush shelters, bird hides, church porches, that sort of thing. I love my tent, that's my favourite place. I have slept in caves, churches or out in the open quite a few times in a field. Once a bed & breakfast I had booked didn't exist. The house was empty and with rain pouring down there was nowhere else nearby to go to. It was raining hard and night time had fallen. I found a barn, moved some logs out of the way and slept in that.

Q8. **What home comforts do you miss when you're out on the road?**

Nothing comes to mind. I do miss my children, Mum and Dad and my sister and brother and their children.

Q9. **What's your favourite food when you're out on the road?**

Porridge with dried fruit, cinnamon, algae and raspberries. Spinach. Nuts. Seeds.

Q10. **And the one food you miss most?**

Vegan apple crumble and almond milk custard.

Q11. **Have you ever got into any scrapes during your trips?**

Only one that comes to mind is when a car decided to overtake a bus despite the fact that I was coming along the road towards him. It clipped the front of the bike as I fell off. I was lucky to get away with just a few cuts and bruises and very lucky not to land on a barbed wire fence very nearby. The driver stopped about three hundred yards away and then cleared off.

Q12. **Tell us about your cuddly companions!**

On the front of the bike :

Albert the Albatross is to remind me of the RSPB's albatross campaign.
Ricky the Robin is a RSPB collection box.
Sid the Frog is a large rainforest frog from the WWT.

On the back :

Scaggy the rabbit, a present from one of my best friends, Lee Dark.
Oscar the Orca (or Wally the Whale), a present from a wonderful young girl, Mary, who birds with her Dad, Tim at my patch, Upton Warren, Worcestershire.

There have been many more over the years but I keep receiving them from kind passers-by and then giving them to children I meet; gorillas, flamingoes, puffins, more rabbits, owls, badgers and last year a very important addition was Bob. Bob was a red squirrel that was the figurehead of a major campaign by the RSPB. I had my Bob proudly on the front of the bike but somewhere between Coniston and Hodbarrow in The Lake District he must have fallen off! I only saw that he was missing on arriving at the RSPB reserve at Hodbarrow and despite cycling miles back along the route, I couldn't find him. Mark Thomas of the RSPB started a Twitter campaign for me, Find Bob. He never did turn up. In my mind though he was found by a lovely child and is safe somewhere. Unlike Colin the Chicken. Colin, a rubber chicken of the squeezy dog toy variety, fell off back in 2010 whilst I was cycling with five lads doing the Land's End to John O'Groats cycle run for a charity called Chase. Once again I searched but to no avail, and on the highest road in England too, Shap, also in The Lake District.

Q13. **And what's with the Smiley-face tie, Gary??**

The Smiley-face tie has been with me since I was a Primary school teacher and reminds me of my love of all children. One of the best things in the World is the sight of a happy child and on my tie there are smiley faces that get larger as you descend the tie. So the youngest children/smiley face are the small ones near the top and the older children/smiley face are at the bottom. One smiley face is bright red, the others are yellow and the red one is me. When I was a teacher I would tell children that I was the red one because I was shy.

Q14. **Tell us about some of the interesting people you've met on your trips...**

I have already said about Phil Jupitus. I have met people who are walking from Land's End to John O' Groats for charity, met people who are cycling the same for the same reason and met some incredible young people who are out there enjoying the world. Some of the young volunteers I have met on the many RSPB reserves I have visited have been amazing. The passion that so many young people have for the environment has been inspiring. The fate of our future is in good hands with young people who care so much and display such commitment and enthusiasm. I am always amazed by the young people that have left the box within a box behind and decided to get out there and do something themselves. Making a life instead of watching someone else's.

Q15. **How do you like to relax when you're not birding or biking?**

Listening to music, reading a good book or watching a non-violent film. Favourite film 2001, music – rock, classical or jazz and book usually political, natural history or classic. Then there's my sporting passion, cricket. I could watch cricket live endlessly, as long as some birds fly over occasionally.

Q16. **Can you describe a typical day?**

Up, wash, breakfast, load bike and plot route for the day. Get on the bike, cycle to location and bird. In the evening find accommodation or put the tent up, collapse. If in accommodation with Wi-Fi, update blog and Facebook, answer emails, write the day up. If not read or write day up. Text friends and family. Sleep. Food I have on the go other than breakfast, the most important meal of the day.

Q17. **How far would you cycle for a bird?**

I cycled 58 miles in five hours on a fully laden bike to see the Citril Finch. I am sure I would cycle more for a good bird for the list or a lifer.

Q18. **Do you have a bogey bird?**

I have never seen a Terek Sandpiper despite having tried to see one on five different occasions.

Q19. **What's your 'one that got away'?**

When I lived in Swanage, Dorset I walked up onto my patch one May morning and saw a bird go over the cliff never to be seen again. Like a headless chicken I ran home, went running around to my great birding friend Gordon Barnes and dragged him up the cliff to try to find the bird I had seen. Having seen a lot abroad I knew what it was but as I said, the bird was never to be seen again. An Alpine Accentor.

Q20. **Do you have any words of wisdom / pithy advice for the teenage readers of 'Wingbeat?**

Get a notebook and write it all down as you find things. Start to draw even simple drawings of birds and label them with what you see. Never be worried about asking someone a question. Nearly every birder loves to share their knowledge. Join **Next generation Birders** on Facebook and **ASK QUESTIONS.** Stay at a Bird Observatory, such as North Ronaldsay in Orkney, Dungeness or Portland Bill and mix with birdy people. Realise you are a very special person because you love birds and nature.

Quickfire questions (choose the one you prefer and say briefly why!)

Mountains or Moors? Mountains. My favourite biome. The physical challenge of walking and climbing mountains, the change in birds and habitats as one gets higher and the thrill of reaching a summit, as well as the views. Mountains every time.

Wetlands or woods? Woods. I grew up spending a lot of time in woodlands around my home in Worcestershire.

Birder or twitcher? Birder! Green birder. I love to constantly be in the field watching birds, not in a car. Cycling allows one to bird while cycling along, listening and watching.

Lycra or camo? Camo. My figure wouldn't suit lycra. I would look like Max Wall! (look him up on Youtube.)

Warblers or Waders? Warblers but only just. Both groups are challenging and fascinating but the extra effort one makes to find and identify warblers puts them ahead, just.

Robin or rarity? Rarity but that's not to say I don't like robins.... Siberian Blue Robin, American robin. . .

Pasta or pasty? Pasta. "Just one lasagne, give it to me!"

Sir Peter Scott or Sir Bradley Wiggins? Sir Peter Scott. I am a birder not a cyclist. Sir Peter was my childhood hero.

And finally, birding or **biking** ? Do you need me to answer that? A bike is just a Green way of getting me to the next bird. Birding. I do love cycling and can't imagine ever not doing it but birding and a love of nature and places is my life.

Thanks Gary. Keep up the good work.

:) :) :) :) :) :)

Saturday 9th January **light S-SW**

Heavy rain showers, occasional thunder.

Starlings, hundreds of thousands of them, leave and go overhead as I sit in the hide early in the morning at Noah's Lake, Shapwick listening to the rain on the roof and the conversation from another early riser, Rob. Rob says that he is down here most days photographing whatever nature puts in front of him.

By 9:30 a.m. the million plus Starlings have all gone and the Great White Egrets have also left the roost. Still there is no sign of the Glossy Ibis.

In heavy rain, I cycle to the main road and hide the bike. I don't want to trudge and push it through the mud that recent bridge repair work has rendered the pathway. Unencumbered, I walk down to the Dusky Warbler spot again and meet someone looking pleased. He has just seen it. Confidence is high once more.

By 3:00 p.m. My confidence has gone over seeing the rare warbler and in over five hours of standing in the rain has not given me even a glimpse of it. I do get a year tick. A couple of **Meadow Pipits** are in an area of cut reed amongst a few pied wagtails. There have been very few other birders braving the foul weather and only one, Paul Williams from Clevedon, has spent the day as I have. He went for a walk some time ago and comes back to tell that he has seen the Glossy Ibis! Well, there's always tomorrow.

I retire to the Railway Inn and buy a couple of chicken rolls. Having only had a packet of Hobnobs and some chocolate bars, the latter of which being given to me yesterday by Pete Drommett, I am in need of some sustenance. No shops around here.

Down to the Noah's Lake Hide again, which is full of Starling watchers. A group of four, two couples have come all the way from Winchester. Together we watch the grey skies and as rain falls and darkness does likewise, masses of Starlings fly over. A Sparrow Hawk tazzes past, almost seeming that it may come in the hide with us. It is carrying one of the Starlings in its talons. Well that makes one million minus one.

Then . . . I shout out . . . **Glossy Ibis**!

There it is, this prehistoric-looking bird, flying low over the reed bed to the right. It lands for a short while out in front of me and then takes off heading left low over the water until it has gone into trees and out of view.

Soon it is completely dark. All people leave and I am left to settle down for the night.

The Green Year list now stands at **102**.

Sunday 10th January **light to fresh S**

Sunny interval with a heavy rain shower band passing.

Not out as early as I should be as breakfast at the Newhouse Farm Bed and Breakfast, Westhay is superb. Out by 9:15 a.m. I head immediately for

Ham Wall RSPB reserve for yet another attempt at seeing the **Dusky Warbler**.

Arriving at the spot I know so well by now I hear it calling. It is there in front of me amongst some thistles away from the water's edge and near the path. The call is a soft tack repeated quite quickly, pale legs obvious to see and the supercilium is whitish both before and after the eye.

It crosses the canal in front of me and keeps low in amongst the ground vegetation only allowing brief glimpses. A very fast, erratic bird, it stops calling and disappears.

Feeling that I really deserve this one, having missed a couple last year by minutes, I celebrate in my time honoured way. "Yes!" I shout with a fist pump or two, Henman-style. No one is around to celebrate with me.

A '16' bird in 2016; I need sixteen new birds above what I achieved last year to take the European record.

I search the reedbeds and lakes adjacent to the muddy path but do not see much of note, except unfortunately I see a black mink swimming across the canal.

Leaving Ham Wall, after almost forty eight hours there, I head for Greylake RSPB reserve and arrive just in time to enjoy lunch; four pieces of Toblerone and some orange juice, and shelter from some heavy rain showers.

Later I reach Taunton for an overnight stop. Describing cycling into the wind mile after mile in rain is pretty pointless.

The Green Year list now stands at **103**.

26.18 miles 950 feet elevation up 861 feet down

Monday 11th January Light to fresh S

Sunny intervals with drizzly showers 7C

Barbara, the owner of the Bed & Breakfast I stayed in last night, has a whole wall of her dining room devoted to world travel. Coloured flags denote where she has been and white flags are stuck on where her bed & breakfast clients live. She is obviously adventurous as the photographs of her with friends atop various European mountains show. What a great bed & breakfast, Heather Croft Taunton. She deserves a plug in these pages.

The day is spent heading south, which is mostly along the A38 until I make a mistake and lose it. The next five miles are spent negotiating a country lane with very questionable tarmac. Finding the A38 replacement I reach Exeter and get to the excellent RSPB reserve, Bowling Green at Topsham. Into the hide, the nearest flock of Wigeon has my target bird, a male **American Wigeon**. There is also a lone **Oystercatcher**, another new year tick and a surprisingly late addition.

With light fading fast I head for the platform where one can see the length of the immense Exe Estuary. It is low tide and amongst a small group of Redshank stands a lone **Spotted Redshank**.

The Green Year list now stands at **107**.

40.25 miles 1798 feet elevation up 1863 feet down

Tuesday 12th January Fresh to strong NW

Showers and rainbows

Sunrise early in the morning at Bowling Green RSPB reserve and the high tide on the Exe Estuary brings in masses of Avocet and Black-tailed Godwits; around six hundred of the former and possibly over a thousand of the latter. The two Greenshank from yesterday are still parading the margins. This time they are accompanied by over forty Redshank. It seems the Spotted Redshank out on the river last night is now in front of me close enough to photograph.

Two birders come into the hide. The first is Dean Reeves, who immediately tells me that last year he was second on the Surfbirds year list list; being second to Lee Evans. He looks at me and remembers where we met before six years ago. Dean it was that woke me up as I slept in the hide at Shapwick, Somerset whilst on my first Biking Birder adventure. Together we remember the birds we saw on that day; Sand Martins and a Long-tailed Duck, winter and summer birds together. We also talk about the Swift species that flew straight through on that day. Giving us only the briefest of views that day, a Pallid Swift was seen an hour or so later in South Wales!

The next birder, Martin Elcoate, comes in resplendent in Lycra cycling gear, which is a good job as he has a Specialised bicycle with him. Martin is a Green Birder! With his patch being the three kilometre square around Bowling Green reserve and Topsham, Martin says that he comes here regularly on his way to work. With a desire to be more environmentally friendly, he and his wife decided that one car would be better than two and so Martin now travels to work by bicycle. So far this year Martin has eighty seven on his Green year list; last year he saw one hundred and thirty five. My own bike, by the way, is a 1984 Claude Butler with an original Brookes saddle. It is a wonderful if rather heavy bike that gives a beautiful smooth ride. I love it!

Brilliant to meet both birders, the conversation is sharp and interesting.

Once the wader flocks had settled after fly pasts en masse, I set off through Topsham to the other, the west side of the River Exe and head downstream along the Exe Estuary cycle path.

A female **Red-breasted Merganser** is swimming lone on the river. There are Stonechats on brambles and Cetti's Warblers are calling along the way. Before reaching Powderham large flocks of **Brent Geese** are feeding in the flooded meadows, especially on the RSPB Exminster Marshes.

Just before reaching Dawlish Warren a farmer named Richard stops me to ask whether I could look on one of his stubble fields for Cirl Buntings. I look but find none, just a large flock of Linnets, a few Chaffinches and a lone Buzzard. He is hoping that Cirl Buntings will come on his land and stop a possible compulsory purchase order and building developments taking the place of his fields.

Down to Dawlish Warren nature reserve, I search the sea for grebes but only find Great Crested. A **Rock Pipit** is close by at the foot of a groyne stanchion. Two **Shags** are out on the sea jumping up before they dive beneath the waves.

The weather makes the walk along the beach bracing with a strong north westerly gale blowing sand into my face. I am here to look for the Bonaparte's Gull but although it has been around Dawlish and Exmouth for over a year I cannot find it.

I go all around the Warren, following the sea around to the hide on the north side. Here there is a lone **Grey Plover** and a couple of Curlew. The tide is extremely low and with the gale blowing hard birds are well spread throughout the estuary and not here.

I head back to the small woodland near to the visitor's centre and look unsuccessfully for the reported Firecrest. There are a couple of Goldcrests here and a Chiffchaff.

Another search over the sea gives just half a dozen or so Great crested Grebes. A day of strong wind, showers and rainbows ends with a lovely sunset.

The Green Year list now stands at **113**. This is **17** ahead of the number I was on this time last year.

20.51 miles **588 feet elevation up** **511 feet down**

Wednesday 13th January **light W**

Warm sunny AM 9C showers cooler PM

The thought that I would get to Tavistock by evening is on my mind when my mobile comes back to life after being in a no signal void at Dawlish. I am on the road west heading towards Ashcombe and the small lane is already a series of ups and downs. A male **Cirl Bunting** is singing in an oak tree. Brilliant to get one, I had expected to have to go to the Labrador Bay RSPB reserve area on the return through this way in about three weeks time. There is another bunting lower down in a bush and closer further down the lane.

Eight text messages arrive in less than a minute. There is a Little Bunting at Dart's Farm, Topsham. Texting birding friends for confirmation before making the decision to turn around and go back, I receive phone calls from Chris Craig and Tony Barter. Seen at 8:30 a.m. I retrace my route and on reaching the main Exeter road head north and onto the Exe Estuary cycle path once more.

At Dart's Farm, once reached, there is a group of around a dozen birders searching a stubble field. The bird was seen at 12:15. It is now 1:00 p.m.

There are plenty of Chaffinches and Goldfinches. With them is a male **Brambling**. Chatting may have cost me the Little Bunting. Whilst talking to a birder who used to frequent Upton Warren, my ex-patch in Worcestershire, John Day, the birder with telescope to our left says that he has just had it, that he had been watching it in a distant oak tree. He didn't tell us this until the bird had flown. No one else has seen it.

Kevin Rylands is the local RSPB conservation consultant and together with John Day I spend the rest of the afternoon searching for the special one, unsuccessfully. A female **Merlin** does pass, dashing one way over a hill crest and then returning about half an hour later. Both are great company, as are other Devon and Somerset birders, some of whom come over for a chat, give good wishes having seen my blog.

The cycle back to Starcross on the west side of the Exe is along the cycle path once more in the dark and with rain falling. With a feeling of complete safety away from roads I put my MP player's earplugs in and sing Pink Floyd songs all the way to a superb Bed & Breakfast, The Red House. Now why haven't I got the Jimi Hendrix song of the same name on the player? A lovely evening is spent talking with the proprietor and a guest, Corinne and Rosella. Corinne talks about her writing a novel about a child with Asperger's Syndrome and Rosella is a Spanish lady from Murcia who is a vet over here. How appalling that she was given a job here on half the salary of British vets with her qualifications due to her nationality.

The Green Year list now stands at **116,** eighteen ahead of where I was at this time last year.

25.33 miles **708 feet elevation up** **778 feet down**

Thursday 14th January **Strong NW**

Cold and sunny

I have only one target today, the Bonaparte's Gull, which hopefully will be at Exmouth. I should have made this the priority three days back and gone there after Bowling Green RSPB Reserve instead of heading for Dawlish Warren. Green Birding on my scale depends on the rare birds I need presenting themselves along the way, with opportunities for the more common species being seen due to visiting as many different habitats as possible. Oh well, today I may rectify my mistake.

The cycle ride around the whole of the Exe Estuary is easy along the superb Exe Estuary cycle way and my old comedy song repertoire keeps me going.

"I'm busy doing nothing, working the whole day through," a Bing Crosby song being sung along with Morecambe and Wise's Positive Thinking song bringing me sunshine.

For five hours I search the Exmouth seafront, looking out across to Dawlish Warren in strong sunshine but with a bitingly cold wind. For five hours I live in hope of an American Gull addition to the list. In five seconds I decide enough is enough.

I retrace my cycle route back to the Red House over yonder without an addition to the year list.

33.88 miles **556 feet elevation up** **560 feet down**

Friday 15th January **fresh to strong NW**

Sunny intervals, hail showers

The road today is going to be hilly. The wind today is going to be obliquely in my face. The weather forecast says showers. I set off.

No birds in the hedgerows today, I pass the spot where two male Cirl Buntings were the other day. The wind is keeping them down. The big push begins and the day alternates between long upward sections through beautiful wood, down steep brake-screeching falls and flat river side roads.

Between Chudleigh and Bovey Tracy there is a road block, possibly due to flooding. I have to go around the diversion.

Beyond Bovey Tracy the climb to get to the top of the Dartmoor plateau is long and tortuous. Today is turning into one of the hardest days for months. Hail showers add to the fun!

The view from the top though is beautiful, with full sunshine as the grey and white curtain of the receding hail shower departs to the south. The two

Tors to the north have brown bracken patches with green pathways and exposed rocky outcrops to tempt the walker to climb.

Day after day, alone on a hill , , , ,

Singing always helps keep me going and I laugh as I change the lyrics of The Beatles' classic song to suit my present situation.

Through Widecombe, all this is taking a lot longer than expected, and up yet another steep and long rise. I turn for Postbridge. The road become one long sheet of ice and snow and *skating away on the thin ice of new day* becomes my task for the next few miles and a Jethro Tull song to sing; the ice and snow slowing me down even further.

Reaching Postbridge, the main road is clear of ice but narrowed by snow. Half way to Two Bridges the views over Dartmoor are stunning; old yellow grass stems poking through the snow. All stand out as the Sun sets.

A very good friend, Lee Dark, has been texting me all day as to my progress and now meets me in the fading light for a brief chat. We are both worried about the state of the road as darkness falls and the temperature drops below freezing.

In the dark, past Dartmoor prison, I plummet off the moorland and down into Tavistock. The owner of tonight's bed & breakfast, Kingfisher Cottage at Tavistock, phones me as I am screeching down the last hill drop. I must change the front brake block! He is worried about me, as it is now near half past six. Two minutes later we are chatting as the kettle boils.

The average mileage for January is now approaching thirty one miles per day. Today's elevation is a punishing twelve feet more than the height of Ben Nevis, Britain's highest mountain. Ouch!

41.09 miles **4423 feet elevation up** **4134 feet down**

Saturday 16th January **Light NW**

Sunny intervals 8C

Dipper seen from the bedroom window of the Bed & Breakfast. Now isn't that a great way to get a year tick? A Kingfisher lands in a nearby bush and a Grey Wagtail lands on the rock vacated by the dipper. All this is before a substantial army-style breakfast from an ex-Army soldier.

Thanking Paul for a great Bed and Breakfast (Kingfisher Cottage, Tavistock), I head into the town to find a cycle repair shop. I need new brake blocks as the downhill screeching heard over Dartmoor the previous evening showed me how slight and dangerous the old ones are.

Martin at Tavistock Cycles has such items and a long chat with another Martin, a customer in the shop with his wife, is about a mutual passion,

Aston Villa. Along the lines of "I was there when . . . ", the customer Martin recalls the 1971 Villa versus Bournemouth match. "What a classic diving header!" I had a klaxon at that match, an old WW2 plunger type that can be heard on Youtube. I dropped it, lost forever when Andy Lochhead got the second to win the game for the Villa in front of 48,000 fans.

https://www.youtube.com/watch?v=UjK_MWnvYE8

After leaving the shop, a phone call tells me that I have left my binoculars at the bed and breakfast. Senior moment.

Standing on the bridge with binoculars retrieved, I watch and video a pair of Dippers downstream.

The road towards my next destination is tough, especially at the spot where I cross the River Tamar at Gunnislake and enter Cornwall. The hill seems interminable and the push is exhausting but I eventually reach Siblyback Lake at around 3:00 p.m. I cycle around to the north end where the bird I am after is a long way from the shore, a red-headed **Smew**.

My evening and night is spent in the bird hide here accompanied by a calling Tawny Owl. The owl is outside!

The Green Year list now stands at **118,** sixteen ahead of where I was at this time last year.

23.16 miles 2356 feet elevation up 1926 feet down

Sunday 17th January light S

Cloudy, a few light showers 8C

Siblyback Lake is still and quiet as I leave my night's accommodation and head back towards the country lanes that will lead me to Hayle.

The Dorset King Stones, an ancient monument, stop me for a while. Having been there from 875AD, the stones have been there a long time.

The A38 is as scary as ever as the road goes through a narrow river valley before Bodmin. The A30 is less so as all can see me on this large busy dual carriageway, the long grey anaconda of a road. I always feel safer on here than on the narrow Cornish country lanes. In fact I feel safer cycling along the A30 than I did in Peru back in January of 2014. A group of us had got up very early in order to go in a canoe up the Tambopata river to a large parrot lick. The area had been devastated by unprecedented floods just a few weeks before and the clay cliffs were clear of covering vegetation. The spectacle of thousands of parrots feeding early in the morning on the clay will stay with me forever. So will what happened next. Instead of going back downstream to the lodge for breakfast, Jorge, the lodge owner, steered the canoe upstream and after a few miles came towards the riverbank. On reaching the mud just beside the smashed up roots of a large uprooted tree, Jorge motioned to myself and a wonderful Peruvian man, Manuel, to go and have a look in the roots. On doing so imagine the surprise on seeing a huge anaconda slowly moving around beneath our feet. She was almost ten metres long and was sloughing, rubbing her scaly skin on the tree roots. Jorge told us that someone had seen her swimming into the roots a few days before and had alerted everyone to her presence. A great memory to focus on whilst cycling.

The day is a fifty mile slog which goes quickly enough and I reach Hayle. I find the bed and breakfast from last year, The Mad Hatter, and leaving my stuff there, after being greeted as a long lost friend by Pauline and Mark, I go birding for an hour along Copperhouse Creek. Singles of Greenshank, Little Egret and Grey Plover I see. The rain, always threatening to fall all day, finally does just that and with some persistence.

57.73 miles 3262 feet elevation up 3972 feet down

Monday 18th January light to fresh E

Cloudy, showers Noon, cool wind

A massive breakfast to last the day and I am off knowing that there are birds available for the year list in the vicinity. The possibility of increasing my total by over twenty five in the next few days is a sure fire motivation.

As usual I have been primed as to the locations of the better birds by Phil Andrews, The Oracle, and for that I am very grateful.

At Hayle Estuary RSPB reserve, an adult **Kittiwake** and a **Spoonbill** ensure a good start to the day.

I cycle towards Penzance. Just after the roundabout, where the road to Marazion is straight over and Penzance is to the west, I spot a fox crouching in a grassy field and stop to photograph it. It sits still and is beautifully photogenic.

Over to Marazion when, on searching for a way to the shore via a back street, I look up to view a very close gull. I shout out "**Glaucous**!" I immediately phone Phil excitedly. I missed out on this bird last year.

A message comes as I am searching the shoreline for the possibly present Hudsonian Whimbrel;

Pacific Diver east of Marazion....now.

I am east of Marazion and I search frantically for the sender of the message. After a few dead end lanes and alleys I find the very man, James Packer, a friend of Chris Craig and he shows me a photograph of what he thinks is the Pacific. I am not sure as the forehead doesn't look right to me though I must admit the neck and bill do point towards Pacific. Anyway we find the diver again bit it is very distant and no way could we tell what it is.

On rocks below where we are is a single **Turnstone** with a couple of Grey Plover and some Redshanks. Meanwhile a diver that does come close is a **Great Northern**. The Green year list goes to **123**.

Nothing much out at sea, a raft of forty or so Shags and a few passing gulls, James and I walk around the coastal path towards Perranuthnoe. We meet a group of four birders who report little. Two of them walk with us, Phil Taylor and Hilary Mitchell; affectionately known as P & H. I dawdle a bit, searching all rocks along the shore and P & H disappear around a hedgerow.

There's the Whimbrel, not far away sitting on top of a rocky outcrop facing away from me. James is only a bit in front of me and I quietly whistle to him and point out the bird. He immediately gets his telescope on it and photographs away like mad. I run to catch P & H, shouting until I gain their attention and so all four of us get to see a Whimbrel species which looks good for Hudsonian. It takes off and the all dark rump confirms that this is our bird. Brilliant, **Hudsonian Whimbrel**, a mega rare bird on the year list and the third I have seen in Britain.

James and I start to walk back towards Marazion as rain falls and we stop to look over the sea towards the ever beautiful St Michael's Mount. I almost tread on a small vole as I sit on a rock.

James finds a **Red-throated Diver** and then goes off to see more birds, offering me a carbon lift to join him. A lift I refuse.

I return to the Hayle estuary and spend an hour looking for the reported Yellow-browed Warbler. I am not too worried over missing this bird, dipping out as birders say. Last year I saw 111 Yellow-broweds on Fair Isle, in cricket terms a Nelson, and my plan for this year is to stay on the Fair Isle for two months.

No luck with the Siberian waif maybe but watching a Kingfisher hunting from a high electric wire is interesting.

I am then off to Carnsew Basin to find a **Red-necked Grebe** and a 1st year Great Northern Diver.

Back at the Bed & Breakfast I start to update my Bubo 2016 year list and find I have omitted to put Red-breasted Merganser seen on the Exe River. That means my spreadsheet list must be wrong and I find that I have omitted Great-crested Grebe from the first day!

The Green Year list now stands at **126,** fifteen ahead of where I was at this time last year.

20.31 miles **963 feet elevation up** **952 feet down**

Tuesday 19th January **fresh SE**

Cloudy, cool wind

I leave The Mad Hatter bed & breakfast with a packed lunch from Pauline and her good wishes.

Heading for Penzance, I stop on the causeway alongside the Hayle Estuary, see the Spoonbill again and find a **Common Sandpiper**.

Onward to Long Rock car park where two **Knot** flew past me heading east along the beach. With no divers to see I cycle to Jubilee Pool, Penzance to look at the large flock of **Purple Sandpipers**, twenty eight of them and Turnstones there. I just love the way the latter walk right past you if you stand still enough. There's a close B**lack-throated Diver** on the sea and I get soaked whilst filming it as a large wave crashes over me.

To Newlyn Harbour next, seeing a R**azorbill** not looking too fit in the surf on the way. Three Great Northern Divers are actually in the harbour enjoying the relative calm compared to the surge outside the walls.

I decide to go along a pathway beside the Penzance Boating Pool and see a small bird go into a privet hedge. I pish a little and a very smart **Firecrest** comes out six feet from my head! Brilliant, one of my favourite birds and it is now on the Year list.

The Green Year list now stands at **132,** fourteen ahead of where I was at this time last year.

12.76 miles **628 feet elevation up** **476 feet down**

Wednesday 20th January **fresh SE**

Sunny AM & warm, Cloudy PM & cool

The plan is to head for Porthgwarra taking in the fields around Jericho farm where Iceland gull has been reported. A text message arrives whilst I talk with a fellow birder, Paul Smith who is staying at the Penzance Youth Hostel and comes from Doncaster. The text reports the Pacific Diver is east of St Michael's Mount again. Paul gives a donation as I hurriedly head for Marazion once again.

Reaching the pathway along which I saw the Hudsonian Whimbrel two days ago, I hide the bike and walk to a far headland point, sit upon some rocks and scan the sea. There is a very close Great Northern Diver and four distant Black-throats swimming together and diving together. No sign of the Pacific Diver though. I keep scanning. I am joined by a local birder, Tim who has Swarovwski telescope. Finding divers becomes easier; two

Red-throated, five Black-throated and three Great Northern. The frustration at not finding the special one is alleviated by finding the Hudsonian Whimbrel again. This time it is with one of it's European cousins and a few Curlew. **Whimbrel** goes onto the Year list.

An adult Mediterranean Gull and three Little Egrets fly past .

The weather changes as cloud rolls in from the south. What had been a pleasantly warm, sunny Spring-like day was now cold and dull.

I walk back to where I had hidden the bike and ride downhill into Marazion. Finding a way down to the shore overlooking the amazing St Michael's Mount, I find a superb male Black Redstart, one of the best looking birds of that species I have ever seen. Searching further along a section of beach that has been covered with thick seaweed debris, there are around fifty **Sanderling** with smaller numbers of Turnstone and a few Redshank.

The Green Year list now stands at **136,** fifteen ahead of where I was at this time last year.

12.47 miles 632 feet elevation up 632 feet down

Thursday 21st January strong S

Rain all day

A day of rest, reflection and conversation after twenty days of cycling and birding. I am happy with progress and the list is a long way ahead of last year and having seen some birds of quality, I spend the day relaxing as the rain pours outside.

Physically the parts of my body that have been aching the most, knees and hands, appreciate the respite and hopefully will show their appreciation by not hurting so much tomorrow.

A chance to look at some websites and blogs that I usually am too tired to look at, the American Birding Blog is a must.

http://blog.aba.org/

Offshoots from that occupy some of my morning.

http://birdgirluk.blogspot.co.uk

A look through Birdgirl's blog is as inspiring as ever and a new blog for me, Positive News, reflects upon positive developments in the Nature world.

http://positivenews.org.uk/tag/nature/

Sleep is restorative and waking in the afternoon I spend the rest of the day with the other people at the hostel. My dormitory companion, Dan, is on his way to the Isles of Scilly and he is amazed at the competitive world of bird listing. I show him world listers, British carbon listers and Green listers. He tells me that his ten year old son is only interested in watching Attenborough programmes on TV but that he he has shown a keen interest in birds. Dan thinks that he will be very interested in all that I have shown him. I hope so too. It is always such a great thrill for me to hear of children interested in any sort of nature.

Friday 22nd January **Strong W**

Very sunny and warm 13C

Out early after both a text and phone call tells me that this week's target bird, the Pacific Diver, has been seen. The wind is behind me as I pedal an unladen bike to the causeway that takes one over to St Michael's Mount. Two Mediterranean Gulls, an adult and a first year bird are on a small island beside the causeway as I walk across to the island. The last time I did this I was eight years old, just a few years ago then, with Mum and Dad, brother and sister on a family holiday to Cornwall. It looks as impressive close to this time as it did back in the Sixties.

I clamber over rocks to get a closer view of the rough sea. Two **Ringed Plover**, the first of the year, fly near to me and land. A Great Northern Diver is close by on the sea but other divers are too far out for me to see properly.

Returning to the mainland before the causeway is covered by the incoming tide, I head for Trenow Beach and settle down on a rock there. Two more Great Northerns are out on the water and a group of three apparently Black-throated Divers appear very briefly as troughs become peaks in the swell.

In an attempt at getting closer to the Black-throated Diver group I pedal into Marazion and find the way down to a harbour wall. Here I meet a local birder, Roger Butts and ask that he allows me the use of his Swarowski. This wonderful man says no problem and I find the three divers. One seems to be Pacific; no white thigh patch, rounded head, overall size slightly smaller than other divers around and so I ask Roger to say what he thinks. He agrees that this is the **Pacific Diver** and so after four days of searching the bird goes at last onto the year list.

He leaves to go off in search of Black Redstarts and I remain, sheltering behind the harbour wall from the strong westerly wind and watch as diver after diver come close, all Great Northerns now.

The Green Year list now stands at **138,** fourteen ahead of where I was at this time last year.

13.41 miles 684 feet elevation up 696 feet down

Saturday 23rd January Strong SW

13C cloudy then rain

I head out towards Sancreed expecting to see lots of gulls in the fields around Trennack farm. There are none. A few Herring Gulls fly over. I wait.

At 10:30 a.m. a lone gull flies around and lands briefly, very briefly. Then takes off to fly around and land briefly once more. Hence I get pretty poor views of the 1st winter **Ring-billed Gull**, an American gull, seemingly rarer than in previous years, looking rather lost despite the fact that it has been coming to these same fields for a number of days.

The day, which had been rather blowy and dry, descends into one of rain and fog. I decide to bird any copse or woodland on the way back to Penzance instead of spending the day searching for Chough around St Just and Land's End.

The Green Year list now stands at **139,** fifteen ahead of where I was at this time last year.

6.87 miles 564 feet elevation up 578 feet down

An email from John Dixon will come in useful in a couple of weeks time:-

Hello Gary,
I gather from Phil that you will be passing through the New Forest soon and need assistance with a couple of species.

Hawfinch: *most reliable site is Blackwater Arboretum, off the Rhinefield Ornamental Drive between the A35 and Brockenhurst: SO42 7QB. Car park and toilets: cross the road and go through the gates to the Arboretum. Hawfinches roost here and can be seen mid- to late afternoon. Get there early (1400-1430) and be prepared to wait, as they sometimes come in early and dive almost straight into conifers to roost: though usually some will sit up. Its as near a dead cert as you will get in birding.*

While you are waiting, this site is good for other woodland stuff, Treecreepers, Nuthatches and woodpeckers including, recently (reported again today) Lesser Spotted Woodpecker. Note that LSW may possibly be in oaks just beyond the Arboretum - stay on the track and through the far gate, then view both sides. It could also be in the Arboretum itself.

Goshawk. *This is common in the Forest but the best place to see them reliably is Acres Down. Acres Down Farm, Minstead, Lyndhurst, Hampshire SO43 7GE is off west side of the road from the A31 to Emery Down, the junction is a crossroads. Follow to end of road and then take the track left uphill through woodland onto the open down. Watch West and South west from the nose of the down accessed west from the main forestry vehicle track. Mornings usually best - light gets difficult after midday. From Acres Down you can see most of the South west part of the New Forest, which contains several pairs of Goshawks. Good views can be obtained here. The site also has the odd Dartford Warbler.*

Hope this helps. If anything is unclear, just ask. Need help with any other species, just ask too. Cheers, John.

Sunday 24th January **Strong S**

13C cloudy, misty then suddenly sunny PM

Off to Sancreed again to try and get better views of the Ring-billed Gull, I arrive to find once again, no gulls. Waiting and searching for almost an hour I do see a pair of Peregrines but no Ring-billed Gull. Another cycling birder arrives, Alex and he tells me that the Iceland Gull has been seen recently at a farm along the Pendeen road. Alex also says that the best place to see Cornish Chough is at Kenidjack.

The wind is sometimes coming from my side, sometimes behind me and I reach the ploughed field suggested by Alex to find it devoid of any birds.

I carry on down to Kenidjack and am thrilled to find a number of **Chough** in the valley by the sewage works. There are a few flying around loosely connected to Jackdaw and Rook flocks. A couple land on a nearby derelict and ruined mine building. One has a number of rings on it's legs.

Having successfully found and seen Chough well, unlike back in 2015 when the BBC Cornwall radio presenter had nailed me with the question of whether I had seen Cornish Chough. I hadn't. In fact in honour of not having done so the RSPB warden of the Marazion reserve had given me a small Chough keyring. This stayed on my bicycle handlebars for almost all of 2015, taunting me until the metal rusted through with the salty air of Fair Isle.

So with Chough on the year list, celebrating what could have been a tricky bird if I hadn't had them here, I cycle to Mousehole to try for gulls; an Iceland Gull was reported there yesterday.

First stop is Newlyn Harbour where a very close Great Northern diver is seen. Two Cornish birders tell me that the juvenile Glaucous Gull is just off the beach nearby and it sure is. Large and pale, the Glaucous stands out amongst the smaller Herring Gulls.

Just before Mousehole I stop for a while beside an allotment where the owner has created a number of figures using whatever materials have come to hand.

Sitting on the rocks beside the car park in Mousehole I add **Gannet** and **Fulmar** to the year list. There are small parties of auks passing and a number of Kittiwakes also.

A friendly local birder with an amazing Deputy Dog-looking hat comes up, Paul Semmens, and together we search for the gull as he talks about his work in monitoring cetaceans in the area. Paul says he records a number of cetaceans over a year, mostly porpoise and dolphins with the occasional whale.

We move around a small headland and meet another two birders Chris and the famous Mashuq. All week whenever I have met Cornish birders they have told me that Mashuq is the gull expert for the county.

Mashuq finds a white winger, possibly the Iceland but half of it is hidden by the rocks. Chris lets me have a look and following their directions I find the bird, seeing a pale mantle and head; the latter looking smaller and rounder than a Glaucous Gull's head would be. Half an Iceland, it doesn't go onto my year list. Maybe it should. The head and mantle were obviously of an Iceland Gull. Darkness falls and after saying goodbye to one and all, I head back to Penzance youth hostel.

The Green Year list now stands at **142,** eighteen ahead of where I was at this time last year.

23.93 miles **1568 feet elevation up** **1594 feet down**

An evening email from The Oracle:-

Here are all the sightings over the last 7 days of stuff you need; will send you an updated list once you are at the Exe (plus live news of anything on your route). Personally I would do the Slav at Stithians, press on swiftly to the Exe and assess situation, then onto Abbotsbury (perhaps quick look at Portland for SEO), Arne / Studland then on to New Forest. After Hampshire a week's hard cycle to Norfolk for lingering winter birds; presently have Pallid Harrier, RL Buzzard, Serin, Shorelark, Twite, Lap Bunt, Snow Bunt, Lsr Yellowlegs before moving up to York

CORNWALL

Slav Grebe - Carmeneleis Causeway, Stithians Res (southern end) 22/1, 21/1, 20/1 Trebah Beach, Durgan (2) 23/1 Marazion 17/1 Perranuthnoe 17/1
Little Gull - Loe Pool, Helston 23/1 Gannel Estuary, Newquay 23/1
Yellow-browed Warbler - Poonsanooth sewage works, sw of Truro 22/1, 20/1, 17/1 Ryans Field, Hayle Estuary 18/1, 17/1
Iceland Gull - St Clement's Isle, Mousehole 23/1 Lower Boslow Farm, Pendeen 18/1, 17/1 Jericho Farm, Newbridge 17/1
Green-winged Teal - Walmsley Sanctuary, Wadebridge 23/1, 22/1, 21/1, 20/1, 19/1, 18/1- IS THIS MEMBERS ONLY??
Water Pipit - Gannel Estuary, Newquay 21/1
Black-necked Grebe - Mylor Churchtown (3) 21/1
Whooper Swan - Dinham Flats, Camel Estuary (4) 19/1, 18/1 Newbridge, SW of Pendeen 18/1, 17/1
Yellow-legged Gull - Newbridge, SW of St Just 18/1 Lower Boslow Farm, Pendeen 18/1
Woodlark - Boscregan Farm, Nanquidno Valley (12) 18/1
Hen Harrier - Crowdy Res 17/1 Bartinney Downs 17/1 (dusk)
Long-tailed Duck - St Johns Lake, Torpoint 17/1
Bittern - Marazion 17/1
Little Auk - Marazion 17/1

DEVON

Black-necked Grebe - Slapton Ley (up to 4) 23/1, 22/1, 19/1, 17/1
Water Pipit - South Huish marsh 23/1 River Teign, Bishopsteignton 22/1, 21/1
Bonaparte's Gull - Exe Estuary from boat 23/1, Dawlish 21/1, Teignmouth 17/1
Red-crested Pochard - Slapton Ley (2) 23/1
Rough-legged Buzzard - Postbridge 21/1
Little Bunting - Darts Farm 21/1, 20/1
Black Guillemot - Brixham 21/1
Slav Grebe - Elberry Cove, Torbay 23/1 Dawlish Warren (up to 2) 23/1, 20/1, 17/1

Little Gull - Dawlish Warren 18/1
Velvet Scoter - Dawlish Warren 17/1

DORSET

Hen Harrier - Hartland Moor roost (3) 23/1, 22/1 Arne / Arne Moors (up to 2) 23/1, 22/1, 21/1, 19/1,17/1 Cranborne 21/1 Lychett Bay 17/1 Morden Bog 17/1
Short-eared Owl - Portland Bill (up to 3) 23/1, 20/1, 19/1, 17/1 Hartland Moors 22/1 Hengistbury Head 21/1 Arne 19/1, 18/1
Black-necked Grebe - Portland Harbour (up to 11) 17/1 Studland (up to 14) 20/1, 19/1 Poole Harbour (2) 23/1
Slav Grebe - Portland Harbour 19/1 Middle Beach, Studland 20/,19/1
Long-tailed Duck - Abbotsbury Swannery (2) 23/1, 22/1, 21/1, 19/1, 17/1
Bittern - West Bexington 23/1 Arne Moors 22/1, 21/1 Radipole 19/1
Black Guillemot - Poole Harbour 23/1, 21/1, 20/1
Little Gull - Chesil Cove 22/1
Water Pipit - Lychett Bay 17/1
Great Grey Shrike - Morden Bog 17/1
Pom Skua - Durlston Head 17/1

HAMPSHIRE

Hawfinch - Blackwater Arb, New Forest (6) 23/1, (7) 17/1
Water Pipit - Old Alresford (2) 23/1, (3) 19/1 Keyhaven 23/1, 20/1 Pennington 18/1, (2) 17/1
Lesser Spotted Woodpecker - Blackwater Arb, New Forest 23/1, 17/1
Great Grey Shrike - east of Ringwood at Stodgmoor Bottom 23/1 Beaulieu Road Station, New Forest 23/1, 22/1, 21/1, 20/1, 19/1, 17/1 Bishops Dyke 20/1, 18/1
Rose-coloured Starling - Eastleigh 23/1 (no other details)
Ferruginous Duck - Kingfisher Lake, Blashford Lakes 23/1
Yellow-browed Warbler - Eastleigh sewage works 23/1
Long-tailed Duck - Keyhaven 23/1, 20/1, 17/1
Slav Grebe - Keyhaven (3) 23/1, 22/1 Pennington Marshes 20/1 Oxey Creek 19/1 Ibsley Water, Blashford Lakes 17/1
Black-necked Grebe - Hayling Oyster beds (4) 23/1, (7) 17/1 Ibseley Water, Blashford Lakes 21/1, 19/1, 17/1
Penduline Tits - Titchfield Haven (up to 4) 23/1, 20/1, 17/1
Ring-necked Duck - Rooksby Lake LNR, SW of Andover (2) 23/1, 22/1, 17/1
Hen Harrier - Alresford Pond 22/1, 19/1
Caspian Gull - Ibsley Water, Blashford Lakes 22/1, 21/1 (roost), 18/1, 17/1
Bittern - Ivy Lake, Blashford Lakes 21/1, 17/1
Crossbill - Holmsley Enclosure, New Forest 21/1
Long-billed Dowitcher - Pennington Marshes 20/1, 19/1

Iceland Gull - Brown down Spit, Gosport 19/1 Southsea 18/1
Velvet Scoter - Langstone Harbour 17/1

Monday 25th January **Strong SW to W**

13C cloudy, some light drizzle, suddenly sunny PM

The day starts with a decision to get a tooth sorted. A bargain of two Fry's Turkish Delight bars, sing along now you older readers who remember the desert located adverts, for £1 had me chewing my favourite chocolate bar yesterday and on swallowing I found a large hole in a bottom left molar. Now I have had problems with this particular tooth for ages and my dentist had said that the next time she sees me she will have to take it out under a general anaesthetic. Last year it was this tooth that first had an abscess and then got cracked even further by a pip hidden inside a chocolate raisin.

Eleven o'clock and I am at a NHS dentist in Penzance. Twelve o'clock the tooth has been cleaned and fixed with a temporary filling. I have to make an appointment with my dentist for the full removal asap as the x-ray shows the extent of the infection below the root. Strange it hasn't caused me any pain at all since the abscess was treated with antibiotics.

On the road again, the day's original plan of trying to see Garganey and Water Pipit at Hayle has changed with the news that the **Rose-coloured Starling** has been seen again at The Lizard.

Through Marazion and along to Helston I cycle past field after field of flowering yellow daffodils. The final ten miles is into the wind. Reaching The Lizard village I start to search by walking the streets, looking at every Starling group. I consider getting a bed & breakfast as the weather forecast for tomorrow is of fifty five m.p.h. gales with heavy rain.

Forty five minutes of searching I look up and the nearest Starling of a small group on telegraph wires is the adult Rosy! It pops down closer onto a hawthorn bush in a garden and gives views that are so much better than last year's bird. In 2015 I had the briefest of views of a superb adult to which this one is dull in comparison. Watching it for the next half hour I wonder when the full pink plumage of a breeding bird comes into play. The other common Starlings spangle in the sun yet the rosy looks greyish-white on the parts that I expected to be shocking pink. Still it is another year tick and a very good one to get.

There are still a couple of hours of light left in the day and I decide to cycle to Stithians Lake to try to get the Slavonian Grebe before the bad weather arrives.

Two hours later, the sun having gone down, I ask a lady for directions instead of looking at the map on my phone. Two miles later, after hurtling downhill for quite some way, I realise that she has sent me to the village, not the lake. A large village sign Stithians tells me so.

Back up the hill I push as darkness falls. I reach the lake with it too dark to see anything and a very close Tawny Owl hoots its derision. A night in the bird hide beckons.

The Green Year list now stands at **143,** nineteen ahead of where I was at this time last year.

46.60 miles 2545 feet elevation up 2180 feet down

Tuesday 26th January Gale force W (55mph)

12C very heavy rain all day

It doesn't take long to see the reported Slavonian Grebe once daylight returns. Last night's clear, star-filled sky has been replaced by thick low cloud and it is raining hard. The promised gale, the remnants of the storm that dumped over two feet of snow on the Eastern USA killing so many, has arrived this side of the Atlantic and the weather is truly foul outside the confines of the C.B.W.P.S. (Cornwall Bird & Wildlife Preservation Society) hide.

The **Slavonian Grebe**, a bird that takes me to **144**, is quite distant and after texting the news I am unsure that I did see it as a little grebe extends its neck before flying closer. I did see the bright white cheeks didn't I? Scanning again I cannot see a Slav'.

Half an hour later the Slavonian Grebe does come closer and I get photographs and a short thirty second video as it bobs up and down on the sea-like swell.

With no intention of cycling in this squall; it would be suicidal to even try, I settle down in my sleeping bag, occasionally reading a book and occasionally watching for birds. Birds are few and far between; four Little Grebes come close catching small sticklebacks and the occasional gull lands on the water to preen. A male Goldeneye stays around in front of the hide for an hour or so.

The book is called Austerity by Kerry-Anne Mendoza and details the current obscenity of Neo-liberalism and the destruction of all that I hold dear; education, the NHS, the Justice system and social compassion.

The other book I have with me is by Roz Savage and is the story of her rowing across the Atlantic. She is eloquent and intelligent and the read is inspirational. “If one is going to be outside one's comfort zone then expect things to be uncomfortable.” I am wrapped up and cosy in this small bird hide; a little different to the sea sickness suffered from a small rowing boat hundreds of miles from land.

Midday with rain and wind still battering the water, I am joined in the hide by Jim, a birder from Newquay. Together we watch as the Slavonian Grebe swims very close by and a Firecrest is seen to the right of the hide; my second of the year.

The Green Year list now stands at **144,** twenty ahead of where I was at this time last year.

Wednesday 27th January **Gale easing to strong W**

Early fog, cloudy occasional light rain

In the hide at Stithians I wait for the fog to lift. The Slavonian Grebe is still here and comes quite close. A party of a dozen or so Long-tailed Tits are in the bushes next to the hide when suddenly the fog disappears and I can see the opposite shore of the large lake. I am already packed and ready to go.

The day is a mixture of pedalling and pushing as I come across hill after hill along this Cornish road. I pass through the city of Truro with its prominent cathedral and push on, literally, towards St Austell. I reach there and find the public house I stayed in last year. The bike is stowed away in the same place and I have the same expansive room overlooking the local church with its interesting small statues on the clock tower. I have forgotten that the church bells in the church tower, opposite my room, ring cacophonously every quarter hour.

26.10 miles **2076 feet elevation up** **2388 feet down**

Thursday 28th January **fresh W**

Sunny AM, sunny intervals & light showers PM

A day of cycling to get beyond Plymouth is ahead of me. I set off on the cycle – push route from St Austell to Plymouth. The morning is sunny and the sky cloudless. It is so warm that a Painted Lady butterfly flutters towards me across the road. I beg it to land onto my bike and it almost does so but it heads off instead over a tall hedge.

Before Liskeard I see a group of eight Ravens circling together and further along the road a flock of around twenty Fieldfare fly over. Winter thrushes have been very thin on the ground.

Hill after hill, the road is a tough one with few opportunities for cycling any prolonged stretch. That changes at Liskeard where I go on the A38.

The next ten miles whizz past.

The ride through Plymouth to get to the house of a great friend parents, Lee Dark's Mum and Dad, Lynn and Alan, is up and down hills again and complicated. Luckily down one stretch of road I am alert as someone has taken the heavy metal grill of a roadside drain hole and there is a deep chasm left in the road!

The evening is spent in the fine company of Lee and his girlfriend Kate as well as Lynn and Alan. A family meal up to a table is the first one I have had for years and much appreciated. A fabulous evening with lovely company.

43.36 miles 3838 feet elevation up 3830 feet down

Friday 29th January fresh to strong W

Heavy rain or thick drizzle

I don't know why but I am having a really enjoyable cycling day. The weather is appalling; either heavy rain or thick drizzle with a strong westerly wind just to make sure I am soaked through. There are no views of the beautiful hilly Devon landscape as it is all lost in the cloud and mist. Yet I am really enjoying the day. The only wildlife of note is, sadly, a dead Dunnock beside a cycle path.

I reach Totnes, then Newton Abbott and finally Teignmouth where the Potter's More Hotel has an attic room with a view over to the sea. Shower, rehydrate and relax.

33.87 miles 2419 feet elevation up 2653 feet down

Email from The Oracle:-

Will send you options for next week on Sunday evening (south coast quiet, option developing around Gloucs / Som) but in the meantime here are the Devon birds of the last 10 days:

Black-necked Grebe - Slapton Ley (up to 4) 23/1, 22/1, 19/1 Laira Bridge, Plymouth 28/1, 24/1
Water Pipit - South Huish marsh 25/1, 23/1 River Teign, Bishopsteignton 22/1, 21/1 end of Milbury Lane, Exminster Marshes 25/1
Bonaparte's Gull - Exe Estuary from boat 24/1+23/1, Dawlish 21/1
Red-crested Pochard - Ireland Bay, Slapton Ley (2) 23/1
Rough-legged Buzzard - Postbridge 21/1
Little Bunting - Darts Farm 21/1, 20/1

Black Guillemot - Brixham 21/1
Short-eared Owl - Exminster Marshes 24/1 over field by river at Bishop's Tawton 27/1
Black Stork - over A30 at Whiddon Down 24/1
Ridgway's Canada Goose (presumed escape) - Matford Pools, Countess Weir 28/1, 27/1, 24/1
Rough-legged Buzzard - possible Denbury, SW of Newton Abbott 25/1
Pom Skua - flew south through Dawlish Warren 27/1

Saturday 30th January **fresh W**

Sunny, short shower PM

To Teignmouth seafront I cycle and a search for the Bonaparte's Gull I missed earlier in the month. The tide is high and the sun is shining; such a contrast to yesterday. No sign of the rare gull, just lots of Herring Gulls of various plumages to admire.

Same again at Dawlish, I go under the railway arches and see the long stone jetty from which I stood with many others looking at Britain's only Long-billed Murrelet a few years ago.

I continue to Dawlish Warren and after seeing nothing other than two Great-crested Grebes and a single Great Northern Diver on the sea, I walk around to the bay at the end of the golf course by the hide. Waders are still roosting there due to the high tide and amongst a fair number of Oystercatchers and Curlew there are some **Bar-tailed Godwits**.

I walk all around the point opposite Exmouth and back along the beach, picking up plastic rubbish as I go.

Golden syrup on chips, actually quite nice, are bought from Chippy Chaps Fish Bar by the railway tunnel and eaten for lunch. An unusual combination I know but it seems to work when vinegar is added.

Along the excellent Exe Estuary cycle path once more, the weather is beautiful if a bit colder than of late. Just north of Exminster Marshes RSPB reserve's car park I see a woman with raised binoculars on the pathway above the level of the cycle path. I ask here if she has seen the reported **Short-eared Owl** and she tells me that it is in the field in front of us. The bird is obscured by a large hawthorn bush from my view but I soon have a sight of it.

The woman's name is Helen Hawke and she asks me how I am getting on as she knows me from my appearance on Springwatch last year and knows of my quest. She asks a young couple to take a photograph of us both and puts some money as a donation into the charity box. Thanks Helen.

To Matford Marsh RSPB reserve next but I cannot see the dodgy small

Canada Goose. I had been warned that it is difficult to see as it stays amongst the reedmace and sedges.

Late in the afternoon I reach Topsham and Bowling Green RSPB reserve. The water level of the pools in front of the hide is a lot lower than when I was here three weeks ago and duck numbers are reduced.

As darkness falls I consider how superb the Exe Estuary is for Green Birding. It has a superb cycle track around it's perimeter, some fabulous RSPB reserves with masses of birds, particularly Brent Geese and waders. The latter amass at Bowling Green when the tide is high. Then there is Dawlish Warren and it's dune system and the sea. Nearby there are woodland and hedgerows with Cirl Buntings amongst the commoner birds. Altogether it is the perfect area for a great day cycling and birding.

The Green Year list now stands at 146, seventeen more than this time last year.

21.69 miles   905 feet elevation up   884 feet down

Sunday 31st January   fresh to strong W

Cloudy AM, sunny intervals PM   mild, 13C

The final day of the first month starts at Bowling Green RSPB reserve near Topsham. Waders in large numbers are coming in from off the estuary as high tide approaches. Black-tailed Godwits number around 800 with a few Bar-tailed Godwits with them. There are also a couple of hundred Avocet and smaller numbers of Dunlin and Redshank. They all take off together when first a Sparrowhawk flies along a hedgerow and then a female Merlin does likewise.

I still need to find the Bonaparte's Gull and with the weather nothing like the heavy rain forecast I cycle to Exmouth. Along the way another cyclist, Max joins me and we cycle together for a couple of miles. He talks of his job and of his two young children.

I spend a few hours along the seafront in Exmouth checking every gull as the tide recedes. There are very few gulls though and around 4:30pm I head off for a nearby country hostel. Reaching it I am greeted by two Midlanders acting as managers of the complex. One has a coffee in her hand, which is in an Aston Villa mug, my own football team sadly.

11.12 miles   497 feet elevation up   430 feet down

And so the first month ends.

January monthly statistics:-

Green Year list	146 birds
Number of birds not seen in 2015	3
Mileage	723.56 miles
average mileage on days cycled	26.80 miles
elevation : up	40,184 feet
: down	40,344 feet

Best Birds : **Great White Egret x 10, Hoopoe, Grey Phalarope, Black Restarts x 6, Lesser Scaup, Cattle Egret, Dusky Warbler, Glossy Ibis, American Wigeon, Smew, Red-necked Grebe, Great Northern Diver x 22, Firecrest x 2, Black-throated Diver x 6, Glaucous Gull, Hudsonian Whimbrel, Pacific Diver, Ring-billed Gull, Rose-coloured Starling, Slavonian Grebe.**

2

FEBRUARY

The sombre stretch of rounds and hollows seemed to rise and meet the evening gloom in pure sympathy, the heath exhaling darkness as rapidly as the heavens precipitated it.

Thomas Hardy, Return of The Native

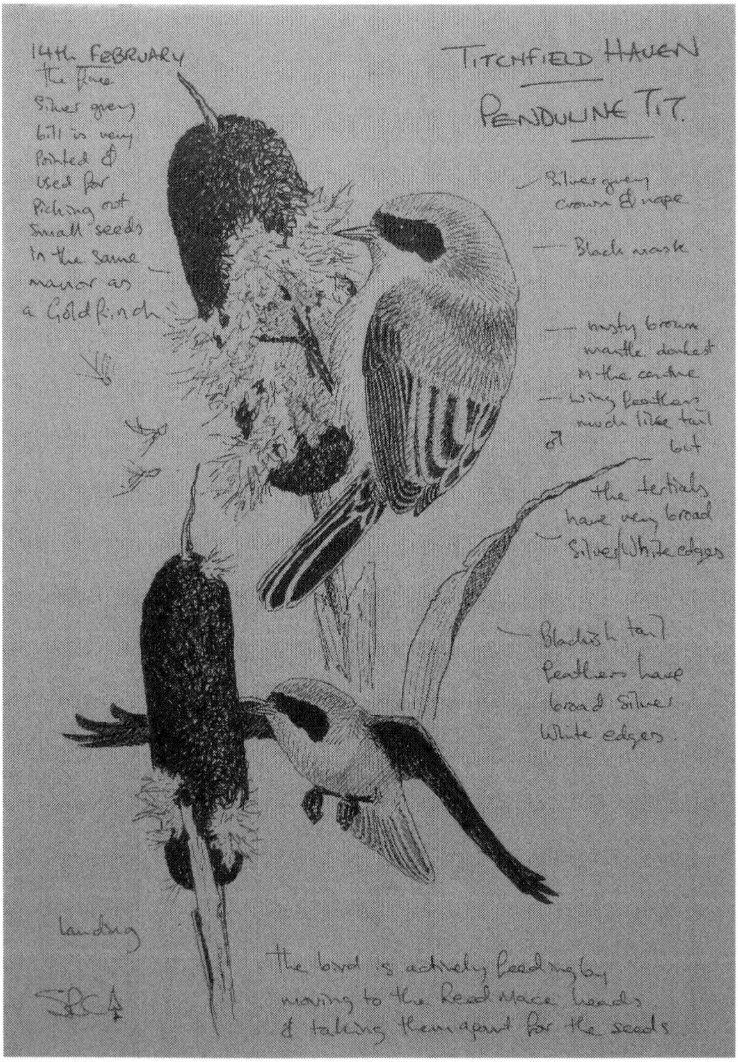

Monday 1st February **fresh to strong W**

Sunny intervals, occasional light rain 13C

There is a report from The Oracle of a Green-winged Teal at Seaton, Devon, which is around twenty miles from where I am at present. With the bike ready I start the cycle. This part of Devon is extremely beautiful but very hilly with deep valleys and lots of trees and hedgerows. The day, it seems, will be one long push up one tree-covered steep hill after another and the going is tough and exhausting.

Through Budleigh Salterton, through Sidmouth, the place where my Mum and Dad had their honeymoon many years ago, and after a particularly steep and long hill climb, I reach a main road with a turn off for Beer.

Unfortunately a lack of road signs takes me down the wrong road. I end up in Branscombe from which to get back onto the right road for Beer there is yet another very steep climb.

Into Beer, I find the youth hostel there and leave the panniers and sleeping bag. With an unladen bike the ride over to Seaton is not that bad and I find the reserve upon which the rare American bird has been seen.

A birder carrying a telescope comes up to me saying that we met on Shetland back in 2010. His name is Tony and together we search for the Teal. I find it whilst peering through some tall reeds. It is almost up against the far bank of the pool, dabbling as teals do along the edge. Distant but great to see, the male, white-shoulder dashed **Green-winged Teal** goes onto the year list; yet another really good bird. Getting a Yank is a superb way to start a new month.

Year list goes to **147**, eighteen ahead of this time last year.

18.66 miles **1993 feet elevation up** **1869 feet down**

Tuesday 2nd February **fresh to strong W**

Sunny intervals, occasional light rain 9C

With the brake blocks changed on the back wheel, I set off and soon encounter the first of what I know will be hill climb after hill climb. In previous Biking Birder years I have cycled east to west, Dorset to Devon, Weymouth to Beer. Today that will be reversed and hopefully I will be in Weymouth by the evening.

A day of cascading rainbows as strong sunshine is occasionally blunted by light, drizzly showers, I reach the Dorset border. I am now into

Wessex,the county of Thomas Hardy, Henchard, Gabriel Oak and Egdon Heath, the vast tract of unenclosed wild. I enter the county that has so many intensely personal memories for me. It is here that I lived with my lovely late wife, Karen, my Irish, Spanish, Gypsy raven-haired, green-eyed love and the four children; Claire, Joshua, Rebecca and Sarah. I remember the many happy times we had here. We lived in Swanage, which is still far to the east.

A long stretch downhill hill leads into beautiful Lyme Regis and I stop on the quay to feed the gulls whilst enjoying the view east along the magnificent Jurassic Coast. A series of beautiful cliffs and headlands stretch into the distance towards Chesil Beach and Portland.

Hour after hour goes by with short bursts of downhill speed interspersed with longer stretches of uphill push. The elevation chart is going to look interesting tonight, like a graph of those tall, undulating and imposing cliffs seen eastward from Lyme Regis, ridge and furrow on a vast scale.

Past Bideford and along the high ridge with views along twenty miles of The Fleet and Chesil Beech to Portland, the sun is still shining and I am singing a repertoire of old comedy songs to keep me going; Sad Eyed Sal by Benny Hill has me tittering to myself.

There's a place near Plymouth Hoe
Where sailors like to go
There's an inn there called the Saucy Pussycat
There's a broken hearted gal
By the name of Fad eyed Fal
On her seat beside the bar you'll find her sat.

She'll whisper sweet nothings in your ear
Sip your wine or swig your beer
Or sing a simple song though slightly flat
She used to juggle with a carrot, four bananas and a parrot
But things got hard and she had to eat the act!

So shed a tear, (shed a tear)
For Fad eyed Fal, (Fad eyed Fal)
All her hopes and dreams will fade and fall apart, (fall apart)
And be sincere, (be sincere)
To your own Gal, (your own Gal)
Remember in your hand you hold a young girl's ....
heart.

https://www.youtube.com/watch?time_continue=24&v=vNBtpfoh8RM

A decorator's van stops and the driver runs across to give me a donation having heard the singing! Thanks Adam.

Now a hill climb I always remember as being very tough is this time a white knuckle descent. Into Abbotsbury I go. Turning down to hopefully visit the famous Swannery, I am prevented from seeing the reported Long-tailed Duck reported there by the place being closed. As the weather is now showery, cool and windy I decide to carry on to Weymouth.

Reaching Weymouth I head down to the RSPB reserve at Radipole. The usual male Hooded Merganser is by the bridge but it won't go down onto the year list. It arrived here a few years ago as a rather timid first year bird. Once maturity was reached it started to join other ducks chasing the bread crumbs proffered by people and so the powers that be decided it must be an escaped bird. Shame really because it is such a smashing little duck.

The Green Year list still at **147**, eighteen ahead of this time last year.

40.32 miles 3507 feet elevation up 3721 feet down

Wednesday 3rd February fresh to strong W

Sunny intervals, 9C

The cycle ride from Weymouth to Arne RSPB reserve is a delight with a strong wind at my back and empty roads with high quality tarmac. It is going to be a great day. I can feel it in my bones.

I feel excited as I approach Arne along a lane from Stoborough. This is one of my top five favourite RSPB reserves with beautiful heathland and woodland habitats beside estuarine arms of Poole Harbour, the World's second largest natural harbour.

After having cycled through some thick smoke coming from an area being cleared of old conifers, more restoring of the original heathland habitat, I reach the reserve and go to the small visitor's reception block. There I meet Luke and Chris, RSPB staff and soon, after stowing the bike away safely, I am off, speedily walking to an area where I am hoping to see my first target bird of the day, Dartford Warbler.

Reaching the area of thick gorse, the exact place where I saw a superb scarce warbler last year, I search and listen for this delightful small bird. The wind is still very strong and after an hour or so I still haven't seen or heard one.

I stand near to some gorse that looks particularly suitable and take out a chocolate bar for lunch. Then I hear something; a small, scratchy sub song. It sounds as if it is coming from quite a way away. I am therefore very surprised when a male **Dartford Warbler** pops up out of the gorse about ten feet away. It moves, unconcerned by my presence, amongst the gorse for a few minutes. Then a female pops her head up too. I get such fantastic views and so close as I stand stock still and watch them exploring the gorse.

New bird for the year and the important one of the three target birds for the day. There would have been only be a few opportunities of seeing one, the bird being restricted to the heathland of mostly Southern England and East Anglia. No matter, it is on the list. UTB. Brilliant.

I walk down to the small cliffs from where one can look over to Long Island and beyond to the ferry crossing at Studland. The tide is receding and four Spoonbills are quite distant out on the mud that starts the Middlebeare channel. There are also a fair number of Avocets and Curlew here. In the distance to the south I can see the famous ruins of Corfe Castle. This was blown up by Oliver Cromwell in the English Civil War after he had captured it from the Royalist army. I take a photograph of it as a large flock of Brent Geese fly in front of it.

Through the large pine woodland and along the side of some large fields, a sign of how benign this Winter actually is is that there are no Winter thrushes on the grass and no finches there either. Usually in a normal, cold Winter there would be hundreds of both.

Also missing are the large herds of Sika, a specie of large deer. They have obviously been culled to protect the habitats.

Back to the Visitor's Centre, which is soon to be replaced by a much larger one, hopefully by Easter, and meet Rob. Now Rob is another RSPB staff member and last year we had a fabulous day birding Arne together. Rob showed me around areas of the huge reserve that I ha never visited before, like the WW2 decoy plateau. Up here during a time of large German bombing raids on the harbour, The Allies had built decoy buildings to divert some of the bombs. Rob also took me to a large clay pit that is reputed to have been the first ever used by Josiah Wedgewood.

After my visit to Arne I head off for Middlebeare, not too far away, where the National Trust has a hide that overlooks the other end of the Middlebeare Channel from where I was earlier in the day. This used to be one of my favourite birding places when I lived in nearby Swanage and holds great memories for me. I haven't been here for around ten years and I am surprised at how high the trees have grown around the hide. The view across the muddy channel looks the same though with the curling dyke down the centre viewable now because of it being low tide. I am hoping a Hen Harrier will go past and that the resident Barn Owl will put in an appearance.

By dark neither have been seen but there have been a number of Spotted Redshanks, Spoonbills, Little Egrets and Brent Geese so life is good. I snuggle down for the night.

The Green Year list still at **148**, nineteen ahead of this time last year.

27.87 miles **1187 feet elevation up** **1210 feet down**

An email arrives from Marcus Ward:-

Hi Gary,

Just caught up on your blog, sounds like a great adventure and for a good cause. I saw your note on Facebook a while back, I might be able to offer you some help when you come to the New Forest.

I have been studying Hawfinch and LSW in the New Forest for a number of years and would therefore probably able to get you onto all your target species with relative ease. I have been studying Hawfinch in particular for past five years, mainly by finding and monitoring roosts (21 Hawfinch roosts found to date accounting for about 400 individuals) we also colour-ring and monitor nesting success with remote camera's. I try to keep it under the radar as much as possible but one interesting phenomenon we have discovered is that many of the Hawfinch roost sites are shared with Goshawk, we think a mixture of habitat preference but also probably down to the fact that the Gos will clear out all the corvids and smaller raptors creating a relatively safe haven for smaller passerines.

LSW are also close to my heart, together with a small band of volunteers we are surveying the whole of the New Forest this year, LSW become a lot easier to find when they start drumming, after around 3rd week of Feb (though I did have my first drumming LSW in the forest this morning).

I would recommend Acres Down/Holm Hill as a good area to try as one of the largest Hawfinch roosts is nearby (counted 58 Hawfinch out of the roost yesterday) and there is a high density of Gos and LSW in the area. At dawn the Gos are very vocal and conspicuous and from late Feb LSW are easy to pick up as they establish their territories. Survey work in this area in 2013 found around three to four LSW territories per square KM in this area.

I am out and about in the Forest most days, generally counting Hawfinch roosts at dawn followed by an hour or two of survey work (depending on weather and work) and you would be more than welcome to join either myself or one of my colleagues or alternatively let me know when you are in the area and I can point you in the right direction for all three species.

Good luck making your way through Dorset!

Cheers, Marcus

Thursday 4th February **fresh SW**

Sunny intervals, 14C

Early morning at Middlebeare, opening up the hide shutter an interesting sight starts the day. Two foxes are well and truly stuck after their night of passion. For two hours they stand back to back, occasionally struggling to separate. They frequently snap at each other but to no avail.

Three Spoonbills are out in the channel and a **Barn Owl** flaps past moth-like.

As for the foxes, I am videoing their predicament when suddenly they're free. The larger of the two just sits looking exhausted. The smaller one jumps around and dashes a few yards left and right before rejoining the partner for some gentle open jaw sparring.

In all my many years of watching nature I have never seen this before, an eight-legged foxy push-me-pull-you.

I cycle to Swanage after looking for Hen Harriers with no luck. Through the village of Corfe and along the undulating road I go to a very dear friend, Perry's house. Unfortunately she isn't in and so I leave a message on the door and start to explore the old places I loved here back when Swanage was our home.

Around to Peveril Point and to the plaque dedicated to Perry's husband, Gordon Barnes, who died over ten years ago. Gordon was the closest friend, other than my late wife, Karen, that I ever had. Gordon was born in Birmingham, like myself, yet in 1960 this young man became the assistant warden at the Fair Isle Bird Observatory. He then became a crofter on that Fair Isle before leaving there in 1975 to sheep farm in Wales. I met him in Swanage, at Peveril Point, after he and Perry had retired from their third farm, a mixed farm in Devon.

Gordon wrote an autobiography of his life on Fair Isle entitled An Unforgettable Challenge. It is a charming read of a tough life crofting on the most remote island in the UK and is available from the Fair Isle Bird Observatory for £5.

I photographed the bike with Gordon's plaque.

A phone call from Perry. She's back and a quick cycle ride to her house is followed by spending an afternoon looking at Gordon's Fair Isle notebooks; notebooks that detail incredibly rare birds that he' saw there. Page after page of his notes and drawings, list after list of birding seen, birds ringed and even one list detailing birds oiled by Fulmars.

Perry has a present for me for the days when it may be a bit chilly cycling, a lovely pair of alpaca wool gloves. The afternoon goes quickly and Perry phones another of my best friends, Pete Barratt, to warn him that I am here. A meal at our favourite Bangladesh restaurant is arranged for the evening.

The meal is as delicious as ever and the conversation is about lost spouses and wildlife, holidays and birding. Pete has been out to Georgia, near Azerbaijan, last year birding and has also driven to Sweden for the same.

The evening finishes back at Perry's house looking through photographs from the happy days when both Gordon and Karen were alive and the five of us used to spend so much time together. Photographs of sitting in the garden on hot summer days, the best photograph to me is of an Alpine Swift flying in front of my wonderful, smiling friends and wife standing in a row along the cliff edge above Peveril. What a fantastic bird and oh, what happy days.

The Green Year list now at **149**, twenty ahead of this time last year.

14.76 miles   776 feet elevation up   659 feet down

The evening Oracle report comes in :

Birds from the last 10 days. Best GGS appears to be Thursley Common in Surrey; not sure how far off your route to Norfolk this is.

DORSET

Hen Harrier - Lychett Bay 30/1 Holton Heath 02/02
Black-necked Grebe - Bincleaves Cove / Smallmouth, Portland Harbour (up to 11) 04/02, 03/02, 30/1, 27/1 Studland (up to 14) 30/1, 26/1
Long-tailed Duck - Abbotsbury Swannery (2) 04/02, 31/1, 29/1, 28/1
Bittern - Radipole 31/1, 27/1
Black Guillemot - off Brownsea Island, Poole Harbour 28/1
Great Grey Shrike - Wareham Forest, south of Bloxworth at Sugar Hill 31/1, 30/1, 28/1 Wareham Forest in centre of recently fenced off forestry area 04/02, 02/02
Water Pipit - North Marsh, Stanpit 31/1 Lychett Bay 02/02
Hawfinch - Stanpit Marsh 30/1
Great Skua - Portland 29/1 Mudeford Quay 29/1
Pomarine Skua - Portland 26/1
Crossbill - Arne (2) 26/1
Sooty Shearwater - Chesil Cove 26/1

HAMPSHIRE

Water Pipit - Drayton Farm Watercress Beds, Old Alresford (2) 03/02, 31/1 Titchfield Haven (up to 2) 28/1 Hook-with-Warsash LNR 02/02
Great Grey Shrike - Woolmer Pond 30/1 NW of Lyndhurst at Stoney

Cross 30/1 Bransbury Common 28/1 Bratley Plain 03/02 1m NE of Linwood & west of Broomy Plain and Amberslade Bottom 04/02
Ferruginous Duck - Kingfisher Lake, Blashford Lakes 03/02, 29/1
Yellow-browed Warbler - Eastleigh sewage works 03/02, 02/02, 31/1, 30/1, 28/1
Long-tailed Duck - Keyhaven Lagoon / Illey Point 31/1, 30/1, 28/1
Black-necked Grebe - Hayling Oyster beds (4) 30/1 Ibseley Water, Blashford Lakes 04/02, 03/02, 02/02, 31/1, 29/1 Langstone Harbour off Budds Farm sewage work (2) 02/02, 30/1
Penduline Tits - Titchfield Haven (up to 3) 03/02, 02/02
Hen Harrier - Alresford Pond 30/1
Caspian Gull - Ibsley Water (often from Tern Hide), Blashford Lakes (up to 3) 03/02, 02/02,01/02, 31/1, 30/1, 28/1
Little Gull - Stansore Point 30/1 Meon Shore, Titchfield Haven (2) 01/02
Velvet Scoter - off Pennington Marsh 28/1
Yellow-legged Gull - Northney Common, Hayling Island 03/02

ISLE OF WIGHT

Snow Bunting - Newtown NR 30/1
Greater Yellowlegs - River Medina, Pinkham (SW of Whippingham) 02/02, 01/02, 31/1
Black-necked Grebe - Ryde West Sands car park 01/02

Friday 5th February **fresh to strong SW**

Rain all AM, cloudy PM

Over to Studland beach, Toytown beach in the Noddy books by Enid Blyton, to look for Black-necked Grebes in drizzly rain and mist. I arrive at the Middle Beach car park and am astonished to see over eighty Mediterranean Gulls here. Years ago when I lived in Swanage it was always special to see just one Med' Gull. Here was a flock of them; of all ages too.

Looking out over a misty, calm sea I can just make out a distant group of six **Black-necked Grebes**, bird number **150** for the list.

Wanting to look in the famous WW2 bunker used by Churchill, Eisenhower, Montgomery and Mountbatten to oversee D-Day landing practise on the beach, I walk around to it. I stand where the four stood so many years ago and try to imagine what the view of the long sandy beach looked like on that fateful day. Leaving the bunker I walk further to try and get closer views of the grebes. The rain gets heavier and the views are still poor. I set off for Wareham.

Past Corfe Castle and through Wareham, the rain has stopped and so my next stop is Wareham Forest, which I reach within an hour. A Great

Grey Shrike has been seen sporadically near Strawberry Hill Enclosure but I cannot find it and neither can two Dorset birders looking for the same.

I need to cycle over twenty miles to Ringwood in order to be there for an early morning start at Blashford Lakes and the rest of the afternoon and early evening I spend doing so.

The Green Year list now at **150,** twenty ahead of this time last year.

45.95 miles **2035 feet elevation up** **2097 feet down**

Saturday 6th **Very strong gales, 55mph plus, heavy rain**

Out into the gale, the quest is for the **Ferruginous Duck** that caused me such a problem last year. I arrive at Kingfisher Pool at Blashford Lakes and am immediately cheered by the view over the pool. Gone is the thick ivy covering of the wire mesh fence. Gone is the seven foot high plastic mesh the fishermen have put up to prevent views. Instead looking across the water is easier despite trees between me and the birds. Another local birder has been searching for the duck also. Tim hasn't found it but I do! The Fudge is out in the middle of the pool drifting left among good numbers of other duck species; Tufted Duck, Wigeon, Pochard and Goosander.

I try to get Tim's telescope onto it but I can't get it to focus through the mass of branches and twigs. I look again and the bird has drifted off. I can't see it. I am frustrated. Will I get a photograph of this bird or not?

I start scanning again and find it again sitting beneath the bushy island; the same one that it had hidden under for hours last year. It comes out into full view. I watch it, photograph it and video it. I kiss, lick and tick it.

Tim is happy with the views and leaves me to watch it for longer. It starts to dive for brief moments.

I move off, pushing the bike along the footpath and back to the main road. There's a thought in my head that the gale may bring down a branch onto my head. I imagine that in the future the Health & Safety fanatics will pollard all trees. We can't have children climbing those dangerous things, can we? I reflect on things I did so long ago as a child. Climbing trees was one of my every day pleasures and one tree in particular was my favourite, a tall cedar tree. At the top the branches spread out to create a platform. Friends and I nailed canvas between the branches to act as hammocks. Thinking back on it now we were so lucky in so many ways. Lucky that on hot summer days we could lie up there unseen by anyone below. Lucky not to have killed ourselves!

Into the hide at Ibsley Water, a group of four lady birders are there and together we bird, finding a close Black-necked Grebe. One of the ladies finds a **Yellow-legged Gull** close by on a spit. Boom, another bird on the list.

To the nearby visitor's centre and into the hexagonal hide, the birds massed outside the darkened windows are mostly Siskins. With them are a couple of Bramblings and Lesser Redpolls, Nuthatch and, more numerously Greenfinch, Blue, Great, Coal and Long-tailed Tits, Blackbirds and Chaffinches with a few Reed Buntings. There's one open window where three photographers are chatting in the language of the photographer; ISOs and shutter speeds, records shots and memory cards. One of them comes over to watch the birds near to me and we start to chat. He asks if I am The Biking Birder and I find it confusing when he says that people ask him whether he is also. I ask his name. "Gary, with two r s." What's your surname? I can't believe my ears. Garry spells it . . . P r e s c o t t!

Once my disbelief has dispelled we laugh at the coincidence. This is the first Garry Prescott I have ever met; same for Garry. I knew there were others but meeting one is strange and special, especially as he is a birding photographer and an absolutely brilliant bloke.

Back to the Ibsley Water hide with the weather getting worse. Two brilliant birders are already in their scanning incoming gulls with scopes, Alan and Lee. Lee points out a bird on top of the Osprey pole on the far side of the lake, an **Egyptian Goose**. I have totally forgotten about this bird knowing that they are a definite 'give me' in East Anglia.

Alan is a big World bird lister with a World total of over 8,000. He tells me of a weekend where he twitched a bird, a Pochard species in Japan! A flight, a plane and a bus, see the duck, turn around and return. The World's highest carbon expenditure for one bird? Possibly. We are different sides of the same I Love Birds coin.

Lee comes up trumps again when he finds the last of the three target birds for the day, a first winter **Caspian Gull**. Thanks to these two wonderful birders I now have four new birds for the year list despite some of the worst weather of the year.

The cycle into Ringwood is tough, gale in the face, darkness and rain, spray from passing cars. No problem. Now on **154**, things are good.

8.26 miles 144 feet elevation up 145 feet down

An email from The Oracle:-

Hampshire birds present in last ten days. Will send you a daily update. Stuff on way to Norfolk incl RN Duck (Bray, Berks), GG Shrike (Thursley Common, Surrey) and Fuggy Duck (Bucks)

HAMPSHIRE

Water Pipit - Drayton Farm Watercress Beds, Old Alresford, NE of Whinchester (2) 05/02, 03/02, 31/1
Water Pipit - Titchfield Haven (up to 2) 28/1 Hook-with-Warsash LNR 02/02
Great Grey Shrike - Beaulieu Road Station (south of Shatterford car park east of railway viewed from railway bridge) 05/02 Woolmer Pond 30/1
Great Grey Shrike - NW of Lyndhurst at Stoney Cross 30/1 Bransbury Common 28/1 Bratley Plain 03/02 1m NE of Linwood & west of Broomy Plain and Amberslade Bottom 04/02
Ferruginous Duck - Kingfisher Lake, Blashford Lakes (view through gap in fence at end of Hurst Road) 05/02, 03/02, 29/1
Yellow-browed Warbler - Eastleigh sewage works 03/02, 02/02, 31/1, 30/1, 28/1
Long-tailed Duck - Keyhaven Lagoon / Illey Point 31/1, 30/1, 28/1
Penduline Tits - Titchfield Haven (up to 3) 03/02, 02/02
Hen Harrier - Alresford Pond 30/1
Caspian Gull - Ibsley Water (often from Tern Hide), Blashford Lakes (up to 3) 03/02, 02/02, 01/02, 31/1, 30/1, 28/1
Little Gull - Stansore Point 30/1 Meon Shore, Titchfield Haven (2) 01/02
Velvet Scoter - off Pennington Marsh 28/1
Yellow-legged Gull - Northney Common, Hayling Island 03/02
Crossbill - West Walk (20) 05/02

ISLE OF WIGHT

Snow Bunting - Newtown NR 30/1
Greater Yellowlegs - River Medina, Pinkham (SW of Whippingham) 05/02, 02/02, 01/02, 31/1

Sunday 7th **Sunny light SW AM, heavy rain, fresh SW PM**

Into the New Forest, I search open moorland first then trudge deep into woodland, seeing common birds such as Redwing, Titmice, Great spotted Woodpeckers, Nuthatch and Treecreeper.

A text from Phil Andrews tells me that a **Great Grey Shrike** is near Beaulieu Road Station and I arrive there within an hour of cycling. The bird is down west of Pig Bush car park and I have to push the bike along a very muddy pathway to get to a ridge that overlooks the area. I can see the shrike some distance away and carry on along the path down to where three birders are just leaving having had great views of the bird. Another birder is walking too close to the shrike to get a photograph. He flushes it and it flies away over a high fence and for a couple of hours I search before deciding to try for Hawfinches elsewhere. As I start the big push back to the road I see the shrike has returned to a few low bushes but still a long way away.

Rain starts to fall and gets heavier as I cycle to the house of two wonderful friends, Kerry and her son, Dominic. An evening with great friends is a delight. Dominic is an incredible young naturalist and their house is a fantastic smorgasbord of books photographs, artefacts from around the World and artworks. It's fabulous and every way one turns there is something to delight, amuse and wonder. Autographed photographs of Dominik with David Attenborough, Chris Packham and Kate Humble, amongst others, shows how Dominik's commitment to wildlife has brought deserved attention to this superb young man. We have a wonderful evening.

The Green Year list now at **155**, twenty one ahead of this time last year.

29.89 miles **1222 feet elevation up** **1240 feet down**

Monday 8th February **Gale force W**

Heavy rain AM, drier and cloudy PM

Storm Imogen has arrived. Outside my dear friend, Kerry's house the weather is wild and wet. The morning I spend inside relaxing.

The afternoon still has the gale but the rain has petered out and Kerry and I go to her place of work, the nearby New Forest Wildlife Park. Kerry is a real life Ellie from the Pixar film 'Up' and she constantly talks to every animal in the park. A winter visit where there is a thrill around each corner; Harvest Mice so close we can watch them feed and wash their tiny paws; owls of many different species and size from Eagle and Snowy Owls to Little and Hawk Owls. Hawk owls! Now there is an ambition bird for many a British lister, including me. Oh for there to be one on Shetland this year!

There are Roe Deer almost close enough to stroke, a running Bison, Scottish Wild Cats with wild eyes, Pine Martins, Wallabies walking amongst the densely packed bushes, Wolves parading through dense conifers and Otters, lots and lots of otters.

All of the animals look amazingly healthy and are excitedly active. To be honest I am not a zoo person, preferring my nature experiences to involve wild animals but I take my hat off to the staff and set up of this wonderful park.

Personal favourites from the visit? Two Giant Otters from South America, immense otters with amazing character and voice. The ultimate experience is seeing the European Lynx on a platform sitting upright in front of us, incredible animal. I may not see all of these superb animals in the wild but I will always treasure the afternoon memories of my visit here with Kerry.

Tuesday 9th February **Light W**

Mostly Sunny, One heavy Hail shower PM

Thanks to some comprehensive birding gen from a New Forest birder named Marcus, for which I thank him profusely, I am confident about the day. Marcus has kindly emailed me with precise details over where I can find the special birds I need to see. I have four target birds today; Goshawk, Hawfinch, Lesser spotted Woodpecker and Common Crossbills.

Marcus relates the success of monitoring projects in the forest and of an interesting discovery. Apparently many of the Hawfinch roost sites are shared with Goshawk. They think a mixture of habitat preference but also probably down to the fact that the Goshawks clear out all the Corvids and smaller Raptors creating a relatively safe haven for smaller passerines.

Armed with maps I cycle through Lyndhurst. I pause at a shop window. I must have what I see there, a dancing Disney Tigger and enter the charity shop to buy such a wonderful item. It goes onto the back of Ophelia the Orca and next to Scaggy the Rabbit.

The charity being supported by the shop is for The Shaw Trust, a charity for helping disabled people into work; a very worthy cause and thank you Penny, the friendly lady at the counter, for pointing out Tigger's features to me.

To Acre's Down, I hide the bike among some bushes and walk up a ridge. As soon as I reach the top I can see a **Goshawk** patrolling over a distant forest.

I walk another few hundred yards along the ridge, through silver birch and holly woodland and out onto gorse and heather heath. From the end viewpoint I sit and watch as the Goshawk still flies along high over the trees.

Another birder, John, an ecologist from Oxford, joins me and we watch as the Goshawk is joined by a larger female. The views of this pair in display flight mode are the best I have had of Goshawk for a number of years. Previously I have watched these magnificent birds of prey at New Fancy RSPB viewpoint in the Forest of Dean, Gloucestershire. This pair are much closer. John finds another one perched up on a tree quite some distance from us. I then see two **Hawfinches** fly past us just after a Raven has cronked it's way past us. Both Sparrowhawk and Buzzard pass us too.

I leave John to explore the woodland down in the valley and immediately notice a small herd of Roe Deer beneath some small holly trees. I kneel to photograph them just as a low flying Goshawk glides past.

Deep in the wood of oak, beech and silver birch I find a fallen tree and sit on it in the hope that birds will pass. A very quick Sparrowhawk does but little else in half an hour or so. Sitting on my perch I start to wonder what the area would be like if just one of the predators I saw yesterday at the Wildlife park were free. The large herds of deer in the New Forest, that decimate the ground flora, may be greatly reduced in number and therefore, just maybe, flowers would have more chance of carpeting this copse in the spring. Rewilding? It won't happen here but the thought of such is exciting. My mind goes back a few years to a time when I was sleeping the car exploring Spain. When in the Gredos Mountain range north of Madrid, I spent an evening with two French astronomers doing the same in their van. They had converted the back of their van into a two-level sleeping quarter, just like a bread oven. Together we drank red wine and watched as shooting star after shooting star fell in the southern sky. The Perseides were hitting the atmosphere, grains of dust that disappeared in a moment. One grain must have been a pebble for it fell almost slowly and far brighter than the others. "Bye bye New York," we joked. Surrounded as we were by the tall, jagged peaks, I stated that I wanted to see the sunrise from one of the nearest. Next morning from the top of it I did just that and was surprised to hear wolves howling in the growing sunlight. The fact that I found out later that the echoing calls came from a few Canadian Huskies that belonged to the warden of one of the mountain refuges down in the valley only diminished the pleasure of hearing the sound at such a time slightly. If I had been a few hundred kilometres north, in the Picos range I may have heard for wolves for real. Maybe before I join the earth there may be an opportunity to do so in Scotland. More of a chance of seeing a beaver there, or of seeing a lynx more likely.

Moving along through the holly and alder trees, negotiating deep muddy depressions, I continue to search for birds yet seeing very few. A few Long-tailed Tits are in the silver birch canopy and there is the occasional singing Robin. On reaching a gravelly bridleway, I stop as a Great spotted Woodpecker is drumming on a nearby oak tree. It tries one branch but it isn't resonant enough. It moves to another and the staccato sound produced is much more to the bird's liking.

A small flock of Chaffinches lands on twigs of a silver birch nearby and then a flock of four **Common Crossbills** lands on a tall oak behind them.

The blue sky has been replaced by threatening, dark grey clouds and the hail that falls so intensely for twenty minutes or so covers the ground like snow.

The Green Year list now stands at **178**. This is nineteen ahead of where I was this time last year.

17.64 miles **908 feet elevation up and down**

Wednesday 10th February **Light NW**

Mostly Sunny

Goodbye to Kerry and Dominik, with a new addition to the Biking Birder Family on the bike, an otter, Oscar, a present from Kerry and Dom', who fits in well with Manu the Frog, right next to Albert the Albatross. I used to call the cuddly toys on my bike 'The Lads' but since receiving a large Orca from Mary back at Upton Warren, named Ophelia they are now the BBF; the Biking Birder Fellowship. Very Tolkeinesque. It is great to have some company on the lonely road. Mind you it always seems to be just a one way conversation. I know exactly what you're saying to yourselves! Now stop it.

Through Lyndhurst once more and along the A35, turning down a small road heading south. The road goes through a superb forest of tall, majestic redwoods and pines, redolent of California, before I reach the entrance to the Blackwater Arboretum. A Hampshire birder has emailed me over this being a place where I could add **Lesser Spotted Woodpecker** to the year list. Through the park and out the back to access a long bridleway, I walk slowly searching the tree tops and carefully listening with birding radar fully primed, after having hidden the bike in thick undergrowth.

There are only a very few birds; Nuthatch and titmice. Then I hear it. The sound of a Lesser Spot' drumming. It is a short burst so much higher in tone than a Great Spotted Woodpecker and unmistakable. I turn around to look in the direction of where I think the bird may be and find a tree to sit against and scan. With my thick waterproof trousers coming in handy, I sit on the leaf litter and wait. It drums again; three bursts in quick succession and now I can see it high in the canopy of an oak tree with some dead branches pointing skywards. I try to photograph it but can only get photographs of out of focus branches. Two Buzzards circle over and the diminutive woodpecker has gone. I sit for around another half hour in the hope that it would return. Two Stock Doves, much in love, flutter around the treetops, flying like slow butterflies in a display flight, a sight I hadn't seen too often before. Three Treecreepers come close as do a couple of Nuthatches but I have no more sightings of the Lesser Spotted Woodpecker. I am thrilled to have seen it though as in 2010 I missed it altogether. Last year I only saw one, at Ynhs-Hir RSPB reserve in Wales and in the same way as today I have failed to get a photograph of it.

It is always so frustrating not to get even the worst of record shots of a bird. How many times have people asked how I verify seeing a bird? On being told about the year list people ask how I prove having seen them all. The honour system they deem not enough. The Guinness Book of Records said the same to me in a letter back in 2010. Well I know what I have just heard, what I have just seen so you will just have to believe me on this occasion. I can take you to the exact tree if you want.

I go in search of another Lesser Spot, walking the bridleways and through the forest along a large stream hoping that my luck will bring the bird. More Treecreepers, they really are showing well today, and the occasional titmouse, particularly Long-tailed but no more woodpeckers of any kind.

Back at the Arboretum, I sit for a spot of lunch, hot cross buns, a bit of Brie and an orange. Then I cycle along the lanes and byways to Keyhaven, past the high tower at Sway.

There has been a Long-tailed Duck reported here and I walk the bike along the sea wall to try and find it. The tide is as high as it can be and the first road is flooded and blocked off. I meet an artist, Lesley Banks of Knightwood Photoart, who is sat photographing a nearby flock of Brent Geese. We chat for a while about her work before I head off once more eastwards along the sea wall.

Through Keyhaven Harbour where Little Grebes and Red-breasted Mergansers are diving amongst the boats. I meet a couple of birders and put their comment of a Long-billed Dowitcher being seen into the back of my mind as they don't seem that hot on birds, despite being friendly and eager to tell me what they do now. If such a rare American wader was in the area my good friend and taskmaster, Phil Andrews would surely have told me about it, wouldn't he?

Along the wall beside Keyhaven Lagoon, Dartford Warblers occasionally show themselves in the dense vegetation and a superb Short-eared Owl quarters the grassland, dives and catches a vole and flies further away after eating it.

Now the couple at Keyhaven had told me that the **Long-tailed Duck** was very elusive and hadn't been seen today so my opinion of their knowledge is further diminished when I find the bird. It is a beautiful drake too, swimming not too far away in a saltmarsh channel with two Goldeneye. I show the bird to a couple of passing lady birders. It's great to share their enthusiasm at seeing such a beautiful bird.

I try to phone my Mum and Dad; I always report a good bird for the year list but I have no signal. Neither can I text Phil, Steve, Jason or Bart, my birding pals.

With two good birds added to the year list today my mood is high and I bird along the seawall enjoying views of geese and ducks, waders and egrets. A flock of a few hundred waders includes Knot, Dunlin and Bar-tailed Godwits. Grey Plovers and Redshank, Curlew and Oystercatchers are on the grassy knolls and the mud. Six Spotted Redshank are close by and a single Greenshank flies past.

The weather is gorgeous and the views over and along The Solent are tranquil and lovely. When the pathway is empty of walkers, I cycle along enjoying it all. I pass the area where the Keyhaven couple had said they saw the Dowitcher and give the pools a cursory glance and scan. I am all alone, no other people yet alone birders are here.

Into Lymington at around 4:00 p.m. I sit beside the yacht marina and my mobile quickly receives two text messages.

"Long-billed Dowitcher at Pennington at Fishtail Lagoon."

"LTD off Keyhaven Marsh. Did you get my Dowitcher message?"

Rude words! I cycle back to where I think Fishtail Lagoon is just as the only dark cloud in the sky comes over. A short shower ensues. It gets dark. It gets too dark. No Dowitcher.

Lesson learnt. Don't let birding arrogance dismiss the words of a couple of 'dudes.'

The Green Year list stands at **160**. This is twenty one ahead of where I was this time last year.

32.17 miles **1121 feet elevation up** **1087 feet down**

A couple of weeks ago I asked the Met Office a question:-

Can you please tell me why the current spate of named storms all have Caucasian sounding names, Imogen etc? Do we not live in a Multi-cultural Britain?

Today I received a reply:-

Dear Gary,

Thank you for your e-mail concerning storm naming. In September 2015 we began our Name Our Storms campaign and asked the public to send in their suggestions for names.

The list announced in October was a combination of suggestions from Met Eireann and the most popular of the thousands of suggestions we received from the public.

If you have any further questions or need any additional information, please let us know. Our Weather Desk team are available to assist you 24 hours a day, seven days a week. Simply reply to this email or give us a call on 0370 900 0100 and one of our advisers will be happy to help.

Kind regards,

Ashley, (Weather Desk Advisor)

Met Office, FitzRoy Road, Exeter, Devon, EX1 3PB, United Kingdom.

Thursday 11th February **Very Light SW**

Very Sunny, cool 5 to 7C after early frost. One quick shower with hail and rainbows

Skating away on the thin ice of a new frosty day, I head off along the sea wall for Fishtail Lagoon on Pennington Marsh. It is a glorious morning, sunny with some mist over The Solent. There is a thin veneer of ice on some of the pools. Maybe there will be Winter this year after all. It has been more like Autumn so far with gales and rain followed by beautiful days like this.

The tide is quickly coming in covering the outer saltmarsh and with almost no wind the view over the sea is mirror-like reflective of sky and shore.

Not having been able to find Fishtail Lagoon on any map on the internet last night, I am grateful for an information board which has a labelled map of the marsh. I proceed straight away to the area, ignoring any birds on the way. I am focussed on the target bird, the Long-billed Dowitcher. I meet another birder, Ian from Christchurch. He has seen it and says he will put the news out on Rare Bird Alert. He describes where he has seen it, "look to the left of where there is a Little Egret," and as we are joined by two other birders, Colin and Ben, Ian leaves and the three of us walk down to the spot to try to find it.

There are waders here, mostly Redshanks with a group of four Spotted Redshanks and a single Common Snipe. Another Spotted Redshank is behind some rushes and a Ruff flies in to join it. After twenty minutes or so a wader flies from behind a nearby gorse bush to join the Redshanks, the Long-billed Dowitcher goes onto the year list.

I watch it over the next hour as just occasionally the rare American wader comes into view. Most of the time though it is hidden amongst or behind the rushes.

Colin is a local birder who tells me that he has been birding here for six decades. Ben is a young man, twenty one, who is extremely keen and eager to learn. Ben spots two Spoonbills flying in. Another Spoonbill comes in but stands away from the first two.

The light today is sharp and clear, the earlier mist has gone and thin wispy cloud merges with the blue.

I start to walk along the seawall to the west and Ben walks with me. He stays with me for the next three hours and together we become a spotting team. There are plenty of great birds to enjoy and we both start a day list. By the time we reach Keyhaven Harbour we both have over sixty birds written down and we stop for a little lunch beside the bridge. We have seen the Long-tailed Duck again and enjoyed close views of Dartford Warblers.

A Water Rail squeals in the reedbed and a pale-headed Marsh Harrier flies over and lands on a distant hedgerow. I then find four Bearded Tits at the far end of the lagoon, tickable but they never give great views.

My target bird for the afternoon is Water Pipit and after saying goodbye and good luck to Ben, "have a great life," I head back eastwards along the seawall checking every pipit. We have already seen Rock and Meadow Pipits and there are more of these, mostly Rock Pipits but no matter what I cannot find a Water Pipit.

A short shower of rain and hail causes a double rainbow to appear and it's reflection is beautiful.

I find the Short-eared Owl perched up and preening at the east end of Keyhaven Lagoon.

Later, with the sun going down I see a young person sitting on a concrete block at the end of a concrete extension out into The Solent. He or she is wrapped in an orange blanket and I am concerned that they might have a problem as it is getting dark and getting very cold as the sun has gone down. A Slavonian Grebe gives me an excuse to go down there. The person turns out to be a young woman who is enjoying the landscape and she tells me she is a foundation year student of art, an oil painter and often comes down here to watch the sunset. I photograph the grebe and leave her to her contemplation.

A day list of seventy one birds, the Green year list stands at 162. This is twenty two ahead of where I was this time last year.

9.52 miles 130 feet elevation up and down

It is lovely when people take the time to email me after finding my email address on the Biking Birder blog. Interesting how many people we meet in life with names that bring a smile. Alison marries Mr Allison, Mr Caroll marries Carol and I won't forget a lad I sat with in cricket scoring box many years ago, Justin Case!

An email arrives from Alison Allison :

Hi Gary,

Great to meet you today. Here is the photo taken just after you had moved on!! Also one of the LT Duck.

Good Luck. Best wishes Alison Allison

My reply:-

Hello Alison,

Brilliant to hear from you. Would it please be OK to put these photos on my blog and Facebook pages please? Coincidentally Carol Caroll got in touch on Facebook this evening. What a wonderful day. Thanks for getting in touch and all the very best, Gary Biking Birder Prescott

To which I get a quick response:-

Hello Gary,

Yes – please use them – I'd be delighted. I look forward to seeing them on your blog. Best wishes Alison

Friday 12th February **Fresh SE**

Rain for most of the day

Fifty shades of Green, my route today will involve three ferries. The first one will take me over to The Isle of Wight, Lymington to Yarmouth. Another will take me on the chain ferry at Cowes, west to east and the final ferry will take me to Portsmouth from Ryde, if I see the reported extremely rare American bird though. If not it will be another night on the island and another search tomorrow. The bird? A Greater Yellowlegs. Guess what colour it's legs are? Actually it is a superb American wader and very special this side of the Atlantic.

So with my Green credentials much diminished I get to the first ferry with seconds to spare before it sets sail, not that it has sails.

Rain is falling heavily as I leave Yarmouth on the road to Newport. Reaching that town I find an excellent cycle path that runs along the west bank of the Medina river. I need to find Pinkmead and do so, finding it to be a large private house within its own grounds, a large garden of cut grass beside the river. With only a single vantage point offering good viewing of the garden I start to scan the area looking for the Greater Yellowlegs, This one is the only one of this species in Britain at the moment and I need to find it; the forty-sixth Greater Yellowlegs on the British list.

I can't.

It is high tide and the rain gets heavier. Godwits, Oystercatchers, Redshanks and Lapwing are here but no sign of the mega rarity. I walk away from this clear viewing position to search for any other place where one can scan the garden but to no avail. It has a border of thick bushes and trees and only small areas can be seen at a time. The tide is at a perfect level to bring all of the river's waders ashore and I am feeling a bit worried that the bird is not going to be here. After all it was last reported last Sunday. My feeling though is that this is due to the lack of birders going over from the mainland to see it and not to the bird having left.

I see a bird on the bank beside a pond-like inlet beside some tall white poplar trees. Bird number **163** goes onto the list and I photograph it after celebrating having found the Greater Yellowlegs.

I text Phil then I look at the photographs again and realise that I have photographed the wrong bird! Instead of a smart American wader I have a very bad photograph of a Redshank! The bird was quite distant but I have no excuse for photographing the wrong bird despite my adrenaline pumped excitement.

I search for the Yank and can't see it. Panic! I need a photograph. Then there it is, much closer than before and I lay down horizontal on the tarmac of the cycle path, in the rain, to steady myself to ensure photographs and video are OK. Phew. That was close to an embarrassing disaster.

Bird on the list after an hour and a half of a soggy search, I carry on to Ryde and celebrate with a cup of hot chocolate and two crumpets at a café. I am soaked but as always, very happy. Yes, I am suffering excessive happiness once more. The young girl serving me sits with me for a chat. She is twenty one and tells of her work with the people of The Jungle, that is the refugee and economic migrant camp at Calais. This wonderful woman volunteers help there and takes van loads of food and supplies out to the people stranded there. She tells me of some of the refugees stories and how they have been conned by traffickers into believing that the people of Britain want them to come to the United Kingdom. Many have been abused as they have travelled through Europe and their hopes and dreams for themselves and their loved ones are smashed as they end up in the squalid and dangerous conditions of the Jungle. Those that do make it to Britain are interred in prison like camps. This woman is a breath of fresh air compared to some of the people I have met down in the south. A girl of determination, empathy and compassion with a sense of humour and enthusiasm. So different to the prevalent mood of too many in Britain these days.

To Ryde to get a ticket I cycle, I board the ferry there, wet through once more due to the heavy rain constantly falling. The Spinnacker Tower in Portsmouth can be seen through raindrops on the ferry windows.

The year list stands at **163.** This is twenty ahead of where I was this time last year.

21.96 miles 1052 feet elevation up 1091 feet down

An email in the evening:-

Hi Gary,

I hope that all is well with you at the moment. Just emailing to say well done so far on your 2016 endeavours; very much enjoying the blog posts and the images on Facebook that you have been putting up, and 162 is a brilliant amount to have seen so far already. Keep up the magnificent work and speak soon for sure!

Kind regards and best wishes, Mark

Another email discusses the location of nearby Penduline Tits at Titchfield Haven Nature Reserve, from The Oracle of course:-

Just had a look at the sightings history since they first arrived in late 2015 - mostly from the West Hide and Meadow Hide. Sightings throughout the day although a peak from 11 am to 2 pm. Also Bittern from Meadow Hide on 06/02.

Then on to Eastleigh for YBW at sewage works, Water Pipit at Old Alresford and up to Bray for RND and hopefully parakeet. Then five days cycle up to Roydon for Pallid Harrier.

Saturday 13th February **Fresh E**

Rain for most of the day

An email has photographs attached of the Long-billed Dowitcher from two days ago sent to me by Alison Allison. Incredible how Alison met and married Mr Allison, the name reminds me of Billy Williams from years ago. William Williams was a student at a Secondary School I taught at in Wolverhampton. Then there was Carol Carroll from last year's visit to Fair Isle. I love names. How about a boy I met many years ago when playing cricket? Was it cruel of his parents to name him Justin when his surname was Case?

It is always lovely to meet people, share the excitement of a bird and then receive a lovely email. Thanks Alison.

A morning rendezvous at a Gosport café, I am thinking I have been stood up when the woman I am waiting for taps me on my shoulder. Thirty two years ago, back when I was a young teacher at a Secondary School, Coppice High, in Wolverhampton, I had the privilege of having a group of amazing, wonderful young children for my form for three consecutive years. From that class there was a girl with a sparkling character, Lisa Gay. Here she is opposite me at the table, now known as Lisa Hillier.

Two hours pass with family talk, memories from the past and future plans, laughs and past teacher character assassination all enjoyed. Goodson, Psycho, Brassneck, Split-lip, Studs and Slugeye; all are mentioned. I had my own nicknames given to me by the children; Noaksy, Stig (of The Dump) and Prezza. Maybe not so insulting as 'Slugeye!'

Lisa's husband, 'Scooter' John joins us and another hour passes. What a wonderful couple.

I cycle off towards Titchfield Haven but notice that my arm is camouflaged instead of covered by Hi-vis. I have left my Hi-vis jacket at the café! Twit. I cycle back and luckily it is still there.

I reach Titchfield Haven and hear from Kate, the young girl behind the counter within the superb visitor's centre, that the Penduline Tits, the birds I am after, haven't been seen since Wednesday. In fact even that report they feel was erroneous. It is Saturday today, my chances don't seem high.

The reserve closes at 4:00 p.m. and I leave without having added to the year list. Does it count as a dip? Hardly but it still hurts. I1 want this European Green Year List record and every bird counts.

In the evening I access the Biking Birder 2016 – The Quest for 300 Facebook page and find a message from a young German birder, Annett Jaegar. Annett had recently got in touch with me over Green Birding and I had asked her about her birding. Here is a reply:-

Dear Gary,
I did share your blog in my (still very humble) Birding Germany Group as well as in Birding NRW (northrhine-westfalian birders and slightly bigger group) I am thinking as my group doesn't have that many members yet it would be too much to ask you to write an article. I will definitely ask you to once my group has grown a little . So thank you very much for your offer.
...So if you happen to know anybody birding in Germany feel free to add people to my "Birding Germany" group. Posts in English or any other language are very welcome.
I started birding quite late (about 3 maybe 4 years ago I think) basically without knowing anything about birds at all. So I still have to learn a lot (not just the gull identification is killing me) .
After not being too ambitious for the first year I am now looking for birds where-ever I go.
Birding mostly in Germany, occasionally in the Netherlands (as I live quite close to the Dutch and Belgian borders). I have been to Iceland for longer visits twice now (but always travelling with a non-birder, which makes it a bit more difficult sometimes.)
Looking forward to Heligoland in April this year, hopefully the Black-browed Albatross will turn up again which I missed last year.
Actually, I do have some lists on bubo,org, as my friend, Mike Wheeler (I think you know him) convinced me to list my birds there. I do find it a bit embarrassing to be yet again the only person who has a Germany 2016 on bubo.org but hey, at least I do stand a chance to end up number one .

It would be fabulous to see more Germans taking up the pastime.

14.49 miles 312 feet elevation up 310 feet down

Sunday 14th February Fresh NE

Sunny intervals

A milestone reached yesterday, 1,000 miles cycled this year so far.

Today starts with more of a push than a cycle. Along the canal pathway south from Titchfield village; the canal being a beautiful brook-like waterway and instead of a traditional tow path with barge wide canals that I am more used to, there is an extremely muddy, in places practically impassable through flooding, walkway. I wade through the water and slosh through the mud.

I stop when a birder shows me a Barn Owl sleeping in hole on a twisted tree. It is a beautiful sunny day and the light is clear and fresh.

The pathway deteriorates further but there is a target bird that has been reported somewhere along this mire and so I persevere, laugh and push, curse and wade. The bird is a Water Pipit and after an hour of searching and getting extremely wet and muddy feet and getting the bike clogged up also, there has only been one pipit. It flew up from a wet area of grassland with rushes but disappeared without giving views.

I continue to search. I continue to push.

A phone call from Phil Andrews can only mean one thing, a very rare bird is somewhere nearby.

"Forget the Water Pipit," he shouts. "There is a Red-flanked Bluetail at Lymington!"

The final half mile of mud and water are negotiated and once on the road again I cycle quickly towards Southampton. I get to Warsash and check the phone for messages. There are two; a voicemail from Sue at Titchfield Haven and a text from Phil.

Phil's is "Sods law mate. Pendulines are showing at Titchfield." Sue's voicemail declares the same. Sue, one of the wonderful staff at Titchfield, had heard of my visit yesterday, knew I needed to see the Pendulines, found my blog and then my mobile number and then sent the message. Partly it is Sue's kindness in letting me know but it is also the fact that I think that I will have more chances to see Red-flanked Bluetails later in the year, I turn around and cycle as fast as possible back towards Titchfield Haven.

On arriving at the reserve, the bike is stowed away in a shed and I run along the path and boardwalk towards Meadow Hide.

On turning towards the hide I see a small group of birders looking towards an area I know from yesterday's visit to have the necessary reedmace. I put my thumb up to ask whether the birds are on view. A positive thumb comes up from one of the volunteers and I run the final thirty yards, well float there really. It's been a tough day so far and I need some good luck.

A female **Penduline Tit** is on a reedmace head plucking, feeding and releasing wafts of fluff towards us.

Over the next two hours birders and interested general public come and go and the Pendulines, two of them, both females stay on view busily feeding. One group of birders are the young at heart RSPB Dorking group. Lovely people.

Just past 3:00 p.m. the birds leave and I head back to the visitor's centre. I thank Sue profusely and sincerely for her message and head towards Fareham. I have seen forty one birds species today including Barn Owl, Cetti's Warblers and Black-tailed Godwits. The Penduline Tits though are a 'good one to get.'

The Green Year list still stands at **164**. This is still nineteen ahead of where I was this time last year.

19.68 miles 556 feet elevation up 543 feet down

The detail that Phil goes to with his emails is phenomenal. In the past, during the two Biking Birder adventure years of 2010 and 2015, the planning route was dictated to by which RSPB reserve I was going to visit next. The routes for both those years had taken a lot of planning as considerations such as weather, timing in order to see certain birds and distance were taken into account. Now the priority was where was the next bird for the Green Year list going to be and how could I get there. Hence the emails and texts from The Oracle have became so important to the success of this year's quest. For instance :

OK mate. Winchester is 18 miles away - do you have enough time to cycle there today after Titchfield and search for Water Pipit at Old Alresford? If yes I will send you site details now.

Winchester to Bray is 53 miles - you would have time to search cycle this and search for RN Duck within 2 days. Won't you get Mandarin at Felbrigg? Water Pipit also at Staines Moor.

Bray to first target (Roydon Common for Pallid and Hen Harrier) is 128 miles (say 3 days cycle). I will advise of any decent birds on route - Iceland Gull being the most obvious. I will send you a summary of the Norfolk birds today to whet your appetite - you really don't need to leave the stretch from Wolfreton to Cley unless you want a punt at the Lesser Yellowlegs at Breydon Water. Think you could clean up in 7-10 days but clearly the longer you leave it the more birds will depart as winter ends.

Kings Lynn to York is 133 miles (say 3 days cycle again). Best birds you may wish to consider getting prior to your event are Richards Pipit and Flamborough and Surf Scoter up the coast at Filey. Whereabouts is your chosen Black Grouse site? Really as soon as your event is over you need to be heading back south.

Which days are you planning to have off so I can factor that in?

All The Best Phil

Monday 15th February **Fresh N**

Sunny!

With a day of cycling ahead and after having received the very sad news of a great Upton Warren friend, Simon Vickers, having died at too young an age, I think about the people who I have met because of a passion for birds and nature. Simon was a larger than life character, full of fun and we met very early one morning when I was sleeping in one of the bird hides at Upton Warren! Simon arrived, woke me up and with a huge lens on an expensive camera started clicking away at every feathered creature. Simon that morning didn't know the names of the birds on view but he soon learnt them. Simon also was soon to be a regular volunteer at the conservation work parties held at The Warren. Immensely well liked and deservedly so, his passing is so sad.

I need to visit the watercress beds of Alresford, Hampshire to search for Water Pipit. The wind is in my face and despite the almost no cloud blue sky, the going is tough. Hills are reached and as chalk starts to appear in the fields as I reach the top, a group of **Red-legged Partridges**, nine of them, become the first year tick of the day. **165**. Thoughts of other chalk downs birds come to mind and maybe a Yellowhammer will be added to the year list at last. I text this thought and the news of the partridge to Phil Andrews, my task master and news provider. The reply states that Grey Partridge and Corn Bunting might be possible. There are Corvids and a flock of around thirty Stock Doves but no small passerines. The agricultural desert of wheat stubble continues. The constant disappointment of the British countryside. How much have we lost?

A large bird in front of me is obviously raptor, one bird species that we have gained over the decades due to reintroduction. A **Red Kite** goes onto the list. Gone are the days when one had to travel to Tregaron Bog in order to see just a couple of these magnificent birds.

Into and through the beautiful village of Alresford, I cycle along the beautiful river and find a small cressbed. No pipits here, there is just a single Lesser Redpoll and a few Moorhens.

A local man tells me that there are more cressbeds down a road to the north and so I find large cressbeds of a more commercial nature along Bighton Lane. They are surrounded by large fences with padlocked fences. My memories of visiting cressbeds in Dorset back in the years when I lived in that fine county are dispelled by the present problem. How can I search for such a small bird without access. I go to the offices of Alresford Salads and am told by a friendly gent that there is a public footpath along the northern edge of the largest beds.

Two Green Sandpipers are the first birds I see once I get to the path and after walking along the eastern edge, outside the fence of course, a group of pipits fly from further down the beds and land in front of me, though at the other side. I start to search and find at least one, maybe two **Water Pipits**. There is a Grey Wagtail with them too. Mission accomplished and a hat-trick of year ticks go onto the year list.

The Green Year list still stands at **167**. This is twenty two ahead of where I was this time last year.

30.03 miles 1875 feet elevation up 1583 feet down

The Oracle sends an update of sightings:-

Here are all the birds you need in Norfolk over the last 9 days:

Twite (up to 8) - Blakeney Freshmarsh 13/2, 12/2, 10/2, 9/2, 8/2, 7/2, 5/2 (25) - Thornham Harbour 5/2
Shorelark (2) - Burnham Overy Dunes 13/2 (3) - Titchwell 8/2, 7/2
Snow Bunting (up to 30) - Cley 12/2, 9/2 (3) - Happisburgh 12/2 (up to 40) - Winterton 11/2, 9/2, 8/2, 7/2 (21) Titchwell 7/2
Lapland Bunting (2) - Ringstead 13/2, 11/2 (up to 5) - Blakeney Freshmarsh 13/2, 12/2, 11/2, 10/2, 9/2, 8/2, 7/2, 5/2
Lapland Bunting (3) - Holme 11/2 (2) - Weybourne Camp 9/2
Hen Harrier (up to 5) - Roydon Common 13/2, 12/2, 10/2, 9/2, 8/2, 7/2, 5/2 (up to 7) - Warham Greens 13/2, 9/2, 8/2, 6/2, 5/2 (3) - Titchwell 12/2, 7/2 Morston 11/2 Horsey 9/2, 5/2 (2) - Blakeney Freshmarsh 9/2 (4) - Stubbs Mill

7/2 Lynn Point 7/2 Flitcham 7/2 Waveney Forest 6/2, 5/2 Ongar Hill 6/2 - Waxham 6/2
Pallid Harrier - Roydon Common 13/2, 12/2, 11/2, 10/2, 9/2, 8/2, 7/2, 6/2, 5/2 Flitcham 11/2, 7/2
Crane (2) - Winterton 12/2 (2) - Somerton Holmes 10/2 Acle 10/2
Golden Pheasant - Wolfreton 14/2, 10/2, 9/2
Bittern - Holkham 13/2
RL Buzzard (up to 2) - Choseley Barns 13/2, 12/2, 10/2, 9/2, 8/2, 7/2, 6/2 Sculthorpe Moor 13/2 Snettisham 12/2 (2) - Docking 11/2 (2) - Holkham 10/2, 5/2 Great Bircham 7/2 Waveney Forest 6/2
Lesser Yellowlegs - Breydon Water 13/2, 11/2
Iceland Gull (2) - East Winch 12/2 Kings Lynn docks 6/2
Water Pipit (2) - Blakeney Freshmarsh 12/2 (2) - Strumpshaw Fen 11/2 (2) - Titchwell 11/2, 10/2, 9/2, 7/2, 5/2 (3) - Cley 11/2
Velvet Scoter (10) - Holme 11/2 (2) - Titchwell 10/2, 9/2, 5/2
Black Guillemot 1 Sherringham 10/2
Great Skua - Sheringham 10/2
RC Pochard - Holkham 10/2
Whooper Swan (45) - Ludham 9/2, 7/2, 5/2
Plus Yellowhammer, PG Goose, Mandarin Duck (Felbrigg), RC Pochard (Titchwell), Tree Sparrow (Flitcham), Corn Bunting, Little Owl, Eider, Common Scoter

I respond:-

Morning Phil,

I'm not too worried about the West London stuff, by which you mean Parakeet and Mandarin I presume. There will be plenty of time after April and may in east Anglia.

Now as for the rest of this week, it has been complicated by family news and not of a very nice nature. I am going home tomorrow and will be back on the road on Sunday. Bad news concerning a favourite aunt.

Today I will get to Farnborough where John has told me of sites for Little Owl.

It's been phenomenal so far and will continue to be so all the way to the record and beyond.

As for yesterday, you should have seen the supercilium on the Water Pipit. Bright white!

Thanks for everything. Gary

Phil answers: *OK mate - I am here to serve. Just let me know what you need and when. Hope everything is OK.*

Tuesday 16th February **Fresh N**

sunny!

It is time for both the bike and I to take a rest. I cycle to my cousin, Rosemary's house close to Aldershot and take the bike into a nearby cycle repair shop.

I am going to have a few days rest enjoying the company of both Rosemary and her son, Paschal. I am also going to take carbon transport, a train, to see my fabulous son, Joshua for his birthday and visit my Mum and Dad.

16.72 miles **756 feet elevation up** **852 feet down**

And so my rest begins. A few days in which to visit my cousin, Rosemary and her son Paschal and then back home via train, leaving the bike at a repair shop for back brake replacement and a service. It is my son, Joshua's birthday on Friday and my daughter, Rebecca is coming down from Newcastle for us all to meet up for a celebration meal. I will also be seeing Mum and Dad. Both are in their eighties and remarkable for their age. Just a few days to catch up with family.

I also need to prepare for the RSPB AGM at York. I am invited as one of the speakers and have been sent emails with attachments. I feel this is a wonderful opportunity to promote Green Birding and will prepare the photograph slide show, the talk itself, a display board and leaflets as well as I can.

So today will be a carbon day; another 'Fifty Shades of Green' moment in the Biking Birder year. As I have said, the bike will be left at the exact spot where I arrived yesterday after cycling through very quiet, and icy in places, country lanes from Alton to Ash Vale, east of Aldershot.

Does this use of carbon transport during a rest period detract from the Green Big Year mantra? The way I see it is that in every way I try to be as Green as possible whilst still occasionally seeing family. When your parents are in their eighties you want to cherish every moment with them.

As for being Green, I don't have a house or a car, no masses of electrical appliances just a tablet. I recycle as much as I can, even collect recyclable items I see whilst cycling. I pick up litter especially plastic litter on beaches and nature reserves. I could never have the time to pick up the mass of litter, much of it recyclable I see whilst cycling. Why do people have to throw this stuff from their car windows whilst going along our roads? I camp around 150 to 200 times a year. I consider food miles. Blueberries from Chile, I think not! My clothes are usually from charity shops. All in all I hope that you understand my Green Year. I would love to have a totally fossil fuel free year but this is the best that I can do.

As for what we can all do, we've got to reduce, reuse, recycle. (repair)

https://www.youtube.com/watch?v=dKdZYYmTT9A

Why do some birders have to make up records? The Red-flanked Bluetail, supposedly at Lymington a few days back, a bird that had been important enough to have me cycle ten miles towards it, turns out to have maybe been a hoax.

RBA (Rare Bird Alert) tactfully states :- **Red-flanked Bluetail** : *Making a sterling effort to usurp two national #1's from the top spot this week was the reported discovery of what would have been a guaranteed show-stopper in Hampshire - Britain's second-ever wintering* ***Red-flanked Bluetail*** *allegedly located in the wooded glades of the New Forest, in the Norley Enclosure across the weekend of 13th-14th.*

The first over-wintering example of this ever-delightful Tarsiger came just two years ago, thanks to the super-showy bird that hopped from Gloucestershire and Wiltshire from February 3rd to March 9th 2014 and this report from Hampshire could have been the focus of attention for bird photographers and birders alike…but was it real? No one seems to know…but the "H" word wasn't far from many locals lips.

The only acceptance of this increasing, more-frequent-than-ever forest dweller for the south coast county came in the more traditional mid-October window of opportunity; one spending six days in and around Sandy Point in 2010.

(…oh how we wished it had been a wintering mainland Western P. ***Rubythroat*** *tho'…)*

Details will come out no doubt but it brings back memories of other such incidents; the Hermit Thrush in Essex and the Siberian thrush in Worcestershire for example.

The Hermit Thrush was 'seen' by a sole observer. The finder (!) later admitted his hoax through the pages of Birdwatch magazine, a double-page spread, apologising profusely for his false record, explaining that he had been goaded by being suppressed from real bird news by other Essex birders. Nigel Pepper's photos of a Hermit Thrush alleged to have been taken in Chipping Ongar, Essex, in 1994, were in fact taken on Mugg's Island, Toronto, Canada.

In a shock confession just published in Birdwatch, the 'finder' of the Hermit Thrush claimed at Chipping Ongar, Essex, in October 1994 has retracted the record. Nigel Pepper, a lifelong Essex birder, has revealed that he made up the 'sighting', in which he used photos taken in Canada as supporting evidence. Despite widespread doubts at the time, which included Birdwatch publishing misgivings about the record, it was accepted by the Rarities Committee as the fifth British record.

The 'occurrence' was surprisingly atypical of other British and Irish American passerine records, being found inland in eastern Britain in a poor year for transatlantic vagrants. It was allegedly present in care from 28 October-2 November 1994, only being seen by the finder and his family.

The Tewkesbury Siberian Thrush, supposedly on the foothills of Breedon Hill goes back to the late 1970s or early 1980s.

On a wet, cold day birders attracted to the area like bees to a honey pot. The honey pot in this case was a male Siberian thrush, still a mega rarity in the UK, but couldn't be found. "No problem," stated the hoaxer, "I've got photographs of it." Weeks later photographs of a Siberian thrush on Breedon Hill did come out, a stuffed one or a maybe a model of one placed in a tree! Allegedly.

Every year in the British Birds magazine there is an issue devoted to 'Report on Rare Birds in Great Britain in . . ' At the back there are always a number of rejected reports. People make mistakes. I know I have made many and will no doubt make many more. People might not have noted every feature necessary for acceptance. Thankfully the birder who feels the desperate need to hoax other birders to increase his credentials and standing in the rarity finding world are very few and far between. Yet the pressure is on. Thankfully actual hoaxes are extremely rare.

Nowadays nearly every record of a rarity is accompanied by a series of photographs. Of the rarities I have seen this year I have managed to get a photograph of nearly all of them. Only four birds have I failed to photograph. Two of them were seen whilst with witnesses so verification is fine. Of the two species I have seen without either a photograph or a witness, trust me!

Music as an ever present Sound. A personal addition.

The demon, whilst cycling, is within my head. It constantly converses with me, bringing up memories and images from the past. It is always there, that little voice that moves so quickly from memory to memory without any apparent conscious control or direction. There are memories that are wonderful; the funny, the momentous and the loving memories that I treasure. Then there are those that I don't want to remember, times of pain, guilt, grief, shame and anger.

Eternal Sunshine might bring solace by the removal of the latter but that isn't a reality away from the film scenario. The good and the bad memories circle around in a cyclical fashion and the fight to suppress the bad is a constant battle. I don't want to remember the latter incidents yet they are what define my life.

Whilst cycling there are hours of time to ponder things and one way in which I divert my thoughts away from cascading images is to sing. Now I will never use an iPod/MP3 player whilst cycling. I think that is extremely dangerous. I like to hear what is coming from behind me. I do sing and whistle though, which is possibly a shame for those people I pass. Songs from the Seventies make up the bulk of the repertoire with the occasional later song or a delve into the Sixties. There is also my comedic repertoire.

There's a lot of Frank Zappa and Jethro Tull with progressive rock bands like Yes, despite the intricate and sometimes impenetrable nature of Jon Anderson's lyrics. *A seasoned witch could call you from the depths of your disgrace and rearrange your liver to the solid mental grace.*

Rock bands and individuals, Hendrix, The Who, ELP, Rory Gallagher, Pink Floyd, Peter Gabriel, Simon & Garfunkel, Led Zeppelin and other older heavy metal bands. The Rolling Stones, The Beatles, U2, Joe Jackson, favourite singles from so many bands and artists. So many songs that luckily I can remember the lyrics to. Comedy songs that I can have a giggle to whilst pedalling; Peter Sellers, Spike Milligan, Benny Hill's Sad-eyed Sal and Eric and Ernie.

And of course there are many Monty Python songs that I can sing along to. Always look on the bright side of life!

Then there are the whistling tunes, the instrumentals, the classical, , the whimsical, the jazz, the Blues. And I can't forget the bizarre moments when it doesn't matter what I do to make a sound, lip dum dums, mouth sounds, tapping and clicking, screams and whoops! Crazy. Obviously music isn't just a diversion. It is an integral to my life. A life without music is unimaginable. It is there within me, constantly and for that I am eternally grateful.

Friday 19th February   Happy Birthday Joshua! Love you Son. Xx

Sunday 21st February

Time to get back to the bike. Time to get back on the road. A train to Birmingham but a coach to Oxford as rail repairs are taking place and between the two cities.

I sit in a seat by the stairs that takes one down to a central exit door. A gentleman comes down the aisle and spots my bright blue RSPB sweatshirt. He sits down next to me and immediately asks whether I work for them. So starts a conversation and a slow realisation of who this is.

Mention of Cardigan Bay dolphins. Mention of freelance journalistic work. Mention of working on a new book. With alarm bells ringing I cautiously ask his name. "George."

Major goosebumps now.

"Are you George Monbiot?"

Sitting next to me is one of only two journalistic heroes. Together with Simon Barnes, there is only George Monbiot who I turn to for articles to read on both political and environmental matters. Simon Barnes used to be with the Times. Used to be. The pieces he writes for the RSPB magazines, which used to be known as Birds but has been renamed Natures Home as part of the major overhauling of the RSPB's image, are always intelligent and thought provoking.

George Monbiot though takes things to another level. Whereas Simon Barnes' book, How to Be a Bad Birdwatcher, is very amusing and very accurate, a book by George Monbiot becomes a reference book. After an initial read it will become the focus for a wide range of studies with so many issues and anecdotal incidents to find out more about. His book, Feral, is one that changes lives, a book that changes one's perceptions. It thrills with every page and here is the author sitting next to me!

On arriving at Oxford station, on saying goodbye and good luck with the new book, I immediately go into self recrimination mode. It is the same every time I have just met someone I admire from the so-called celebrity world. I start to think of what I should have said, what I should have asked and how I should have said what I feel about that person and their work.

My son, Josh, will tell you of an occasion when Freddie Flintoff was coming towards us. We had gone to Taunton to watch Lancashire play Somerset in a County Cricket match. Despite the occasional stop by some enforcing father for a fixed smile photo with a son, I saw that Freddie wasn't in the mood for such and just wanted to get off the pitch. I didn't stop him because of this and hence my son didn't get his desired photo. Sorry Josh but today . . . HAPPY BIRTHDAY! Xx

Monday 22nd February **light to fresh W**

Sunny 9C

The bicycle is all shiny, serviced and ready as I collect it from Geared Up Cycles, Ash Vale. New chain and gear system, new brakes and cables, new back wheel with a new Marathon Schwalbe Plus tyre and a new cartridge; the bike looks fabulous and the ride is perfect after Stephen and Stephen, Dad and Son, are paid.

Goodbye to cousin, Rosemary and Paschal is followed by a simple, reasonably quick ride to Virginia Water around fourteen miles north east.

Entering the park via the eastern entrance, the cycle path starts after a large new café and goes around the lake. It has been improved since my last visit ten years or so ago. I search the cascade in the south east corner but don't find any of the brilliantly attractive ducks that Virginia Water is well known for. I head for the tall totem pole, a present for Queen Elizabeth from Canada and stop at a place where a small pool is cut off from the main lake. People are feeding a number of common duck in amongst which are four male **Mandarin** posturing at each other for the attention of the lone female.

Two **Ring-necked Parakeets** fly over and land reasonable nearby and so in the space of just a few minutes, today's target birds are added to the list bringing that to **169**.

Three Red Kites fly over, two of them in a sort of close together display flight. London is so lucky that the Chiltern reintroduced birds have multiplied and spread to such an extent that London skies frequently contain these magnificent birds. I just hope that they continue to increase their numbers so that more people can enjoy their elegant spectacle.

Through Staines and north to the west of Heathrow, I reach a public house just outside West Drayton that two of my best friends will remember well; the Paddington Packet Boat. So named because . . .

I want to stay here for the night because back in 1984 it was a directional landmark for a teacher with three young students who were searching for a special bird, a Ferruginous Duck.

I was that teacher and the students, Alex 'the Bear' Barter, Jason John Oliver and Richard Southall. For the three Wolverhampton boys it was their first experience of rarity searching, carbon twitching as it is called. That day so long ago we had already been successful seeing a famous Siberian bird, an Olive-backed Pipit. Having been seen in the back garden of a Bracknell garden; this bird had caused queues of birders to stand outside a house in Bracknell, Berkshire, waiting their turn to go into the lounge of the bird's finders to watch the stray waif in comfort.

When we arrived early in the morning, after driving through the night, despite my wife's dire warning of impending doom that she psychic-like predicted, there was a note on the door asking that birders gave the occupants a rest. Instead we went around to the nearby Primary school's playing field where the bird could be seen. We did, we saw it and feeling happy we left to go get the next bird on the lads' want list that day, Smew at Kingsbury.

Back in the days before pagers and SatNavs things weren't quite so easy over getting accurate gen (information). Our happy troupe were buzzing with excitement as we went through some large gates to get to the perimeter road that went around the large Wrasbury Reservoir.

Some workers busy painting those gates even waved us through and wished us luck. Those workers left the same gates locked when we returned an hour or so later!

Now trapped inside the reservoir grounds,we drove around the reservoir. We hadn't found any Smew and we were now stuck inside the reservoir grounds with apparently no way out. No mobile phones to get help. We found a gate that we thought we could lift off the hinges and so escape. We heaved, we laughed, we couldn't lift it. As we tried to escape a police car arrived and the officers heard of why we were the other side of the gate to them and why we were trying to get out. They had had a report from a member of the public that some lads were trying to steal the gates. "We'll send someone to let you out," the police officers laughed.

Two hours later an old man on an old squeaky bicycle arrived with a key.

Still upbeat despite dipping on the Smew, we went the short distance to the Paddington Packet Boat. The large gravel pits was supposed to be the home for a male Ferruginous Duck but we couldn't find it. We searched but only found an area of bomb crater-like pits where some locals had been digging out old Victorian bottles. Two dips and a Siberian bird, we drove home to the Midlands.

It later turned out that we were at the wrong place at Wrasbury. The Smew were on another pool near to the reservoir. As for the Ferruginous Duck, that had been hiding under a tree almost next to the car and we had missed it.

As for the lads; one, Jason is still a very keen birder who takes his young son, Jack birding most weekends. Richard is occasionally seen birding around his home town of Wolverhampton but loves dragonflies more than birds. Sadly Alex, 'the Bear,' died all too young. An undiagnosed heart condition caused a heart attack and a great, very close friend had gone.

No room at the Inn, I backtrack to West Drayton where a hotel has a bed. The daylight fades as large flocks of ring-necked parakeets fly into an adjacent park to roost, hundreds of them.

So the Green Year list is now **169**, nineteen ahead of this time last year.

27.15 Miles 786 feet elevation up 920 feet down

Late evening an email arrives from Ponc Feliu Latorre, the current European Green Year List record holder:-

Hi again Gary!

Great you are trying again in 2016. I wish you all the best. Everything is OK, here! We are all very well, and I keep cycling and birding.

Last 2015 I did 8100 kms and just 220 species (not a birding focused year, though. Many sport cycling days around home, for the same places and mountain not far from home). Since January, I have done 1100 kms and just 110 species. Too much work with the kids and my job!

I don't have Facebook, but I'll tell all my friends to take a look at your page.

Great you gave help to the Manu project in Peru. Good choice! Great place!

Details of Ponc's Big Green Year can be found on his blog at:-

www.ecobigyearcatalunya.blogspot.cat

Tuesday 23rd February **light to fresh N**

Sunny 6C

In the morning I go down to breakfast and notice that the other punters are looking at me in a funny way. On returning replete to my room I find out why. Last night I cut my hair with my newly purchased hair clippers and before breakfast I had noticed a bit at the back that I had missed. With the cord from the clippers too short to reach the mirror I had cut the missed bit.

Unknown to me at the time I had forgotten to put the number 3 comb onto the clippers. Looking in the mirror after breakfast I find that my scalp has a fully shaved trench amongst a number 3 haircut! I shave it all off!

What's this? I am actually enjoying the cycling this morning, through the north west suburbs of London. The roads aren't too busy, the tarmac isn't too bad and the way is attractive.

Turning towards Elstree, the road becomes a little too steep for me to cycle up and so a long restful walk begins. I start to notice that the ditch alongside is full of rubbish, plastic mostly; bottles, bags and even lots of plastic red pipes. There are drink cans, dozens of them and fast food polystyrene boxes, does it matter? The ditch is being clogged by this mass and the rubbish is getting covered by sludge. Where does it all come from?

After passing the famous film studios I find out as a small side road leading to a large bridge designed for horse traffic over the A1, has pile after pile of fly-tipped waste.

Despite disappointing road side verges, the views on this splendid sunny day are lovely and three Red Kites fly over. There is even the occasional Nuthatch calling. Spring is around the corner.

I stop just north of Potter's Bar as a red traffic light instructs me to do so. A white van stops next to me and the passenger window comes down. Without a word I am passed a large, heavy and cuddly Bagpuss! The lads in the van have seen the lads on my bike and thought that it would be a laugh to add to the collection. It is! I can't stop laughing as they drive off. Bagpuss goes next to Wally the Whale, Scaggy the Rabbit and Tigger.

52.25 Miles **2199 feet elevation up** **2007 feet down**

An email from Dave:-

Hello Gary, well done last year ! Are you coming to East Anglia this trip? You know you are welcome to stay at Brandon
regards Dave .

Now Dave, who got in touch after seeing an article about my adventures on the Rainham Marshes RSPB blog, has a bungalow in Brandon, Norfolk and it is wonderful that he has once again offered it as a place of rest and refuge. The kindness of people never ceases to amaze me. Thanks Dave.

Wednesday 24th February **light to fresh N**

Sunny 5 to 7C

The frost is thick and the air is cold as I cycle along the A10 north. A bird flies over becoming a year tick that I had expected to have on the year list weeks ago, a male **Yellowhammer**. It lands on one of the very few bushes to be seen some distance away. This chalky landscape is dominated by immense cereal fields with few, if any hedges.

Through Royston and on towards St Ives. A green form of transport passes me with a hello and turns further down the road, a speedy horse and cart.

Into St Ives where I am just about to enter a shop when a lady comes up to me and inquires as to whether I recognise her voice! I do. The memory of meeting a couple who were waiting for their cycling son to pass a roundabout in Cheshire last April comes back to me. Their son was cycling for a homeless charity in Cambridge called Winter Comfort,

"John," I ask. "And Janice," she responds. We go for a coffee and a chat. Janice is in St Ives to look after her 90 year old mother whilst John is at home in Dorset. I love lucky meetings like this and an hour passes before we say goodbye.

Trying to get out of St Ives I take a wrong turn and end up on a large maze of a housing estate. I ask a passer-by for directions. I am told by her, Chris, that she looks after orphaned hedgehogs. She takes me to her house, introduces me to her husband, Errol and shows the cages where the sleeping hedgehogs lie. They have helped hedgehogs for over twenty years, returning them to the wild once fit and well. They support the nearby Hinching Country Park. Kindly they add to the menagerie on my bike by giving me a cuddly toy hedgehog, Wilfred Prickles!

So the Green Year list is now at **170**, eighteen ahead of this time last year.

53.51 Miles **1442 feet elevation up** **1686 feet down**

Whilst cycling through the South of England, a birder commented on Birdforum that he wanted me to approach my Green Big Year with the same commitment of the D-Day Landings of World War 2. In his honour I rewrote a famous speech from that time :-

I shall go on to the bitter end,
I shall bird in Britain.,
I shall bird the seas and oceans,
I shall bird with growing confidence and growing strength on the bike,
I shall bird our Island, whatever the cost may be,
I shall bird on the beaches,
I shall bird on the feeding grounds,
I shall bird in the fields and in the streets,
I shall bird in the hills;
I will never surrender.

Thursday 25th February **light to fresh N**

Sunny 5 to 7C

A message on Facebook from David Gray tells me that there are five Bean Geese about five miles from me. I am surprised that I haven't received any text messages from The Oracle, Phil Andrews.

Two miles out of Whittlesey I receive six messages on my mobile in quick succession, mostly from The Oracle. Bean geese at Nene washes RSPB reserve. I pedal there as quickly as my short, fat, hairy legs can go.

It is a beautiful clear sunny day and the cold accentuates the sound of whooping from a pair of **Cranes** quite a distance away.

No sign of the Bean Geese unfortunately, the list grows though as a couple of **Whooper Swan** family parties flies by whooping.

In beautiful sunshine and a cool northerly breeze I explore around a gravel pit that has a lot of duck and geese on it and disturb a couple of Muntjac. The way they dash off with their white tails held vertical is interesting, making them very visible amongst the tall vegetation. A couple of Peregrines buzz around too disturbing large flocks of Golden Plovers and Lapwings.

I leave to go search of a Rough-legged Buzzard at Thorney. Three hours of searching gives me only a single Common Buzzard and a very distant Barn Owl.

The Green Year list is now at **172**, nineteen ahead of this time last year.

37.96 Miles **417 feet elevation up** **429 feet down**

Friday 26th February **fresh N**

Sunny 5 to 7C

A day of cycling into Norfolk from Wisbech to get to Hunstanton along the side roads. I wish to avoid the very busy main road to Kings Lynn.

A couple of Muntjacs are quietly walking beside a railway line. The first attempt of what will probably be many attempts for the lone male Golden Pheasant at Wolferton is unsuccessful and a long walk over the adjacent heathland is beautiful but the Woodlarks here last year haven't returned yet.

The amount of road-kill today is extremely sad. There are Muntjacs, Hares, Badger, Fox, Brown Rat, Song Thrush, Collared Dove, Red-legged Partridge and plenty of the most commonly seen squidged, Pheasants. Carnage!

A Red-tailed Bumblebee is on the floor. It is alive and I am sure it appreciates it when I pick the sleepy creature up and put it onto a flower, giving it a careful stroke first.

To the cliff edge at Hunstanton where the tide is at its lowest and huge sandbanks are out in The Wash.

32.80 Miles **993 feet elevation up** **936 feet down**

Saturday 27th February **fresh NE**

Sunny 5 to 7C

Out to cycle to Burnham Overy via Choseley Barns, near Titchwell, I see a head of a bird poking up from a crop field on the edge of Hunstanton. **Grey Partridge** goes onto the year list.

There is almost no wildlife to see at Choseley; just a few Yellowhammers and a couple of Hares. I push the bike along field edges to search for the reported Rough-legged Buzzard but have no joy.

To Burnham Overy and along the seawall to the beach. I spend the rest of the day pushing the bike along the tideline searching for Shorelarks. I see a small number of **Pink-footed Geese** on the way along the wall.

To Holkham Gap and back and then west towards Scolt Head. I have no luck with these and seem to be missing birds that may be vital for the list.

The Green Year list is still at **172**, nineteen ahead of this time last year.

23.06 Miles **578 feet elevation up** **636 feet down**

Sunday 28th February **fresh NE**

Sunny intervals 5 to 7C

Another long push along the beach in search of Shorelarks follows an early morning Barn Owl, seen from the Holkham Woods bridleway. Waders on the beach won't be roosting for long despite the high tide; dog walkers are on their way.

I meet a fellow birder, Steven Holloway, at the start of the Burnham Overy boardwalk. We chat for half hour or so about birds, Norfolk's birding history and birders old and new as well as Steven's present employment status.

News of a possible White Stork at Welney WWT reserve has me cycling towards Hunstanton. The bird has rings that show it has Polish origins. I need to see it and the adrenaline of a really good bird clicks in. I try to remember the last time I saw a White Stork in Britain. A group of five in Oxfordshire not too long ago had The Birding Clams, my close twitching friends' group, heading that way. We crashed on the motorway though as heavy rain caused the car to aquaplane. We survived and stopped spinning just in time for all of us to get out of the car and witness a pile up of vehicles about a hundred yards away, back along the carriageway. More devastation due to speed and water.

As I cycle through Thornham the Oracle's next text tells me that the White Stork has flown off and I turn around to bird at Titchwell instead.

Bramblings at the feeders by the café, waders on the shore; the birding is superb in the wonderful clear sunlight and the day list goes past seventy.

Common Scoter on the sea, a year tick, and Water Pipit are the highlights but then again having a Robin come onto my hand to collect some cake is just as much of a thrill.

The White Stork is back at Welney! My plans change and I am off again.

The Green Year list is still at **175**, nineteen ahead of this time last year.

18.53 Miles **448 feet elevation up** **386 feet down**

The Oracle sends and email:-

Will aim to send up the summary every day whilst you are in Norfolk which hopefully will become shorter as you tick stuff off; looks like you may just be a week too late (something to consider for 2017 ?). I have rearranged in it a rough geographic order around the coast which may be more useful.

White Stork - Welney 27/02

Pallid Harrier - Roydon Common - 20/2, 19/2
Hen Harrier (up to 4) - Roydon - 26/2, 25/2, 20/2 (up to 3) - Snettisham 26/2, 23/2 (up to 3) - Titchwell - 26/2, 20/2 Choseley 24/2 Brancaster Staithe 25/2 Blakeney Freshmarsh 26/2 (up to 6) - Warham Green - 27/02, 22/2, 20/2, 19/2
Twite (up to 21) - Thornham Harbour - 26/2, 25/2, 24/2, 20/2 (up to 7) - Blakeney Freshmarsh - 26/2, 24/2, 23/2, 22/2, 21/2, 20/2, 19/2 Strumpshaw Fen – 21/2 Haddiscoe 25/2 (up to 3) - Stubbs Mills - 27/02, 21/2
Lapland Bunting - Choseley 27/2 (up to 10) - Blakeney Freshmarsh - 27/2, 26/2, 25/2, 24/2, 23/2, 22/2, 21/2, 20/2, 19/2
RL Buzzard - Choseley Barns - 25/2, 24/2, 20/2 Docking - 21/2, 20/2 Brancaster (Field House Farm) 25/2 Haddiscoe 27/02, 26/2, 25/2
Shorelark (3) - Burnham Overy Dunes - 25/2, 24/2, 22/2, 21/2, 20/2, 19/2
Snow Bunting (up to 20) - Burnham Overy Dunes - 22/2, 21/2, 20/2 (3) - Holkham Gap 25/2 (11+) - Arnolds marsh, Cley 27/2 Winterton (up to 40) - 26/2, 21/2, 20/2
Red-crested Pochard - Holkham Park -22/2, 20/2, 19/2 (also birds at Titchwell?)
Velvet Scoter (2) - Holkham Gap 26/2
Serin - unconfirmed report of 2 - Felbrigg - 19/2
Little Gull (2) - Trimingham 23/2 Sidestrand 26/2
Great Skua - Trimingham 23/2
Bittern - Whittingham 23/2
Twite - Breydon Water - 20/2
Lesser Yellowlegs - Breydon Water - 20/2, 19/2

Still also Corn Bunt, Willow Tit?, Golden Pheasant, Tree Sparrow, Eider, Little Owl, Woodlark?, Common Scoter, Barnacle Goose? etc plus chance of Bean Goose.

Monday 29th February **light N**

Sunny, 5 to 7C

The Polish White Stork is still at Welney as I cycle towards there. It is another day when I am enjoying the cycling and progress is quick enough to get me to Downham Market by 11:00 a.m.

A text from the oracle, Phil Andrews tells me that the stork has gone. Then another text saying that it is now present in front of the Friends' hide. I don't know whether I am coming or going!

I arrive at the visitor's centre and am greeted like an old friend by all the WWT staff.

With a keen twitcher from Heathrow, met whilst I jog over the bridge, I go to the hide not expecting to see the White Stork as the staff at the centre believe the message sent to the East Anglia birdline was erroneous. They think the birder who reported a stork saw a Great White Egret. At the hide we can see neither White Stork or Great White Egret and after two hours or so we decide to go back to the centre and hope that the bird comes in to roost.

It doesn't.

The Green Year list is still at **175**, nineteen ahead of this time last year.

51.04 Miles 1277 feet elevation up 1323 feet down
February Monthly Statistics:-

Green Year list	175 birds
Year ticks seen in February	29
Bird species had, not seen in 2015	1
Mileage in February	643.33 miles
Total mileage for the year	1,366.89 miles
average mileage on days cycled	27.97 miles
elevation : up	25,583 feet
: down	25,596 feet

Best Birds *:* ***Green-winged Teal, Great Grey Shrike, Caspian Gull, Ferruginous Duck, Long-billed Dowitcher, Penduline Titmice, Greater Yellowlegs.***

28 year ticks

An evening email from Ponc Feliu Latorre, the current European Green Birding Year List record holder from Barcelona, Spain:-

If you do 305 I'll have to do it again in 2017!
We keep in touch! Good luck. Ponç

3

MARCH

There is only one true morality for every man; but every man has not the same true morality.

George Bernard Shaw in Major Barbara

Tuesday 1st March **light NE**

Heavy rain all AM, occasional showers PM

The Polish White Stork is 'plastic!' It seems the stork was brought over from Poland by plane to recuperate from an injury. So a dip on a plastic bird is a new experience when Biking Birding.

The day is spent catching up with things on a computer in the library in Downham Market.

Wednesday 2nd March **light NW**

Heavy hail showers

Heavy hail showers occasionally hit me as I cycle back to the North Norfolk coast. The shower cap over my cycling helmet protects my scalped scalp from the hail.

Another try for the lone Golden Pheasant male at Wolferton is as successful as when myself and the Coppice 'Birding Clams' group used to try every time we went birding to Norfolk in the 80s and 90s. That is not successful at all. I just hope it doesn't become a piece of Norfolk road kill before I can get back here in May.

To Titchwell RSPB reserve to ask for new RSPB logo laminates to put on the bike. I like people to know why I am doing this, to raise the profile, to advertise and hopefully raise some money (hint!) for the RSPB. To my great surprise I am offered not only a coffee but cake and a chicken roll as well! Thanks Richard and Frances, Sue and Pam.

Sue is a World big lister, that is she travels the world seeing as many species of birds as possible. Sue is off to Estonia and Lithuania next week. Here's a link to her blog for more information.

http://www.freewebs.com/suebryan/

Red-crested Pochards are said to be out of the reedbed and on view on Patsy's Pool so I make my way there. Nine of them are on the pool, another for the list. A RSPB volunteer, Paul Fisher, is sitting there and we talk about birds and I realise that I am in the presence of an absolute legend. Paul is a lovely man who has a proud history with the RSPB, helping to create so many reserves around South Essex, as the regional project manager.

http://www.wildlifeextra.com/go/uk/wr-canveyisland.html#cr

Interested in my quest, Paul asks me what else I need for the year list and as I say "**Hen Harrier.**" Blow me! One appears in front of us. The moment went like this:

"What else do you need?"

"Hen Harrier, like that one there!"

Brilliant. The photograph of the ringtail I take doesn't do it justice but it soon goes behind some trees and is gone.

Maybe I should have said Pallid Harrier.

We talk for over an hour in the cold before deciding that the conversation could be carried on more comfortably in the café. In fact we chat until we are thrown out! A wonderful, inspirational man.

So the Green Year list is still at **177**, twenty two ahead of this time last year.

44.48 Miles 1247 feet elevation up 1243 feet down

Thursday 3rd March light W

Very sunny until late PM

Staying in the excellent Wells Youth Hostel means that the ride to Blakeney Marsh for a target bird, Lapland Bunting, is a breeze in the early morning sunshine with a light breeze behind me.

There's a lot of duck on a pool at Blakeney Quay; Blue-winged Teal, Garganey, Ross' Goose, Puna Teal and a male Ferruginous Drake. As they are within a fenced off area I may not count them! Puna Teal!

The Lapland Buntings couldn't be easier to find as a group of ten or so birders are watching as one by one the birds come up onto the fence. Unfortunately views are brief and not that good due to the birds being in line with the strong sun. Two Barn Owls are hunting in the area and I see another as I cycle towards Cley along the repaired sea wall.

After the iconic views of Cley's famous windmill from the long sea wall, I go to the environmentally friendly Cley Marsh visitor's centre for a drink and cake. I am invited to sit down by two strangers as all of the tables are taken.

Out onto the reserve, I cycle along the East Bank, also with it's path redone, and push the bike along the shingle searching for the reported Snow Buntings. Not finding them, I chain the bike to the fence and proceed down to Salthouse. It is amazing to see how far the shingle was taken inland during the terrific storms of two years ago. In some places the shingle is two hundred yards away from its original position. I am interested in why areas of shingle have been moved so much where as in other places it hasn't. Also interesting are the brick walls and posts revealed which I presume are from WW2 defences.

Back to the bike I can see three people who have binoculars trained down on a shingle depression near to it. The **Snow Buntings** are next to my bike!

A couple of bird photographers ensure that the birds don't stay too long and the flock flies off down the beach. After an hour or so they return and I sit down rest against a fence post and watch fascinated as they feed by flicking over small pebbles in search of seeds. Occasionally individuals squabble, a wonderful privilege to be able to sit quietly and watch them close by.

The Green Year list is **179**, twenty four ahead of this time last year.

23.63 Miles **699 feet elevation up and down**

Friday 4th March **fresh N**

Very sunny and cold

The target today is the Rough-legged Buzzard at Choseley barns near Titchwell. The bird was seen last night and it is obviously an important bird to get for the year list. If I do succeed today then it may save me many miles of cycling later in the year.

It is cold today and the wind is fresh though from the side. There is almost no traffic as I cycle west, which is a blessing.

Lots of Partridge, Red-legged and Grey, are in the fields as I proceed and two Barn Owls are daylight hunting again. So many Barn Owls in the last few days; eleven so far. I wonder why they seem to be doing so well in Norfolk compared to other counties?

I search the Choseley area for a couple of hours but only see Partridge and Yellowhammers. I even count the Hares, over a hundred, in order to keep searching.

Lunch at Titchwell and a walk down to the sea to look for eider. None there but plenty of Common Scoter and a few Goldeneye on the sea. Bar-tailed Godwits are here in good numbers along the shore and close too. I love Titchwell beach and as usual it's wide expanse is empty of people.

Out on the freshwater marsh the water level is extremely low so that a predator proof fence can be built around the large islands to improve wader breeding productivity.

Back to Choseley.

Three hours of pushing the bike along roads and bridleways. There has been a couple of Common Buzzards and yet another Barn Owl. This one was sitting on a garden fence. What a garden bird to have!

The sun is setting and I watch as a small group of Greylags flies over. What's that beneath them?
It's a 'there it is!' moment. **Rough-legged Buzzard** goes onto the list.

So the Green Year list is **180**, twenty five ahead of this time last year.

31.16 Miles 970 feet elevation up and down

Sunday 6th March fresh N

Cloudy and cold

Time to head off for Lincolnshire. I feel a little light-headed after such a late night last night in Wells Youth Hostel drinking brandy and red wine. Now this is a very rare thing for me to do yet the company of such a great group of Spaniards was wonderful. Why is it that Spanish people have these times when friends, couple and families get together on a holiday somewhere? In Peru it was the same, wonderful to be taken in as a new friend and share the laughter and camaraderie. Another similarity was the way the ladies retired whilst the men carried on until the early hours.

Another Barn Owl quarters a field as the route today takes me inland in order to cut the north west corner. I reach Wolferton for yet another attempt for the Golden Pheasant. Yes I know that the best chance of seeing it is at 7:00 a.m. but at the moment I feel too tired to camp there. I will camp later in the year if I don't get it today.

I don't!

Instead I see a couple of Green Woodpeckers and explore Dersingham Heath hoping for Woodlarks. They haven't returned yet so that's another reason to be here again in May.

29.58 Miles 1318 feet elevation up 1308 feet down

An email from The Oracle and I wonder how many of the birds Phil has listed I will actually get to see:-

New birds seen in Lincs and Yorks (with a small extension into Cleveland and Co Durham) in last eight days:

LINCS
White Stork - Bourne 4/3 (I would imagine this to be the ringed escape)
Garganey - Willow Tree Fen, Spalding 3/3, 2/3, 1/3, 29/2, 28/2
Bittern - Wisby Nature Park 28/2
Twite - Marston sewage works 5/3 (75) - Donna Nook 26/2 (80) - Tetney Marshes

27/2 Great Gonerby 1/3
Velvet Scoter (2) - Saltfleetby 29/2

Shorelark - Buck Beck, Cleethorpes 4/3, 3/3, 2/3, 29/2, 26/2

YORKSHIRE
Long-eared Owl - Blacktoft 29/2 Fenwick, Doncaster 28/2
Bittern - Old Moor 29/2, 27/2 (3) - Potteric Carr 28/2 Potteric Carr 2/3 Swillington Ings 27/2 Flamborough Head 5/3, 3/3
Iceland Gull - Potteric Carr 5/3 Hampole, South Elmsall 27/2 Wintersett 26/2 Swillington Ings 28/2 (fly-by) - Flamborough 28/2 (up to 2) - Rufforth, York 4/3, 2/3, 1/3, 29/2, 27/2, 26/2 Upper Poppleton, York 3/3 Wheldrake Ings 28/2, 27/2 Nosterfield 2/3, 1/3
Kumlien's Gull - Nosterfield 28/2, 27/2 Hazel Lane, South Elmsall, Doncaster 2/3 (up to 3) - Hampole, South Elmsall 1/3, 27/2 Wintersett, Wakefield 2/3, 1/3, 26/2
Richard's Pipit - Swillington Ings, Leeds 29/2, 26/2 Flamborough Head 5/3, 3/3, 1/3, 29/2, 28/2
Possible American Herring Gull (fly-by) - Flamborough Head 5/3
Woodlark - Flamborough 29/2
Velvet Scoter (7) - Flamborough 27/2
Surf Scoter - Filey 4/3, 3/3, 2/3, 1/3, 27/2, 26/2

CLEVELAND
Long Eared Owl - Haverton scrub, Billingham 1/3, 27/2, 26/2
Bittern - Saltholme 29/2, 28/2, 27/2
Shorelark (2) - Hartlepool Headland 3/3, 2/3, 29/2, 28/2, 27/2, 25/2

CO DURHAM
Richard's Pipit (2) - Blackhall Rocks 2/3, 1/3, 29/2, 28/2, 27/2
Iceland Gull - Cleadon 29/2
Mealy Redpoll - Hebburn 28/2
Mealy Redpoll - Ryhope 28/2

Phil also sent a list of some needed birds seen in Norfolk:-

Sightings since 20th February -

CORN BUNTING
Chooseley Barns 1/3 (6), 26/2 (5)

TREE SPARROW
Believe there is a population at Abbey Farm, Flitcham

BITTERN
Titchwell 21/2 Holkham Freshmarsh 27/2 Cley 25/2

LITTLE OWL
Abbey Farm, Flitcham (2) 28/2 - plus lots of sightings earlier in the year

BARNACLE GOOSE
Snettisham 1/3 (8), 24/2 (1) Burnham Overy Marshes 25/2 (5), 21/2
Holkham Park 26/2, 25/2 (16), 24/2, 23/2 (25), 21/2, 20/2
Holkham Freshmarsh 23/2

Scratching around this year trying to find Tree Sparrows! Back when I was a birder in my twenties they used to be everywhere. There was even a flock on Penn Common, my patch back then on the southern edge of Wolverhampton. A 93% population decline since 1970, yet another sad loss involving one of my favourite birds.

Monday 7th March **fresh NE**

Sunny intervals and cold

A day of cycling as far as I can towards Boston, Lincolnshire starts with a walk through Kings Lynn's town centre; well after three large fresh fruit-covered pancakes for breakfast. The Grange hotel, Kings Lynn isn't one of my favourite hotels for no reason. Jane, the bubbly Australian manageress, who in herself is a good reason to revisit, has brought not only three pancakes covered in raspberries, blueberries and banana but she has also put an extra four in foil for me to enjoy later. There's also the bottle of Canadian maple syrup with which to enjoy them with.

So after shopping for a little something for a gift to my daughter Rebecca, who is going to San Francisco to give a presentation in a couple of weeks as part of her PhD, I set off along the country lanes along the south end of The Wash.

Heacham passed, I cycle across the car park of a large café which has two armoured vehicles, a large RAF aircraft and a number of large missile shooting guns. A recruitment trailer for the army is parked here and there are 'Help The Heroes' flags flying.

I need a pee. One does occasionally when one is drinking two to three litres a session. The only private place is a broken down ruin of an old cottage and the deed is done inside, There's no roof so with the forecast for heavy rain tomorrow it will soon be washed away. Another few litres of fresh water saved as I won't be committing the sin of flushing urine with the precious liquid.

I reach Frampton after singing The Who repertoire for half an hour. The Bell Boy arrives at this fabulous RSPB reserve all newly born, my Biking Birder uniform and bike tells a volunteer and a staff member who I am. Simon, the RSPB staff member greets me like an old friend. Last year he helped me see a rare American White-rumped Sandpiper here back last June. The volunteer, who's name I can't recall sorry, shakes hands as Simon tells me that he will tell Chris I am here. Who's Chris?

Into the visitor's centre I buy myself a hot chocolate and a packet of chocolate raisins. I wonder how much profit the RSPB get from the small packet of the latter. I am sure they, and I would get a better deal if they bought much larger packets of chocolate raisins from Lidl and sold them at £1!

Simon comes on in with Chris Andrews. I had totally forgotten that the brother of The Oracle, Phil Andrews, worked here and the surprise has me laugh out loud.

Recently Phil has not only been sending around fifteen to twenty texts a day over birds available for the year list ahead of me. He has also started to add possible ten day itineraries to the comprehensive list of birds seen in the last week in the counties around me! Phil has two wonderful small boys and a beautiful wife. Where does he get the time? No matter, he is a vital cog in the professional team that is The Biking Birder.

Tree Sparrows come to the feeder where there are already Goldfinch, Chaffinch, Greenfinch, Yellowhammers, Robin, Blackbird and Dunnock. The list grows by one.

As by now it is late afternoon I head for the 360 hide where a Little Ringed Plover was seen earlier in the day. A Barn Owl flies over. How many of them have I seen in the last week? There are flocks of roosting Dunlin and a sleeping Ringed Plover stays as that. No sign of the LRP, I leave the reserve and get to Boston. New bird for the year and target place reached despite the cold, and it has been a very cold day and the strong wind in my face. Music kept me going!

So the Green Year list is now at 181, which is still twenty four ahead of this time last year.

41.23 Miles **439 feet elevation up** **454 feet down**

Tuesday 8th March **light SW**

Sunny intervals and cold

A day of cycling ahead in order to get as far as I can north. I don't think I have told you much about the bike and what it has to carry, other than me and 'The Lads & Lasses.' The bike is a 1984 Claude Butler, Black Diamond. On it there are four panniers, two at each end. Inside those are clothes, a small laptop, food, drink, a couple of books, cycling tools, repair kits and two spare inner tubes, a torch, toiletries and a first aid kit. At this time of year most of my warm clothes and waterproofs are on me. Later on I will need to carry them in the panniers. Add to the weight of all this a sleeping bag and a tent and one can imagine that sometimes it isn't possible to lift the bike.

Two special birds are available; Richard's Pipits at North Landing, Flamborough and a first winter Surf Scoter at Filey.

At last there is a light wind this morning and almost behind me too. The first road is very straight and very flat.

Through Horncastle and Wragby; north to Market Rasen and I stop to buy a large Danish pastry from an independent bakers. Nearly all of the products are in plastic cases sealed in a plastic wrapper. The Danish pastries aren't wrapped in such a wasteful fashion and the young shop assistant is confused when I ask for the bought item to just be given to me. I don't want a paper bag. I am going to devour it straight away. "I can't do that," she says.

To Caistor and the mostly gentle falls and rises becomes a steep chalk hill to climb. The route along the ridge top gives views for miles to the west and a steep bendy downhill stretch takes me into the village of BIGBY, a village well named for a Biking Birder to travel through.

For those who don't know the term BIGBY let me explain. A few years ago there was a film with Jack Black, Steve Martin and Owen Wilson called The Big Year. Based on the real adventures of three Americans; Sandy Komito, Greg Miller and Al Levantin, the film told how each wanted to be the birder who had the biggest 'carbon' birding list in the USA in a particular year. The book of the same name by Mark Obmascik is fabulous. The film I like, it being more an exploration of relationships. Anyway a 'carbon' year list chase of epic proportions is called A Big Year.

BIGBY is for the birder who wants to avoid carbon as much as possible. A pure BIGBY is when a birder doesn't use any fossil fuel transport at all in a whole year. My personal BIGBY has the use of a few ferries to get me to Shetland and Fair Isle. This is allowed as long as I am honest and say that when placing my list on record. I wonder if one will ever have to say how Green one is in other ways as well?

Bigby. I like it! Oh sorry, it stands for Big Green Big Year.

Through more country lanes and onto a dual carriageway towards the Humber Bridge; I turn off at the past roundabout before it and go down into Barton-upon-Humber. Here I find a guest house, which is superb and the owners, Rachel and Simon are very friendly. I have cycled over sixty miles today and gosh, don't I feel it. My knees feel swollen and my hands feel stiff, being stuck in a grasping attitude. C'est la rue!

61.94 Miles 1963 feet elevation up 1873 feet down

Wednesday 9th March light to fresh NE

Heavy rain all day and cold

There is another couple in the breakfast room this morning, Lesley and Mark. They tell me that they send shoe boxes full of things to send out to our troops and, as well as giving me a donation for my charities, pass me their card. Here's a link to their website. A brilliant couple.

www.forcesshoeboxappeal.com

Rachel has done me a packed lunch to help me on my way at no extra charge. Thanks Rachel, much appreciated.

It is raining heavily and there is a fresh wind in my face as I go over the immense Humber Bridge. Sprays from passing vehicles contains salt that I can taste on my lips. This is going to be a fun day!

Thirty five miles later I reach Bridlington. I find a hotel. I go to bed. Once cosy under the covers I search Youtube for some comedic moments from long ago. I come across a Les Dawson video where the great piano playing comedian is performing in the Royal Variety show of 1987. I watch and I laugh, giggle and smile. Then suddenly, after asking what happens to the rest of the frog once they've had their legs taken off by the French frogs' legs eaters, Les goes into a monologue about the being the President of the Society for the Preservation of the Black Infested Swallow-backed Duck of Southern Bridlington! I sit up and concentrate on the dialogue. The coincidence of the duck's location being the place of tonight's rest is incredible.

Apparently Les was an ecologist! You have to watch this link to hear more details about the poor drake's fortunes.

https://www.youtube.com/watch?v=LQ0G2Z8k1Gg

38.51 Miles 924 feet elevation up 1016 feet down

An email from Michael Szebor of the RSPB:-

Dear Gary,

Hope you are not getting too wet out on the bike today!

I wonder if you might be able to help with an image. I am currently sourcing images for a historical timeline display about our Arne reserve, and the designer is in need of a shot of the Arne anti aircraft position. I notice that you have a shot of this on your blog from last year. Would you be able to grant us use of this image? The version on the blog looks like it should be big enough for us to use.

Many thanks,

Michael Szebor, MSc, BA (hons) *Picture Researcher*

UK Headquarters *The Lodge, Sandy, Bedfordshire SG19 2DL*

My pleasure! I respond.

Many thanks Gary,

I understand that internet access is not always a constant when you are travelling around, so I appreciate you getting back to me as soon as you did.

The timeline display will be in the new visitor centre at Arne, hopefully in place in a month or two. We will credit the photo to yourself.

Thanks again and good luck with the rest of your 'Quest for 300'.

Michael.

PS. I might have to pick your brain about cycle touring tips. I'm heading off to Iceland in July for a 10 day trip in the saddle.

Thursday 10th March **light NW**

Misty, cloudy with some brighter periods . . . and cold

Past the harbour hoping for an Iceland Gull but not getting one, I follow the cycle path and then take the road to Flamborough. To North Landing, I search the fields along the cliff edge for the reported Richard's Pipits. There are only two other birders doing the same, a couple who have just started birding, Steve and Judith from Wakefield.

With three large fields scanned after a couple of hours I haven't found the rare Pipits. With some time spent enjoying the massed ranks of Kittiwakes and Guillemots on the cliffs, and enjoying watching Gannets, Auks and Fulmars flying past, I head back to the bike for lunch.

Steve and Julie had left an hour or so ago and as I reach the first field, the field nearest to the cafés and car park, a Crow lands in it. I use my binoculars and experience another 'oh there it is' moment. **Richard's Pipit** goes onto the year list.

I text Phil, The Oracle, the good news and he asks how many. Looking back I can see there are two of them. Brilliant, a possibly tricky to get scarcity is seen.

Now there has been a Bittern seen close by each evening for a while and 'The Oracle' Phil suggests seawatching and then the Bittern. I have other ideas. There is a Surf Scoter twelve miles away at Filey. I set off to find it.

An hour and a half later, and after meeting two lovely couples who are out either walking the dog, Lise and Dave or birding, Julie and Trevor, who used to live on Fetlar, I cycle along the cliff top and easily find the first winter male **Surf Scoter**. One hundred and twenty miles in the last three days is well worth it. Two very good birds are added to the year list. Result!

I chain the bike to a fence and clamber down the muddy cliff to get to the shore. I am interested in the rocks that I have seen from the top and want a closer look. Does anybody want to hazard a guess at what the coral-like structures are in the limestone?

The Surf Scoter is a little closer and seems to like the company of a Great-crested Grebe. I sit down on some rocks and am surprised when I hear a loud cough. Twenty feet away are two small Grey Seal cubs! They're staring at me but aren't too concerned. They yawn and roll and stretch. To be so close to two such wonderful animals is, here comes that favourite word of mine, a privilege.

So the Green Year list is **183**, which is still twenty two ahead of this time last year. Almost coincidentally the 182nd bird I saw last year was Surf Scoter at Hoylake on the 14th of April.

23.95 Miles 1099 feet elevation up 1012 feet down

Friday 11th March light SE to fresh

Sunny 7C

After all of the effort of the last few days since leaving Norfolk I decide a rest day is deserved. I head for the Brigg in lovely sunshine and with only a light wind from the south east, things are a tad warmer. Spring is just around the corner. I keep saying that.

Carrying the bike down the muddy cliff path, I reach the limestone pavement at the Brigg's base and after chaining it to a bench I start to walk to the far end. There are two ecologists from Hull University on their way out to Laminaria beds exposed because the tide is incredibly low.

The area is fascinating with many seaweed species, some shore crabs and periwinkles. I hadn't realised just how far the Brigg extends out into the sea. It reminds me of the Giant's Causeway in Northern Ireland and it's limestone structures seem to me to be just as interesting as that more famous place. I remember visiting the causeway when on the first Biking Birder tour in 2010. The most impressive view was when I turned my back on the sea whilst standing on a hexagonal piece. The high cliffs are magnificently impressive here.

Birds are passing, mostly heading south; Gannets, Guillemots,

Kittiwakes and Fulmars. The Surf Scoter is as faithful as ever to his blue plastic bottle left floating out on the sea as a marker for a line of crab pots. There are a number of Shags and Cormorants feeding close by.

The two young seal pups are still on the rock ledge close to the muddy cliffs. They seem to be extremely relaxed and don't react too harshly even when a border collie goes over to sniff them over. People come and go all morning, taking photographs of the sleeping pair. I am amazed when one particularly brave or foolhardy girl puts her head almost against one of the seal pup's head for a selfie. Amazed that she isn't bitten that is.

Returning to the bike I sit and seawatch as more people come to see the seal pups. I am talking to one couple when a bird flies past from off the sea. I jump up and chase after it. It's a male **Ring Ouzel**! Unfortunately it just keeps flying and is soon off over the cliff top. I text Phil about what I feel is an almost unbelievable sighting. To see a Ring Ouzel at this time of year and coming off the sea is incredible and I am buzzing, telling anyone who comes by and will listen for ages.

A couple I met yesterday. Lise and Dave, arrive with their two dogs. Lise is a keen birdwatcher eager to learn more. Dave is a photographer who likes to photograph birds yet confesses to knowing nothing about them. Together we watch and chat. Maybe it is because the hour is getting late but there are now a few **Puffins** flying past as well as the masses of Guillemot.

The wind has got up during the day and the temperature has correspondingly fallen. It is downright chilly!

I decide to go and search for birds in the sheltered trees and hedges along the cliff tops. On the way back up the cliff path two birders replete with scopes on tripods come down to look for the Surf Scoter. I wave goodbye to Lise and Dave and stand with the two birders and get great views of the Scoter through one birder's telescope. Hence I meet Tim Isherwood and Adrian Johnson. Tim tells me he started birding as a kid when his Mum and Dad put up a red bag full of peanuts. The birds attracted to it were so diverse and colourful seeing them started Tim's life of loving birds. Adrian's story is more unusual and totally amazing.

Many years ago Adrian, before he was a birder, saw a bird in his garden that he didn't recognise. Local organisations dismissed his report as a Redwing. It wasn't. It was a spring male Eye-browed Thrush! A CMF* of the first order. How can one top that as a garden tick?

The Green Year list is **185**, which is still twenty four ahead of this time last year.

3.69 Miles **245 feet elevation up and down**

* Please refer to Bill Oddie's Little Black Bird Book for the meaning of a

rather naughty birding expression.

Saturday 12th March **light S**

Hazy sunshine 11C Happy Wedding anniversary Mum & Dad xx

My day starts watching a Youtube video about the biggest Green day list ever; Scott Robinson and Ted Parker's amazing walking and canoeing day back in 1982 in the Manu, Peru. They saw 331 birds that day, still the Big Green Big Day record. It's a fascinating watch. Scott's talk about going for the Big Green Day record at Cocha Cashu in The Manu National Park in Peru. It is also very touching when Scott tears up emotionally when recalling his friend who sadly died too young.

I laugh out loud at the thought of doing a BIGBY, a Big Green Big Year along The famous Manu Road. Maybe a dream; Lima with San Isidro Park, the Miraflores beach and Los Pantanos de Villa reserve would start the year. Then the cycle along the coast to the Paracas. I wonder if a yacht would take me out to the islands? Up and over the Andes via Cusco, Ollantaytambo and the sacred river; canoe to Machu Picchu! To Huarcarpay and the lake there and then the long Manu Road itself down to Chontachaka and Salvacion and beyond to areas that I haven't been to .. yet. Dream on. The thoughts of my daughter, Rebecca, come to mind as I go through the route in my head. On mentioning this idea my daughter, Rebecca gives me an epitaph for my future gravestone : "killed by bandits!"

https://www.youtube.com/watch?v=TUXAEwWw-LQ

On my Facebook page I see the sad news that Keith Emerson has died and so immerse myself in his music for the next hour whilst uploading some photographs to my blog. A member of one of my favourite rock bands back when I was at college, ELP. So sad to hear that another Rock music hero has gone.

It is going to be a tough day. I need to cycle as far as I can along the North Yorkshire coast towards Teeside. At least the weather is with me. The sun is shining and it is warm enough to cycle without a coat. Also a light wind is behind me at first.

Through Scarborough and the hills begin. Up the road goes to moorland heights and a couple of Stonechat are on the heather.

Yesterday's Ring Ouzel is on my mind; the earliest ever seen in Yorkshire so I am told. I am confused over it. I can see it passing me in my mind's eye and I wonder how it had got there. Was it on Flamborough before coming over the bay? Or did it just come over the whole of the North Sea to get here? Do Ring Ouzels usually migrate at night? How come it came in during the afternoon? Lots of questions.

Just to keep the strange avian theme going, I see a Lapwing flying around in display. The unusual thing is that it has a totally white hand; the primaries on it's right wing are white. Just on one wing but so distinctive.

Further on a large male Pheasant is sitting stunned in the middle of the road. I pick it up and put it into a field. It may get a bit more life before the bird murderers get to work.

This main road is a veritable graveyard for so many species. The usual load of Pheasants and Hares are here. Also the road verge has a Yellowhammer, a Barn Owl, a Moorhen, a few Blackbirds and a couple of Wood Pigeons. Mammals dead by the road include Fox, Badger and Rabbit. Later on there is another of the bird murderers favourite birds dead by the road, a Red Grouse. How the evil hunting community gets away with murder, especially of Britain's birds of prey, is beyond me. Search out a breeding map for the hen harrier in Britain and see how the gaps coincide with grouse shooting areas. Coincidence Botham?

This depressing total of car-nage is relieved when a couple of very much alive Short-eared Owls I see over the moorland with just nine miles to get to Guisborough. A **Red Grouse** is there too, alive this one and yet another bird that takes the Green year list to 186.

A few miles later two females and a male Red Grouse are very close to the road and easy to see.

So the Green Year list is **186**, which is still twenty four ahead of this time last year.

45.65 Miles 3027 feet elevation up 2718 feet down

Sunday 13th March light S

Hazy sunshine 11C

The sun is a-shining to welcome the day, hey ho. . . .

Cycling and singing I get into Middlesborough and go past the 'stockings', by Anish Kapoor and photograph the Transporter Bridge through it's rings.

http://www.bbc.co.uk/news/10281554

There is a crowd of people at the Transporter Bridge. They are there to watch young person after young person abseil down from the top. It is a sponsored event for a World Challenge event. Fabulous to watch the young people's faces when they reach the cobbled ground.

The cycle path takes me towards the A19 and, after passing a park with very large jigsaw dinosaurs (!), I cross the River Tees via another tremendous bridge.

To a favourite RSPB reserve, Saltholme and I am soon out of the visitor's centre to go and find a **Long-eared Owl** for the year list. With the help of a birder, Dave from Carlisle, the bird is located as hidden as ever in an elder bush. Dave is a bit credulous over the fact I cycle everywhere and thinks I catch trains to get from place to place. I suggest he looks at my list of routes on mapometer!

Dave is happy with his views of the owl and a couple from Sheffield, Susan and John, arrive to look at the sleeping bird. It is great to meet such a close couple and I must admit to being a bit jealous. Oh to have a ... come on Prezza, don't go there!

Back at the centre to celebrate the new year tick with a cuppa, I meet two birders, Morris and Dave, who are talking about my British nemesis, Chris Mills. We chat about birding, Green Birding and the like. Morris says that he has been many times with Chris on many of Chris' tours. Knowing Chris' personality it must be fabulous to go on one of his tours and to go again and again shows how good they must be. Nemesis is a joke term. Chris is a fantastic birder and friend.

http://www.norfolkbirding.com/

Dave asks where I am off to next and when I say it is to try to see the Shorelarks at Hartlepool, he asks whether I would like to stay at his house that night. The kindness of strangers once more pops its head up and I accept the kind offer gratefully.

Leaving Saltholme eventually, after checking out the long-staying red-head Smew, I cycle off towards Hartlepool. Birders are standing rather dangerously beside the road looking for the Penduline tits seen from there and I stop briefly to search for them myself, unsuccessfully. A lovely couple pass a donation over saying that they knew what I was doing. Thanks.

Before reaching Seaton Carew another cyclist comes up along me. It is Dave whom I had just met at Saltholme and together we cycle the maze of Hartlepool Harbour. We reach the Jewish Cemetery and the large waste ground that the Shorelarks have made their winter home. A couple of birders are obviously looking at something and we cycle over to them. A dog walker disturbs three birds, Snow Buntings but the birds I need is in the opposite corner. **Shorelark** goes onto the year list; a very good one to get as this may mean I won't have to cycle to Norfolk next winter. A just reward for the previous weeks cycling, having searched the beach at Burnham Overy and then having travelled up Lincolnshire missing a couple of Shorelarks at Gibraltar Point, I feel getting these and getting the Richard's Pipits and Surf Scoter, makes the long distance cycled north worthwhile.

David and I cycle to the World War Memorial Park on the headland to see a Black Redstart there.

So the Green Year list is **188**, which is twenty six ahead of this time last year.

Monday 14th March **light SE**

Hazy sunshine 11C

I pass a sight you don't see every day, a house covered in empty aluminium drink cans! I am about to go to the door to ask about all of this when a passer-by tells me that it is empty, the owner having died. Looking up the story of the house later I find a Youtube video:-

https://www.youtube.com/watch?v=ppelxJNY4LQ

In fact there a few of them, videos that is, not can houses and a long film too. Brilliant. I love coming across the unexpected like this and remember the shark sticking out of a terraced house roof in Oxford and the windmills made of recycled plastic artefacts that filled a pensioner's garden in a village near Salisbury. There must be so many bizarre creations around the UK waiting to be seen and enjoyed.

I find a disused railway cycle path and take it for ten miles or so, enjoying the sunshine and occasionally walking instead of cycling. It is a beautiful warm Spring-like day.

My intention is to visit the Wildfowl & Wetland Trust reserve at Washington and I reach there around lunchtime. I love this place with its grass-covered visitor's centre, the wildfowl collection in the usual WWT-style pens and areas for wild birds with lagoons down by the river. After a cursory glance over the reedbed in the vain hope of seeing the apparently wild Ferruginous Duck, I walk down to the largest of these lagoons and enter the hide just as a male Goosander flies in. There is another couple, John and Kate from Durham in there who are both keen and knowledgeable birders. They tell me that their daughter is the Golden Eagle project officer in Dumfrieshire where they are releasing birds. Now that would be good. There are already a few pairs there, and if more could be helped to build up the numbers, there may be a chance that the lonely male at Haweswater in the Lake District might at last have a female who appreciates all of his nest building efforts.

As well as the Goosander, there are a dozen Avocets here; possibly the most northerly breeding Avocets in Britain. Talking with the reserve manager, Gill, later she tells me that there is evidence that some of these birds have been seen over wintering at Cadiz in Spain. It is great to meet Gill again and every visit to the WWT Washington has been an absolute pleasure. Thanks Gill.

Leaving here late in the afternoon I negotiate the complex route of roads and cycle paths to take me down to the Millennium Bridge that takes me over the Tyne. It swings both ways, blinking like an eye when a large ship needs to go upstream, across the Tyne. I spend the evening with my daughter, Rebecca. Here I am going to have a couple of days of rest, wash my clothes and catch up on things generally. I hadn't bargained on being here until mid-April but the birds have been so good along the way that I may as well enjoy the time with Rebecca before another big push.

38.27 Miles 1696 feet elevation up 1591 feet down

Wednesday 16th March

It is an incredible thing, reading a blog. My blog, **Biking Birder 2016 – The Quest for 300** makes me realise how the love of nature can link people from all over our wonderful globe.

The statistics today show people from the United Kingdom make up the bulk of viewers but it is wonderful to see that people from many countries look in too. The list is in order of number of views :-

United States
Sweden
Ireland
France
South Africa
Spain
Australia
Germany
Portugal
The Netherlands
Peru
Cyprus
China.

Thursday 17th March

I have been looking at the Green Birding tour completed by the American Dorian Anderson today. Dorian is the current World BIGBY record holder; the birder with the biggest Green Year list.

His blog is a tremendous read not only for the birds for the wide breadth of environmental issues that he talks about within it.

For those who don't know, Dorian Anderson back in 2014 cycled around the US of A for the whole year. Dorian took the BIGBY, Big Green Big Year, record from 326 up to 618! A phenomenal effort with absolutely no carbon fuels used for transport, Dorian cycled 17,830 miles.

His blog can be found here :- http://bikingforbirds.blogspot.co.uk/

An interview on ABA's site (American Birding Association) may be found here :-

http://blog.aba.org/2015/01/an-interview-with-dorian-anderson-pedal-powered-big-year-champ.html

Saturday 19th March **no wind**

Cloudy but high, cool 5C

After leaving Rebecca place in Newcastle yesterday and having reached Castleside, near Consett by dusk, I leave the wonderful Castleneuk Bed and Breakfast to head for Langdon Beck. Jan the B and B owner has filled my water bottle with juice and chats about her years of hitch-hiking back in the 70s. She tells stories of hitching across Europe and India evoking memories when hitching was my preferred taxi service in Britain in the same decade.

Deep in The Pennines now, the road is alternatively steep up and steep down before I reach the Sea to Sea route 7 cycle path. It has already been a wonderful day for displaying birds with Lapwing, Snipe, Golden Plover and Curlew all sky dancing, diving or drumming to a backdrop of Skylark song and Red Grouse clutterings. A single Red Kite glides over. I worry that it will suffer the same fate as the Black Isle kites in Scotland from two years ago. There over sixteen Red Kites were poisoned and there has been no action taken.

I stop at a café and B and B near Waskerley owned by the friendly Lorraine. This must be a perfect stopping point for cyclists using the route and a full house must be an exciting place to be in a late evening when the drink is flowing and the tales are being spun. There's a family with a young seven year old dancing in the first café room. They and I are joined by a group of cyclists out for the day. They want to know my tale and receive a Biking Birder sticker for their patience in listening. Lorraine then tells tales of the mad Red Grouse that attacks passers by and of how long she has had the establishment. Great place.

White knuckle downhill section to Stanhope, a car stops in front of me and four young people get out. One shouts "are you the Biking Birder?" They, three men and a woman, Caroline, Steven, John and Mike, are out for a day's birding and turned their car around to say hello when they passed me. Yesterday the driver of a van shouted "hello Gary," as he drove past and a couple of cars pipped their horn at me in recognition of either me or the RSPB and WWT posters on the bike.

The young people are a brilliant enthusiastic group and it is inspiring to think that maybe in some small way I am inspiring others.

After a quick shop for some provisions in St John's Chapel and after photographing the war memorial there, I turn towards Langdon Beck, the signpost telling me that I have five miles to go. I can see that this is going to take some time as the road heads towards the moorland top where small patches of snow are gathered in crevices. Headphones on, I mostly push the bike whilst singing to the fields. A few cyclists pass on their macho climb and most say hello.

At the top there are three young stunt motorcyclists who have been laughing at my rendition of Money for Nothing. They show me a few 'one wheel, look Mum – no legs on the bike' tricks and chat about Newcastle's chances of staying in the Premiership, the Big Game tomorrow against Sunderland and where my team, Aston Villa, will be next year. Thanks lads!

Down the other side I can see black lumps in a distant field. Binoculars up, **Black Grouse** go onto the year list, bird number **189**. There are twenty two males here eyeing each other up but mostly just feeding. Occasionally a pair will turn away from each other showing their white backsides. They are a few hundred yards away but show no sign that a bright yellow-clad cyclist is causing them any concern.

I cycle on past the Langdon Beck Hotel and after finding the youth hostel closed I go to a farmhouse bed and breakfast where Michael and Emma greet me kindly. A superb house with a number friendly and not so friendly dogs and a male Peacock; sheep out on the hills. A mass of rosettes around kitchen doorways shows the quality they are and a few cows in barns are waiting for the Spring grass to start growing.

Spring, first day of Spring day after tomorrow, migrants are coming!

The Green Year list is **189**, which is twenty six ahead of this time last year.

23.96 Miles **2807 feet elevation up** **2037 feet down**

Sunday 20th March **no wind**

Very sunny AM, clouded over for PM, cool 2 to 8C

A glorious morning greets me from my farmhouse cottage bedroom window and after breakfast I am off on the physical challenge of the year. My planned route is across the Pennines via part of the Pennine Way. I have no idea on the surface of the pathway yet know that no matter what it may be I can either cycle or push and still enjoy it on such a beautiful day.

Naive? I will see later.

The road has frosty imprints from a few passing vehicles and there are a few Lapwings sky-dancing. The road takes me to a large reservoir and I take a route that gets me to The Pennine Way just south of a large dam. A pair of Red Grouse are on a small island beneath a powerful water shoot.

The tarmac has gone and the track is cycle able, just. After a farmhouse it changes again though as the way is made of a new covering of stones. I push.

A Small Tortoiseshell butterfly flutters by as I cross a stream. Birds are few and far between out here, just the occasional Red Grouse and Curlew. A single Meadow Pipit lands on a wall quite close.

Mile after mile of pushing, I reach a turn in the path where the stony way changes to boggy grass and small boulders. This is going to be fun!

Downhill to a river, more tough pushing and then over a bridge. More stones and a bouncy push uphill, I meet a walker, the first of the day.

Half a mile later two cyclists stop for a chat. Their bikes are built for this terrain with huge wide tyres. Photographs are swapped and respect.

There are no birds singing here and I decide to listen to some of my favourite songs and sing along to them. Meat loaf and Status Quo songs head across the moorland. Suddenly there are crowds of people. So far today I have seen three people. Here there are dozens and they are all at this spot because of the incredible, magnificent view. I am reached the top of High Cup Nick and a group of people tell me that it is nicknamed 'The Grand Canyon of the North.' The valley is U-shaped and surrounded by steep cliffs with views over the plain far below over to the Lake District.

People want to know why a happy singing man is pushing a heavily laden bike across the moor and a couple kindly give a donation into the robin collection box. Thanks.

I start to head towards the way down. The path goes along a cliff edge and bumping the bike over the rocks is fun and difficult. A purple-haired girl helps push over one particularly hard part. My hands are getting battered by all of this and once the steep path down is reached I find that with care I can white knuckle ride.

Reaching the village of Dufton after 15 miles of mostly pushing I can at last relax and cycle. The small country lanes takes me through valley after valley, village after village in the direction of Haweswater.

Stopped by a cyclist named Lee, he questions my reasons and sanity and tries to lift the bike. He makes complimentary comments about my legs as his wife, Ribby, puts a large donation into the collection box. Brilliant.

Over the A6, over the M6, and with the Sun now having set, I find a bridleway that cuts a corner and find a secluded area to set up the tent for the night. I am a bit tired.

27.98 Miles 2329 feet elevation up 2997 feet down

Monday 21st March light NW

Sunny intervals, cool 2C to 8C

I open the tent flap to find a cloudy day and a quite cool one too. Packed I am off towards Haweswater. The views along the bridleway to Rosgill and the stone-walled country lane downhill to Brampton are superb. I can see Haweswater from this elevated position flanked by two wooded sentinels. To the south the valley where I failed to find Ring Ouzel last year. The Golden Eagle ridge is just peeking above more nearby hills.

It is all so lovely with snow still on the tops in the distance. I get to the RSPB offices at Naddle Farm.

I leave and head for Leighton Moss RSPB reserve.

Was it really only a week ago that I was talking about the lone male Golden Eagle getting a passing female from a re-introduction scheme in Dumfrieshire?

"Hello Gary. What have you come for? Says Lee, an assistant warden at the RSPB reserve. "To see the Golden Eagle," reply I naively.

"We think it is dead!"

Not having been seen over the whole Winter period since the horrific floods in December of last year, the RSPB hadn't put the news out for fear of hoaxes and mistaken identity phone calls.

Up and over Shap, the highest A road in England and boy does it feel it, and down to Kendal where I find a hotel to collapse in for the afternoon and evening, The County Hotel. Brilliant, it has a deep bath in the en suite.

http://www.rural-roads.co.uk/shap/shap1.shtml

27.38 Miles 1751 feet elevation up 2479 feet down

A Facebook message from Lisa Hanson gives pause for thought. It details a pale phase Gyrfalcon:-

Did you see this? It's not exactly in your vicinity I guess but so many rarities up in the Hebs you could cache a few superb spots!

Arctic wanderer takes up residence on the Western Isles

http://www.stornowaygazette.co.uk/news/arctic-wanderer-takes-up-residence-on-the-western-isles-1-4074789

My response to Lisa on Facebook:-

It would be a dream to see this bird Lisa. Thanks for telling me. 460 miles from where I am! 1,000 mile round trip . . oh well.

The support of people either through Facebook, emails or just when meeting them on the way, has been a wonderful thing. Messages such as this one from Lisa really cheer me up.

Tuesday 22nd March **light W**

Sunny intervals, cool 2C to 8C

To get to Leighton Moss RSPB reserve involves a shortish cycle along the A6 south from Kendall. It all seems to be downhill and a smooth ride gets me to the Arnside area quicker than expected. I reach the reserve and I am greeted by Lesley and Sophie in the RSPB shop. They want a photograph of the Biking Birder for the reserve's Twitter page.

Out onto the reserve there are plenty of Black-tailed Godwits to see from Lillian's hide. Some are in beautiful summer plumage. With a small group of Redshank are a couple of spangly-backed Ruff and a couple of Little Egrets walk around the reedbed edge.

Next to the Grisedale hide where a couple of female Red Deer are quite close before quietly walking and disappearing into the reedbed. A female Marsh Harrier is sitting on a branch away to the left of the hide and I sit and relax, enjoying watching the duck on the water. There are Wigeon, Pintail and Teal and the occasional group of up to four over-flying Buzzards.

With the afternoon drawing to a close I head off for the causeway where a couple of Bittern were seen last Sunday.

A couple of residential volunteers, two young girls, are also looking for the Bittern. They were the birders who saw the Bittern on Sunday but report that to them the birds seemed to be leaving. Darkness falls and Water Rail pig squeal but no Bittern are either seen or heard. All I get are a number of insect bites on my neck and head! Oh well, it would have been nice to get Bittern, not bitten at Leighton Moss but there's a couple of months in East Anglia to come.

19.16 Miles 976 feet elevation up 1119 feet down

Wednesday 23rd March No discernible wind

Cloudy, cool 6C

I get to the reserve very early and enjoy birding around every trail and from every hide. The insect bites from last night have blistered and the lumps are hot and swollen, oozing orange lymph. Ouch! These are worse than any bites I received last year but need to be far worse to beat the ones I received from horseflies back in 2010. Sausage lips!

I keep a day list and by the time I reach the Lower Hide at the far eastern end of the reserve I have forty-nine bird species on the page. An adult Mediterranean Gull flies past, fifty up.

Back to the centre for a drink in the superb upstairs café, I meet Kevin who was the laughing RSPB staff member to my right in the wonderful Biking Birder – RSPB reserve sign photograph from last year. He is going to Fair Isle this Autumn and it's great to know that we will meet up there on the magical isle.

Before leaving the reserve to start the long ride back over the Pennines I go to the top of the high sky tower; a strong steel construction from which one gets a panoramic view of the whole reserve. It is superb to be above a male Marsh Harrier flying past.

Time to leave, it has been lovely to visit this favourite RSPB reserve; well one of them. It has everything; great birds, lovely staff and diverse habitats as well as a great ambiance and café. What more could one want? A broad walk? There's a long new one which takes one to the causeway through the reedbed. A tower? Already mentioned and fabulous. Nature's Home garden ideas? It's all there. A superb RSPB reserve.

6.66 Miles 352 feet elevation up 323 feet down

Friday 25th March light to fresh SW

Sunny or sunny intervals warm 11C

Carnforth is full of giant garishly decorated eggs attached high on the walls of houses and businesses. Well it is Good Friday.

It is a pleasant day with some warm sunshine and only a light wind. The route back towards the East coast over the Pennines takes me to Kirby Lonsdale. I had wanted to go another way but the bridge over the River Lune must have been damaged in the December storms as the road that way is closed.

I can tell that it is going to be one of those tough days where my inner voice dwells too long on the negative things from the past. Every part of my body that has ached over the days and months of cycling seems to be doing so once more, especially my left knee. I could do with some music on the MP3 player but I never listen to it whilst cycling on the road. Eternal Sunshine!

The A65, the road from Kirby Lonsdale heads south-east towards Skipton, is horrible. A sign states that Skipton is thirty two miles away. Not that the road isn't beautiful. The landscape is superb with Ingleton and other high flat Pennine and Yorkshire Dales peaks providing a gorgeous backdrop. The greenery at this time of year is muted awaiting the Spring blush. The trees are still bare and distant woodland looks grey.

No, I can't fault the scenery. It is the traffic. Constant traffic of cars mostly, with a lot of motorbikes and the occasional large lorry to keep the decibel level extremely high. At no time do I feel in danger though as I tuck in along the kerbside.

A couple of texts arrive with one changing the mood completely. Carphone Warehouse's offer can be deleted as the spam it is but the other is a Happy Easter message from a very dear friend, Diane. The dark mood of guilt, blame and shame of relationships past are immediately replaced by a flood of memories of adventures and scrapes with Diane. Diane was a fabulous girlfriend over twenty five years ago. Sunrise over Beachy Head, somersaulting car on black ice near Thurso, when 'hit me with a peat bog' became a mantra for anything surprising for a few years, just as 'well forgive me' was the same in the film, Fisher King.

Another text of Easter wishes from my cousin, Rosemary and her son, Paschal. It is great that these texts arrive when I am feeling my lowest.

Things come in threes and a car stops me and a silver-haired gentleman starts a conversation and is reluctant to leave. His name is Steve and he tells me that he was a violinist. I mention some of my personal favourites; Ian Underwood, Jean Luc Ponty and Stefan Grappelli yet Steve was a string quartet player before arthritis set in. He was also an advertisement photographer and is now retired. Steve is eager to talk and the conversation includes his love of opera, particularly Wagner. Indeed Steve has a ticket for the Wagner festival. The cost of the ticket, £5,000, means that I will have to give it a miss.

I reach the charming, small youth hostel at Earby, near to Colne. Colne was where my first ever experience in front of a class of children occurred over forty years ago. My first teaching practice at Colne High School back in 1974 was an adventure. I was with a group of teacher training students that had been taken by minibus to the nearby Nelson and put up in a bed and breakfast. I remember the mass of food the landlady gave us all as one evening we watched an England football match on the TV. A memorable moment to me as an Aston Villa player, Brian Little came on for a substitute cameo. This was the first Aston Villa player I had ever seen play for England. We still don't have many!

A memory from the teaching practice was when the head of science had me kill and dissect an earthworm in front of all of year 10's students! At nineteen I wasn't much older than this crowd and this baptism of fire, with boiling water to kill the worm, dispelled any nerves for future lessons.

41.74 Miles 2336 feet elevation up 1878 feet down

Saturday 26th to 30th March

Earby Youth Hostel, Yorkshire where I stay for a few days in order to relax and prepare for the coming RSPB Members' Weekend at York.

Previously the home of Katherine Bruce Glasier, an evangelical socialist who helped form the Labour Party. The days I spend in this small, very quiet Youth Hostel, included spending time reading up on the life of both her and her husband, John Bruce Glasier. If you're of a mind for a love story about two passionate socialists then there's obviously an entry on Wikipedia but by no means does it tell the whole story. Called The Enthusiasts, the book is a superb read about two such influential members of the pre-Labour Party Socialists.

It feels incredibly special sharing a living room with the original furniture and the ghosts of such great people. George Bernard Shaw asked her to marry him on a number of occasions before John succeeded in getting the hand of the strong, independent woman. Maybe George was on one knee in this very room.

The oil painting on the wall in the lounge shows a real stateswoman and one can only imagine how marvellous she would have been if in the current Labour Party.

After staying and relaxing here and after one day when, on waking to find it snowing heavily and therefore enjoying walking in the not oft seen these days heavy snow, eventually it was time to carry on towards Fairburn Ings RSPB Reserve.

Watching from the Youth Hostel garden, Dipper and Grey Wagtail from the Earby Youth Hostel garden early doors, I pack and head off towards Skipton.

With the wind, light to fresh coming from behind me, the cycling is easy despite hills. Actually most of the way is downhill with long stretches of just relax and hold on.

Through Leeds and down to the river, the evidence of the immense floods recently suffered in the area is draped high on every riverside tree; plastic and lots of it. The cycle path is extremely muddy in places and badly damaged in others. Eventually though I reach Astley Lake and enter the excellent bird hide overlooking it. A Garganey has been reported there but no one in the hide believes the report. Two **Sand Martins** fly past, year tick number **190**.

The oracle texts me to say that there is an Osprey over Fairburn Ings NOW!

As fast as I can I cycle there but the Osprey has flown on, probably it went over my head whilst I cycled.

It is wonderful to be at one of my favourite RSPB reserves again with Tree Sparrow covered feeders and mating toads to carefully step over. I explore the lakes to the east as the Sun sets.

50.94 miles 1918 feet elevation up 2394 feet down

Thursday 31st March

Early morning sunshine with lots of bird and beautiful views, who would believe that I am so near to so many urban conurbations? I adore Fairburn Ings and such a start bodes well for the rest of the day. In fact the weather looks too good, too sunny for migrants to drop in. Just to prove me wrong sand Martins drop in at around 8.00 a.m.

I cycle to the visitor's centre and am greeted by the staff. Photographs are required and so we all go into the kid's garden for frolicking photographs after the rather formal few are taken by the centre itself.

With the thought of the frog face RSPB advert in mind it is decided to do leap frogs photographs. Great talent is displayed by the young staff and one old codger.

Onto the huge wooden dragonfly for more fun, my waterproof trousers don't allow me to slide down the tail and it is rather a painful journey down to the ovipositor.

I need Willow Tit for the year, as The Oracle constantly reminds me. My promise of 'I will get one within the hour' sent at 9.00 a.m. is broken but at 11.00 a.m. one comes onto a feeder beside a screen like hide and onto the list this scarce titmouse goes; bird number 191.

Willow Tit secured, I leave the hide to explore the rest of the reserve and actually walk around five miles in order to walk every pathway. I go first to the high ridge to the south and follow the path along the largest lake side, through the birch woodlands and visit all of the hides. Spring blossom is out, Chiff Chaffs are chiff chaffing and it is a beautiful day.

The walk back takes me to a new pathway that circumnavigates a few high rise, reed-fringed lakes. I sit on a path and think that I have heard a distant sound of a Bittern boom. Just a couple of booms, I wonder whether I have imagined it. I carry on along the path and do hear Water Rail and Cetti's Warbler.

Arriving back at the previous bench I hear what is definitely a Bittern and again .... and again. Bittern, bird number 192 onto the list.

On leaving Fairburn Ings for the ride towards York, I cycle along very quiet country lanes, thankfully, and the first Swallow of the year flies over a large ash tree, bird number 193.

14.94 miles 741 feet elevation up 689 feet down

Green Year list	193 birds
Year ticks in March	18
Bird species had, not seen in 2015	0
Mileage in March	645.06 miles
Total mileage for the year	2011.95 miles
average mileage on days cycled	32.25 miles
elevation : up	26.930 feet
: down	28,907 feet

Best Birds : Rough-legged Buzzard, Richard's Pipit, Surf Scoter, Black Grouse, Willow Tit.

4

APRIL

It was a very small fledgling, and had no dreams of soaring to the heights which it had reached

Emily Wilkinson, Co-founder of the RSPB

Saturday 2nd April

A day standing with my bike and with The Lads; Albert, Manu, Oscar, Colin, Ricky and Tigger, and the Laddies; Ophelia, Acorn and Scaggy, beside my Biking Birder table at the RSPB's members' weekend at York University.

Meeting RSPB members is a thrill, always a delight to hear their stories and share their birding moment anecdotes.

Mike Clarke, the RSPB Chief Executive, comes over for a chat and photographs are taken. His handshake is firm and sincere.

I occasionally walk around the hall in order to see the other exhibits. The work of the RSPB and Birdlife International is fascinating, especially the success of the Albatross Campaign. Albert, my own cuddly Black-browed Albatross, who is slowly turning into a Sooty Albatross with all of the grime collected from his being on the front of the bike, is particularly happy at seeing that the numbers of his cousins killed by long-line fishing has declined since the campaign started in 2006. Back then it is thought that an albatross died every five minutes, caught and drowned on a hook. Deaths are down by 85%. Still some way to go and there are still albatross species in danger of extinction but there is now a lot more hope than there was.

https://www.rspb.org.uk/join-and-donate/donate/appeals/albatross/

Sunday 3rd April

I said it before over Freddie Flintoff, I am never comfortable when I meet one of my 'heroes'. I remember failing to say thank you to Sir Peter Scott, the founder of The Wildfowl & Wetland Trust, way back in the early 1980s. Sir Peter came into the Miller's Bridge hide at Martin Mere with Dr Janet Kear. I desperately wanted to say thank you to him for answering my schoolboy letter sent when I was around 10 years old. My shyness was maybe a little due to my attire. Birding in a vividly bright lime green floral shirt with shocking Bermuda shorts, well I'll leave it to your vividly bright imagination.

That return letter from such a famous personality from The Sixties was so special.

So it was today when David Lindo, the Urban Birder passes my table. No one has done more to promote Urban Birding than David and his philosophy inspires thousands. Birds are everywhere no matter what the location. Just look up!

Last Christmas I asked Santa for the two autobiographies of the solo rower, Roz Savage. I was incredibly disappointed with the first book and

the second has gone to a charity shop unread. David's autobiography though I found unputdownable.
I hope he will forgive my copying the following from his website. David puts it so much better than I ever could:-

I'm David Lindo, also known as The Urban Birder. I'm a broadcaster, writer, naturalist, photographer, public speaker, tour leader and oh, I have been known to do the odd bit of birding!
Born and raised in London, I love anything nature, but for as long as I can remember birds have been my particular obsession. When I was three I went missing during a family party and caused my mum great panic. The police were called and a search party dispatched and I was eventually found standing outside a graveyard watching some Magpies.
I never switch off when it comes to urban birding, I'm forever on the lookout. If you saw me strolling down a street you'd think I was in Manhattan for the first time, gazing up in wonderment. The sky is my canvas and it's amazing what you can see when you look up; birds of prey, swirling swifts, migrating thrushes, raucous crows. It's a beautiful world up there.
My main passion is for urban birds and I spend my time doing as much as I can to promote the appreciation and conservation of the birds that share our city lives. I now travel the world encouraging citizens and organisations to step outside wherever they may be to enjoy urban birding. Through my TV appearances, writing, talks and tours I try to inspire people to re-look at their urban environments. I believe wildlife in urban areas is so easy to engage with. All we have to do is open our eyes, ears, hearts and minds and soon we will be linked into the nature around us.

A few urban birding tips to get you started:

- *See your urban environment as how a bird would: The buildings are cliffs and any green areas are an oasis for nesting, resting and feeding.*
  Don't stress about learning the names and songs of all the birds you encounter, just enjoy them.
- *Learn at your own pace.*
- *You don't have to wear green anoraks; you can look cool and fashionable, I find the birds prefer it too.*
- *Get your friends involved.*
- *Find a local patch to regularly visit.*
- *Think that anything can turn up anywhere at any time.*
  That still works for me to this day.
- *Don't go out expecting to see anything. That way you'll never be disappointed but most likely be surprised.*

My message is simple - ***Look up!***

I saw someone I thought was David on Saturday but failed to say "hello". That innate shyness with 'celebrities' again. Today I manage to ask him over to say thanks for being such an inspiration. The hug I receive is bear-like and appreciated.

Now someone equally as inspiring came to sit with me by default. A lady in need of a chair and a table upon which to write her thoughts on the weekend comment sheet comes over to me. And so I met the lady I spend most of the rest of the day with, 93 year young Mary from Stevenage.

Mary immediately tells me how she loves cycling and only stopped at the tender age of 89 because she was worried about how to get off her bicycle safely.

Together Mary and I, arm in arm, went to see David Lindo's talk. Brilliant and I won't give anything away except to say, if you have the opportunity to see David speaking I hope you like Long-eared Owls.

Next Mary and I go to the final presentation of the RSPB Member's Weekend, designed to mobilise the troops via a collection of films and talks, the first of which is by two incredible young people from Northern Ireland.

First Matthew Scott, tall and lucid, tells of his many RSPB volunteer experiences. It is like a list of my favourite reserves. Then Orlagh McLoughlin shows the cutest photograph of a determined toddler eager to love nature, before describing her way into the nature loving, conservation world. She is about to have some children's books published and promises to say when they are available. I will be first in line to buy them. Two superb, strong and eloquent young advocates for Nature. We even hear from Seamus, an RSPB staff member from Northern Ireland that the politicians at Stormont are nervous of meeting them.

Preceding this had been a powerful short film on the creation of the new and immense reserve at Wallasea Island. Amazing.

Next was some fun with not only news of the very large Sherwood Forest project but a Robin Hood ' Play Your Cards Right' quiz. Mary and I won a Robin Hood hat.

The CEO of Birdlife International gave a talk. What a fabulous organisation.

Finally Mike Clarke, the CEO of the RSPB wraps things up with a speech that includes the good news that RSPB membership is still rising.

Mary and I go to lunch together. It is my crafty way of getting two helpings of apple crumble and custard. Well I have to take a small and a large portion for her to choose from to our table, didn't I? Luckily she chooses the small one for herself. I force the larger portion down.

The weekend is over. Yet another demonstration of how the RSPB is such a powerful force for Nature and is therefore working for all of us. The audience may have been made up of mostly young in heart people. The people running the show, though, are young and vibrant; such caring, enthusiastic and up for fun, wonderful young people. None more so than Sarah Houghton; this was her first time at organising the event and she can hold her head high and know that it has been a job extremely well done.

All too soon it is pack up time and head to the nearest public house, well after all of the goodbyes and thanks.

What happens next, as I watch the final of the 2016 Cricket World Cup between England and the West Indies, is summed up by ...

6, 6, 6, 6.

:(:(:(:(:(:(

Not everything goes smoothly when on an extended cycling adventure. My poor little laptop finally gave up the ghost and required replacement. Last October, whilst staying in the Bod at Scatness, South Shetland, it had been accidentally placed onto a hot hob as four young birders prepared their pizza and beans dinner. The large melted circle on the base of my laptop affected the battery and I am surprised it has lasted this long.

The next few days were recorded via the old and trusted method of a notebook; a piece of birding equipment I would feel naked without.

4th April Weldrake to Tophill Low

Early morning misty walk around the flood plain nature reserve, Wheldrake Ings, east of York, is followed by a long ride along mostly small country lanes. A male **Blackcap** is the first of the year, heard and seen whilst cycling.

Tophill Low Nature Reserve – a walk with a brilliant birder and warden, Martin. **Little-ringed Plovers,Willow Warblers** and **Garganey** are added to the year list, now stands at **197**.

5th April A day off with a visit to Beverley Minster and the town's library.

An email in the evening is from Martin Hodges of Tophill Nature Reserve. We had been discussing the wind turbine issue:-

Hi there Gary,

Hope you had a good kip in the youth hostel. It was a pleasure to meet you today.

To save you searching, everything about Tophill can be found on this website should you wish to furnish your notes on your day out.

http://tophilllow.blogspot.co.uk

And here is mine which offers a different look at Tophill from the one the visitors see.

https://esticadinhonature.wordpress.com

I'll try and dig some stuff out for you on the Algarve Barao wind farm turbine shutdown on demand project I worked on last autumn just for your info in case you end up bored for a few hours. The published stuff on the internet is very little and not up to date as E.on are the customer, but I might be able to find some relevant stuff... even I could read the Portuguese instruction leaflet!

Say safe, and I wish you the best of luck on your quest, I'm just reading your blog for last year... mad, but very impressive.

Take care   Martin

Now the wind farm issue is a difficult one. I actually love the aesthetic of them, surprising as that may be and appreciate that we need alternatives to fossil fuels. Yet I am concerned over their positioning and there is no doubt that they do kill some birds. I saw a Greater Back Backed Gull last year with smashed wings beneath a turbine when on Westray, Orkney.

6th April Cycle ride from Beverley to just south of Horncastle.

A day cycling south involved enjoying the views over the immense Humber Bridge and then heading towards the tiny village of Bigby. The whole day was just one of head down cycling before camping in a daffodil-filled graveyard.

63 miles.

7th April An afternoon at Frampton RSPB reserve.

Meeting RSPB staff and volunteers is always a pleasure so thanks to Toby, Sarah, Chris (Andrews!) and others.

Explored every pathway and hide, before walking out along the long promontory to the mouth of the River Wytham in the evening as high tide approached. I end up falling asleep in a WW2 pillbox as a heavy thunderstorm passes by.

Corn Bunting, Yellow Wagtail and **Wheatear** are added to the year list, which reaches the major landmark of **200**.

8th April Morning at Frampton RSPB reserve, cycle to Kings Lynn in the afternoon to the 'pancake' hotel.

Early morning **Little Owl** takes the list to **201**.

9th April Laptop bought and off to Dersingham/Wolferton.

An afternoon at Dersingham Bog gives **Woodlark** for the year list **(202)**, whilst the evening is spent in the splendid company of Trevor Girling, a superb Norfolk birder. He hears **Woodcock** making their whiplash call over the traffic noise of the adjacent main road. I don't.

10th April Early morning Golden Pheasant, Snettisham wader roost and then to Titchwell RSPB Reserve

Up at 5.00 a.m. to listen for the lone male **Golden Pheasant** (the plastic pheasant!). It calls about twice every minute for half an hour or so around 6.00 a.m. and then stops. At around 7:00 a.m. it starts calling again from somewhere 100 yards away. Don't see a feather! Bird number **203**.

Determine that the bird must be somewhere close so keep trying. David Lindo comes to mind. Look up! Golden Pheasant sitting on a branch! Oh, never thought of that.

To Snettisham RSPB reserve and with a high tide, views of tens of thousands of mostly Knot packed together on a gravel bank.

News of a Wood Sandpiper has me heading towards Cley but updated news as I approach Titchwell RSPB reserve has turned it into a Green Sandpiper.

Rest of day spent at Titchwell.

11th April Titchwell and Holme

Over seventy species of bird seen during the day with **Sedge Warbler** and a cracking male **Redstart** at Titchwell and a rather tame male **Pied Flycatcher** at Holme NWT. **(206)**

Accidentally deleted the amazing sunrise photographs and those of the birds mentioned. Twit!

12th April Holme and Titchwell

Arrive at Holme and am searching for a male Redstart at a spot next to the last house before the reserve entrance, when a Hoopoe comes out of some pines and immediately disappears over the sea bank to the north. I run around to get to the path but the bird can't be found. I text Phil Andrews who put the news out on RBA – Rare Bird Alert. Other birders arrive but still no sign of it. Frustrating, one always wants to share such a bird with others.

Frampton RSPB Blog has an article about me this evening :

The Biking Birder

I have now been an Intern at Frampton Marsh for almost two months and during this time I have had the opportunity to meet many interesting people. Many of whom have travelled hundreds of miles in the pursuit of their passion for birds. However one visitor has a particularly cool story, Gary Prescott, also known as the Biking Birder.

He is currently taking part in The Big Year competition for birders, the aim of which is to see who can identify by sight or sound the largest number of species of birds within a specified area. It started in America as early as the 1930's and has only become more popular since. Some birders, including Prescott take this one step further and go green. This means taking on the challenge whilst making as little environmental impact as possible, called the Big Green Big Year (BIGBY). The biking birders' aim is to get the most species in Europe, a title he shared in 2010 with Chris Mills of Norfolk. During that year he travelled to all of the RSPB (Royal Society for the Protection of Birds) and the WWT (The Wildfowl and Wetland Trust) reserves, covering thousands of miles.

Gary's current year list, the 2016 BOU Year list, may be seen on the Bubo listing site:

http://www.bubo.org/Listing/view-all-lists.html?showlists=1,BOU,1,2016,0

I saw him most recently a couple of weeks ago, looking remarkably chipper for a man who had spent the previous night camping in a graveyard. He'll often camp along the way, and as he said, he wasn't exactly bothering the neighbours! I had the opportunity to have a chat with him this time, and actually ask him why he does it. This year's target is to beat the current holder of the European title Ponc Feliu Latorre, which currently stands at 304 birds. However this is not his only goal, his main drive (no pun intended) is to raise as much money for the charities he cares about as possible, which are the RSPB, WWT, Asthma UK and Chaskawasi-Manu, a project giving the children from the Manu rainforest in Peru the opportunity to go to school and get an education. As you talk to him you can see the passion he has for these charities and what a great way to support them. He has funding pages for each of these which I'll attach at the end. He's always looking for new ways of raising money for the charities he supports, so if you spot him now you'll have a choice of a lovely range of pin badges too.

So for 2016 he has a plan, a leaner version of his previous attempts with fewer out of the way reserves in order to reach this year's goal of 305 to regain the European title and seems well on his way to achieving it. You can follow his progress on his blog http://bikingbirder2016.blogspot.co.uk/ which includes updates of his total bird count as well as some stories of his adventures along the way. And as always the very best of luck, a win would be very well deserved. **RSPB Frampton Marsh**

13th April Titchwell RSPB Reserve, Burnham Overy Dunes and Holkham Freshwater Marsh

An exploration of the famous RSPB reserve with all lagoons and paths birded before I head to the beach where a passing male **Eider** is added to the list. A **House Martin** is amongst some Sand Martins and once again over 70 species seen. Not a bad reserve.

By the café when suddenly two birding heroes, Mark Thomas and Tim Jones appear. Fabulous to see the pair.

Off to Burnham Overy, **a Cuckoo** flies past; bird number **209**. Three Ring Ouzels are on the landward side of the dunes.

A Great white egret is at Holkham.

14th April Holkham

Early morning rain, Spoonbills and more of the usual birds seen before retiring in the afternoon to the nearby Wells Next to the Sea Youth Hostel.

281.85 miles 6627 elevation feet up 6791 feet down

Sunday 17th April Light to fresh W

Sunny intervals, two short hail showers

Cuckoo cuckooing in the early morning reminds me of Mary back at Upton Warren. Mary frequently birds together with her Father, Tim, at Upton Warren and Mary has an uncanny ability to make a perfect Cuckoo call. One of the things I always find thrilling is watching young children show an interest in nature. Mary started to come to the Warren when eight years old. I remember her father holding her up to a telescope to look at some particularly special bird. Now she is fourteen and still has a passion for birds, as well as the ability to sound like a Cuckoo!

Nearby Willow Warblers and Chiff Chaffs are singing as Cetti's Warbler erupt; these sounds start the day with still a cool wind blowing from the West.

I set off for Minsmere RSPB Reserve, the iconic and magnificent reserve, which has hosted Springwatch recently, with a light wind mostly from behind to help me on my way. The small country lanes are empty so early on a Sunday morning and there are small undulations in the landscape to give me short rests as I cruise downwards after each short uphill section.

Signposts with mileages start to tell me that I am going backwards. Not really, it is just that in the centre of Loddon the sign states five miles to Beccles. The next two signs each say six miles despite being over a mile further. Oh well, keep pedalling.

On reaching the main Lowestoft to Ipswich road at Blythburgh there is a splattered stoat on the road, which I photograph for my 'car-nage' project; a sad collection of around forty species of bird and mammal that I have seen and photographed dead by the side of the road. A hundred yards later there is a dead male Wheatear. So sad to think that this bird had migrated all the way from Africa to die on a British road side. I check it for a ring but it doesn't have one.

Minsmere is a truly wonderful place and a short hail shower passes over as I cycle down the seemingly never-ending entry lane.

I meet a gentleman who is telling everyone that he is a local bird guide, Alex Bass and together we walk to the Mere Island hide. Bearded Tits are easy to see here and a number of Bitterns are booming. A **Reed Warbler** not too far into the reeds yet still unseen, is singing and so becomes bird number **210** on the year list.

Around the walkways and through the oak forest, I head for the scrape. There is a cacophony of Black-headed Gulls' noise and a number of Avocets and duck. The Black-tailed Godwits are acquiring summer plumage yet their single Bar-tailed cousin is still in its silvery winter attire.

I find a **Common Tern** sitting on post number four. The islands used to be named after biscuits way back long ago but now there are numbered signposts to help birders locate the different species. Common Sandpiper, look right of number two. Mediterranean Gull, look by post number nine.

A Sandwich Tern flies out to sea as I push the bike along the sandy path.

I circumnavigate the scrape, visiting every hide before heading back to the Island Mere hide for the evening. Well, I do so after enjoying a coffee in the café, taking up a position on a picnic bench overlooking the Sand Martin cliff. The Sand Martins are here in good numbers, flying frantically around and occasionally landing next to holes in the sandstone. They don't seem to be entering them though, just hanging onto the cliff edge.

I try to imagine what it must be like for new visitors to the reserve. On leaving the visitors' centre they walk down a short path. Suddenly on turning a corner they come across a golden yellow streaked with orange sandstone cliff with maybe a hundred swirling Sand Martins. A beautiful introduction to one of the RSPB's flagship reserves.

My evening is spent in the Island Mere hide. Most people have gone home but four ladies, who are staying in accommodation on the reserve, are enjoying the peaceful sunset.

An Otter swims nearby not too concerned about being so near to the hide. I cup my ears and hear the bird I have cycled here for, **Savi's Warbler**. The bird is a long way off over the far side of the large mere yet it is quite a distinctive trill. Now-a-days a very rare breeding bird in Britain, I remember seeing them in the 1980s singing on bushes not too far from this spot. The Savi's I really remember though was at my patch, Upton Warren Nature Reserve, back in 1984. That bird could be seen reasonably close singing on a now long gone bush near to the Moors car park. I remember seeing it one evening, a lifer for me and then returning before dawn the next day to get more views. A male Garganey was beside it on the water; a lovely pair.

The Green Year list now stands at **211**, twenty eight birds ahead of this time last year.

33.13 miles 1052 feet elevation up 1055 feet down

Hi Gary,

Hope you found Fowlmere after our chance encounter with you in our village today. Another ½ minute and our paths would not have crossed!
It was very interesting and enlightening to talk to you and we have lobbed a few quid into the charity at Chaskawasi - Manu and hope it helps.
Good luck with your quest for the 300, we will be following your progress with interest.
Regards
Adrian & Pat George

Monday 18th April Light to fresh NW

Cloud built up during day yet dry. Cool 8C with chilly wind.

A Tawny Owl is hooting as I cycle along the road through the oak woodland. A Cuckoo is cuckooing as I walk up the ramp to the Island Mere hide at 5:00 a.m. It is still, cold and cloudless. Bitterns are booming and Water Rail are squealing. The Savi is reeling away again but still a long way away so no chance of views.

Two early morning photographers come into the hide before six, one of whom tells me that I met his wife, Claire last week. Three otters decide to swim across the far left corner of the mere. Two Bittern decide to show themselves by flying over the reed bed as Marsh Harriers sky dance. The photographers' cameras go wild, ratcheting out shot after shot. Gone are the days of 36 photos on a film, which then had to be sent off for processing. Now a photographer with a large enough memory card can reel off hundreds in minutes. Machine gun photography. Personally I am thankful for the innovations. I dread to think what photography cost me over the years before digital.

Along to the visitors' centre, I go straight past and down to the **Stone Curlew** field. A distant bird is standing up on the far side. Another year tick, **213** and a bird that will save my legs from having to cycle to Weeting Heath to see one there. Shame really as I love Weeting Heath and the staff and set up.

I spend the morning in the North Scrape hide with Robin Harvey, the site manager for the reserve and all-round brilliant birder. With a team of seven wardens, he and others run the Minsmere Reserve as well as a couple of nearby RSPB reserves. A little-ringed Plover lands nearby and a House Martin flies over, Robin's first of the year.

Later in the day, after a meal in the café and after publicity photographs for the RSPB Suffolk Twitter feed, I see my first **Swift** of the year speedily flying over the scrape.

I meet Robin again in the evening. He is heading around the scrape and off towards the ruined priory to the south. I can see him birding there as ten Whimbrel fly around just behind the south scrape hide before heading off north. Later another group of Whimbrel, twenty five of them, fly past over the sea, also heading north.

The Green Year list now stands at **214**, thirty birds ahead of this time last year.

THIRTY BIRDS AHEAD!

Tuesday 19th April **Light to fresh NE**

Very sunny all day. Cool 8C with cold wind.

Early morning with **Nightingales**, three of them singing in turns and occasionally coming out to give unobstructed views. I am sitting on a grassy knoll amongst gorse bushes, listening to the wonderful song. The usual Spring migrants, Cetti's and Willow Warblers, Chiff Chaff and Blackcap, all add voice to the chorus. Such pleasure from sitting there for half an hour or so.

I head back towards Minsmere and stop to walk a public footpath to search for Whitethroat. The area looks perfect for them with thick bramble patches and sporadic bits of hawthorn hedge. I chat with a local woman out for a walk in the bright sunshine. A **Whitethroat** comes out onto the topmost twig of a hawthorn and scratches its song. Bird number **216**. It is crazy how I search so diligently for a bird that will soon be in almost every hedgerow, along every country lane in Britain.

To the Island Mere hide just in time to see a Bittern fly over the reeds to land nearby in the dense reed bed. Four Bearded Tits, including two males do the same. There is the briefest glimpse of an Otter way over the back of the mere amongst the reed bed edge.

Once more to the scrape with my mobile staying as silent as the grave. Every minute I am hoping for news of some rare bird having been found within cycling distance but nothing. The wind and weather conditions are all wrong. Cold northerlies and full sunshine is either stopping migrant birds from moving in large numbers or some are flying straight over with no reason for stopping.

I spend some time on the internet in the café before heading once more for The Scrape.

Apparently, The Scrape was the idea of the first resident warden at Minsmere, the famous Bert Axell. The area had been flooded during World War 2 to prevent any possibility of German tanks finding an area to invade. The wetlands created attracted Avocet, which bred for the first time in over one hundred years. These attracted visitors and Bert came up with the scrape idea for the Avocets in the early 1960s, an idea which has been copied around the world. When the RSPB were given the opportunity to buy the area they had to quickly raise £240,000 and thankfully they managed to do just that.

At the scrape, two Common Terns are flying around as three more rest on a muddy island. The Bar-tailed Godwit is still here as are a number of Mediterranean Gulls.

Afterwards I head around for the sea and spend an hour sea-watching, seeing three Harbour Porpoise and a single Red-throated Diver heading north low over the sea.

A male Stonechat is atop some gorse near the north walk looking superb in the sun. There is no sign of the Stone Curlews in the field but seven Red Deer are relaxing there.

Once more through the woods I head for an evening at the Island Mere hide, stopping on the way to watch a superb male Redstart fresh in, and watch as Otters and Bitterns give great views. Outside, in the cold wind, and RSPB staff member is logging booming Bitterns, mapping the booms so that she can collate results with other colleagues later and see how many booming males the reserve has.

The Green Year list now stands at **216**, still thirty birds ahead of this time last year. Yippee.

Wednesday 20th April **fresh to strong NE**

Very sunny all day. Cool 8C with cold wind.

After a cold night, I am up around seven and head down to the Island Mere hide. Despite the early hour there are a number of photographers in here and their machine gun clicks start almost immediately as three Otters strut on top of a large pile of cut reeds nearby. The Otters, not the photographers, eventually swim along the reed edge and disappear. Oh, I am such a grump at this time in the morning!

I walk off in the direction of the Bittern hide, stopping every so often to look for any migrants in the trees. Black caps and Chiff Chaffs oblige.

From the North hide overlooking the scrape I find two well hidden Snipe and chat with a couple from Stoke on Trent, Nick and Helga, who tell me that they follow my adventures on the Biking Birder 2016 blog.

After a day walking around all the paths of the reserve and with the café closed, I sit for my tea at one of the picnic benches and immediately a male Pheasant, a Red-legged Partridge, a Magpie and a number of Chaffinches come down to search for titbits. I go to the West Hide at the scrape. This I feel will be warmest place with a setting sun providing warm as long as the shutters are shut. As evening falls and the sun sets, a large Full Moon rises over the sea bank. Five Common Tern look almost chocolate brown in the fading light and a Peregrine looks to have rosy underparts as it chases a Bar-tailed Godwit. The Godwit survives, just, by diving into the water.

Thursday 21st April **fresh NE**

Very sunny all day. Slightly warmer at 10C

I decide to walk down to the Sizewell Nuclear power station after a lovely bright sunrise. The wind is still north easterly and cool at 6:00 a.m. It interests me how the high Cirrus clouds are heading north, albeit slowly.

With still no news on any new bird for the year list anywhere nearby, the only ones being those that will be easy to get later, it seems only sensible to explore all areas of Minsmere. The low dunes and sandy pathway with low Hairy Birch, willow and oak with sporadic pines look good for any migrant warblers and so it proves. There is a **Lesser Whitethroat** to add to the year list, **217**.

Lying in my sleeping bag the previous night, instead of counting sheep, I counted regular occurring birds that I still need for the Green Year List. I made it fifty. That means I would need thirty four rarities, one a week from now to the end of the year to beat The European Record. I will take that at this time of year.

A text from 'The Oracle,' Phil Andrews asks whether I am up to cycling to Bedfordshire to see a White Stork and the sole Lady Amhurst's Pheasant. "Of course I am," I reply, "but only if the White Stork isn't plastic." I bird on at Minsmere not too confident that the stork will be a real wild bird. There is a Greenshank on Lucky Pool and three Brent Geese head north along the beach.

After searching for but not finding the rare Whorl snails near the

Minsmere sluice, it is rather strange to see a Fulmar coming from over the scrape. It heads out to where one would expect to see it, over the sea.

From the elevated position of the sea wall path I can see over the scrape and notice a large Peregrine tucking in to a large prey item. I go to the public platform and get great views of the raptor tucking into an unfortunate Godwit, despite heat haze and distance.

There are a number of waders nonchalantly close to the feeding bird; Black and Bar-tailed Godwits and Dunlin. All of them must be thinking that the Peregrine will be some time eating and so in the meantime they feel safe.

Walking back towards the north walk four Whimbrel come down the beach. Three carry on towards Lucky Pool. The other one turns and heads north.

Bearded Tits show as I walk towards the visitors' centre and the Sand Martins are tazzing around the sandstone cliff as I go towards the café. Once inside one of the staff, Doreen gives me a cheese scone. Delicious and it goes well with fruit crumble and custard. Maggie, another café worker comes over and chats about her twenty years of playing the French horn in the North Opera Orchestra. The RSPB attracts volunteers from all walks of life, wonderful people.

There is a pregnant Wood Mouse by the RSPB's solitary wasp tower at the visitor's centre and people gather to watch her as she walks and bounds around our feet before disappearing into some leaf litter.

It is late afternoon. I walk into and through the large woodland area marvelling at the amount of fallen trees and dead wood. The woodland though is silent and I spend the time looking at the wonderful variety of patterns on the trunks and stumps.

Another reason to enjoy the walk is the total lack of anyone else around. Don't get me wrong, I love people but sometimes I just want to be alone.

The trail takes me towards Dunwich Heath and along a sandy track. I come across a wasp species creating a circular hole. I sit down to watch. Must look up the species and find out what it was actually up to. Is it a parasitic wasp that has buried a paralysed prey item and lays an egg on it, whereupon the poor creature waits knowing that upon the hatching of the egg it is on the menu? Always fascinating, I find parasitism one of the most incredible things in nature. Now what's the name of the mite that lives in our eyelashes? Eyelash mite, *Demodex folliculitis*.

A sandy area on the heath has evidence of another interesting creature, the capture pits of the Antlion. Like the sandy hole that so many are thrown into by Jabba the Hutt in Star Wars – The Return of the Jedi, the Antlion has made a pit into which an insect might fall into. If one does the Antlion grabs it for a tasty meal.

Down to the shore with not a bird to be seen out at sea. Minsmere at the moment is definitely not the place for a protracted seawatch. Once on the North Wall path to enter the RSPB reserve, there are birds as Bearded Tits that ping and fly.

Back in the shelter of the North Hide overlooking the scrape there are four Mediterranean Gulls to watch with one pair exchanging loving glances and green weed. A male Redshank has loving intentions too and pipes whilst moving ever closer to his desired love. Always a comical moment, he takes off full of amorous hope and whilst hovering lower and lower over the girl of his choice. He must be gutted when the female, at the last moment before intimate contact, flies off. It was ever thus.

The Green Year list now stands at **217**, still twenty nine birds ahead of this time last year.

Friday 22nd April **fresh E**

Cloudy with occasional light rain. Cool 8C with cold wind.

The Oracle's text from the previous evening states that there are two Black Terns at Alton Water south of Ipswich. Now this is a bird that I have never managed to see whilst Biking Birding cycling so would be a great addition to the list. After fixing the back brake in the shelter of the South Hide and after a chat with an early rising RSPB staff member, I set off south. Leaving Minsmere is strange after having four days here. Each day has been different and feeling I know the reserve a lot better now having explored every pathway, it is time to move on. This could easily become my favourite RSPB reserve; such incredible biodiversity.

By 9:00 a.m. I am at Blaxhall Youth Hostel and having no word from Phil about the terns, I book in. Coffee and washing up takes the next hour. Then my phone receives two texts and I miss a phone call. The terns are still there! With apologies to Amy, the hostel manager, and after being reimbursed the overnight cost, I set off once more as the weather deteriorates and spitting rain falls.

Through Woodbridge and Ipswich, making the mistake of following the convoluted Route 1 Sustrans cycle path instead of the straight main road, I get, eventually, to Lemon's Hill Bridge. A gentleman in a car calls my name. Chris Baines, a Facebook friend whom I had last seen whilst watching a Bluethroat near The Hook on Blakeney Point four years ago, calls me over and together we watch distant terns. A year tick, seven or more **Arctic Terns** are over the water. A **Black Tern** comes into view. Brilliant. It is cold and raining slightly so photographs are appalling, but both birds are on the list, **219**. Black tern becomes the latest '16' bird, which is one that I didn't see last year. Remember I need sixteen of these over and above the

289 I did see. Now maybe it is the cricket fan in me but I break the sixteen down into four birds per quarter, that is four '16' birds per three month period. January to March gave me four : Dusky Warbler, Hudsonian Whimbrel, Glaucous Gull and Greater Yellowlegs. April has given me two already, Savi's Warbler and now Black Tern. Things are looking good. Little targets to keep the spirits up and keep the legs pedalling.

Another pleasing thing from the bridge is the number of Hirundines hunting flies low over the water. They are mostly Swallows with some Sand Martins and the occasional House Martin.

Saying goodbye to Chris, as I am now starting to shiver, I head off along the circumnavigating the lake cycle path. A helicopter comes low and lands in a garden backing onto the path.

Three miles later I am warming up with a large mug of hot chocolate and enjoying the company of Gina and Andrew, the owners of the café at the south end of the lake. Mentioning the helicopter I am told it belongs to a city banker. He lives in a large house adjacent to the lake and commutes in such a fashion.

The only other customer in the café is Doreen, a local originally from Anfield, Liverpool. The four of us chat awhile before all too soon it is closing time and I carry on to search the lake for other birds. Three Little Gulls, which were reported this morning, have moved on.

The Green Year list now stands at **219**, thirty birds again ahead of this time last year.

50.69 miles **1473 feet elevation up** **1443 feet down**

Tuesday 26th April

It is now early on Tuesday morning and I am in Margate, Kent. After a day of rest yesterday, it is time for me to get back on the bike and head for Dungeness, forty five miles to the south west. A Bean Goose has been seen there recently and Pomarine Skuas have gone past the headland.

The rest was due to the previous three days efforts, 168 miles from Minsmere to Margate, cycling. Why Margate? An **Iberian Chiffchaff** in a local park had been seen and luckily, very luckily, I turn up there on Sunday evening and not only hear it but get close views of the rare Chiffchaff with a funny, squeaky, repeated call. Bird number **220** onto the Green list and one not on my radar.

So eighty five to go in order to get the European record and around fifty 'regulars' still needed.

Still feeling very tired, I manage to cycle to Grove Ferry* and Stodmarsh Nature Reserve. I spend the day pushing the bike along the many paths with the hope of hearing a Grasshopper Warbler in the evening. There are occasional heavy showers and a cool north-westerly.

Common Terns are over the largest pool and a few Sedge and Reed Warblers are to be heard adjacent to the pathways.

The highlights of the day do occur in the evening when first a **Hobby, 221,** flies past and then a Hen Harrier, ring-tail, comes down to roost in the reed bed.

***message from Alcalabirder on Biking Birder 2016 blog** :*

Very interesting. I feel exhausted just reading about it. Just to let you know before anyone else points in out, but it's Grove Ferry not 'Grove End'. People often call it the "Grove Ferry end" or just the "Grove end", but that isn't really the place's name.

Wednesday 27th April

A cycle down to Dungeness is relatively straight forward. Arriving at the RSPB reserve in mid afternoon, I spend the time searching Denge Marsh for the Bean Goose reported to be there on the previous day. A dip. Can't find it.

Thursday 28th April

With the wind only alight westerly early morning I head off for Pett Levels in East Sussex to look for two Velvet Scoter reported there.

A flock of thirty-plus Whimbrel and very obliging Yellow Wagtails delay me at Scotney Gravel Pits on the way to Rye.

Taking the Rye Harbour roadway I soon reach Pett Levels and with the help of Steve, a Kent birder whom I had met at Grove End two days earlier, have **Velvet Scoter** to add to the year list, **222**. The long present Glossy Ibis puts in an appearance too.

Back to Rye Harbour I take time to enjoy its birds as by now the westerly wind has freshened up and a lunch break there is rewarded with views of nesting Mediterranean Gulls and Sandwich Terns.

Friday 29th April

Back at Dungeness, I head for the seawatching hides by the nuclear power station, seeing a ghostly Barn Owl and a couple of Whimbrel on the way.

At 'The Patch' there are a good number of Common Terns, around seventy five. Once in the shelter of the hide, the birders present say that one Arctic Skua went past at about ten to six and a few Manx Shearwaters. It is now 6:30 a.m. and only Common Scoter are going past in any numbers and even they aren't too numerous.

Seawatch finished, I go to the Dungeness Bird Observatory and book in for the night. I love staying at observatories. They are so cheap! More importantly birders stay at them and therefore the evening conversation is guaranteed to be birdy. Dave Walker, the long-standing Warden of the Observatory, takes my accommodation money and I decide not to use the bike for the day, instead I will walk to Lydd to get some food and bird on the way there and back.

Into the willow bushes near to the Observatory, an almost tailless Fox stands on the path not thirty yards away and looks back at me with disinterest.

Bumblebees take my own interest and there seems to be two varieties out in the cold, hazy sunshine, Garden and Red-tailed.

Lesser and Common Whitethroats are vocal and on reaching the ARC pit a superb summer-plumaged Black-necked Grebe is sheltering from the fresh westerly breeze.

In fact the wind is gathering strength and after looking around the Cathedral in the Marsh, All Saints in Lydd; where a poem from the First World war is accompanied by two original WW1 crosses, the wind is strong and cold.

Back to Dungeness RSPB reserve via the back bridleway, only Greylags and Canada Geese are on Denge Marsh.

Back to seawatch the evening away; Andy, a birder whom I had last met at Sumburgh Lighthouse last Autumn, immediately sees a distant passing **Bonxie,** the preferred name for the **Great Skua** and passes me his telescope so that the pirate can be added to the year list, **223**.

Two **Manx Shearwaters** pass and the operation with Andy's 'scope is repeated. Finally two **Arctic Skuas** pass. Jokingly they seem closer to France than England! What a fabulous evening.

The Green Year list now stands at **225**, twenty five birds ahead of this time last year.

Saturday 30th April **Light to fresh N**

Sunny intervals with one prolonged heavy shower PM

Early Saturday morning after a comfortable night in a bed for a change at the excellent Dungeness Bird Observatory. The sun is shining and there is a light northerly breeze; very different to yesterday's south westerly gale.

A cycle to Lydd for more food with Whitethroats singing from apparently every bramble patch. An almost unladen bike to ride, luxury.

To the RSPB reserve for the afternoon, the summer-plumaged Black-necked Grebe is now on the pool in front of the visitor's centre, giving more distant views than yesterday.

Of interest along the pathway is the only colony of *Andrena vaga*, a small bee in the UK. Concertinaed Green Tiger Beetles are amusing, a piggy back of four.

Into the visitor's centre just as a very heavy rain shower hits. I spend some time reading the history of the reserve display and marvel at the wooden slat shoes worn to aid walking over the shingle years ago. The name Bert Axell features large again with ideas used to assist the breeding birds to be found here many decades ago, forty pairs of Kentish Plovers! Dream on.

Outside Swallows and Sand Martins perch on branches to rest during the rain.

April Monthly Statistics:-

Green Year list	225 birds
Year ticks	32
Bird species had, not seen in 2015	3
Mileage in April	651.19 miles
Total mileage for the year	2,663.14 miles
average mileage on days cycled	29.60 miles
elevation : up	14,899 feet
: down	14,966 feet

<u>Best Birds</u> : Garganey, Savi's Warbler, Black Tern, Iberian Chiffchaff, Velvet Scoter.

5

MAY

"The surprise which was first excited by what appeared . . . disappears on further reflection."

Sollas, a Paleontologist talking about the hoax, Piltdown Man

Sunday 1st May **light SW**

Sunny, warm!

Today is all about distance. A Rufous Turtle Dove, ssp. meena has been reported just north of Sevenoaks and I need to see it. I set off early and appreciate not only the lack of wind and the warm sunshine but also the flat road for the first fifteen miles. Yellow Wagtails are along the roadside just north of the RSPB reserve entrance.

Mile after mile, the ride is not strenuous and with two litres of milk and a litre of blackcurrant juice, I have plenty to drink along the way. I stick to a one hour a drink, one hour some food regime with maltloaf and jam sandwiches for the food.

A cruel reminder of my football team's present fate is seen as I cycle through Tenterden. A house is named after Villa Park. How different a prospect for Aston Villa to that of Leicester City this year, yet I was there when it was the other way round. Highbury, 1981; Aston Villa lost 2 – 0 to Arsenal yet still won the First Division due to Ipswich losing at Middlesborough. My brother, Paul, my Dad and I were at that match. Wait a minute, I must watch the highlights on Youtube.

https://www.youtube.com/watch?v=WUjpzEdEqLg

Enjoyed that. A few tears. Fourteen players used all season and it got better the next year and yes, I was there for this one too, the European Cup Final in Rotterdam, 1982.

https://www.youtube.com/watch?v=m6xSbPjybok

Later, back at Villa Park, I even managed to drop the cup after being photographed holding it! A long time ago. Back to today.

Congratulations to Leicester City winning the Premiership. These days, when money decides position, Leicester winning is the best thing that has happened in British football for a very long time.

Back to today, miles go by and, eventually, the benign, flattish roads take me to steeper sections. Whilst pushing up one particularly steep hill I come across a sleeping tiny Fox cub. As I reach down for my camera it wakes up, notices me and disappears into the fox den. I think my chance has gone but another small cub waddles over and doesn't notice me. Wonderful moments of watching a beautiful little creature.

Further along the road, I see another somewhat older Fox cub take his life in his hands crossing a main road. It tries once and a car just misses it as it dives back into cover. Then moments later it tries again, luckily successfully.

I arrive at my destination, a place made obvious by the crowd of birders who are all looking at something in a nearby tree. I see one of my best Wolverhampton friends, a Birding Clam no less, Steve Allcott. He sees me and shouts for me to look quickly through his telescope. **Rufous Turtle Dove** goes onto the year list in moments as the bird is seen first with his glistening back to me. Then it turns around to make sure I see all sides.

Another crowd of birders are further down the road, closer to the bird and I go along to them leaving the bike against a wall. Another Birding Clam, Jason Oliver, is with them and together we laugh and celebrate such a rare bird. Other birding friends are there too; Jumbo and Pete who I had met on Fair Isle last year, Geoff and Carol from near Leicester, John Pringle from Essex.

Birders come up to hear of the ride from Dungeness, fifty eight miles, almost exactly the same distance that I cycled last year for the Citril Finch at Holkham. Some kindly give donations for the charities. Brilliant.

The bird? Oh it flew off after twenty minutes or so to be seen again much later. Being of the meena sub-species, this is a new bird for me. I saw the Chipping Norton orientalis bird in the pouring rain a few years ago and the hope is that the scientists will decide that these two are separate species one day.

The Green Year list now stands at 226, still twenty seven birds ahead of this time last year.

76.80 miles 2869 feet elevation up 2787 feet down

Monday 2nd May light NW

Sunny, warm

Along the cycle path I know so well from previous Biking Birder tours, I head east along the North Kent coast to Cliffe Pools. **Black-winged Stilts** are added to the year list.

Memories of taking four Wolverhampton schoolboys in a clapped out Nissan Cherry car to Titchwell to see the Black-winged Stilts that bred there in the late 1980s.

On arriving we found out that they had left overnight. Now what was the chance that the stilts decided to fly to our local patch, Belvide Reservoir in Staffordshire. That is precisely what they did and we all saw them there later in the day.

The stilts here at Cliffe become bird number **227** on this year's list.

20.58 miles 515 feet elevation up 571 feet down

Tuesday 3rd May light NW

Sunny, warm

A cycle to Rainham RSPB Reserve for lunch. I couldn't miss out on one of my favourite RSPB reserves, could I? The cycle path along the Thames takes me straight there and also takes me away along the great river before I head inland for Dagenham.

A crash … and my fault! I have sunglasses on for the first time this year and the traffic is stuck along a long road. I can get through along the inside, just. Unfortunately, to avoid a drain hole, I swerve and hit a car's side mirror. I immediately stop and hence meet Marcia. My fault, my cost.

The cycling is rough due to going through the north-eastern edge of London. Reaching the Lea Valley Reservoirs gives me a break from suburban roads and, after watching a fox strolling around a large horse field, a cycle path heads due north along the canalised river to some prism-shaped lodges that make up London Lee Valley Youth Hostel. **Garden Warbler** seen whilst cycling along the canal is an addition for the year list. **228.**

37.84 miles 1881 feet elevation up 1677 feet down

A lovely email from someone whom I met recently:-

Hello Gary,
Met you today @ the RSPB, Such an amazing chat with you, I could have stayed for hours, I will never get over the amount of countries you have cycled through, & the massive amount of miles you must have clocked up.
We live in the Upminster/Hornchurch area, A127/A12 ish area. Should you ever be nearby/passing our neck of the woods, you would be more than welcome to park your bike & sleeping bag for a stop-over, "No Sweetcorn Beer" I'm afraid.
I am so pleased that I told you about that basking sealion, having a sunbath on the mud, over the other side today.
I was fascinated about your stories from Lima/Peru, I wish you every success & happiness & if one day you hang up you bike clips, park your bike & make yourself a home on that football ground you told me about.
I know you're a busy busy fella, but I would love 2catch up with you again sometime, all-be-it "on-line"
So4now my friend, you take care, go easy on them pedals & beware of the undercover H&S people.
Cheers & Many Best Regards, Ernie Wright (BIG ERN) to his friends

Wednesday 4th May **light SW**

Getting hot! Sunny

Off early in the morning to get to the Lady Amherst's Pheasant location. This is the only one, a male, left in Britain, so I need to see it. It may soon be gone.

A stop to see one of my very best friends was as wonderful as ever. Coffee and chat, catch up and deep friendship.

Arriving at the village graveyard, I push the bike up through it and out along a grassy footpath. Finding the rare pheasant's haunt, I peer into the scrub, searching for this amazing looking bird. The Lady Amherst's Pheasant calls repeatedly; a three note call softer than the double note utterance of the Common Pheasant. I wonder what this lone male feels like having a lady's name. It reminds me of an occasion when I was a teenager at Redditch County High School in Worcestershire. Way back in the late 1960s the school was converted into a Comprehensive and the staff wanted to change the name. I well remember the day of the pupil's strike over the chosen name, Lady Harriet's. This was even broadcast as a news item on BBC Midlands TV at the time. Suffice to say the school became Abbey High instead. Student power!

As for Lady Amherst's, I don't see it and set up camp nearby amongst the brambles.

43.21 miles **1881 feet elevation up** **1677 feet down**

Thursday 5th May **light S**

Sunny and hot 24C

Up early after listening to the Lady Amherst's Pheasant coaxing me out of my sleeping bag. It proves almost impossible to see and yet doesn't seem to be moving around the dense undergrowth. Garden Warbler and Blackcap sing in bushes adjacent to the wood and a Cuckoo flies over. Three more birders arrive to help with the search; Laurence and John from Cirencester, and Peter from Cornwall.

Around 8:00am I find it! **Lady Amherst's Pheasant** onto the list as it shows in a less-than-a-metre area next to a pine tree trunk about forty yards in front of us. The photograph I get of this bird is a rare thing these days.

Bird secured I need to get to Norfolk.

The rest of the day is spent cycling to the Ouse Washes RSPB reserve. Once there the evening is spent in the brilliant company of Steve, the RSPB farm stock coordinator there. Together we sit in the office and he tells me every tale of cows over the ages he knows for about two hours.

As the sun goes down and darkness falls I hear and watch drumming Snipe.

60.45 miles 1288 feet elevation up 1579 feet down

Friday 6th May fresh E

Very sunny and hot 24C

Early morning birding at Ouse Washes RSPB reserve, moving from hide to hide to view over the wet grassland and pools. There are a number of male Garganey and I count five before reaching the visitor's centre for an early cup of tea with Steve.

A Short-eared Owl is a surprise for this time of year. Fifty species of bird seen before breakfast, always a good sign.

The oracle sends a text detailing a Purple Heron at Heacham. I set off but I am too tired, shattered by the recent cycling distances. I reach Welney WWT reserve and decide to stop for some lunch. News from Gill and Amanda about a **Temminck's Stint** having just been found takes me to the hide where the bird can be seen. Bird number **230** and another good one to get. A Great White Egret pokes it head out from behind some tall rushes.

Back at the WWT café I just get some soup when Amanda comes up to me, again to say two Curlew Sandpipers have been seen right at the far end of the reserve. We both walk there but the birds aren't on view.

Leaving Welney, after eating my soup eventually, wonderful carrot and coriander soup, I leave but can only cycle as far as Downham Market. A bed is available at the best value Bed & Breakfast in Norfolk and I am soon in bed. Only after having a relaxing bath though, and drinking a mug of hot chocolate. I am truly bushed!

29.21 miles 430 feet elevation up 364 feet down

Saturday 7th May fresh E

Sunny and very warm, 24C

After an immense breakfast I set off for North Norfolk. One last word on this Bed & Breakfast; in a county renowned for B and Bs being expensive, at £35 a night, Chestnut Villa in Market Drayton is superb value for money. A lovely bedroom with en suite, coffee, cup-a-soups, tea and hot chocolate, chocolate bars and milk. The bathroom has anti-

antiperspirants, shampoos, creams and shower caps. June is a lovely host and so welcoming and helpful.

OK, advert over.

I soon reach the cycle path that takes me off the main road and allows me to sing along to The Who's Quadrophenia on the MP3 player.

Dotterel are today's target and to get to Choseley quicker I take the back roads after Sandringham. It is very hot and soon two litres of milk have been drunk.

Reaching the spot that Dotterel seem to have made their annual migration resting stage, I join other birders and search the distant stubble fields for the special birds. There is a terrific, mirage-like heat-haze making viewing almost impossible. Someone says they have one in their telescope and proffers the eyepiece for me to get a view. There is a bird in the centre of the view but there is no way I can say it is a Dotterel. An eyestripe, a bit of breast and maybe a wing, all shimmering and indistinct. A view of a different, closer bird is better and so Dotterel can go on the year list.

I cycle along the lane towards the famous barns and stop on the hill adjacent to the Dotterel-filled stubble. Here at last I get excellent views of four Dotterel.

There are only three of us at this spot and I can't remember how or why but the discussion goes onto suppression. I mention to one gentleman to my left that a famous case of acting against suppressors was when an Essex birder claimed he had seem an extremely rare Hermit Thrush. He hadn't seen this incredible North American passerine but was so fed up with certain Essex birders suppressing the news of rare birds that he made up a whole tale saying that he had. His fabrication was accepted, with suspicions and so his Hermit Thrush went down as the fifth British record.

"That was me," says the other gentleman in our trio.

Unbelievably it is too. Nigel Pepper, who in 1994 did such a birding 'crime'. He came clean in Birdwatch magazine with a double page spread explaining his reasons. A hero for making a stand against suppression or a villain for carrying out the birding cardinal sin of a hoax? Take your pick but here is the man standing right here with me. Now what shall we talk about? I hear his explanation.

To Titchwell for the afternoon, a Little Gull there in the morning has moved on. Both Temminck's and Little Stint are here.

I go to the beach and see a number of **Little Terns**, bird number **232**. I return to the hide to find that a Wood Sandpiper has just flown over. Missed it.

I head for the reed-bed where a Grasshopper Warbler was reeling this morning. It isn't now.

A text from The Oracle.... Alpine Accentor at Gibraltar Point nature reserve near to Skegness; ninety miles away. With the sun setting I set off.

51.36 miles 1669 feet elevation up 1579 feet down

The thought of suppression and perpetrating a birding hoax has me thinking. The recent phenomenon amongst younger people has been the incredible popularity of a Disney film called Frozen. In the film there is one song that has received over a billion Youtube views, Let It Go.

Birders will understand the terms hoax, suppression and how these two words cause so much anger, angst and aggression. Changing the lyrics a bit, here is my version of the song.

I don't want to go into it all but the following lyrics are about a fictional birder finding a bird new for Britain and how he or she agonises over telling other birders.

Chalet by the way is on Fair Isle, a fabulous place to find rare birds. Stay at the famous Fair Isle Bird Observatory . . . you know you want to!

A Connecticut Warbler is, as you may have guessed from the name, an American warbler that hasn't occurred in Britain . . . yet.

A warbler creeps here at Chalet tonight
No other birder to be seen
I think that it's Connecticut
In Britain it's not been seen
This thing is skulking
but it's still within my sights
I should phone the Obs
Even think I might...

Don't let them know
Don't let them see
Keep this rare bird right here
just for me
suppress, conceal
don't let them know
don't let them know!

let us know let us know
don't suppress us all any more
let us know let us know
there's a mega on our shore

I should care
that it may fly away
Let the bird now stay
Their scold never bothers me anyway

It's funny how persistence
makes birds just start to crawl
And the fear that it may disappear
Doesn't get to me at all

It's time to see what it will do
Will it stay here, keep in view
No right, no wrong
No rules for me
I'm free

let us know let us know
For this bird we all will try
let us know let us know
You'll never see us cry
With you we'll stand and with you we'll stay
Let us get the bird

I start to run across the grassland oh so fast
My goal is tell you all of the bird that I've just found
And one thought crystallises like an icy blast
The bird might be dead
It could be in the past

Let it live Let it live
Be alive 'til way past dawn
Let it live Let it live
The perfect bird not gone

Here it is in the light of day
Turn the cameras on
I told you it would be here another day

Sunday 8th May **fresh ESE**

Sunny and warm 24C

Awake in my tent at an early hour, I listen and hear Woodlark and Tree Pipits singing. Getting out of my sleeping bag, getting dressed and walking from the woodland to the heath, I see Woodlark and **Tree Pipit**; the latter is bird number **234**.

I take my tent down and pack, making sure that my rhododendron surrounded clearing is clear of anything not there before.

It is still before 6:00 a.m. and I feel like a 'Big Day.' Coal Tit, Goldcrest and Nuthatch are all seen before leaving Dersingham, I head for Snettisham. Last night's reason for heading this way, the Alpine Accentor at Gibraltar point, has flown away overnight, done a moonlight flit so to speak and therefore I think I will head back to Titchwell via Holme. Can I get 100 birds today?

Arriving at Snettisham about an hour after the high tide mark, there are still a good number of Knot and Oystercatchers at roost. It is around 8:30 a.m. and hot already. It is pleasant to shelter from the sun inside the bird screen. I say screen as this structure is like a bird hide but with no back. The closely packed flock of Knot have a few more red, summer plumaged individuals than a few weeks ago yet most are still grey. There are two silent bird photographers in here. They have their lens focused on the Knot flock and ignore the action as a Peregrine causes Starling-like murmurations of Knot flocks over The Wash. They also ignore a rather humorous clash of two male Black-headed Gulls. A rogue male is trying to seduce another male's female. He hovers about a metre over the female as she keeps trying to peck him. Eventually the pair's male attacks the interloper and together they fight with beaks locked on the shingle. They roll around for a few minutes before disengaging and posturing.

Not a click from the cameras. Each to their own, I prefer the behavioural stories to image perfection, which is a good job considering my own photographic attempts.

A text from The Oracle, Bonelli's Warbler specie. Singing at Gibraltar Point. I set off. On reaching the main road the news is that the bird hasn't been either seen or heard again and so I decide to head for Hunstanton and Holme.

Walking along the cliff path at the former a pair of Mediterranean Gulls fly past.

After lunch in the Norfolk Wildlife Trust, NWT, café and after a chat with an ex-president of the NWT over farming subsidies and the Norfolk beef industry, well more like an argument really, I go through the Norfolk Ornithological Association's Bird Observatory area and wave to the warden who is busy on the phone. Reaching the plank walkway along the sand dune ridge, I push and cycle to Thornham and onto Titchwell.

A birder calls me over. He has found a **Whinchat** and wants to share it with me. Lucky me, another new bird to see for the year list. Another birder shares his telescope a little further along the path so that I can see two **Wood Sandpipers** and add them to the year list too.

A birder from Willenhall, near to Wolverhampton one of my old home places, tells me that he has seen two **Spotted Flycatchers** nearby and soon enough we are watching them as they fly catch from perches in the willows. Three new year ticks in quick succession, can't be bad.

The day list is seventy five and with Titchwell still to explore properly, the list climbs steadily. Brent Geese are still her in good numbers and a Greenshank has replaced the Wood Sandpipers. A Short-eared Owl quarters Thornham Marsh and is chased by a Marsh Harrier spectacularly.

Year listing isn't finished for the day yet as a **Grasshopper Warbler** reels and by climbing on a bench, I get a very brief view of it before it drops down into thick cover.

Red-crested Pochard on Patsy's Pool takes the list to ninety-eight for the day and despite the sun having almost set I decide to cycle to nearby Choseley Barns to try for the final two birds that would take me to the magic 100.

The sun sets and the thinnest of crescent Moons is in the clear sky. The Dotterels aren't on view but a male Yellowhammer is singing and easy to see.

Ninety-nine.

All the Partridge seem to be Red-legged but using my camera as a telescope I can just make out a dark belly on a distant bird. Grey Partridge, bird number **100** for the day. Brilliant.

So the year list now stands at **238**, twenty nine birds ahead of this time last year.

30.4 miles 691 feet up elevation 801 feet down

Monday 9th May fresh ESE

Sunny and warm 24C

Very early morning starts at Titchwell with a nuclear bomb-like sunrise; one where a small area of sky appears glowing red just before the bright yellow orb peeks above the horizon.

Bitterns boom and birds can be added by song and call to the day list. I head off for Holme. Arriving at the golf course west of the NWT nature reserve, **Turtle Doves** are purring and give glimpses from dense cover.

The wind has freshened and the branches bend in the breeze. I take the coastal path around the outside of the Holme reserve and find a very tiny Small Blue butterfly and a Common Toad sits on the path rather prone. Other butterflies sheltering include Small Coppers and Wall. Both Common and Lesser Whitethroats are singing here too.

On the far side of Holme's reserves, I find a Grasshopper Warbler that goes from one clump of thick vegetation to the next and so on, giving brief glimpses.

The tide is very high and covers part of the car park at Thornham as well as covering all of the saltmarsh there. From here I decide to meander along North Norfolk's country lanes and hope for news of a rarity, or at least a year tick. Dreams of finding one myself filter through though and indeed almost happen as I come across a small flooded area of a winter wheat field. This time though I have already seen the bird I find but this one is so much closer and in such a strange spot. A Wood Sandpiper stands next to the puddle.

Cycling along towards Burnham Norton an even better bird has me leap off the bike and shouting with delight; a male **Montagu's Harrier** flies by and is gone in a minute or two. Superb new bird for the year, Montagu's Harrier was one bird I was nervous about missing and here is one in front of me. Snatched photographs are poor but what the hell, they show the bird and the excitement.

Elated I continue along and take an inland route to Wells-next-the-Sea instead of following the coastal road. This takes me behind the extensive wooded grounds of Holkham Hall. It is great to have singing birds in hedgerows that grow tall and thick beside every road. Common Whitethroats outnumber Lesser Whitethroats but both are in good numbers. Both of these outnumber the 'little bit of bread and no cheese' Yellowhammers.

On reaching Wells, I book into the Wells Youth Hostel. At £10 a night I can't complain and I am soon asleep. Truth be told I have been very ill for the last three weeks with probably a cold first off. This affected my asthma and filled my sinuses with painful rubbish. Today has been the first day without the feverish, sweaty feeling. The first day I feel I have this thing beat.

So the year list now stands at **240**, nineteen birds ahead of this time last year. Birds seen on this date and the day before it last year included the Citril Finch and Moltoni's Warbler.

30.23 miles 1006 feet elevation up 978 feet down

Wednesday 11th May fresh ESE

Sunny intervals, 16C

After a day in bed, a dilemma presents itself this morning. Do I walk and bird Blakeney Point, that tapioca pudding shingle walk of hell, or wait for news and bird Cley?

Everything about the weather says that there should be birds on the point yet I tarry, procrastinate more like, and start the day list with common waders.

Red-backed Shrike at Burnham Overy dunes, just beyond the west end of Holkham Pines!

I peddle as fast as I can and get there.

12:45 p.m. **Red-backed Shrike** UTB. I watch it for the next hour or so mostly by myself. The shrike keeps disappearing into bramble and hawthorn and occasionally turns up some distance from its last location. The best views though are when I am sat on a small sand dune, tucked in from the cool breeze, and the bird hunts from a nearby barbed wire fence.

Throughout the hour-long view I meet four other birders, one of whom, Paul, supports Aston Villa. We cry together over our team's sad demise whilst watching the shrike. I remember a scene from the comedic birdwatching film A Big Year with the Steve Martin's character being likened to a shrike. Randy Lerner, the current Aston Villa chairman and owner is a similar beast. In fact this analogy would be an insult to a shrike. I recommend any birder to watch the film. I don't recommend supporting the Villa at the moment!

I search the dunes but cannot find any other birds of note amongst them and the pines. Mediterranean Gulls are out over the marsh and a pair of Stonechats along the marsh edge.

I head off for Titchwell, Little Gull reported there again and this is fast becoming a bogey bird.

Reaching Titchwell the Little Gull has moved on. I spend the afternoon walking around the reserve and the evening sitting in the Parrinder Hide watching as Curlew come into roost. Highlight birds amongst the day list of sixty nine include two Temminck's Stints and a Little Stint, a Whimbrel, Bittern booming and a fly over Spoonbill heading east.

The year list is **241**, exactly twenty ahead of this time last year.

19.04 miles **440 feet elevation up** **430 feet down**

Thursday 12th May **fresh NE**

Sunny 12C

I should head off for Frampton RSPB reserve in Lincolnshire. There is a Wryneck there and Curlew Sandpiper. I don't. Instead I steadily bird Titchwell starting with a scan of the freshwater lagoon. There is a gorgeous male Garganey out in the middle and a lone Wood Sandpiper on one of the islands. Both are soon gone though.

I walk to and then along, alone, on the immense beach that takes me to Thornham Point. I photograph items of interest on the beach and marvel at the millions of washed up, empty Razorshells. Along the tideline there are also mats of dead Bryozoa and the occasional sea urchin and Piddock. It's the Razorshells though that are sometimes packed in deep drifts of thousands and I enjoy crunching them as I walk along. Helping to make more sand on the beach, I think, as I always do when I walk along a beach that there are more stars in the Universe than there are grains of sand on every beach and in every desert in the World. A constant reminder to me of the immensity of our incredible universe.

The thick thorny bushes alongside the leaning ruin of a World War Two lookout tower look as though they should hold a migrant. They do but not the hoped for Icterine Warbler or White-spotted Bluethroat. A Chiffchaff is the only bird apart from a couple of Dunnocks and a Wren.

A Cuckoo comes close being chased by a couple of angry Meadow Pipits.

Back at Titchwell I meet Trevor Girling again, the superb Norfolk birder friend and news comes in that a Bee-eater has been seen and heard over Cley and is heading west. We position ourselves on the West Wall Walkway and scan hopefully.

A Pallid Swift is reportedly seen twice over Blakeney Marsh and is heading this way also. We scan over the reedbed and watch every Swift carefully.

Three hours later and after having moved onto the meadow trail boardwalk, we have to admit that neither bird has come our way or is looking likely to do so.

Trevor leaves and I walk off towards Patsy's Pool. I stop for a while under the willow bushes to watch a passing group of nine baby Long-tailed Tits being fed by two workaholic parents. A birder excitedly runs up to me. "Did you see it?" An Osprey had just flown over and has disappeared in the mist heading east.

"No."

15.93 miles 345 feet elevation up 333 feet down

Friday 13th May Fresh to strong NW

Sun, increasing cloud, cold to very cold with wind chill.

I set off for Frampton with the news that a Broad-billed Sandpiper is now there with Curlew Sandpiper and a Wryneck. T-shirt weather soon changes as clouds gather and the pleasant side-on wind that takes me to King's Lynn becomes a strong and extremely cold and painful gale in the face.

A stop for some chips and a fish cake, living it up by having some lunch on a picnic bench at Sutton Bridge. The cycling is tough but the three available year ticks keep me going.

The A17 is as busy as ever and I avoid it as much as I can. It would be lethal to cycle along it in this howler. Cycling along one small back road stretch I see a Stoat come out of the grass in front of me. I stop and it passes right beneath my feet!

Eventually I reach Frampton and quickly head to the spot where the Broad-billed Sandpiper has been seen; a small group of birders marks the spot.

It has gone, flown off with a flock of Dunlin. There is a **Curlew Sandpiper**.

"It will be back," I am told of the Broad-billed.

Late evening, the bird hasn't returned and looks like it has gone. A Temminck's and three Little Stint, as well as three Curlew Sandpiper and a lack of the Wryneck, also gone, make for mixed feelings.

Frampton has been the best RSPB reserve for waders since it was created just a few years ago. Indeed a series of Golden Willie trophies, awarded to the RSPB reserve that each year has the most wader species seen, adorn an office shelf.

67.40 miles **1289 feet elevation up** **1319 feet down**

Saturday 14th May **Fresh NW**

Sunny intervals, not so cold.

A friend from the Midlands appears, Rob Wardle, and together we walk to the spot where the Broad-billed Sandpiper was last seen yesterday. Dunlin and Ringed Plover are the only birds on the pools. Then I receive a text jingle and a message from The Oracle states, *'the sandpiper is on site.'* I look across to a small group of birders adjacent to the car park and notice one birder waving to us frantically, beckoning to us to come on down!

A run and a lifting of my binoculars, the **Broad-billed Sandpiper** is a close bird, greyer than the many Dunlin that surround it, with zebra head

and obvious large drooping bill. Brilliant, a bird I haven't seen before whilst on a Green journey and only my third ever.

With the bird UTB I have another go at searching for the Wryneck and collect two carrier bags full of strandline plastic. This all goes to be recycled but my efforts aren't rewarded by the Wryneck turning up. *I believe in good Karma; what you do will come back later!*

I set off for Abberton Reservoir in Essex, as you do! After all it is only 125 miles away! There is a Franklin's Gull, an American bird, that has been showing up there for the last few days.

With the wind behind me at last the cycle is pleasant and reasonably fast. Through Holbeach and Wisbech, I reach the village of Three Holes and a text arrives; *two White-winged Black Terns at March Farmers.* I turn to the west and head that way.

Evening time, **White-winged Black Tern** goes onto the list despite being quite distant on the far side of the flooded meadows. Thanks to Nigel and Amanda from Deeping for the use of their telescope. Two Short-eared Owls are much closer and there are a number of Black Terns out over the water also. One of the editors of Birdwatch magazine is there so who knows, maybe my exploits will grace the magazine's pages. More importantly it would be fabulous to see an article on Green Birding in there.

With two more birds of superb quality added to the year list I cycle on.

69.49 miles 440 feet elevation up 423 feet down

Sunday 15th May light W

Sunny, cool to warm

Another target bird has appeared, a Great Reed Warbler at Paxton Pits and I detour in that direction.

Just south of Huntingdon my mobile tells me there is a cycle path but it is a bumpy, grassy mountain bike only affair that goes along the banks of the beautiful River Ouse. It is lovely and I would love to push the bike along this stretch and enjoy the pastoral scenes but there is a rare bird to see and I return to the main road.

Paxton Pits is reached with birders looking through gaps in the hawthorns to look over to a patch of reeds. The bird is singing away almost none stop but getting a view takes over an hour. A brief flight view and trembling reeds to show where it has landed are all I see. Then suddenly the **Great Reed Warbler** climbs a reed to near the top and so having seen it, kissed it, licked it and ticked it, another very rare bird goes onto the year list. **245.**

53.17 miles 1010 feet elevation up 968 feet down

Monday 16th May **light W**

Sunny, warm

Cycling along the country lanes south of Cambridge, Corn Buntings and Yellow Wagtails are seen.

Something is up with the bike, a puncture, the first of the year and the first since last June in fact, so I can't complain. It is the front tyre and it takes me thirty one minutes to repair and replace the punctured inner tube.

Still the bike feels sluggish but I put it down to feeling very tired after cycling 180 miles in the last three days. Along one narrow lane and whilst cycling uphill a car comes behind me and seems reluctant to overtake. I feel irritated as I get off to let it past and feel embarrassed when the lady driving, Monica, calls me over to give a donation. She has seen the RSPB sign on the back of the bike and wants to give some money to them. There are lovely people out there and I shouldn't let my tiredness make me grouchy.

I reach Abberton Reservoir in the late afternoon after negotiating an excruciating and convoluted maze of small lanes. Two birders from Minsmere, both RSPB staff, have been here all day but haven't seen the Franklin's Gull.

Two other birders arrive and after an hour or so one calls out that he has got it. It doesn't inspire confidence when I look through his brand new Swarovski telescope and find a **Little Gull**, not the Franklin's that he is claiming. Still it is another bird for the year list, a first summer bird almost lost amongst Black-headed Gulls and Common Terns and distant in the mirage-like heat haze.

Another hour of searching passes and the same birder shouts that he has got it. His friend and I don't get onto it. All I can see is a distant Lesser Black-backed Gull heading south. They go onto a bird identification app. on a mobile to check the identification. I hear, "Yep, that was it."

They leave satisfied that they have seen the rare gull. I continue to search, satisfied that they haven't.

Alone for a while, I see a Hobby and a couple of Yellow Wagtails. Then a birder arrives, Geoff Keen from Weybridge, and together we search.

It is late evening. The gulls have started to fly catch in the fading light with the sun almost setting. One gull catches my eyes and I scream, "There it is!" and indeed there it is, thirty yards in front of us flying past. When in Lima, Peru Christmas Day 2013, there had been tens of thousands of Franklin's Gulls. I am more excited by this lone bird. Partial dark hood, dark, long wings, black bill; this is the real thing and my extremely hastily taken photograph in the gloom does it no justice at all. **Franklin's Gull** goes on the year list, unbelievable but oh so good. **247**.

51.05 miles 1860 feet elevation up 1890 feet down

Tuesday 17th May fresh SW

Sunshine to cloudy, cool 15C

The bike is still sluggish, especially up hills and I stop to check it out. I find that a spring on a front brake block has stopped retracting the block from the wheel rim; repairs take a while. I have no battery left on my mobile phone and decide to get to Malden to charge it at the local library. With no news available I am cycling towards a bird, a Red-footed Falcon, which might not be there.

I spend two hours in the library, charging the phone and updating the news on Facebook, checking emails and the like.

I reach Vange RSPB Reserve, south of Basildon, at around 3:00 p.m. The rare falcon hasn't been seen since one o'clock.

By dusk it hasn't returned and with the weather now cold and breezy, it seems as though it isn't likely to either. A dip and luckily I haven't suffered too many of those this year.

One pleasant thing, as per usual is the company of other birders. One in particular stands out, Tom Bell, a very enthusiastic young man, whose patch is Rainham Marshes RSPB reserve. He delights in talking about the birds he has seen and the places he is about to go birding to; Minsmere and Skomer, very good; Alaska and California, brilliant.

Time to head north, back to North Norfolk for an appearance at the excellent Norfolk Bird Fair this weekend.

Last six days cycling:- **320 miles 7283 feet elevation up 7128 feet down**

19th and 20th May

Three days of cycling only with birds seen along country lanes; Lesser and Common Whitethroat, Blackcap and Garden Warblers, Yellowhammers and Chaffinches and the occasional Kestrel.

A quality Bed & Breakfast, Pickwick Guest House in Stone le Clare, is as exceptional as described.

A night at Dave Lovatt's house in Brandon is comfortable. Dave has kindly said that the house is available any time I cycle through Brandon. Finally, before reaching the Norfolk Bird Fair, I have a night in the tent tucked away from prying eyes between two large hedgerows at Fowlsham, near Fakenham. This day, the 20th of May, I have cycled from Brandon, stopping at a large church in a small Norfolk village for a rest. Imagine the surprise when on entering the church I find a large model railway! It is not every day one finds a very detailed model railway layout with track, trains and cars etc. in a church.

Saturday 21st May Norfolk Bird Fair Manninton Hall, Norfolk.

Day 1. Saturday Stand number 52 - The Biking Birder

Bike is loaded and the main attraction sit together atop saddle and tool box. People want to be seen with The Lads. Selfies with a cuddly albatross and frog are taken. It is great to see that my stand is opposite the WWT stand and that on it is Emma from Welney. Emma, not Amanda that I have always thought her name was and have put on my blog and Facebook pages. Must change that.

Also opposite is the superb Wader quest group with Rick and Elis Simpson. I can't help but have a chat with these excellent people, new friends hopefully.

Www.waderquest.org

The public enter the large marquee and I start a competition with anyone who comes up to the stall. How many bird species, wild ones, have I seen this year? You all know the answer, 247. I have a separate children's competition with the same question and amazingly a young boy, Connor guesses exactly the 247. I tell him to go around the fair and find something he wants for £10. With his Mum and three sisters he goes off and comes back wanting a large photograph of a hare from the B & J. Legge stand. The hare photograph is his.

I really want to go to some of the lectures but feel that I can't leave my stand. The first lecture is by Yoav Periman, Director of the National Bird Monitoring Scheme at the Israeli Ornithological Centre. Incredibly after his talk he comes to find me. He has a proposal. Would I like to take part in the Champions of the Skyway bird race in Eilat, Israel in March in 2017? It would be an honour and a privilege to do so. I need to get a team of the best Green Birders. Would Chris Mills be up for it? Nick Moran from the BTO?

Maybe we should have an international field. How about Ponc Feliu Latorre, the current European Green Year list record holder and why not ask the World record holder, Dorian Anderson?

Wait a minute, these would be hares to my tortoise but that can't be helped.

What a prospect.

I am still in delighted shock at this invitation when another huge surprise occurs. Cath Mendez, a lady who I met on Fair Isle last year, has made it all the way up from South Wales to see the Bird Fair. She stays with me for quite a while and tells me that she will be a volunteer at the Fair Isle Bird Observatory later this year for three months, August to October. Brilliant to see such a great friend.

The day flies by and the evening has a pig roast followed by cheesecake, a favourite combination. I sit with three ladies. One is Liz Huxley, a bird photographer:-

www.lizhuxley.co.uk

She is the birder who found the Franklin's Gull at Abberton; the bird I was very lucky to add to my list earlier in the week. In fact I believe I was the last birder to see it. The other two are bird surveyors from Scotland, Laura and Amber.

Soon time for sleep and I make the mistake of placing my tent in a field too near to the site generator. Two sleepless hours listening to that from Midnight with frequent hoots and squeals from nearby Tawny Owls. Mind you, I lie in my sleeping bag writing notes from the thoughts buzzing around in my head from the day's events and people met.

Sunday 22nd May Norfolk Bird Fair, Mannington Hall.

Day 2.

The WWT are so lucky to have such a sunny personality in Emma. She is here again and has lots of children at her stand making badges. I have a feeling Sir Peter Scott, the amazing Man of the 20th Century, founder of the WWT Wildfowl & Wetland Trust, will figure large in today's Fair experience.

Still opposite are Rick and Elis Simpson. It is a privilege of travel to meet amazing couples that show so much love for each other. Not withstanding the fantastic work they both do for waders around the world, they exude a passion both for each other and their cause.

I buy a book off their stand and join Wader Quest, making a donation too as I feel the £5 joining fee is a little 'as cheap as chips'.

My little competition with 'guess my year list' of 247 has another winner. Michael, with his wife and two boys, has guessed correctly and has one of Dave Gosney's superb DVDs to go home with.

I go to the lecture by Rick Simpson's from Wader Quest. I am a little late and he is showing photographs of waders that are found in New Zealand and explaining their problems. Elis, his wife is there and she prompts him when he forgets to say the name of a particular wader. Brilliant.

Lewis, Carol, no not a typo but the names of a wonderful couple who come to meet me. They have followed me via the frequent Birdforum updates that The Oracle, Phil Andrews posts. Their Birdforum name is Jabberwocky of course. They kindly make a donation and share the same laugh as we include the opening of the film of the poem in our conversation; the unforgettable sequence of the flesh striped peasant and his head tossing agony.

Mike Linley comes to my stand! An immense personality is chatting with me. Mike worked with Sir Peter Scott on the survival series and with Sir David Attenborough on Life on Earth. Forty minutes pass by in a flash. WOW! Star-struck Biking Birder.

http://www.wildlife-film.com/-/Hairy-Frog-Productions.htm

Talking later with Rick (Wader Quest), another birding legend approaches, David Tomlinson. Birders of a certain age will remember the iconic **Big Year Race**, British variety of course, where two teams raced around East Anglia back in 1982 and the book of the race, documented in two witty sections detailing the race experiences of each team, became a must-have birding classic, as well as opening up British birders to the whole bird race for charity and fun craze.

In fact the Secondary-aged students of a Wolverhampton school with a certain teacher were so inspired that the annual Coppice High School Bird race day became a feature. My team never did win.

I gabbled away, star-struck again, with both David and his wife. Charming and approachable.

The day draws to a close. A massive thanks to Jill and Robert, the event organisers, and it is time to go. Goodbyes and an empty marquee, A birder named Andrew has something to show me. Now there are trophies that sport's fans hold as sacred; the football World Cup trophy, the large plate for Wimbledon, whatever that is called, Golf's Ryder Cup trophy and my personal favourite, the little Urn that is presented to the winning cricket team, be that Australia or England.

In British Birding there is the original **Big Bird Race** trophy. Andrew has it in his car. His team has just won the Norfolk Big Bird Race 2016 back in April and David Tomlinson has given Andrew the trophy! Together Andrew and I hold the trophy with reverence.

So it is that Sir Peter Scott completes my experience of the Norfolk Bird Fair with his presence. Within the Holy Grail shaped trophy is the egg of an Hawaiian Goose, a Ne-ne, signed by . . . . Sir Peter Scott.

Monday 23rd May **fresh NW**

Sunny intervals

The previous evening I spent at Kelling Heath listening to maybe four Nightjars churring around me. Before dark in fact, before the colours faded to greys, Turtle Doves had been purring and a male Dartford Warbler had sung from a perch atop a nearby gorse bush.

Nightjars takes the list to **248**.

The same birds I see again in the early morning. Well I don't unfortunately see a Nightjar in the morning but one keeps intermittently churring. This morning's Dartford Warbler is a female.

I cycle down to Weybourne and take the road west and the bridleway north to access The Quags. Egyptian Geese have five well grown youngsters.

The day list grows with common birds and there are a lot of Hirundines flying around. I notice that Sand Martins frequently go past with two following one, flying closely together. I imagine that this may be two young birds learning from an adult. I walk all the way to Salthouse, not wishing to cycle and instead push the bike so that I can take in the lovely, if rather chilly morning. There is a new hide just off the road as I approach the famous East Bank. Time for breakfast, spicy fruit loaf with peanut butter. I read the notices and see that the extension to the Norfolk Wildlife Trust's Cley reserve, an area of fifty three hectares, has cost £2.6 million. I ponder. Almost £50,000 an hectare, why so much?

Next to the beautiful, Green grass roof-covered Cley Nature Reserve visitor's centre for a permit. Down to Daulkes hide to watch the many Hirundines over the scrapes. A Hobby comes past twice just to prospect without hunting too seriously. A small group of Black-tailed Godwits come down with a couple of Knot. All of these delights are enjoyed by myself and a group of Dutch birders. The last week has been rather exhausting, what with cycling almost 400 miles as well as the two days at the Norfolk Bird Fair. I make my way after walking around the reserve, to Morston. Here I enter the church and sleep on a pew for three hours! I hadn't intended to. I had entered the Holy place to look at the memorial to the village's War dead.

A cycle ride to Wells, a quick shop for provisions, a short reading session in yet another church and into the excellent Wells Youth Hostel for the night.

The year list now stands at **248**, twenty five ahead of last year at this stage.

34.83 miles **1165 feet elevation up** **1348 feet down**

An email arrives:-

Hi Gary

It was simply a great pleasure to meet you in person at last this weekend. We admire what you do a great deal and always feel drawn to people who do things that are a passion rather then something they feel they ought to do.

Don't forget, if you are ever in the vicinity of Newport Pagnell, you will be assured of a warm welcome even if it is just for a cuppa and a chat. Can't always guarantee a bed for the night, but if we know you are coming we'll do our best to accommodate.

Thanks for agreeing to join us as a Friend of Wader Quest, much appreciated, we need all the friends we can get! We also appreciate the additional donation you pledged on your application form.

I have attached the last newsletter. the next will be out in July and, if you ever have the time and want to write a wader related story about your project just let us know and we'll slot you into the newsletter for sure.

I hope it isn't too long before we meet again and thanks again for keeping us entertained over the weekend the event was certainly enlivened by your presence there.

All the best and keep safe.
Rick and Elis.
Rick Simpson: Chair.
Elis Simpson: Treasurer & Membership Secretary.
Wader Quest Board of Trustees.
www.waderquest.org
rick@rick-simpson.com
waderquest@gmail.com
https://twitter.com/waderquest
https://www.facebook.com/WaderQuest

Tuesday 24th May **Strong NW**

Sunny intervals but feeling cool

A quick ride to Titchwell RSPB reserve, a favourite of course with such diversity of habitat and bird. The usual birds are their usual places and my familiarity with them is growing have had so many visits here this year. A Water Rail is in the ditch by the feeders. Reed Warblers are singing loudly in the reeds just after the willow bushes disperse. Bearded Tits are seen tazzing over the first long and straight ditch from reedbed to reedbed.

Down to the beach once more, it never ceases to amaze me, it's length and breadth seem never ending and yes, my usual more suns than there are grains of sand analogy pops up again.

Lunch is simple fare taken in the cafe with Steve Cale's fabulous diorama as a backdrop. Not often you see a Ross' Gull in May. There's one on the wall.

The rest of the day I spend wandering and watching. What a wonderful way to spend a day.

12.69 miles 327 feet elevation up 343 feet down

Wednesday 25th May fresh NW

Persistent rain

Feeling very tired I walk alone around Titchwell and eventually sit alone in the Parrinder Hide. Six summer plumaged Knot are close and a single Greenshank out beside a small island where Common Terns are sitting.

I head back towards the visitor's centre for breakfast. I meet two RSPB staff, the first one is out to litter pick, the second is out to see what birds are around. Both are superb people, as usual.

One says he is following the blog and that my journey is really about the people I meet. Now there's a thought. Every day I am privileged to meet the most amazing people, people with stories, people who in their own way are incredible and friendly.

Another RSPB staff member must be one of the best 'Meet & Greet' people in the RSPB. I tell him that and take his photograph. His name is Ian and he is the same with everyone he meets, friendly with a huge smile with a sunshine personality.

Breakfast is taken in the café, a Stilton and mushroom baguette with salad. Two ladies wave through the window. I met them both on Fair Isle last year, Jane and ... I must look up their names in my notes. Great to see them both again. They're so happy to see me again. Lovely.

Another friend comes to sit with me, Chris. We actually talk about match fishing in the 1970s. Back then I used to match fish in the Midlands and I met so many famous fishing characters during my teenage years. Chris was a match angler too of some repute and so the names flood back the memories of great days. Clive Smith, Kevin and Benny Ashurst, Ivan Marks, Roy Marlow, Barry Brookes, Tony Reece, Ken Giles Max Winters; all fabulous to watch and learn from. Great days.

I return to the hide to watch as Avocets have territorial disputes and courtship displays as the cameras click with rapidity.

I fall asleep!

This is bad news as I have received an invitation to stay at one of the most special places in Britain, the lighthouse that was the home of Sir Peter Scott in his younger days in the 1930s.

I text the owners to say I will be late.

Three hours later I arrive, soaked and hot, at the lighthouse that now belongs to Doug and Sue Hilton, Sir Peter Scott's Lighthouse.

35.82 miles 860 feet elevation up 852 feet down

Let me tell you the tale of how I ended up staying the night with a wonderful couple, Sue and Doug Hilton, in the bedroom of Sir Peter Scott.

Last year I found out one evening that after a day birding at Cliffe Pools and Northwood Hill, both RSPB reserves, and whilst being on a tour of all the RSPB and WWT nature reserves, I had missed three RSPB reserves that were back at Cliffe. It was back in early January 2015 and I was tucked up in my sleeping bag in a bird hide, reading a thin booklet about the RSPB reserves of The Hoo Peninsula.

In the morning I retraced my tracks and found them all and decided that as a reward I would have a full English breakfast in a café I had seen the day before, located beside a huge chalk pit not far south of Cliffe village.

On entering the establishment I noticed one of my favourite books, Paul Gallico's Snow Goose, on a top shelf. It was the special edition illustrated by Sir Peter Scott's beautifully painted plates and a bright blue dust sleeve jacket. Back in the day when I was a Primary school teacher I used to read this story to the children. A very special, beautiful and heart-rending tale, the story tells of an disfigured artist, Rhayader living alone in a lighthouse far out on a lonely saltmarsh in Essex. A young girl, Frith, scared because of village gossip, overcomes her fear of Rhayader and takes an injured bird to him, a snow goose. Rhadayer heals the Snow Goose, a poor lost Princess and a friendship grows between the girl and man but only when the Snow Goose is present. As soon as the Snow Goose returns to the North Lands, the girl leaves.

The story develops until one day Rhayader goes to help rescue the British soldiers on the beach at Dunkirk. "God speed, Rhayader."

The Wildfowl & Wetland Trust have re-issued the book with the same artwork by Sir Peter and I urge you all to get in touch with the WWT and buy a copy. The WWT's webpage details the following text:

The Snow Goose

A novella no thicker than a love letter, in which every sentence seems to shiver with the salt-laden chill of the desolate landscape in which it is set.

It is a love story between an uneducated village girl who comes to visit the hunchback outcast artist in his lighthouse bearing a wounded Snow Goose for him to heal is so well-known, perhaps because of its fable-like quality. The silence and growing sympathy of the first two-thirds of the novella, broken only by the cries of the wild birds, is in stark contrast to the noisy clamour of the conclusion, related entirely in dialogue between soldiers in the pub and officers in their club, who witnessed the man in his little boat and his heroic attempts to rescue the stranded men from the Dunkirk beaches.

It has been hugely influential to work over the years and we believe it still has the power to inspire today. Michael Morpurgo cites it as an influence on War Horse, The inspiration for William Fiennes' The Snow Geese, Lisa Allardice's Guardian Winter Reads 2011 - "It may not be free from sentimentality, but this sad, sweet tale has an elemental power that makes it soar"

Peter Scott

Peter Scott was the father of modern conservation founding WWF, the IUCN Red List of Threatened Species & WWT, whose 70th anniversary is this year.

Not only did he illustrate the best selling 1946 edition, but he also inspired the book itself as an Olympic medallist in sailing, who kept a wildfowl collection at his lighthouse before the war and served at sea during it.

This book I still read regularly and my old battered copy with torn dust sleeve jacket is a treasured item with those wonderful, atmospheric paintings by Sir Peter. I used to read this to Year Five Primary school children as part of their World War Two project. It would always bring me to tears.

So, back at The Snow Goose cafe, with my breakfast ordered, I chatted with the ladies behind the counter and asked why the book was on the shelf. They explained that the owner of the café and lake ran a nature conservation charity called the Snow Goose Trust. They phoned the owner, Doug Hilton and despite being very busy and needing to get to the House of Commons to lobby the MP Eric Pickles over a local environmental issue, he came and sat with me for over an hour telling me the story of why The Snow Goose.

http://www.snowgoosetrust.org/

Doug told me the whole story of how Sir Peter met Paul Gallico and invited him to stay at a lighthouse, a lighthouse far out on a lonely saltmarsh.

Here the two collaborated on the Snow Goose story and book. Doug embellished the story with many details of a love of an artist for an American ice skater unrequited and made the links between the story of Header and the life of Sir Peter in the lighthouse; artist, wildlife lover and WW2 hero.

Back in 2010 Doug bought a lighthouse far out on a salt-marsh in Lincolnshire, the home of a certain Sir Peter Scott from 1933 to 1939. Then Doug repeated Sir Peter's invitation to Paul Gallico by inviting me to stay at the lighthouse!

So here I am, over a year later, cycling up the long lane towards the ex-home of my childhood hero.

Into the beautiful home that Doug and Sue, his wife, are carefully and painstakingly restoring to its former glory. Doug gives me the full tour. Into the lighthouse with dining table in the bottom floor room we enter and via a misshapen door and stairway, access the upper rooms. Up the next flight of stairs and into Sir Peter's bedroom. Up a steeper set of steps and into another empty room and up an almost vertical set of steps and into the light room with its view along the channel to The Wash, now half a mile away. When Sir Peter lived here the sea was just outside the window.

Outside where a long pool with attendant wildfowl could have been taken from Slim bridge, the HQ of the WWT, itself. A bridge over the lake is modelled on a Monet picture and the one end of the lake is landscaped to take on the southern features of The Wash.

Red-breasted Geese, a small group of Pink-footed Geese showing still the effects of the guns that brought them to this sanctuary and ….., of course, Snow Geese.

An evening with Doug and Sue flies by as conversation about aspirations for not only the lighthouse, with a planned visitor's centre about to be built but also of Dog's conviction to help nature in practical ways through future housing development planning laws, is one of those wonderful experiences. One could listen forever and wonder at the energy and commitment of this wonderful couple.

To bed and where else could I sleep but on the first floor of the lighthouse, Sir Peter's old bedroom.

The morning tour and photographs and goodbyes. I cycle off towards the next bird but stop after just a few hundred yards. There is a pair of Barnacle Geese beside the river and with them . . . a Snow Goose.

26th to 28th May Brandon, Dave's bungalow

Asthma and sinusitis have taken their toll and maybe the amount of cycling done also. I am exhausted, full of mucus and with a temperature. I struggled yesterday to get to Brandon but made it after a forty three mile cycle ride and have been to the local doctor in the town. Antibiotics and rest prescribed, I stay mostly in bed and read. I could never travel without a favourite book or ten and so I have a Penguin copy of The Mayor of Casterbridge by Thomas Hardy to read. Well thumbed from multiple readings over the years, I let Henchard, Elizabeth and Farfrae fill my waking hours and let my Lucetta, my Elizabeth-Jane fill my Wessex dreams.

Sunday 29th May Fresh N

Mostly cloudy with drizzle, cold.

So, after a rest for a couple of days at Dave's bungalow at Brandon and with antibiotics to hopefully get rid of my sinus problem, I set off for Minsmere RSPB Reserve yet again. A Purple Heron has been seen there and obviously that would be a really good bird to get. I have never seen one whilst cycling, so it would be a '16' bird., one of the sixteen birds I need over last year's total of 289 in order to get beyond Ponc Feliu Latorre's European record of 304. OK, I know I keep repeating this but it focuses me to keep reminding myself of my quest this year, 300 and then some.

Cycling towards Thetford, the smallest of grass snakes is on the road in front of me. I stop but this tiny ribbon of a snake is gone, quickly disappearing in the roadside grass.

Now in twenty nine months of Biking Birding, twelve months in 2010, twelve in 2015 and five this year, I have only seen two dead snakes along the road. After the beautiful, small live grass snake, I see two dead snakes within the next ten miles, both adders. Shame. More 'car-nage'.

Late afternoon, I arrive at the Island Mere hide. Standing on the wooden walkway up to the hide, I watch as a Bittern comes regularly past to access an area beside the hide in the reeds. She comes out and lands just yards in front and parades through the short reeds.

Marsh Harriers quarter the reeds and Bearded Tits ping; the Savi's Warbler reels once more over the far side of the mere. No sign of the Purple Heron but it has been reported earlier today.

The evening is cool with a northerly breeze. Darkness falls. Four young people arrive, four members of the fabulous Facebook groups: Next Generation Birders; Jess, Jake, Drew and Dan. In the dark they have come to try to hear the Savi's at the end of a birding day that started at Spurn, Humberside. How brilliant is it when one meets four driven birders of such passion? Long may the NGBs have such people.

51.63 miles **1367 feet elevation up** **1443 feet down**

An evening email:-

Hello Gary,

I hope you enjoyed the rest of the RSPB conference. I never regret going every year!

Well, I had my last couple of bike rides from Pooley Bridge last month before the full hip replacement on 27th April.

On the 24th, I was lucky to find 3 male Redstarts in the valley and one of the loveliest views I had that day was a right royal line up on a fence - a pair of Stonechats, Meadow Pipit and male Wheatear all facing the same way, ready for the 100 metres sprint! 2 brown hares crossed in front of my path and the place was teaming with Wrens!

Obviously, I am still unable to drive so have had to forego hide guide duties at Saltholme. However, I have been no slouch!

One of the chaps had written down 100 birds he has seen every year since the reserve opened. Earlier in the year, we lost a large number of sheep in lamb when some idiot let his dogs loose on them a few times. We decided to try and raise money to counteract the loss by putting together a booklet of these 100 Saltholme birds. 3 of the guys are really good artists and have drawn the birds and to accompany each one we have a snapshot paragraph. I have put together 67 of them and Dave Braithwaite seems to approve! The book should be on sale when you next visit so do look for it!

I have just today sent a letter to the Architects Association and enclose a copy. I am hoping friends in Kendal will start pestering these organisations, councils and their own MP!! Do the same if you have time!!

I have been watching the behaviour of a pair of G S Ws frequenting my garden throughout my incarceration. Absorbing! They both have created their own personal anvil in my lilac tree for nut battering!!

Happy cycling and birding!
Barbara

Monday 30th May **Fresh N**

Cloudy and cool.

Early morning, and by that I mean 4:00 a.m. I am up and hoping that a Purple Heron will come out of the reeds. After an hour it hasn't. Two photographers arrive and tell me that it was last seen in front of the Bittern hide yesterday evening. I wait.

6:30 a.m. I move around to the Bittern hide.

7:10 a.m. The Purple Heron flies in front of the Island Mere hide.

7:30 a.m. I return to the Island Mere hide.

18:00 . . . . **Purple Heron**!

Those intervening ten and a half hours I spent sitting in the same chair mostly with a wonderful fourteen year old birder-photographer, Harry, sitting next to me. My reaction to getting Purple Heron on the year list was euphoric. Well, it would be wouldn't it after waiting so long? I danced around the hide, I fist thumped, I shouted!

Harry had arrived at the hide with one of his Dad's friends, Dave. Both had great photographic equipment and as Dave went off to explore the reserve, Harry stayed behind to try to get a lifer for himself, the Purple Heron.

The hide was full for most of the day due to the presence of BBC's "Springwatch". It seemed funny when people's telescopes are trained on the three presenters during their rehearsals in the afternoon instead of the birds and otters. It is also strange to think that this time last year they may have been training their scopes on Chris Packham and me, as we went through the strict afternoon rehearsals; for last year I was one of the main guests one evening.

The usual Bitterns, Marsh Harriers and Bearded Tits gave views all day, yet the best sighting, before the rare heron, occurred when an otter swam around in the middle of the mere. It was fishing and caught a number of small fish, which were immediately eaten. This wonderful male thought it was a dolphin and breeched a number of times as he dove deep. The sound of gasps and delighted exclamations from the crowd was brilliant, especially from a very excited small boy next to me with his sisters and Mum and Dad. I love seeing children enjoying nature. I love seeing children enjoying life!

The crowd thinned as the evening approached but I wasn't going to leave my spot. I had been told where the Purple Heron had landed earlier in the day, a spot way off to the west deep in the reed-bed, and despite the jokes that it could have walked to Ipswich by now, I waited.

Grey Herons kept coming out of the reeds, flying a short distance in the northerly gale.

Then a darker-looking heron came out.

I shouted, "There it is!" I changed my mind, "no it isn't." Looked again all in a split second as my final cry confirmed to everyone still present that the Purple Heron was indeed flying. "It is the purple!"

With everyone now on the bird, the special one flew around in the distance before coming a lot closer and landing in the reeds opposite the hide.

Up again and off towards the Bittern Hide, Harry and I went there and met a BBC producer, who was co-ordinating a nest search for the programme.

Harry's Dad, Dave and the friend Dave arrived with sausage rolls and doughnuts for all.

Purple Heron, bird number **249** and such a good one to get.

Tuesday 31st May **Strong N – gale force**

The day starts early once more with a loud thunderstorm accompanied by intense rainfall. The water is coming in despite the hide shutters of the East Hide being shut.

Two birders come in to shelter at around six. Ian from Watford describes how he has had six holes cut into his skull in order to remove a brain abscess.

Simon is the geography master at Harrow school who talks about his experience of being in Sri Lanka on a school trip when the tsunami hit their holiday resort.

Why stay in and watch TV when one can be out meeting the real deal in the shape of these fascinating characters?

A couple of RSPB staff come in to bird and enthral the crowd of three. A first summer Little Gull is out on the scrape and the adult Long-tailed Drake. Now what on earth is he doing here and in six inches of water? Summer and winter out on the scrape together.

I spend the morning circumnavigating the scrape before heading off for lunch.

4:30 p.m. a text from The Oracle, *Greenish Warbler at Lowestoft.*

7:30 p.m. I am in the corner of a sports field with a few other more local birders.

Dark falls – no Greenish Warbler. Oh well, there's always tomorrow.

27.43 miles **841 feet elevation up** **824 feet down**

Green Year list	249 birds
Year ticks in May	24
Bird species had, not seen in 2015	8
Mileage in May	1023.25 miles
Total mileage for the year	3726.84 miles
Average mileage on days cycled	40.93 miles
Elevation : up	27,442 feet
: down	27,330 feet

Best Birds : ***Rufous Turtle Dove, Black-winged Stilt, Lady Amhurst's Pheasant, Broad-billed sandpiper, White-winged Tern, Great Reed Warbler, Franklin's and Purple Heron.***

6

JUNE

"Come, this is life! How splendid it is! This is how I should like to live!"

Leo Tolstoy, spoken by Oblonsky in Anna Karenina

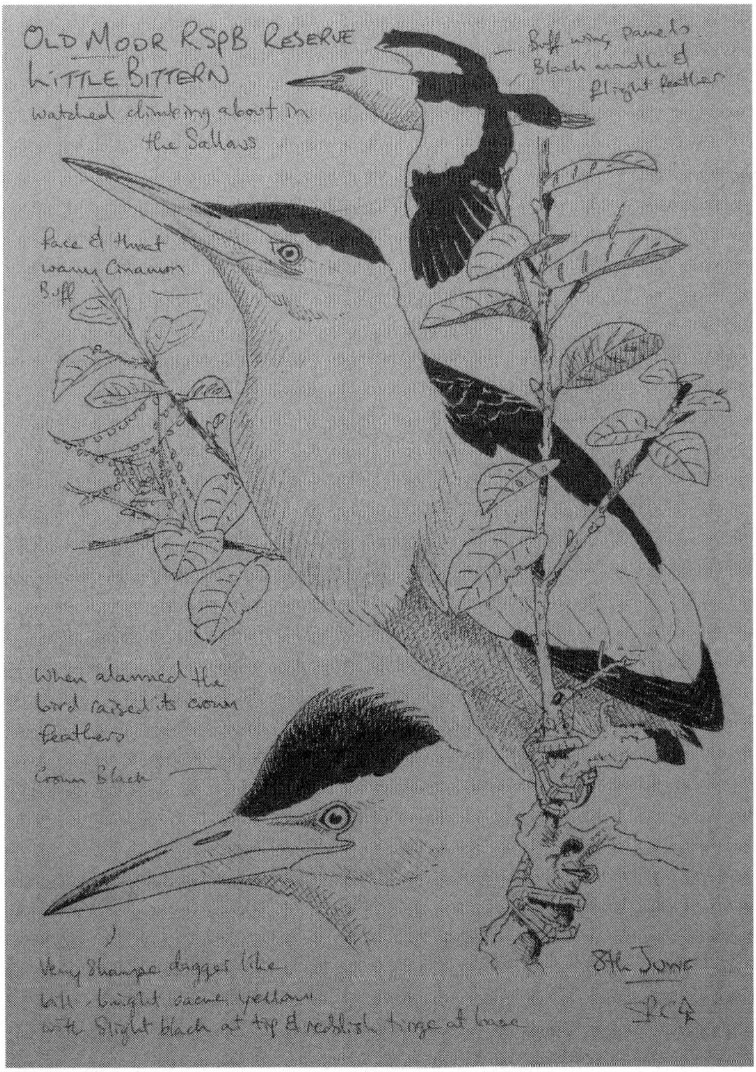

How much of The Biking Birder year is about meeting the most incredible people? Since leaving Doug and Sue at the Sir Peter Scott lighthouse, there has been a wonderful procession of wonderful and inspiring people. Maybe too many to remember them all, here are some details of the ones it has been a pleasure and privilege to meet over the last three days:-

1. Charlie, an ex-soldier crippled whilst on exercises and invalided out of the army. Became homeless but now has an ice cream van and organises beach cleaning!

2. Steve and Lindsey, met in the Island Mere hide and they deserve a full posting just for them! Lindsey has started a butterfly education programme where she goes into schools with characters she has produced herself, Bob and Bobette, with various cuddly caterpillars. Have a look at her website . . .

http://www.butterfliesofbritain.co.uk/home/about-me/

3. Trevor, a black currant and apple farmer, who loves swallows and house martins. He encourages them to nest in his barns by placing a lot of platforms in the roof space of his barn.

4. Four fantastic young birders; Dean, Dan, Jake and Jess. Actually I didn't see them! We were listening in the dark for Savi's Warbler. This wonderful group of Next Generation Birders had just come down from Spurn and, after hearing the Savi's, they head off to Norwich, their home. Very keen birders, the next generation (of) birders is in safe hands.

https://www.facebook.com/groups/386321508160072/

5. A fantastic young fourteen year old photographer and keen to learn birder, Harry, who sat with me for ten hours to try and see the Purple Heron at Minsmere. Harry is a superb young photographer and his enthusiasm is inspiring. With his Dad, Dave and his Dad's friend, Dave, the three made the long, long wait fly by.

6. A birder from the Midlands, Steve tells me the tale of another well known Midland birder who saw what he thought was a White Stork and put the news out on Rare Bird Alert. His initial view wasn't the best and on looking again he found out that it was plastic. No, not an escape with leg rings but literally plastic! A large plastic heron bought at a garden centre. Oops, a reputation ruined

and a story that will define him forever.

7. Ian told me that despite an appearance that told of an age around fifty that he was actually only thirteen. Thirteen years ago Ian had had a brain abscess and had a series of operations that meant he had to relearn everything he had ever known. Six holes through his skull and a new life, a great sense of humour and a vivacity that is understandable with the chance he has been given to live his youth again.

8. The geography and cricket master at Harrow school, Simon and myself made an incongruous trio of birders with Ian but we had a great half hour or so as thunder and lightning flashed outside the east hide at Minsmere.

9. Zack and Dad, Mark. Zack is the winner of the Junior category of the Wildlife Blogger of the Year competition for 2015. A superb young man, it is great to see how confident he is when being interviewed for Springwatch with a TV camera almost in his face. Zack has just attended the BTO Boot Camp, another brilliant young person to watch.

http://yearofnature.blogspot.co.uk/

10. The fabulous Gibbin and Martin families; Mums and Dads with entourage of 'out loving nature' children.

So many wonderful, interesting and diverse people.

3rd to 5th June **light to fresh N**

One day of cloud and drizzle, then .. Sunshine .. what is that blue stuff in the sky? Warmer .... to 20C

3rd June to Brandon

After two days of just cycling with a migratory urge to head north, today my aim is to reach Dave's bungalow at Brandon via a cycle ride of forty seven miles. Car-nage, WW1 memorials, WW2 pillboxes and interesting weather vanes punctuate the journey as I stop to photograph them all. Hares, Pheasants, Blackbirds, foxes, rabbits .. all dead and mangled by the side of the road. How many creatures are killed on our roads?

WW1 memorials show the horrific slaughter of people and one day I will put all of them onto a Facebook group/community page. I have been photographing as many as I see around Britain for the last seventeen months. Horrific lists of the dead, "For the Glory of God and for Country/King" Variations on a theme. Sons, brothers, fathers, uncles . .

The pillboxes I photograph are for a man I met in Kent last year, Paul Hayesmore. Another reminder of war, each box must tell a story.

In a lighter vein, the weather vanes show a household's main interest, foxes, pheasants and on one house, a whale!

Brandon reached, I do my laundry, take a shower and get an early night.

4th June to Frampton

Blue and yellow, the sun is a shining to welcome the day! Warm t-shirt weather, the vagaries of the British weather, it was only a couple of day since I was wearing thermals and waterproofs.

Sixty one miles today, though not all of it as intended. I think that I will reach Long Sutton and camp there but the weather is so conducive to cycling that I may carry on.

Retracing the tracks of a few weeks back, I get to the final A17 bridge before the turn off towards Frampton. Realising that dusk is falling I think about the possibility of a Little Owl being on a telegraph post.

Around a corner and there on the very next telegraph post, a little owl. It stares at me in dusk's gloom.

A mile or so on, after the sun has gone down, another Little Owl is perched on a barn roof. It dances as it checks on whether I am alive, head nodding side to side.

5th June Frampton to Lincoln.

Close Avocets to start the day, one pair with a lone tiny chick, grebes and gulls; after chat with Sarah, the resident staff member in the visitor's centre, I am off again and once more into the wind. When will this constant northerly turn? Day after day of cycling into this is not doing my mental state any favours. The sun is shining again though so count blessings and get on with it. Flat landscapes and reasonably empty roads, I reach a fabulous nine mile cycle path that follows two large canal-like features. With a tarmacked surface, this is the best cycle path I have been on since the Exe Estuary one way back in January.

A weasel comes out in front of me and stretches his neck to check me out. Unfortunately I am not quick enough to get a photograph but my mind's eye will remember this smashing little creature. With yet another forty mile plus cycle ride completed I find a hotel and what a hotel, The

Old Palace behind the cathedral. Luxury room and screaming Peregrines around the cathedral tower. I am asleep by eight!

3 day mileage . . 149.79 miles

6th to 9th June **light N-NE**

Mostly very sunny and very hot, 20C plus

6th June to Hotoft Bank reserve, north of Anderby Creek

The morning plan of a cycle to Old Moor RSPB reserve, one of my top ten favourites, changes when the news of an all singing, all dancing Marsh Warbler, over on the Lincolnshire coast, comes in from The Oracle.

Back along the cycle path east, the superb path I came along yesterday, has me feeling very relaxed, despite the about turn, listening to some of Frank Zappa's guitar music as I cycle. I so prefer Frank's instrumental work to his monologue-style, songs with puerile sexual lyrics.

To Horncastle along mostly roads empty of traffic and then along a busy, noisy A road. Up a steep chalk hill I push before a turn off towards Alford gives me more peaceful, reflective roads. Do people realise how obtrusive loud traffic can be?

Arriving at the reedbed reserve, I find that I am alone and that other than the occasional burst of Sedge Warbler song, there is silence. That is there were no mimicking calls or songs from the rare acro. No one else is here and no sign of a Marsh Warbler.

A nice Spotted Flycatcher is fly catching and for an hour or so the Sedge Warbler and flycatcher are the only birds of note. A Cuckoo cuckoos nearby.

Then low down in the bushes that runs along the southern edge of the path, I see a small Acrocephalus warbler. It looks good. From what I initially see I think 'Marsh.' I photograph and video it.

The bird disappears into the undergrowth. Moments later a couple of local birders arrive and have brief views. They think the same as me, Marsh Warbler.

They leave happy with their identification, leaving me alone with my thoughts.

Now many years ago when in my early twenties I had a personally embarrassing experience over such an easy bird to identify yet mega rare back then, Pallas' Warbler.

I had found one in Well's wood, the Dell, and had run like a headless chicken to find my friends. Instead of them, I bumped into a group of far more experienced than me at that time birders and blurted out a description of stripes and wing bars. I forgot to say the yellow rump! I remember even now blushing at their laughter which was probably well meant but that embarrassed me at the time.

Sitting in the hide in the evening, with images on the viewfinder of my camera, I start to be unsure of my identification of the warbler. The differences between Marsh and Reed are subtle.

Phil Andrews, The Oracle has received my initial text:

18:23 – wish I could get these photographs to you! This looks good . . . . short bill, no warm brown to the rump . . .

And in return Phil texts:

Ready to declare 251 Marsh Warbler?

I am not. I am just not sure any more.

20:50 Sorry mate. I don't think it is. The feet look too dark. Not singing.

I camp nearby and sleep comes as I reflect on what I had on the bird.

An evening email from Mark Ballamy:-

I was in Scotland last year have been going there 3 times a year for the last 10 year and I think I just missed you last year cycling through Castle Douglas.

Hope you get the 300.

Best Wishes   Mark Ballamy

7th June to Blacktoft RSPB reserve.

No sign of the Marsh Warbler in the early morning, it is time to try again to get to Old Moor RSPB reserve for the Little Bittern that is being reported there. No it isn't, a Red-necked Phalarope is at Blacktoft Sands RSPB reserve!

After seventy two miles of cycling in the heat, over the high lump of chalk between Louth and Market Rasen and after the flat landscape of North Lincolnshire, I reach the reserve to be told by the RSPB staff in the visitor's shed (!) that the phalarope has gone. "It hasn't been seen for a couple of hours."

A lovely, friendly and enthusiastic volunteer, Penny walks with me towards the hide furthest away from the middle of the reserve, the place where the phalarope was last seen. Two birders just coming from there tell us cheerily that the spinning wanderer is still there!

Asking permission from Penny, I cycle as fast as I can to the empty hide and soon find it. Bird number **251, Red-necked Phalarope**. The final countdown, fifty more birds to see to reach the magic 300, has begun.

Now 251 is a special number to reach in itself. Back in 2010 this was the number of bird species I saw that year, so equalling the then British Green Big Year record held by Chris Mills.

The spinning, frantic, fly catching wader is distant but easy to see. It's tiny size is emphasised when a Pied Wagtail walks close to it and there isn't that much difference.

Black, Summer-plumaged Spotted Redshank, Avocets and a group of Black-tailed Godwits are here too. The latter don't like the small phalarope and peck at it whenever it comes close.

The hide fills up in the early evening and the banter is fun. A mother and son combination brings in a very keen fifteen year old who will become a birding star in the future. Stupidly I forget to put his name in the notebook; a senior moment I regret as I want to tell you all of the immense pleasure I get when I meet a young person is so passionate about birding and nature. Well you already know that. I remember his Mum's name, Karen.

8th June to Old Moor at last!

Into Goole for breakfast and another long, mostly country lane cycle gets me to the Trans-Pennine cycle path that takes me to the bridge into the wonderful RSPB reserve, Old Moor. I love this reserve. It has everything and the thrill to me is that it was created from the old mining industry pits and slag heaps. The main reserve is just one of a complex of close together reserves which are being added to as more projects come on line and more land is bought.

I am excited but extremely tired so I don't rush to the Bittern Hide where the barking Little Bittern may be heard but probably not seen.

Instead I am thrilled to meet the people I have met on previous visits; Craig, Lauren and Matthew, and new RSPB staff faces too; Bill and Joy.

The incredible Dave is here, wonderful man who deserves a lot of credit for the success of the reserve.

I am given cake and coffee and sit at a table on the balcony overlooking the garden, writing the cost of both down in my notebook, treating the kindness of the café's staff as a donation. The amount written down is approaching £100. I will be busy on my Just Giving pages and the Chaskawasi-Manu donation webpage when I can get on the internet. Remember I am doing all this for four charities and any gift, like the coffee and cake, is a donation in my mind. Thanks Kevin and Michelle!

Late afternoon and I casually wander down to the Bittern Hide. The Little Bittern is barking unseen at the back of a bush surrounded reedbed.

Three hours of standing on the small bridge with around ten other birders, the Little Bittern hasn't even shown us one of his resplendent feathers.

A married couple find a way through the tripod legs and birders and head off for the nearby hide.

The Little Bittern decides it is time to go to roost and climbs up a willow. Unfortunately it does this at the back of the tree and is unseen until it takes off and gives me a split second banking view as it heads off to the left.

Birders all rush into the hide to find that the Little Bittern has disappeared into the far reedbed. The husband of the couple is distraught. He missed it. So did all of us except for one lone person who, despite no interest in birds at all, had the best view, the wife! Brilliant. One can but laugh at the vagaries of birding. Those who wanted great views didn't get them. She, who didn't really care, did.

9th June Old Moor RSPB reserve

Internet accessible in the café, all funds are placed into the various Just-giving webpages for the charities; the RSPB, Asthma UK and the WWT, as well as 32 Euros into Chaskawasi-Manu so my notebook figure is deleted until more donations are given.

I have arranged to bird with Dave and together with a number of birders we are all gathered once more on the bridge first thing in the morning. A large number of Common Swifts *Apus apus* are swirling around overhead. I love the Latin name. My favourite bird always has me dreaming of joining them....

Can't keep my mind from the circling skies, tongue-tied and twisted, just an earth-bound misfit I.

The **Little Bittern** is barking once more and decides to give everyone the best of views as it climbs a willow in front of us. I take a video of it doing so. Bird number **252** and what a bird.

After this another great bird to see, a common one but one not often seen well, is sitting in a large tree, a Tawny Owl, back near the visitor's centre.

A privilege today, I am given permission to join the Greater Bittern monitoring team. Think about this. This is a nature reserve almost completely man-made and here we have two pairs of nesting Greater Bitterns and a calling Little Bittern. Add nesting Avocets, Cetti's Warblers and the presence of a lot of Little Egrets to the mix and who would have thought such was possible in industrial Yorkshire. Well done RSPB!

In the hide with Foggy, Clegg and Compo, oops I mean Steve, Paul and Gerry, we four sit and map all movement of the female Bitterns as they return to the nests and go off to either get more food or relax in the heat.

There is cricket Test Match on today and I use my Smartphone to see how England are faring against Sri Lanka. TMS, Test Match Special on the BBC webpage is asking for photographs to show where people are playing cricket whilst at work. There are already two boring office-type photographs. Surely we lads could do better. A stick is found for a bat, a few Kestrel pellets for the ball and a rucksack for stumps, plastic bottle for bails, myself in to bat, Gerry waiting for the snicked catch as wicket keeper, Steve bowls with a reverse swing action. Paul is on camera to capture the action.

The first ball is hit straight at Paul, a fair straight drive. He shells the easy catch. The next ball/pellet is pulled through the shutter for six!

The final pellet, another one found on the floor, is hit straight back at the bowler, who also drops the easy catch.

The resulting photograph is emailed to TMS at the BBC and at 12:33 appears on the BBC Live Score feed. Result!

Twice bittern once shy cricketers of Old Moor RSPB reserve.

Lunch in the superb café and procrastination over leaving. This reserve has so much and I would love to have the time to see all of it again and again. Springwatch should come here!

I eventually head off once more along the Trans-Pennine way and get to Doncaster. Here I get a bed at my favourite Doncaster Bed and Breakfast, The Balmoral. Here Nurse Gladys was almost trapped into a weekend of passion by Arkwright many years ago.

3 day mileage .. 163.62 miles The last seven days mileage of 362.96 miles is a new seven day record for me, with an average of 51.85 miles a day.

Sunday 12th June

People look at my bike and smile at the collection of 'friends' I have on it. There is a reason for each and over the next few weeks I am going to introduce you to each character and explain why they travel with me. They provide so much inspiration and although sadly any conversation with them is one way, I wouldn't be without them.

The Lads on the Bike – (1) Manu the Frog and Acorn the Parrot

Manu's name was originally Sid. Indeed this followed the name of every one of my pets over the years. I named them all Sid in deference to Sid James of the Carry On movies fame.

Nowadays I only have one pet and he is far too heavy to travel with me on the bike. Sid is back in Worcestershire; a large metamorphic piece of rock from the Pyrenees. In fact he is from the French Pyrenees. Back in 1991 I was walking there with a wonderful girlfriend from my past, Diane. Together we had walked from Gavarnie village, south of the famous Catholic sanctuary of Lourdes, to the highest waterfall in Europe in La

Cirque de Gavarnie. After taking a number of photographs of each other next to the noisy cascade, we could hear the imploring cries of someone not too keen on water nearby.

"Aidez moi, beaucoup trop de leau."

We searched and we found the large rock. He told us that he had been at the base of the waterfall for centuries and that he was fed up. He wanted a different life. Picking him up and drying him off, we carried him the five miles or so back to the car and from there back to Britain. He didn't have to go into quarantine.

Sid is now in my sister's garden with his family. In 2009 I went back to Gavarnie to search for his wife and children. I found them in the same spot as where I found Sid and brought them back.

OK enough silliness. Back to Manu and Acorn. Manu the frog is from the Wildfowl & Wetland Trust; in fact I bought him from the WWT shop at Slimbridge. As I said originally Sid, he was on the front of the bike for the whole of 2010, the year of the first Biking Birder tour of all of the RSPB and WWT reserves. In 2010 he represented the magnificent Wildfowl & Wetland Trust. He still does but ever since my trip out the the Manu National Park in Peru, he has taken on a dual role. The name change to Manu is to show this.

As I have said before whilst on the Peru trip I had the immense good luck to meet two incredible sisters, Herminia and Maria.

Herminia was at Chontachaka, a Reserva Ecologika centre, which is across a river from the famous Manu Road. To get to it one has to brave the road, an exhilarating and sometimes terrifying ride. Then after a walk down a jungle trail, one has to cross the river on a zip wire.

This is my review on Tripadvisor:-

At 30 US dollars a night, the Reserva Ecologika Chontachaka offers a cheaper way of getting to know the Manu than other hostels and lodges. This includes all food (vegan) and transport to and from far away Cuzco. Just getting here is an adventure!
To be greeted by Herminia, a Spanish lady, on arrival, introduced to the volunteers and then being asked "do you want to see Cock of the Rocks?" was fabulous. Meeting Paola also, a wild yet tame howler monkey was amazing.
Right, let's quickly be honest. This is not a hotel! It is a basic, open to the elements accommodation place where one can bird or choose to join in with the ecological program. I did both.
The bedrooms are open all around and mosquitoes nets are provided. They weren't too bad and the only ones that got me were when I forgot to put repellent on.
Showers are cold but that doesn't bother me none. If it bothers you - look away now. The better option is to shower in a waterfall not too far away. Wash away your worries and

your cares beneath an Amazonian cascade.
Food as I've said is vegan and there is plenty of it. Inspirational to me.
The five volunteers there when I was were fabulous company, as was the previously mentioned Herminia. Meeting local people increased the intense pleasure I derived from my stay. Augusto and his father Mario gave guided tours for free to parts of the reserve and locale. In fact being part of the entertainment at the Augusto's son's birthday party was a privilege.
Be warned, there are bugs. I love them! Butterflies and cockroaches in the kitchen, birds in the gardens. Others you may not be keen on include millions of ants, leafcutters mostly.
One final thought, Access is via a basket zipwire across the large river. Brilliant fun!
So, as you may be able to tell, I loved each day of my stay. Each day starting with a 4.30 a.m. walk to a Cock of the Rock lek, which gave very close views of up to five males and three females. I loved the work that I chose to join in with and I loved the company. The open to the air bedrooms are right up my Street, the food was fine by me and the general ethos of the place as an ecological reserve goes with my philosophy on life. If you're expecting full mod cons - go elsewhere. If you want to experience something deeper and more meaningful, this is the place.

If ever you are considering a visit to the Manu and not just a bird-tick fest of mega proportions, then a visit to Chontachaka would be brilliant. Are you brave enough to go down The Manu Road?

On a later visit to the area I was invited to meet the incredible children of the Amazonian forest in The Manu, Peru.

They stay at the Student Shelter called Chaskawasi Manu, which is located in the town of Salvacion, the capital of the Province of Manu (Peru), within the geographical area corresponding to the cultural area of the Manu Biosphere Reserve.

The Manu Biosphere Reserve is located south west of Peru, partially located in the regions of Madre de Dios and Cuzco, in the provinces of Manu and Paucartambo with an area of 1,909,800 hectares is divided into three main areas:

- The National Park, with 1,532,806 hectares.
- Reserved Zone, with 257,000 hectares.
- The Cultural or Transition Zone, with 120,000 hectares.

The Manu National Park was established on May the twenty ninth, 1973. It is located in the departments of Cusco and Madre de Dios.

Manu National Park has been recognized as a World Heritage Site in 1987, and in 1977 UNESCO recognized it as the core of the Biosphere Reserve area.

Manu National Park is part of the great biological diversity of the Amazon. It is likewise one of the most important gene banks worldwide. According to its recent management plan, it contains more than 3,500 registered plant species, many of them still unidentified. The variety of

Manu Wildlife is impressive: 160 species of mammals, more than 1,000 species of birds, 140 species of amphibians, fifty species of snakes, forty species of lizards, six species of turtles, three species of alligators and 210 species of fish.

The Student Shelter Chaskawasi Manu was created with the intention of addressing social and environmental problems, especially among children and adolescents, in the area of Salvation in Manu Biosphere Reserve, Madre de Dios, Peru.

Currently twenty children and adolescents with poor access to education, from Amazonian native and peasant communities are living in our shelter which ensures their access to education, identity and health, so that they can exercise their basic rights of children and adolescents due to them.

A word from the Chaskawasi-Manu project manager, Maria:-

Located in the Manu National Park in Peru, the Chaskawasi –Manu project gives the opportunity for children from deep in the rainforest to get an education.

It gives one a chance to meet, study and enjoy the company of the amazing children and adolescents from remote Amazonian communities.

Two of the students to mention, Yuri is sixteen years old. He is in the final year of high school. He wants to be a forestry engineer and to work to protect the forest in which he has lived with his family, the Manu.

Parari loves animals and it now seems clear his vocation will be with the nature he loves. He can recognise a dozen birds simply by how they beat their wings.

These children spend nine months of the school year at the shelter away from their homes and parents. They need to feel loved, supported by the values of solidarity, generosity and community living as they would in their homes. The children also need food, medicine, transportation, books, notebooks and a long list of basic items that every child in the world needs to go to school. To get this many things we need to do a lot of fund-raising.

The project's main aim is to educate and to give voice to children in a culture excluded from our everyday reality. The forest is the centre of the life of a Matsigenka, their whole way of life, beliefs and culture depend on it. The project looks out from the forest to enrich and teach anyone willing to approach these children. For the cost of a latte or a day trip on public transportation, Yuri can take care of their Amazon rainforest; protect it from illegal logging and preserve the environment of his community. Parari can protect the colourful species of the jungle. The Matsigenka, through the quality education of their children, will continue to live in peace in the land they love. The Manu rainforest we all need will be protected by them.

By making a donation you will support the future of the forest through it's children. The future of the forest depends on it.

To support their work please go to the following website :

http://www.chaskawasi-manu.org/en/

My support of the project comes from my visits there in 2014. To meet and become friends with such incredible children and staff was a tremendous occurrence. The childrens' love of each other and their rainforest shines through their everyday actions and through their commitment to their education. They, these brave and lovely children, spend months away from their families in order to learn how to ambassadors for their way of life and communities. They have dreams and ambitions like all children. Their commitment deserves our support. So please visit their website and meet the children.

It is also to this project that I will be returning to in 2017, once the Biking Birder experience in Europe is finished.

Acorn the parrot was stuck in a drain manhole in Essex and I rescued him, cleaned him up and now he is great friends with both Manu the frog and the new girl aboard the bike, Bobette the Caterpillar. It has been great to see how the three get on with each other!

The Lads on the Bike – (2) Albert the Albatross

The original Albert the Albatross was given to the, previously mentioned and amazing Mya-Rose Craig aka Birdgirl. Back in 2010, when Mya-Rose was seven years old, I met her with her Mum and Dad, Helena and Chris Craig and over an evening meal together I asked Mya-Rose which was her favourite bird. The confident answer of 'Black-browed Albatross' was a surprise. When asked why Mya-Rose stated, "because I saw one!" Mya-Rose had been with Mum and Dad atop the high cliffs at Porthgwarra, Cornwall when a Black-browed Albatross flew by.

I had a cuddly and noisy Black-browed Albatross, like now, on the front of my bike and so he had to go. Mya-Rose still has him, Albert. I managed to get another.

On writing this Mya-Rose is now fourteen years old and in 2015 saw her 4,000th (yes, 4,000!) bird species. Her blog is a pleasure to read, lucid and always entertaining.

As I said, I got another one for the rest of 2010 and gave it away to another incredible young nature lover who birds Upton Warren WWT reserve, Birder Gladys, Mary. You remember the girl who can make a perfect cuckoo call. Mary was there when I finished my 2010 adventure at the same place I started, Upton Warren Nature reserve.

On January the first 2015 Mary was there for my start, once more at

Upton Warren with her father Tim and other Upton regulars. She brought Albert with her to give to me for the journey. He took his place on the front of my bike and is still there. Mary took home someone mentioned in the next part, Mani.

Albert is a symbol of the incredibly successful Save the Albatross campaign.

Please access the following web page to find out more:-

http://www.birdlife.org/worldwide/news/high-seas-heroes-saving-albatrosses-extinction-decade-success

The Lads on the Bike – (3) Ophelia the Orca

Last year, 2015, behind me for the Biking Birder journey, placed atop sleeping bag and tent,was a large mammoth, Mani. He was a gift from my niece Emily and a wonderful addition to the entourage.

For the whole of 2015, a cycling trip of around 9,000 miles, Mani the Mammoth maintained a rather morose presence. Never much conversation, Mani seemed to only come to life whilst we travelled together through the Ice Age sculptured landscapes of Wales and Scotland. He revelled in the huge u-shaped valleys of the Highlands. Wistfully he would sigh as though dreaming of past times. He was an animal from the past with no future.

Let's go back to January the first, 2016. I am at Upton Warren Nature Reserve for the day; a Worcestershire Wildlife Trust treat. Friends are here to see me off yet again, another Biking Birder year begins.

Two of those friends include Tim and Mary, father and daughter. Mary has a new occupant for the bike, an Orca – or in old-speak, a Killer Whale. Wally the Whale, Mary proudly announces but I prefer Oscar the Orca. He is large, black and white and he presents a problem. Where will he fit on the bike?

Mani suggests a solution. He doesn't want to endure a year on the road once more. Last year was enough with roads, cities and sterile farmlands. He wants a quiet life in a place where he can be left to his memories. Mary offers her bedroom and Oscar takes Mani's place atop the sleeping bag and tent.

The journey begins and the first two months have The Biking Birder heading south west, down to Cornwall's Lands End before turning to cycle along the British South coast.

Oscar thrills at the seaside landscapes of the southern counties, from the granite headlands to the Jurassic coast of Dorset. He is hoping to see his cousins; the porpoises and dolphins to which he is related.

In Hampshire, in the New Forest, two of Biking Birder's best friends, Kerry Reynolds and her wonderful, wildlife ambassador son, Dominik, give him an Otter for the bike. Kerry works at the excellent New Forest Wildlife

Park whilst Dominik has received many awards for his superb work for nature.

By the strangest of coincidences the Biking Birder, that is I, finds out during his visit that Oscar the Orca is actually a female Orca! A female stowaway amongst The Lads.

Ophelia the Orca takes her place as usual on the bike. Oscar the Otter is now on the front. By the way, Oscar the Otter has a great rapport with Ricky the Robin. Great to see the friendships and partnerships developing.

Ophelia the Orca is a symbol for the Marine Conservation Society, a charity devoted to improving all habitats and environs around our extensive United kingdom coastline.

From beach cleaning to lobbying for great marine protection zones, the work of the MCS id phenomenal and it is a privilege to have a representative with me to remind me that it is not just terrestrial habitats that need protection.

Whilst I was at Spurn Nature Reserve week before last, I collected each day I was there, a number of carrier bags full of plastic rubbish washed up on the beaches. This I felt was my way of saying thank you to Spurn for the rare birds I saw there. Sadly I am sure that I could do the same every day for a whole year and there would always be more arriving to deal with.

How I would love every birder to do the same; pick up some rubbish every time they go birding. Pick up 3!

I remember meeting a lovely very old lady at Dungeness who says that every day she goes out and collects a plastic carrier bag full of rubbish. Every little action helps.

Maybe a link to Albert the Albatross comes in here. After all so many of his kind are starved to death by the ingestion of plastic particles and discarded pieces.

This September the Marine Conservation Society are having their annual beach clean campaign. Now this coincides with a time that I will be on fair Isle. Last year I cleared a long beach of plastic, mostly one use plastic bottles and discarded fishing tackle. I hope to do the same there this year. Well, no actually I hope to find no plastic on the beaches but expect masses of it.

Don't forget that there are still many others. Each has a reason for being with me. Scaggy the Rabbit (a gift from a close friend, Lee Dark), Colin the Stone Curlew (Weeting Heath Nature Reserve), Ricky the Robin (the RSPB collection box), Oscar the Otter (The New Forest Wildlife Park) and Tigger (My nickname since college days many years ago) are all on the bike. Love them all, which one might feel is a rather sad thing for an ageing Biking Birder to say.

Gordon Barnes

It is now well over the ten year anniversary of the death of the best friend I ever had, Gordon Barnes. The privilege of saying 'friend' will stay with me always.

Sitting here in the Spurn Bird Observatory, having just come across the Fair Isle Bird report for 2006, there is an appreciation of the wonderful man by the respected Nick Riddiford, a previous Warden of the famous Fair Isle Bird Observatory, who knew Gordon very well.

Gordon was a wonderful man. A phenomenal birder with amazing knowledge of birds, as well as a superb botanist. The stories from his life on Fair Isle are legendary and Gordon is still talked about by the crofters there that knew him. From 1960 to 1976, Gordon, originally from my own birth city of Birmingham, lived on Fair Isle. Originally going there as an assistant warden at the Observatory, Gordon was given the croft and land called Setter. Here he met a young National trust volunteer, Perry, married her and together they crofted and had two children, Alan and John. They started the Fair Isle Museum together in their house and according to many on the island, saved Fair Isle with their dedication and extreme hard work.

There is an autobiography available and if you would like a copy then please email the Fair Isle Bird Observatory for a copy or message - email me. It is well worth the read and at £5 plus postage, cheap as chips.

Tonight I am sitting with a brilliant young birder, Dan Branch; a very enthusiastic twenty-one year old and in him I can see reflections of Gordon back when he was that age. I have only faded black and white images of Gordon from then. In 1976 Gordon, Perry and the boys, left to start a new life with a sheep farm in Wales.

I can see Dan having a similar career in birding. He and other 'Next Generation Birders, young RSPB wardens, volunteers and keen unaffiliated youngsters like Jack Bradbury and Mya.Rose Craig, are one of the biggest thrills when meeting them during a Biking Birding experience.

Dan and I have just come back in from an attempt to see whether two Caspian Terns, that we have been told left Gibraltar Point, Lincolnshire at 19:15 heading north, would come past Spurn. They didn't but we did meet the man top of the BOU Year list at the moment on a BUBO listing webpage, Gareth Hughes. Top 'Carbon Twitcher' meets The Biking Birder. I am fourth by the way on that list. Top man, Gareth has seen 295 birds having added the Golden Oriole to his year list yesterday. We met last year when he was seawatching from atop a sand dune in Northumberland. Smashing to talk to, Gareth's enthusiasm for birding and year listing is inspiring.

http://www.bubo.org/Listing/view-all-lists.html?showlists=1,BOU,1,2016,0

Now for Spurn Bird Observatory. For the last three nights I have stayed at Spurn; spending two nights almost alone in the old Bird Observatory building with its artefacts and original furniture, history and ambiance. Last night was spent in the new Bird Obs; a plush modern affair with spacious kitchen, plush lounges with good bird book library and beds with linen and all others without so a sleeping bag is required. WiFi is available here hence the updates. The birding has been generally low key, well it is June and yet I have seen two of the best birds of the year; **Bee-eater** and **Golden Oriole**. So with the list now on **254** I head towards a birthday, and it's a big one, a rest and the EU referendum.

Thinking about monthly targets, and thinking that I need exactly fifty birds to equal Ponc Feliu Latorre's European record of 304. Fifty to go. I wonder how each month will go. So far each month has exceeded expectations and I hope my good luck continues. I can almost taste the record. It's the final countdown.

15th to 17th June **light to fresh N-NW**

Mostly cloudy and cool

15th June

"There be Quail, Captain." A text from Tim Jones tells me that there are Quail around the North Duffield area. I am on my way around lunchtime though leaving the comfort of the new Spurn Bird Observatory is tough. Thanks Spurn, delivered as always. Bee-eater and Golden Oriole added to the list.

Through Hull and along the lanes, I head for North Cave Wetlands reserve,a superb Yorkshire Wildlife Trust reserve with gravel pits and Black-headed Gull nesting on every island.

Leaving a hide I meet a scout troop that have been doing some conservation work. Their leader and a local birder, Barry tell me that there is a probable Lesser Scaup on the other side of the reserve. I head that way after looking at Mediterranean Gulls amongst the many Black-heads. Interesting to see how mature the Black-headed Gull chicks are here. There are lots and some have fledged already.

Once around the north side I meet two Garys. There won't be many times when such an occurrence will occur again, three Garys together. A recent news item predicts that the name will be extinct in the future as no one is naming their child such a magnificent name any more. So, with North cave's highest lister, Gary; Yorkshire highest 2016 year lister, Garry and myself, Britain's highest Green lister, we look for the Lesser Scaup. Unfortunately it has flown and Gary, the local, is not sure of it's full credentials anyway. Seems there is too much white on the upper wing and it may be a little too large. He has told me that there is a nearby spot that has had Quail in the past and so, as the other two go in search of the maybe rare American duck, I head for a nearby ridge and camp there for the night hoping to hear the resonant 'wet-my-lips' call.

I don't.

16th June

There is a metal bench conveniently placed at this remote spot and after packing away the tent, I lie on it hoping that any Quail will call. Once more they don't but I do hear Skylarks, Corn Buntings, Yellowhammers and Yellow Wagtails whilst lying with eyes closed.

I fall asleep.

There is another possible Quail site not too far away, as one was reportedly heard there the previous evening. I therefore head for North Cliffe wood.

It all looks a bit like a needle in a haystack as there are a lot of possible fields with high crops that could conceal a Quail or two. I start to stop and give each field a few minutes before moving onto the next.

At one particularly large barley field I think I have heard one call and so stop and push the bike the length of the long field. No joy.

Now I am still in an area ten miles or so before the one mentioned by Tim Jones and so I decide to head that way.

Half a mile or so later I think I have heard a Quail. I stop beside a large barley field at a junction with a road that heads down to Carr Farm.

Wet-my-lips! **Quail** UTB. It calls four times and like so many times when I have listened to them in the past, that's it. A few years ago I lived in a VW-LT35 campervan. I remember clambering onto the top of my van with a deckchair and sitting up there for a whole evening. I was hoping to see one of the three Quail calling in a large field of tall grass awaiting cutting. I still haven't seen a Quail in Britain.

I text The Oracle with the news and location details for Rare Bird Alert. Bird number **255**.

I set off for Wheldrake Ings, yet another Yorkshire Wildlife Trust reserve near to York. I had visited here the day after the RSPB Member's Weekend back at the beginning of April. Then there were large areas of flooded fields and the river was in spate. Now it is lush, the meadows are dry and green and the trees and bushes leaf laden. Banded Demoiselles and Blue-tailed Damselflies flutter along the pathway and the occasional Willow and Sedge warbler sings. A peaceful afternoon and evening alone walking around this extensive reserve.

17th June to York

In York I find a cycle shop and hear that the bike will probably be in need of too much of a repair. A replacement bike will have to be found. A crash back in November 2015 has left its legacy and the frame is ruined at the front. How I would love to throw the bike at the car driver who hit me back in Aberdeenshire last year! I had half expected this news and leave the bike for Andy, the shop owner to do his best.

I wander through the streets of York, buy a ticket for the train back to Worcestershire and head to York library. I am having a 'carbon day' to go back to my constituency and parent's house in Worcestershire, to vote in the coming EU Referendum.

I am meeting my daughter, Rebecca this evening at York Station, for the journey back to my parents' house and so have a few hours to fill.

Horrific news filters through, about the Labour MP Jo Cox being murdered. The hatred displayed by too many during this EU campaign fills me with despair. A few days ago, when I was cycling towards Spurn, a crowd of Leave supporters were gathered by a dual carriageway asking for support. Their vile, foul-mouthed comments on hearing of my desire for us to Remain in the EU cannot be printed here.

3 day mileage . . 163.62 miles

Biking Birder Monthly targets for the rest of 2016

My Green BOU (British Ornithological Union) Year List is currently 256, which includes a heard only Quail. Now to beat Ponc Feliu Latorre, who holds the European Green Year List record at the moment with 304, I need forty nine more. Now to non-birders this may seem a particularly small number, especially when one considers that there is still six months left. This is not the case. Other than a few British breeding birds I have yet to see and some birds only found in Scotland, that I will detail in a minute, the available birds in the coming months will be those incredible ones that are vagrants. These are rare birds in British terms that have got lost either by a process caused reverse migration or through the action of weather conditions that have forced them away from their normal migration route. Some of these birds, such as Yellow-browed Warblers, are virtually guaranteed if one is on a certain famous island during September and October. Despite originating from their summer breeding grounds in Siberia and migrating in our direction, in good years hundreds of these beautiful, small lost waifs end up in Britain.

Then there are the super rarities, the birds that are so rare that planes would be chartered by the fanatical few, the mega twitchers after a mega.

An American magnolia warbler on a cliff face on Fair Isle was such a bird. A Cape May Warbler on Unst, Shetland and the legendary Golden-winged Warbler in Maidstone, Kent are two others. The latter caused the biggest twitch ever to be seen in Britain when thousands of twitchers descended on a modern housing estate on the outskirts of the town in 1989 trying to see the bird. It was chaos! The locals couldn't drive for the crush of birders. Buses couldn't get through.

I was there with birding friends a couple of days later after the initial rush. A freezing cold day, it took seven hours of searching with by now a much reduced crowd, yet still around a hundred or so. At one point we had retreated into the warmth of a large Tesco store's café only to have a birder rush in shouting "it's here!" Leaving our food on the tables, we rushed out to find that it was a Waxwing. Nice but not the mega bird.

We eventually saw this incredible small warbler on a cotoneaster bush that surrounded the door of a small town house. One of the Birding Clams, Ian Crutchley had found it that day. UTB. Under the belt and one that will probably remain a mega blocker to anyone who didn't see it. That is the chances of another one occurring here are extremely slim. Will another cargo ship coming up the Thames after a cross Atlantic trip bring one in?

Actually, unknown to all birders there who had the Golden-winged, there was nearby another American warbler, a Common Yellowthroat at the same time as the Golden-winged but the information on that was suppressed until it had gone.

Back to now.

What follows are the details of the bird species that either are available or statistically will or may be available for me to cycle to and add to the year list.

This time last year I knew I wasn't going to beat 300 let alone beat Ponc. This year I am confident that the 300 figure will be beaten. All I have to do is keep pedalling.

I return to the road on Friday after having collected the bike from the cycle shop where major repairs are, hopefully, being carried out. If the bike is beyond repair then a new one will have to be bought. Whatever the outcome I will be heading for a woodland near Scarborough to try for Honey Buzzards.

There follows a long cycle to an area in Northumberland. I need to get here as fast as possible as there is a very rare Bonaparte's Gull that has been seen for the last few weeks. I missed the Boney's available in Devon earlier in the year, despite spending a few days searching for it and obviously this bird would be a major addition to the list. Just up the coast from this bird there is a colony of Roseate Terns, a very rare British breeder. My problem here is that they are on a small island offshore, Coquet Island, a RSPB reserve. I will need to see them from the opposite shore as I am not allowed to take a boat out to see them. No carbon in this case. Anyone got a canoe?

So for June, who's original target number of year ticks was five, I may end up seeing ten!

July Targets – Scotland (Mull and Cairngorms/Abernethy)

Ten birds : **Osprey, Black Guillemot, Hooded Crow, Rock Dove, White-tailed Eagle, Golden Eagle, Crested Tit, Ptarmigan, Capercaillie and King Eider**

In 2010 I had the good fortune of seeing a Pacific Golden Plover during this month. Last year the unexpected bird was a Spotted Crake heard on Coll, so maybe another surprise may occur . . or two.

August Targets – Orkney (North Ronaldsay)

Ten birds hopefully including **Storm Petrel, Sooty Shearwater, Icterine Warbler and Wryneck**

For August I enter the world of the rare lost migrant, excepting a few regular seabirds. Staying at the beautifully located North Ronaldsay Bird Observatory, where there is an excellent hostel, I expect to spend hours in the seawatching hide on the north-east coast of the island.

September Targets – Fair Isle

Ten birds including the almost certain to see **Yellow-browed Warbler, Common Rosefinch, Barred Warbler, Little Bunting, Bluethroat and Barnacle Goose**

The return to Paradise. I adore Fair Isle. The people, the landscape and of course the birds. The perfect combination of magical elements that come together every Autumn with rarities in every wet ditch, amongst dry stone walls, clinging to vertiginous cliffs or in the hands of the supreme Bird Observatory staff after having been caught in a mist net or Heligoland trap.

Using old Fair Isle bird reports I have created a spreadsheet to not only see what birds have turned up in the last eleven years but also work out the chances of them being there this year. [see appendix . . . .]

The statistics also give an average for the number of possible year ticks for this month. That figure stands at nineteen! The maximum number of year ticks for me would occur with a repeat of the birds of September 2006. That year would have netted me twenty five year ticks, including Yellow-breasted Bunting and Aquatic Warbler.

September 2009 would only have given me twelve year ticks. This would still be more than my target number of ten though. Confidence is high.

There is also **Mealy Redpoll** and associated races. I will not be counting any I see on the European list although I will on the British. The different listing authorities treat the bird differently. With BOU Mealy is a species; with AERC it isn't.

Then there are the more than 50:50 birds: Pectoral Sandpiper, Citrine Wagtail, Red-breasted Flycatcher, Olive-backed Pipit and.....

Lanceolated Warbler. Yes this amazing mega has occurred in six years out of eleven years.

As well as these there have actually been forty eight other bird species seen over these years. By the way, add Twite to the list. There are good numbers of these on Fair Isle.

October Targets – First week Shetland followed by the rest of month back on Fair Isle.

Ten birds including some sure to be incredible surprises whilst mopping up some of the not so rare migrants that didn't occur in September. Siberian Rubythroat would be good.

The Birding Clams, the great group of birding friends, are coming to Shetland for their annual birding fix. If the weather allows the Good Shepherd to sail back to South Shetland, I will go and see my best birding friends, Jason, Steve, Tony, Rob and Martin. Adam will be sorely missed but how wonderful that he will be concentrating on a wedding to the beautiful Nadia. Two incredible birders destined to be together will be celebrating their marriage with a honeymoon in Costa Rica. All the very best to you both. My plan is really to stay around South Shetland but that might change if a mega turns up elsewhere on the wonderful islands. A lifer on Unst might tempt me to undertake the two to three day trek north; especially if The Fife Birding crew are there at that time.

Once The Birding Clams leave then it is back to Fair Isle for the rest of the month.

Once again I have done a spreadsheet of possible birds and probabilities for the month. [see appendix . . . .]

Without omitting the most likely September year ticks, there is an average of eighteen year ticks over the years. The same most likely birds as the previous month dominate the table, adding Little Auk and Waxwing later in the month, which both have a more than 50:50 chance of occurring. As well as the top thirteen there are another eighteen bird species that have turned up. These include good chances for Siberian Rubythroat, Short-toed Lark, White's Thrush and Arctic Redpoll. Now wouldn't a tame 'snowball', Hornemann's Arctic Redpoll be great?

November Targets – Scotland

Five birds

Target bird, Bean Goose, should be a gimme with flocks around the Falkirk area, especially the RSPB reserve at Fannyside. With by now hopefully less than ten birds required to reach 300, the task will be to get to any birds available. Snow Goose? Blue-winged Teal or Ring-necked Duck somewhere; I do hope so.

December Targets – Who knows? Back in England and back towards The Midlands, eventually.

Five birds

I have already had some of the major Winter birds; Shore Lark and Rough-legged Buzzard for instance. If the Pallid Harrier returns to Norfolk I might head that way. So whatever I need I will go for.

Finally, just to wet my appetite for the rest of the year, here is a list of the best rarities I saw from last year, 2015 that I haven't seen yet this year. Some probably will be listed before the end. Some it would be miraculous if I saw them again : Chestnut Bunting! Arctic Warbler, Red-flanked Bluetail, Blyth's Reed Warbler, Chestnut Bunting, Citril Finch, Radde's Warbler, Citrine Wagtail, Subalpine Warbler, Moltoni's Warbler, King Eider, Lanceolated Warbler, Laughing Gull, Siberian Rubythroat, Little Bunting, Night Heron, Ortolan Bunting, Pallas' Grasshopper Warbler and Pallid Harrier.

Sunday 26th June **Very light N**

After my few days rest, during which I celebrate my 60th birthday with my family and vote Remain in the EU referendum, I cry over the result and I am soon back on the road heading north from York.

The bike has been serviced and repaired, despite the dire prediction from the bike shop when leaving the bike there and I reach Thirsk on Saturday evening and camp.

Nine hours solid sleep, I cycle on Sunday to Blackhall Colliery. I have been feeling very low due to the EU referendum result yet three things occur along the way that brings me back to my usual optimistic, happy self.

I call in at the superb RSPB Saltholme nature reserve again, north of Middlesborough and meet a lovely couple who share my feelings and opinions over the referendum. Talking about it with like-minded people is therapeutic. Refreshed by a drink in the visitor centre café, I continue north through the land of the Monkey Hangers, Hartlepool. OK, this needs to be explained.

Legend has it that during the Napoleonic Wars of the early 19th century, a shipwrecked monkey was hanged by the people of Hartlepool, believing him to be a French spy! To this day, people from Hartlepool are affectionately known as 'Monkey Hangers'.

A French ship was spotted floundering and sinking off the Hartlepool coast. Suspicious of enemy ships and nervous of possible invasion, the good folk of Hartlepool rushed down to the beach, where amongst the wreckage of the ship they found the only survivor, the ship's monkey, which was apparently dressed in a miniature military-style uniform.

Hartlepool is a long way from France and most of the populace had never met, or even seen, a Frenchman. Some satirical cartoons of the time pictured the French as monkey-like creatures with tails and claws, so perhaps the locals could be forgiven for deciding that the monkey, in its uniform, must be a Frenchman, and a French spy at that. There was a trial to ascertain whether the monkey was guilty of spying or not; however, not unsurprisingly, the monkey was unable to answer any of the court's questions and was found guilty. The townsfolk then dragged him into the town square and hanged him.

So is the legend true? Did the good folk of Hartlepool really hang a poor defenceless monkey?

There could perhaps be a darker side to the tale – maybe they didn't actually hang a 'monkey' but a small boy or 'powder-monkey'. Small boys were employed on warships of this time to prime the canons with gunpowder and were known as 'powder-monkeys'.

Over the centuries the legend has been used to taunt the residents of Hartlepool; indeed still today, at football matches between local rivals Darlington and Hartlepool United the chant, "Who hung the monkey" can often be heard. Most Hartlepudlians however love this story. Hartlepool United's mascot is a monkey called H'Angus the Monkey, and the local Rugby Union team Hartlepool Rovers are known as the Monkeyhangers.

The successful mayoral candidate in the 2002 local elections, Stuart Drummond, campaigned dressed in the costume of H'Angus the Monkey, using the election slogan "free bananas for schoolchildren", a promise he was unfortunately unable to keep. However this appears not to have dented his popularity, as he went on to be re-elected two more times. Whatever the truth, the legend of Hartlepool and the hanged monkey has endured for over 200 years. Great story!

Eventually in warm, sunny weather, I reach Blackhall Colliery, a small town along the coastal road towards Sunderland. A woman with two young seven year old boys waves me down, having herself parked in a lay-by. They want to give me a donation having passed me and seen the collection cans and 'friends' on the bike. Hence I meet Jac and his Mum, Zoey with Jac's friend, Lennon, who proudly tells me that he was named after John Lennon and so was his Dad, John! They were from nearby Hesledon and give me a small furry cuddly for the bike. It looks like a small Tribble from an old Star Trek episode. The boys name it Maximore. I am unsure of it's gender!

As I cycle on up a slight incline a gentleman gestures to me asking whether I need a drink. Hence I meet the lovely Jan and Ron. An hour or so I spend in their lovely home, enjoying a coffee with them and a chat. Ron used to be an electrician in the coal mines, back when such things existed in Britain. He talks of the train that went seven miles out under the North Sea, taking the miners out to the coal face. A fabulous couple, so kind of them to help a stranger.

By now it is early evening and rain has started to fall. I pass a large, rough-looking pub and ask whether they do bed and breakfast. Immediately I am surrounded by a few loud and in your face tough lads. The bike is carried inside into the bar and the girl behind the counter tries to ascertain what I want through the loud music blaring out. The lads one by one try out their strength in lifting the bike. As each lad expresses their opinion over each one's strength, they each put coins into the collection boxes and ask what I am up to. Salt of the earth I believe the expression might be, I eventually manage to get upstairs to a superb bedroom. Newly furbished, it is comfortable with bath in a large bathroom. Perfect.

Three occasions of kindness restore faith in humanity. I sleep happier than of late. Personally though I will state from now on that I am European in the future.

An evening email from The Oracle:-

Revised following departure of Musselbrough King Eider and St Abb's Woodchat and arrival of WW Scoter.

Sun 26/06 - leave Thirsk (75 miles)
Mon 27/06 afternoon - arrive Ashington; get BONEPARTE'S GULL
Tuesday 28/06 - leave for Amble
(13 miles)
Tuesday afternoon - get ROSEATE TERN and stay in area that night
Wed 29/06 early - leave for Grangemouth
(118 miles)
Sat 03/07 late - secure GULL-BILLED TERN and start journey to Oban
(121 miles)

Tues 05/07 midday - arrive Oban with a detour via Loch Lockmond for WOOD WARBLER

Wed 06/07 - late ferry to Mull (unknown mileage depending how easy GOLDEN and WHITE-TAILED EAGLES are)

Mon 11/07 - ferry back from Mull

Detour to Coll / Tiree IF Spot Crakes are confirmed and you still need

Monday 11/07- head to Abernethy

(110 miles via Laggan)

Thurs 14/07- arrive Boat of Garten (or similar)

Fri 15/07>Thurs 21/7 - allow a 7 days for CRESTED TIT / OSPREY / PTARMIGAN / CAPERCAILLE

Fri 22/7 - head off for Aberdeen via Murcar for WHITE-WINGED SCOTER and Ythan Estuary for KING EIDER

(96 miles)

Tues 26/7 - arrive Aberdeen

Tues 26/7 late - catch ferry to Kirkwall

Monday 27th June **Fresh N to strong W**

After a massive Full English breakfast I am off into a fresh northerly wind heading north. It is about time this weather changed, that is I would love to have a wind behind me for a change. I know I keep asking for this sort of thing but bear with me, it is tough when one cycles into the wind day after day.

Through Sunderland and South Shields, over the Tyne to North Shields, I take a road north to the A189. Cycling along the busy dual carriageway I reach the high bridge over the Wansbeck Estuary. Taking the bike down the precipitous grassy slope beside the bridge down to the water's edge, I arrive at the spot where a Bonaparte's Gull has been seen for some time now. You may remember that I had dipped out on a Bonaparte's down on the Exe Estuary, Devon back in January. I had spent four days searching for that bird.

I scan along the shoreline. It takes seconds to see it. Black-headed Gull, OK...... oh there it is..... **Bonaparte's Gull** on the list, bird number **257**. A great addition to the year list, the bird wades along the water's edge quite nearby and occasionally flies for a while before always returning to the same spot.

After an hour or so and after enjoying some tea whilst watching it, I continue north to Cresswall Ponds and enjoy watching Avocets, Dunlin and Curlew as the strong, now westerly, wind blows.

Tuesday 28th June **Light W**

An early morning of glorious sunshine has me on top of a sand dune looking over to Coquet Island, another RSPB reserve which has nesting Roseate Terns. Out over the bay there are plenty of terns yet there is no way I can be totally convinced that any of them were Roseates. None of them come close and I decide to try the harbour and adjacent rocks at nearby Amble. Arctic Terns are here and a few Sandwich Terns too but still no Roseates. I retire to a café for lunch.

Back on the beach again in the afternoon, by now rain is falling yet my hopes are still high as the tide is very low and I can get a lot nearer to the island.

A figure appears on the distant sand dunes and proceeds to walk towards me. Gareth Hughes! Brilliantly Gareth had decided to do some tern watching whilst on the way to Aberdeen. A bit of a detour on the way to see a White-winged Scoter at Aberdeen but here he is and almost immediately a **Roseate Tern** flies over our heads. Bird number **258** and a witness to witness the event.

Rain falls, we watch and then walk to some nearby freshwater pools, hoping that some Roseates would head there to wash. Indeed a couple of Roseate Terns are there.

After this we eat fish and chips together and talk bird listing.

Wednesday 29th June **Light SW**

A day with my daughter, Rebecca, we head together for The Farne Islands in a hire car. Yes, I am having another carbon day and any birds I see cannot be counted on my Green Birding Big Year list. How strange to be travelling north in a carbon-fuelled vehicle and along roads that I will have to cycle along tomorrow.

Onto a Billy Shiels boat at 10 o'clock, we head out to the Outer Islands, to islands I have never been to before. The Birding Clams and I came this way a couple of years ago to see a very rare Bridled Tern but that was on the Inner Farnes. This time we are to stand on an island free of head-pecking Arctic Terns. Instead there are thousands of very close Guillemots with good numbers of Puffins and Kittiwakes. Shags, Razorbills, various gulls, Rock Pipits and Oystercatchers are also here in smaller numbers. All the birds are so close and not bothered at all by the close proximity of the milling people.

Back to Alnwick with rain pouring, we visit Barter's Bookshop and meet up with Rebecca's wonderful boyfriend, Les. Coffee and cake, the best flapjack of the year, they buy me a book, The Big Year by Mark Obmascik; the book of the story made into a film, The Big Year of the Big Year of

1998. The story of three carbon twitchers. I wonder if Green Birders will ever make it into a book and a film? Maybe me! I wonder which actor will be chosen to play The Biking Birder. A Norman Wisdom-type would suffice. Don't laugh at me, for I'm a fool.

Thursday 30th June **Fresh W**

Breakfast is in the beautiful dining room of The Sun Hotel. Zoey, the staff member, is one of those wonderful sunshine people that it is so great to meet every so often. Zoey tells me of her passion for rubber ducks. She has over 500 of them! I give her my enamel badge of one.

On the road north the sun is shining and the way isn't too bad. In fact it is stunningly beautiful with views of castles and Holy Island passed. Bamburgh Castle must be one of the best sights and sites in Britain.

North of here a cycling American, Beau, stops me for a chat. He is brash and confident and laughs about the condition of the cycle path, Route 1 that he has just followed south of Berwick. I know it well. Last year the cycle path disappeared into a field of cows and mud. Beau is from Florida but works as a ski instructor in Montana. Fascinating man.

I reach the cycle path that Beau had mentioned and find sheep there this time. No tarmac or grit, just a six inch wide mud pathway to negotiate. It reminds me of those death-defying cycle pathways that are high in the mountains. Videos of death-defying cyclists are so popular on Youtube.

Reaching a tarmac road once more after a couple of miles of sheep dung laden dirt, I hear a Quail. Stopping I try to ascertain where exactly the bird is calling from and text a message to Jason Oliver, a Birding Clam, to ask him to alert Rare Bird Alert.

Later I miss a turn of the cycle route and end up on the A1. This takes me to Berwick where I stop for the night. Finding a Bed and Breakfast I find that the bumpy cycle way has snapped the back pannier rack. I will have to do something about that in the morning.

I am asleep by eight.

The target for June was five so I am thrilled to have seen nine. The Green Year list now stands at **258**, twenty one ahead of last year at this stage.

Statistics for June 2016 :

Green Year list	258 birds
Year ticks in June	9
Bird species had, not seen in 2015	4
Mileage in June	719.88 miles

Total mileage for the year	4,985.05 miles
average mileage on days cycled	39.99 miles
elevation : up	17,564 feet
: down	17,522 feet

Best Birds *:* ***Greenish Warbler, Red-necked Phalarope, Bee-eater, Little Bittern, Golden Oriole, Bonaparte's Gull, Roseate Tern, Quail.***

7

JULY

O ye'll tak' the high road, and I'll tak' the low road, And I'll be in Scotland a'fore ye, But me and my true love will never meet again, On the bonnie, bonnie banks o' Loch Lomond.

Unknown author, lyric from The Bonnie Banks o' Loch Lomond.

Friday 1st July **Fresh E**

Sunny intervals

Kenny, the owner of the B and B, has repaired the snapped rack overnight! Thanks Kenny. The kindness of strangers . . . .

I cycle along the A1 north. Traffic isn't too bad and the wind is mostly from my right, the east.

Into Bonnie Scotland, I will be here for possible five months. Will it be a midge-filled delight of biting insects, spectacular views and incredible birds interlaced with inspirational people. Of course it will, this is SCOTLAND!

After twenty miles or so I reach a cycle path crossroads and with my head down due to strong wind now in my face, I take the Sustrans Cycle Route 1, which is actually a footpath adjacent to the main road. Suddenly it ends with a large fence and looking up, I see extensive road works. All this is opposite Torness Nuclear Power Station.

I cross the road to the cycle path there and two workers in a van come to tell me that I have missed the cycle path closed signs. They advise me to walk to the end of the cones and rejoin a different cycle path. Once there I meet two police officers who check me out and once satisfied that I am genuine, point me in the direction of a cycle path that goes beside fields, far away from the main A1, takes me to Dunbar.

Some way further, with rain falling, I go into a lovely café, Voradani, in East Linton. Mince and tatties (potatoes) for lunch and the best carrot cake I have had in ages. Donations too from the owner, Jane and from a customer, Lynda.

By six o'clock I am shattered and I pitch the tent in long grass beside a field of oilseed rape hidden from the roads by a long line of conifers. A hare and a Roe Deer career off at my arrival.

I am asleep by eight with the book I am reading, The Big Year, still in my hand.

A rather long email from The Oracle to read and think about:-

(Here are my thoughts on the route dilemma. Personally I would stick with what you had originally planned i.e. Mull first then Abernethy then Aberdeen. I imagine the scoter flock will linger for some time. My main concern is that you will need to go to the Hebrides which will add significant miles if you have done Cairngorms first (although time wise it doesn't appear to make much difference). Main considerations are:

(1) Are there pure Rock Doves on Orkney or Shetland? Don't recall seeing any? Presumably easy enough on Lewis?

(2) Is it confirmed there are no Spotted Crake on Coll or Tiree (whichever you saw

them on last year)

(3) Unless there is a bird in Findhorn Valley think you will struggle to tick White-tailed Eagle in east Scotland due to the reintroduction position. If you are not going to tick a perfectly good Marsh Warbler than that should be a no-brainer ;)

(4) Goldies are do-able in Abernethy / Cairngorms but easier on west coast

(5) How easy are eagles on Harris / Lewis?

(6) The new route relies of Wood Warbler being encountered on North Ron or Fair Isle

However the difference time-wise is minimal - there is also an occasional Black Duck near(ish) to Ullapool that comes in play). Have sent message to Gordon Hamlett anyhow re availability of birds in Abernethy / Cairngorms. So the two routes are:

PHIL'S SUGGESTION

Fri 01/07 Leave Berwick (122 miles)

Sun 03/07 Arrive Loch of Lowes - get OSPREY

Mon 04/07 early - leave LoL (96 miles)

Wed 06/07 late - arrive Oban (If detour via Loch Lochmond for WOOD WARBLER then journey increases to 147 miles)

Thurs 07/07 - ferry to Mull

(unknown mileage depending how easy GOLDEN and WHITE-TAILED EAGLES are)

Mon 11/07 - ferry back from Mull

Detour to Coll / Tiree IF Spot Crakes are confirmed and you still need

Tuesday 12/07- head to Abernethy (110 miles via Laggan)

Fri 15/07- arrive Boat of Garten (or similar)

Sat 16/07>Fri 22/7 - allow a 7 days for CRESTED TIT / OSPREY / PTARMIGAN / CAPERCAILLE

Sat 23/07 - head off for Aberdeen (96 miles)

Wed 27/7 - arrive Aberdeen after dropping into Murcar for WHITE-WINGED SCOTER and Ythan Estuary for KING EIDER

Thurs 26/7 late - catch ferry to Kirkwall

GARY'S SUGGESTION

Fri 01/07 - leave Berwick (181 miles)

Mon 04./07 late - arrive Aberdeen

Tues 05/07 - Murcar and Ythan for SCOTER and KING EIDER

Wed 06/07 early - leave Ythan for Abernethy (83 miles)

Fri 08/07 - arrive Boat of Garten

Sat 09/07>Fri 15/07 - allow a 7 days for CRESTED TIT / OSPREY / PTARMIGAN / CAPERCAILLE / OSPREY

Sat 16/07 - set off for Ullapool (84 miles)

Mon 18/07 - arrive Ullapool. Take ferry

Tues 19/07 - allow three days on Lewis / Harris for eagles

Fri 20/07 - take ferry back to Ullapool
Sat 21/07 - leave Ullapool early (120 miles)
Tues 24/07 - arrive Thurso.
Wed 25/07 - catch ferry to Orkney

Either way given you will be nearly stationary in Aug and Sept you might as well push yourself in July, especially if you aim get to Aberdeen first. Scoter will be much easier whilst the twitchers are still visiting in good numbers and have decent (large) scopes as opposed to your pea-shooter. If you can get there in four days that would be great mate!

All the best, Phil

Saturday 2nd July **Strong W**

Heavy rain showers

Early morning, it is raining. The book is unputdownable and I want to stay here for the day.

I get up and pack.

The hare has come back and doesn't run off as I approach.

Eventually it does and the day's cycling begins. The wind is strong and westerly and I am heading west. Around every hour or so a heavy shower passes by as I shelter beneath trees waiting for them to pass.

Through Edinburgh, and after being stopped by a young man eager to make a donation, Jethro, who runs a RSPB Phoenix group locally and does bat and bird surveys for a living, I find the cycle path out of the city that takes me to the Firth of Forth Suspension Bridge. To the west the new cable stay bridge has three large sections yet to be joined up to each other. To the east the railway bridge looks as magnificent as ever. I cross over the bridge for the first time on a Biking Birder trip and reach Rosyth.

<u>Last two days</u> **:- 76.6 miles 3111 feet up elevation 3055 feet down**

Sunday 3rd July **Very strong W**

Heavy rain for most of the day

I am in a bed and breakfast and appreciate the comfort. The weather outside is pretty appalling and I have chosen to have a rest day to gather my thoughts and recharge the leg batteries.

I try to think positively about the coming months. Aesthetically these will be the most beautiful with the Scottish Islands and Highlands providing the backdrop to my cycling days. The birds will be incredible with the autumn migration months to be spent on North Ronaldsay, Orkney, Shetland and Fair Isle.

Before then there are target birds to get on the Scottish Mainland and Mull:-

Black Guillemot, Hooded Crow, White-tailed Eagle, Golden Eagle, Crested Tit, Capercaillie, Ptarmigan. Osprey, Rock Dove and Wood Warbler

There may be a chance of a Spotted Crake and at the moment there are two rare ducks near Aberdeen; King Eider and an extremely rare, I need it for my Life List, White-winged Scoter. This last one is a vagrant from America. Ten birds you will remember is the target for July.

So after a week that has seen me cycle over 250 miles, 261 to be exact with an elevation up of 8,498 feet, I awake this morning feeling a tad tired.

I don't think I have ever talked about the physical aspect of the trip, the actual wear and tear (tears!) that cycling almost every day as far as possible or necessary does to me.

Every day is painful. I never know exactly where the pain will be but the usuals are my knees, my thighs and especially my hands. The heavy weight of the bike, with it's panniers, tent, sleeping bag and entourage, ensures that I can only go at around eight to ten miles an hour, so try to imagine six to eight hours plus that I manage every day.

The weather over this last week hasn't been kind. Nearly every day there has been wind in my face and the last two days have been particularly tough with a fresh to strong westerly. According to the forecast today's wind will be the same.

Oh well . . . . .

Monday 4th July **fresh to strong W/WSW**

Heavy rain, 12C

Setting off from Forsyth, I cycle to Stirling via an old bridge over the Forth. An uneventful day of head down into the wind, a stop in a wooden bus shelter for lunch, a dry off and a read of The Big Year.

I stop cycling early once I reach Doune where, having crossed the river, I find a beech-covered footpath. Here I erect my tent and read before sleep.

30.95 miles **972 feet elevation up** **942 feet down**

Tuesday 5th July **Fresh W**

Cloudy 12 – 14C

Up early and off towards Callander along the busy A84, I stop for some cherries for breakfast at the start of a cycle path, route seven, that takes me for the first part along a disused railway track. Good quality tarmac in places, the cycle route proceeds away from the main road and into the hills of The Trossachs. A beautiful way along which I meet some wonderful people. Eric and his very chatty, can't get a word in sideways, wife, a retired couple from Somerset who, despite age and arthritis, walk from Callender to the next village north. I push the bike to walk slowly with them and enjoy her conversation.

After fifteen or so miles the path zig zags its way up a steep high bracken-covered hill. At one corner I am confronted by a mother with three children. She is delighted to meet me and I am sure quite surprised. Vicki, the Mum's name says that they have just seen an article about me in the teenage RSPB's magazine, Wingbeat. Badges for the children and chat and fun, a selfie for Facebook and a small green caterpillar with a yellow face, we eventually say goodbye after a rendition of the Duck Song. Thanks Jenna! Lily, the oldest was the only child who would hold the caterpillar. Alexander, the energetic and cheeky youngest, dropped it as soon as it was on his hand. It is a lovely meeting and I continue on my way pushing the bike up the hill.

After a half a mile or so I can hear someone shouting. A young man on a mountain bike stops me and passes me my coat. I had dropped it at the spot where I met the family. Inside it was my wallet with all my plastic and driving license, RSPB bird badges and a couple of Bounty chocolate bars. I am grateful for his honesty but he is off before I can ask his name.

A stop for lunch at Balquhidder, sitting on a stone wall with a view to misty mountains and hills funnelling a large loch. I continue along the route seven and am stopped by a very young effervescent girl who is practically dancing along with two women. The woman aren't dancing but they are enjoying the walk as their child prances towards me. She has an ox eye daisy in her hand and she proudly says to me, "I've got a flower." "It's beautiful," I reply.

"You can have it."

This is such a wonderful moment that I am quite emotional about receiving such a precious gift. I carefully place the daisy next to Oscar the Otter on the front of the bike as the little girl dances off. "I gave that man my flower," I hear her say as the trio walk off.

Back on the main road to Crainlarich, there is no room at the Youth Hostel there; just a rather rude, very abrupt receptionist.

Twelve miles later, with my tent up once more, I am comfortable beside a small river and asleep soon after.

51.66 miles **2961 feet elevation up** **2613 feet down**

An email from Vicki has a photograph attached and a message:-

Hi, It was great to meet up with you on the road to Strathyre today. We all had a fabulous time chatting with you - you made our day. Hope you have a good evening at Crianlarich and onwards to Mull. Vicki

Wednesday 6th July **Light to fresh W**

Heavy rain!

The early morning is dry and after packing up and after a conversation with a lovely German lady from Munich about the EU and Brexit, I head off towards Oban.

It soon starts to rain and the rain gets heavier as my progress along the main road takes me towards my goal. Along Loch Awe I search for Osprey having seen them here in 2010. No luck I continue on my way until a wooden bus shelter, how I love them, offers me a dry place for some late lunch. I phone the Youth Hostel in Oban and yes, there is one last bed available.

I arrive there a couple of hours later soaked to the skin in the trouser department. My torso is dry which surprises me as I had thought my coat wouldn't be waterproof enough for this sort of downpour.

The year list at this time has had a new wet and bedraggles addition to it, five **Hooded Crows** were sitting on a branch of a cherry tree just a mile before the town. Birds had been few and far between since Callander with meadow pipits being the most commonly seen bird. No Corvids until this group, they are the first of the four target birds that have brought me over here. The next target bird is sitting on the low tide water in front of the hostel, **Black Guillemots**, the comical black seabird with white wing panels and over large reddish-orange feet. **260** achieved with almost no effort. Who am I kidding? One hundred and thirteen miles cycled in the last three days, surely that's enough effort to allow me such easy rewards. Now for the eagles!

The hostel is full of German teenagers and a group of them sit with me for the evening; in fact two girls, Julia and Anja sit with me until midnight, telling me about their Russian ancestry and talking about the EU referendum and life in general. Julia wants to be a computer artist. She is passionate about the artwork that can be achieved for multi-levelled games and programs. The quieter of the two girls wants to be a psychiatrist. How good to see that not one of the group of around twenty students has a mobile or a tablet out. All are involved in the age old art of conversation.

30.6 miles **1623 feet elevation up** **2181 feet down**

Thursday 7th July **fresh SW**

Showers and mostly cloudy

An early morning taking carbon transport, a ferry, that takes me over to Craignure, Mull. Seabirds on the way include forty seven Manx Shearwaters, mostly sitting on the water.

Once on the road south and west of the harbour I soon reach the first seawater inlet at Gorton. Scanning the distant wooded hill I can see a huge **White-tailed Sea Eagle**; bird number **261** and the first of the hoped for eagles. Now to find Golden Eagles, hopefully.

The road starts to go up and I have to push the bike up a hill through a conifer forest. After a dip and another rise, a car has two birders standing beside it motioning for me to have a look and a chat. Martin, a Northern Irish birder from Carrickfergus is with his grandson, Dylan. They show me their camera screen. A large overflying Golden Eagle fills the frame. They delight in saying it flew over my head! I remove my helmet for the uphill struggles.

The road continues through high-sided mountain passes and a policewoman in a police van stops me. PC Claire tells me that just a few miles further is a place where I will see Golden Eagles. I just hope she's right. Actually Claire doesn't seem to mind stopping traffic in order to tell me this.

Time goes on and with the pressure mounting to find the Goldies, I see a large bird carrying sticks flying overhead. It disappears behind a rocky crag and comes out again before landing. **Golden Eagle**, bird number **262** onto the list, I can relax and watch the close spectacle. There are two of them sitting on a ledge and I can hear the chips of a hungry youngster nearby. An excited lady stops her campervan to come and have a look, M.A. From Edinburgh tells me that she is a RSPB member and goes to the Edinburgh RSPB local group.

I go a little further along the road as I can see a couple with a telescope. Katherine and Mick are from Wigton, Cumbria and Mick gives a running commentary as the eagles sit on their ledge. The young eaglet can just be seen in a dark smiley-shaped cave some way from it's parents. This is the first time I have ever seen eagles at such a close nest site and an hour or so passes quickly. This is obviously a well known spot as a wildlife tour minibus stops here as well.

The hostel tonight is full of a different mass of German teenagers. They are from Berlin and memories of my time with my daughter, Rebecca there a few years ago has me listening to The Ramones for the evening. Why The Ramones? Well the best museum dedicated to the band is in Berlin.

The Green Year list now stands at **262**, twenty five ahead of last year at this stage.

27.01 miles **1938 feet elevation up and down**

Saturday 9th July **Light S - AM**

Dull, misty to very thick fog, drizzle

7:30 a.m. - I am sitting on the ferry that takes one to the wonderful Hebridean Island of Coll, which lies north west of Mull. The trip takes just under three hours. The ferry is unable dock at Coll due to very thick fog and is carrying on to the next island Tiree. Standing on the aft deck, it is sad to see pieces of plastic floating in what sea I can see. Nicer to see Manx Shearwaters sitting on the water before skittering off into the fog.

The Captain has posted three staff members at the front of the boat as he inches his way towards Coll harbour. Visibility has slightly improved but still great care is taken as rocky reefs and buoys are passed.

Once off the ferry in the afternoon I cycle to the RSPB reserve at the south west corner of the island. The rain is heavy but at least there is only a light north easterly.

A female Hen Harrier is quartering the moorland despite the rain. Four **Rock Doves**, real ones not the tatty feral pigeons back in England, fly past becoming Bird Number **263** on the Year list.

Into the RSPB visitor's centre with it's sandy floor, to dry off and have some late lunch. No chairs, I sit on a plastic box full of leaflets and read a book my Dad has given me, ***My father and Other – Working Class Football Heroes*** by Gary Imlach. I read about Gary's footballing father, Stewart Imlach and his part in Nottingham Forest's FA Cup Final victory in 1959. A very emotional read and almost unputdownable.

Unfortunately I am feeling very tired and I close the book, put my head in my hands resting against the wall and fall asleep.

Awake again, the rain has stopped but a strong south easterly has sprung up. I walk around the machair, that special flower rich habitat so well known on the Hebridean islands. Immediately I hear a Corncrake crexing . . . . crex crex . . . . crex crex........

Two Snipe are drumming in the dull skies and Meadow Pipits are on fence posts. The latter are soon dispersed when a superb grey with black wing tipped male Hen Harrier flies past.

Down to the beach I look at a good number of Pyramidal Orchids on the way. It is a very low tide and rocky outcrops stretch out into a calm sea; the area being sheltered on this the north west side of the island.

Back at the visitor's centre I talk to the RSPB warden. The bird I had hoped for, Spotted Crake is not present. There had been one a number of weeks back but it hadn't been heard whipping since. Oh well, it was worth the effort.

Last year I came to the reserve on my tour of all of the 232 RSPB reserves and was surprised when on arriving I immediately heard a Spotted Crake. Shame history hasn't repeated itself but you can't win them all.

I start to head back to the ferry and whilst walking into the strong wind a couple of **Twite** land on a fence nearby; Bird number **264**.

More Corncrakes are calling as I walk the flat road by the island's airport.

By now the strong wind is behind me which makes a pleasant change. The ride back to the harbour is quickly done with a stop to watch a pair of Red-throated Divers on a small loch.

Into the harbour waiting room to read and wait for the ferry back to Oban.

The Green Year list is now at **264**, fully twenty seven ahead of this time last year!

**14.64 Miles		457 feet elevation up				457 feet down**

Sunday 10th July

The fates are with me! The weather forecast, thanks BBC, states that Sunday in Oban would be a day of heavy rain. The day starts that way and I take the tent down as it pours down. I decide to see whether there is a bed available at Oban's Youth Hostel.

There is so a day relaxing instead of cycling to Fort William. Sleep in the lounge after a breakfast of Lidl's pseudo Hob Nobs, chocolate of course. An afternoon is spent watching Andy Murray win Wimbledon.

A text from the Oracle, Phil Andrews.

Apparently the Snow Geese on Coll are tickable, a category C2 - BOU population

. . . . just like Mandarin.

Last year Phil and I had talked about these geese after I had searched them out and saw a group of twenty one of them, including one juvenile.

Plastic fantastic was Phil's verdict back then and I didn't count them on my 2015 Green Year list.

Great, **now** he tells me that I should have done back then and that I could have done if I had seen them yesterday.

Actually I had looked for them yesterday but not with any real conviction as the rain fell and a strong gale blew.

From the comfortable lounge of the Youth Hostel I determine that I will go back to Coll tomorrow.

Meanwhile the weather in Oban? Drizzle and light rain for the morning followed by a dry afternoon with a south east wind.

Monday 11th July **Fresh WNW**

Dull AM to sunny PM

The ferry at 7:15 a.m. is easy enough on flat sea and on reaching Coll, the cycle ride to the area where the Snow Geese are usually to be found is an easy ride too.

For the first time in a long time I do a day list of birds and before finding the Snow Geese I have seen around thirty species. I have also heard five Corncrakes but as per usual no views of them.

The **Snow Geese** are in same field as last year. My memory tells me that back then I saw twenty plus a young bird. This year there are seventeen. They seem more animated this year and when a couple of walkers pass through the field they all fly out onto the sea.

I feel good about seeing this iconic bird this year.

It is the Seventieth anniversary of the Wildfowl & Wetland Trust and to celebrate they are reissuing an edition of the Paul Gallico – Sir Peter Scott book,The Snow Goose and seeing them close to and not in an enclosure or as a white spot in a flock of six thousand Pink feets is as good an experience of them as I am likely to get in Britain. Now watching the huge flocks in The States would be good. One day perhaps.

It feels good too as it is the bird for Doug Hilton's Snow Goose Wildlife Trust down in Kent, as you may remember from a few weeks ago.

http://www.snowgoosetrust.org/

Bird number **265**, now twenty eight ahead of last year and one that I didn't count last year yet as they are category C2 on the BOU list they are countable and maybe I should update last year's list to 290.

Having watched the Snow Geese in the field and on the sea, and having seen them swim away around a headland, I take a closer look at a beach. It has a mass of plastic rubbish on it.

Two hours later I have cleared two thirds of the beach and there are three large fishing crates full of it to be collected.

I head back to the hidden bike and make my way to the south western tip of Coll.

Pushing the bike to the north of the RSPB reserve here I find another beach and spend some time on a cliff watching the birds go by; Manx Shearwaters, Shags and Gannets. I lay my head back and fall asleep for an hour or so.

On waking I look around me and the sun has come out. Everything looks so different with the light colour of the granite outcrops looking almost Pyrenean limestone white.

I go down to the rocky beach and collect all the plastic here too. This time though I collect it in two large carrier bags and take it back to the RSPB car park to deposit it in a large lidded skip. Having done so I then I return to the beach for some more and set up my tent to camp on the grassy area overlooking a very large and beautiful sandy beach that curves away to the south.

Leaving the tent to dry out after the other night's heavy rain, I walk along a headland and find a number of Frog Orchids *Coeloglossum viride*; tiny in stature with dark reddish mauve lines on the cowls.

In the evening cloud comes over as I settle into my now dry tent. The fresh breeze is making everything feel and look cool with the granite taking on a darker grey appearance. From where I am I can see over some ancient sand dunes to a high hill on the Isle of Tiree. I am asleep before sunset.

12.5 Miles 394 feet elevation up 354 feet down

Tuesday 12th July Light WNW

Sunny intervals after one brief shower.

I spend the morning intermittently waking up, reading and sleeping in turn. With no reason to rush, as the ferry back to Oban isn't until 17:40, I can relax and take the opportunity to get into a philosophical and scientific book.

Looking out of the tent to the beach I wonder which beaches in the World are considered the best. Bondi? Copacabana? Surely neither of these can be as beautiful as this long, white sand one and there isn't a soul to be seen here. I have the whole area to myself.

I can still bird whilst inside the tent and I have a list of four by the time I decide to get up; Raven, Meadow Pipit, Wheatear and Herring Gull have all been calling, cronking or tacking just outside the tent. One doesn't need to see them to know what they are.

More plastic on this beach and by I collect four large carrier bags of it and take them to the skip two bags at a time. The reason for the double trip is that on reaching the skip the first time I see that I have lost a pannier somewhere in the sand dunes and going back to retrieve it I decide to collect some more plastic.

On reaching the skip the next time I see I have lost my cycling gloves and have to go back yet again to search for them! Twit.

Whilst lying in bed this morning I was thinking about various things from the past and I don't know why but a repetitive ditty from the Reading Rock Festival days from the 1970s. That one was about marijuana. I change the words . . .

And he would pedal, pedal, pedal.
The Biking Birder.
He would pedal, pedal, pedal.
A little further

He would cycle in the rain,
Usually in some pain,
Up a hill, down a hill
And then get lost again.

And then he'd pedal, pedal, pedal,
A little further,
Until he saw the bird.
He'd give his pencil a lick,
And then put down the tick,
And then he'd pedal, pedal, pedal . .

One more time!

I have been thinking of the fundamental differences between Carbon Twitcher, the more normal sort of birder, one who uses a car or aeroplane to get to the birds, and my own Green Birding pursuit of the same.

My birding is 99% perspiration with 1% inspiring moments, to paraphrase Edison. Those moments of rapture though may come from landscape beauty as well as flora and fauna moments. They can come from a more intimate relationship with the environment than a Carbon Twitcher ever gets driving along the same roads.

A crazy bit of thinking involving scale and perspective; there are a few midges in the tent this morning and I think of how immense I am compared to a midge. A crazy thought with large error margins is that were a midge to be my size, I would be around four kilometres high to keep the scale comparison going. I wonder what the relative masses of us both they and I would conjure up?

9.96 Miles **414 feet elevation up** **448 feet down**

Wednesday 13th July **Light WNW**

Heavy showers & sunny intervals

The Black Guillemots are out on a jetty as I leave Oban. Heavy showers alternate with sunny intervals as I cycle towards Fort William. Magnificent scenery all the way with sections of superb cycle path that takes me away from a busy road for long sections.

A stop for a snack at a small café brings about a meeting with a fellow Brummie (someone born in Birmingham). Not just a Brummie but someone who lived in the same area, King's Heath, that I lived in as a young boy. A bacon, black pudding and apple sauce bap wasn't a Brummie creation that I remember but it was tasty enough.

Through Fort William, as I head north along yet another section of cycle path, a young lady on a bike comes alongside me and asks if I am the man cycling to all of the RSPB reserves. She had seen the article in Wingbeat, The RSPB's teenage magazine for the Phoenix members. A physiotherapist by trade, she cycles with me for a couple of miles, a pleasure to meet and chat with.

To Spean Bridge and after a gift of a small white rabbit for the bike to be named June from June, a local lady on her way to the pub, I search a woodland there for Wood Warbler. No joy, just Treecreepers, Willow Warblers and titmice, I set up the tent and relax.

54.28 Miles **2495 feet elevation up** **2263 feet down**

The evening email from The Oracle:-

Wednesday 13/07- head to Abernethy (110 miles via Laggan)
Call in at Spean Bridge for WOOD WARBLER and Insh Marshes for OSPREY and SPOT CRAKE en route
Sat 16/07 late- arrive Boat of Garten (or similar)
Sun15/7>Fri 22/7 - allow a 6 days for CRESTED TIT / OSPREY / PTARMIGAN / CAPERCAILLE
Sat 23//7 - head off for Burghead (41 miles)
Sun 24/7 - arrive Burghead for WHITE-BILLED DIVER
Mon 25/07 early - depart for Aberdeen
via Murcar for WHITE-WINGED SCOTER and Ythan Estuary for KING EIDER (74 miles)
Wed 27/7 late - arrive Aberdeen

Where would I be without you? Thanks Phil!

Thursday 14th July **Light WNW**

Sunny intervals

Up early to explore this expansive woodland in the hope of finally getting Wood Warbler onto the list. At this time of year the wood is almost silent and only a Blackcap gives a brief snatch of song.

I walk pathways, try sit and wait tactics but no luck after four hours or so. There have been a few birds, same ones as last night with Willow Warblers high in the canopy, Treecreepers on the low trunks and titmice at all levels.

I set off for Insh Marshes with forty miles of road to negotiate. It is mostly uphill until a series of lochs, The first one has a dam at the west end yet the water level is fifty foot down on the highest possible level. It has been this way for a long time as the vegetation is lush all along the old lake valley.

After shopping in Newtonmore I am surprised to arrive at Kingussie. I thought I still had around ten miles still to go but here I am almost at Insh Marshes. Brilliant.

I cycle past the ruins of the Ruthven Barracks on top of it's glacial mound left after the last Ice Age; the mound that is not the ruins, and get to the visitor's centre. Now this fabulous wooden structure has a balcony on top with magnificent views over the whole valley. This really does have one of the best views of any RSPB reserve. I watch as a female Roe doe cleans her young fawn. A couple arrive who I have met before this year, Vickie and Ryan from Blackpool. Great to have a catch up chat.

Downstairs and into the centre, the views from inside are equally good. A truly wonderful reserve. Tomorrow's exploration of it is going to be tremendous.

42.72 Miles **2111 feet elevation up** **1699 feet down**

Friday 15th July **Fresh SW**

Heavy rain

My hope for an exploration of the RSPB reserve is dashed by the heavy rain that arrives mid morning. I do get to the hides that flank the centre. The views are atmospheric as drifts of falling rain pass in front of the hills and over the marshland. Roe Deer are out there and occasionally a bird shows itself, Redshank, Lapwing and Curlew. The rain gets heavier and I spend the afternoon in the centre reading the noticeboards and the RSPB leaflets, especially the ones on climate change subjects.

In the evening, as the rain stops and the sun decides to show itself briefly, I cycle first to Insh Loch and watch **Ospreys** coming to the island there. Bird number **266**, not a bird I was worried about missing as there are a number of them in the Speyside area.

I then return to the west side if the Insh Marshes to try to listen for Spotted Crake, a very rare breeding bird here.

First I set the tent up near a lay-by that I had been told was near to where one could hear them.

Midnight. No sound at all, it is cold and cloudy and after walking along the B-road for an hour or so with hands cupped to my ears to amplify whatever sounds there, I haven't heard any whip-like call. Sleep per chance to dream.

11.90 Miles 873 feet elevation up 737 feet down

Saturday 16th July Fresh SW to 50 mph at the summit

Occasional showers of horizontal rain, very cold at the summit. 6C feeling minus 5C with wind chill.

The cycle towards the Cairngorm mountain range is lovely and a butterfly atop a grass stem gives me hope for a warm, sunny day. No mobile phone signal so no chance to check on a weather forecast, I reach the superb Cairngorm Youth Hostel. Here I have to wait for the postman.

Nationwide Building Society had, unknown to me, blocked my debit card. Yesterday I had tried to book a night at the hostel and my card had been declined. Knowing that I was a long way from being skint I phoned Nationwide. "We've stopped your card. We thought that there was some fraud." No text, no phone call, no email; Nationwide had sent a new card to my parents' address back in late June. Great!

Mum and Dad found it amongst my post and sent it to the hostel, recorded delivery. Now I have to wait.

Noon, postman arrives, I have my card and I am off on an unladen bike up the mountain. Actually most of the way is a push. Super strong cyclists pass me as I use the excuse of looking for a Crested Tit to push up the steep road.

Reaching the Ski Centre, I hide the bike and set off up the valley's central pathway, which is somewhat sheltered from the wind. The higher I go the stronger the wind gets. There is a smirk of snow in a cirque of rock and I head for that. Last year the slope to the left, north of this snow was where I found over twenty Ptarmigan, today's target bird, and I am confident of finding them, despite the extremely cold gale that is scouring the rocks.

I find some Ptarmigan pooh! They must be around here somewhere. I scramble up to the summit just as a particularly heavy rain shower hits with the cold weather adding hailstones to the rain drops. It soon passes and after a spot of lunch, taken crouching down behind some larger rocks, I start the search for the birds in earnest.

A Mountain Hare dashes off at my approach. I see it three more times over the next two hours, or maybe I see three different ones, as I zigzag across the blasted rock landscape; first with the wind at my back before turning and facing the gale. My fingers are starting to feel painful with the cold, despite gloves and the occasional rain shower stings my face.

The Ptarmigan café is just a couple of hundred feet below me, teasing me with the promise of warmth, hot chocolate and cake. I need to find **Ptarmigan** for real though and I am thinking that I may have to come back another day, maybe even in November, when one shows itself. I am so pleased I even shout, “we've got one!” Ghostbuster style.

Just one but after a photograph for evidence I decide that one is enough and am soon tucking in to a delicious flapjack with a large mug of the dreamed of hot chocolate.

On leaving the warmth, I start the descent and what should be walking up the path? Six Ptarmigan who have got more sense than me taking advantage of the shelter of the fencing along the path.

Six Wheatear and a single Ring Ouzel are seen to add to a very sparse day list. Meadow Pipits have been the most frequently seen bird up here. A single each of both Pied and Grey Wagtail and a single Carrion Crow, a fly over Herring Gull, a few titmice and a Willow Warbler make up the rest of the list. Not a lot but I can't complain when Ptarmigan goes onto the Green year list, bird number **267**.

Green Year list is now thirty ahead of this time last year! Brilliant. Surely the 300 is just a matter of time this year. I can imagine the moment when I see the 300th bird. Dream on Prezza.

29.88 Miles **3767 feet elevation up** **4121 feet down**

Sunday 17th July **Light SW**

Cool and cloudy

I want to find today's target bird, Crested Tit, not at a feeder conveniently set up at the RSPB Loch Garten reserve nearby but somewhere out in the immense Abernethy Forest. To that end I am up early at the Youth Hostel to enjoy a large breakfast before setting out to explore. The area I plan to walk is one I have never been around before and

I am looking forward to new views and landscapes. I am particularly looking forward to finding a large variety of fungi. Yesterday's examples had been in superb condition and I expect a lot more today. Red Squirrels are possible and hopefully I will hear the trilling call of a Crested Tit during the day.

In fact Red Squirrels prove to be easy. They run across the lawn at the hostel as I eat the substantial fare. Curious how they have white, bleached-out looking tails.

Now I don't know why but when I see a hill I have a hankering to climb it. So it is today. The path from the hostel goes up. It goes up beyond the tree line after going through fir plantations of row after row, same sized firs. No birds in here, a few Meadow Pipits are in areas where the trees have been removed. Scots Pine skeletons punctuate the slopes.

Why am I going up here? The wind is strong at the top and light rain is falling. It's cold.

I want to see the other side of the hill. The trouble is when I arrive at the summit and shelter against the cone of stones, the cloud descends and I am in a whiteout. I relax against some stone and eat my lunch. A small moth crawls in front of me.

The clouds lift and I descend down a steep heather-covered slope down to the forest again. It is so sad to see how much of the area is just regimented conifer blocks and how little is original pine forest.

Eventually reaching a sort of dirt road, I head back towards the hostel. Listening all the way I hear a **Crested Tit** in the high canopy of some of those cultivated pines and find it. Bird number **268**. A photograph proves impossible amongst the branches. I do however manage to get one of a Spotted Flycatcher in the same area. A few hundred yards later another Crested Tit is once again high in the canopy.

Green Year list is twenty eight ahead of this time last year. Last year at this time I had three birds on the island of Islay; Rock Dove, Arctic Tern and Golden Eagle.

7.57 Miles 1502 feet elevation up and down

An email from Ben Jones, warden of the RSPB reserves on Coll, gives his thoughts on the Snow Geese flock on the island that I saw few days ago:-

The Snow Geese have been around about 40+ years and my understanding was that there were originally 40 that escaped. I've only ever known the highest adult count to be around 25 and over my time here they have dropped off steadily. Apart from anything else the small gene pool and inbreeding must be taking its toll!!

Thanks for doing beach cleans. It's a never ending job, when we get a gang of people together you should see the load we take off to the council depot. Humans aren't we just great for the planet. See you next year? Ben

Monday 18th July **Light SW**

Cool and cloudy, early morning heavy rain

Another walk in the Cairngorm area with an aim to circumnavigate Loch Morlich and a hope of finding a Capercaillie. Rain falls as I make my way along the Old loggers Pathway towards the south west end of the loch. There are plenty of fungi along the pathway but each specimen is damaged in some way; Boleti sp. with holes caused by slugs, Amanita with damage caused by twigs and pine needles. Why should every photograph of these superb organisms be perfect? I start my collection of fungi in less than perfect condition. A new Facebook group beckons . . . Funny Fungi.

Rain stops for brief moments and birds are very few, just a group of Coal Tits come to the first pishing session. A few Common Hawkers are hawking as I follow pathways deeper into the forest. Most of the forest seems to have been planted. I must check on this as the history of the area would be fascinating.

Off the path, I search an area of seemingly open and original forest. The trees are of all different ages and sporadically spaced. The heather, moss and rush are up to my thighs and I almost put my hand into a Wood Ant nest. No Capercaillie here.

I arrive back at the loch side and take the dirt road north east. It has been a very quiet walk with very few birds, just the occasional Coal Tit or Willow Warbler with a few Swifts overflying the trees.

Then a Long-tailed Tit crosses the path in front of me. Then another. I start to pish. More birds are coming and going as a large titmice flock is passing, mostly high up in the trees. I pish harder and birds come close; Willow Warbler, Siskin, Goldcrest and a few Long-tailed Tits. Then a very close Crested Tit is on a branch. I click and the camera focuses on a leaf!

The flock passes. The chance for classic Crested Tit photograph is gone.

I walk on and pish a male Redstart. It is definitely the way to see birds here in the forest. Psssht. Psssht. Psssht......

Trout in the stream, flowers form a head band on a young Danish girl; Clara the youngest is wearing a beautiful yellow hawkweed headband made by her sister. Mum and Dad insist on a photograph. A family from Copenhagen. Great!

Back at the youth hostel again, an evening of watching The Matrix is followed by Rolling Stones music. Perfect.

6.38 Miles **462 feet elevation up and down**

Tuesday 19th July **Light SW**

Very warm, 26C and very sunny!

Off to Loch Garten RSPB reserve in the Abernethy Forest, the iconic Osprey nest site. The sun is shining and the hills are free of cloud for the first time since arriving in the area. I know it must be warm and sunny as a Song Thrush is sunbathing just outside my Youth Hostel dormitory. The temperature is climbing and what little wind there is as I cycle is behind me. Hence I am in a fabulously good mood and singing all the way.

The ten or so miles to Loch Garten pass quickly enough and after stopping to photograph both a house that looks French and a very large Boletus sp. fungus, I go out onto the small boardwalk that overlooks a small rush and horsetail filled pool. Four-spotted Chasers, Libellula quadrimaculata are chasing each other and a few damselflies include Large Red, Emerald and Northern.

Three people from the US of A join me and we chat about American politics, Brexit and nature. John is from New York, his wife, was from Chicago originally and her sister is from Boston. They are a delightful trio and a pleasure to be with.

From here it was a short cycle to the visitor's centre and after meeting Sarah in the entrance kiosk, another superb RSPB staff member, I go into centre to view the famous Osprey nest. EJ, the resident female Osprey is on a tree by the camera pylon and her two offspring, Rowan and Willow, are on the nest devouring a large rainbow trout, brought in by EJ.

Odin, when he arrives, only brings in a small fish. Apart from the Ospreys there are some bird feeders that attract a good number of Siskin and Chaffinch, as well as a few Greenfinch, some titmice and a juvenile Great Spotted Woodpecker.

Outside for a strange lunch; brioches with jam, peanut butter and apple sauce; well it's all I have, I meet a fantastic family from Ipswich. Mum and Dad with their two sons, Oscar and Max. They talk about birds and their holiday and are an inspiring group. I had really wanted to see a RSPB staff member from last year, a man who really made his mark on me last year, a Maltese man named Nimrod. Unfortunately he is having a day off but I am told by Sarah that he will be in tomorrow.

With that in mind I head off into the magnificent Abernethy Forest to find a place to camp.

18.18 Miles **581 feet elevation up** **970 feet down**

Thursday 21st July **Light SW**

Warm, 20C sunny intervals

Off to Loch Garten RSPB reserve again from my deep in the forest camp site. It had been a wonderful, if unplanned rest, due to the violent thunderstorms the previous day, with books read and lots of sleep.

Tent is packed quickly and the road reached. No early morning Capercaillie on the way, just a pair of Grey Wagtails catching flies on the tarmac. The forest is extremely quiet, a serene silence and so beautiful.

Nimrod is in the kiosk at the reserve and comes out to give his friend a hug. He is eager to tell me his news, that he is in love with a Danish girl and that they will make a life together once he returns to his native Malta.

I had met a lovely couple from St Albans, Tricia and Duncan along the road and they arrive at the kiosk. As usual, it is great to.

meet a couple who bird together.

Nimrod introduces me to a residential volunteer, Donna and together she and I walk the path to the centre. Once more the Osprey family are present, though the juveniles are without a fish today.

After a snack or two, Donna comes over to ask whether I would like to go in the forward Osprey Observation Hide. Would I!? I had always wanted to see the inner sanctum of this iconic place.

Two hours inside with Donna and another res-vol', residential volunteer, Jane is a pleasure and a privilege.

Donna is from Doncaster originally and used to live in Dudley. She had been to Worcester University, where one of her lecturers was a friend of mine, Mike Wheeler. Small world. Donna is a keen birder and fascinating to listen to.

By now the afternoon is getting on and I decide to head off towards Carrbridge. On getting back to the bike I realise that one of the girls, one of my cuddlies, is missing, the small white rabbit June. Julia, the retail manager, gives me another rabbit to replace her, naming her Ginny. I determine though that June must be found. I have to retrace my tracks and find her. I can't leave her alone in the forest. I find her along the small track very near to where I had pitched my tent. Phew!

As if some sort of karma is deserved I pish a titmice flock nearby and two Crested Tits come very close. At last I manage to take a good photograph of one.

Once back on the bike it is a case of 'All aboard' and with everyone accounted for with one new addition, we head off.

12.68 Miles **610 feet elevation up** **682 feet down**

Friday 22nd July **Light SW**

Warm, 20C sunny intervals

Elizabeth, the owner of The Ferryhouse Bed & Breakfast, has a Spike Milligan vinyl or two to show me after breakfast. One of them partners him with Jeremy Taylor with songs about Pot and Lift Girls! The other piece of vinyl has Spike Milligan narrating Paul Gallico's The Snow Goose. I didn't know that Spike had done such and I find it on Youtube. Listening to it I am somewhat disappointed by the stupid sounds that accompany a moment when the 'Sky Princess' goes into the kitchen. Spike's narration is short with sporadic phrases each followed by orchestral themes. The record fails in my opinion to capture the atmosphere of the saltings and the emotion of the relationship between Fritha and Phillip. More of Spike's narration would have improved it.

Away and off north towards Carrbridge, I enter a large coniferous forest north of the town. I have been given instructions on how to find Capercaillie here and proceed to do exactly not what I have been told. I enjoy exploring various parts of the forest. The ground is extremely difficult to navigate, with thick clumps of heather and moss. A large stag Red Deer watches my progress carefully. Clegs, horseflies, are following me. I am very allergic to them and hope that my repellent works well. I remember my children calling me Quasimodo due to one bite on my eyebrow years ago during a holiday in Switzerland. Then there was the 'sausage lip' week back in 2010. I always get a large area of swelling when bitten by a Cleg.

A Cleg bites below my left wrist. No blood as I brush it away so hopefully not too much swelling later.

The trees are very dense for a few hundred yards and I enjoy ducking and diving through it finding a few interesting fungi and mound after mound of Wood Ants.

I come across a huge area of deforestation and devastation. Out in the middle a young stag Roe Deer seems to be stuck, totally unable to find a way across the area. I watch it from a hidden position for quarter of an hour or so as it keeps turning and trying different ways to get out. Trapped by the piled up debris of branches and twigs, I can't see it ever getting out, poor thing. If I approach it I am sure tat it would only panic and rip itself on the sharp dried branches.

A male Sparrowhawk glides close by and I walk around the broken trees to get back to an area where the trees have been removed to allow a line of pylons and telegraph wires to pass through. Method in my madness, I want to walk down this tree break from an elevated position, which would allow me to see down a large expanse. The heather and moss clumps are high and there are water-filled dips between them hidden and therefore easy for me to fall into. Progress is difficult and I keep my hand on my camera expecting a black explosion any second.

It happens! A male Capercaillie comes out of a tree from the left. It flies fast to the south, downhill it goes low over the heather. After a hundred yards or so it veers off into the forest. Gone.

Bird number **269** onto the list and another good bird to see.

Clegs persuade me that my time in my forest is up. The target bird has been found and I return to my hidden bike.

I cycle a long way around the Nethybridge and find the place where I camped a few nights ago. Food bought from a shop, I enjoy a picnic in the late evening sunshine before settling down for the night.

The Green year list goes to **269**, twenty six ahead of this stage last year.

19.50 Miles 1003 feet elevation up 923 feet down

Phil, The Oracle, emails John Dixon, the provider of the Carrbridge Capers info, with the good news:-

Hi John,

Just a quick note to say that your Carrbridge site produced the goods today; Gary is very appreciative.

Many Thanks Phil

Saturday 23rd July Light SW

Cloudy, muggy, dry

I make my way to a pine forest north of Nethybirdge. I am looking for crossbills. Beyond a large quarry, up a steep hill and into the forest proper, I pick bilberries that stain my hands and, like miniature blueberries, provide some sustenance. No biting insects here, I spend four hours and see six crossbills. None of them land though, they just chup as they pass, first three, then two then one.

I return to my tent just before heavy rain starts. The rain lasts well into the night.

9.44 Miles 616 feet elevation up and down

The evening email from The Oracle:-

Based on what is currently available:

23/07-27/07: Searching for SPOTTED CRAKE and PARROT CROSSBILL
28/07: Aviemore cycle fair
29/07-30/07: Cycle Aviemore to Strathbeg (105 miles)
31/07: Bird Strathbeg for WHITE-RUMPED SAND
01/08 Cycle Strathbeg to Murcar (35 miles)
02/08-03/08: Allow 2 days for WW SCOTER
03/08: Catch ferry to Kirkwall
04/08-05/08: General birding on Orkney
06/08: Catch ferry (9am) to North Ron

The earlier ferry leave Kirkwall on Tues 02/08 so do-able if you secure Scoter quickly.

John replies:-

Hi Phil, and Gary,
Glad to help. Four days of dipping Caper must have been grim! I doubt you'll be after anything else I can help with, but I'll keep an eye out in case. Presumably if anything turns up on Shetland while Gary's on Fair Isle it will be straight on the pedalo :-)
Good luck on the finishing straight!
Cheers John

Sunday 24th July **Light SW**

Drizzle, followed by an evening of heavy rain

I make my way to a pine forest north of Nethybridge once more and enter it via a public footpath conveniently placed to the west of the quarry.

I walk to a sort of elevated hide, the sort used for shooting deer. Drizzle is falling and two crossbills land on a nearby pine. Unfortunately due to the inclement weather, photographs are poor. Also unfortunately the birds are silent. Still they are obviously not Common Crossbills, having a strong neck and broader bill so maybe I can claim half a year tick. After all they must be either Scottish Crossbill or Parrot. After all Adrian Riley counted one, well five actually, without a sonogram during his Big Carbon Year of 2002.

The rain gets heavier and I sit in the hide and count a large flock of Mistle Thrushes as they pass by, over one hundred and fifty of them. This is the largest flock of Mistle Thrushes I have ever seen.

Six crossbills chup past but don't land.

The rain stops and I head back towards the hidden bike. A Willow Warbler pho-eets nearby and I pish quietly not expecting much. I am soon surrounded by a fair number of titmice, mostly Coal Tits with Chaffinches, more Willow Warblers and a Treecreeper.

Back at the tent my lonely evening is spent reading, typing notes and studying the photographs of the crossbills. What I would give for some equipment to record the sounds the crossbills make when flying past. Is it just my hopes that makes the crossbills that fly by the tent sound so different to the ones I have seen in the Nethy Bridge forest?

6.74 Miles 354 feet elevation up and down

Monday 25th July Light SW

Not feeling well, sinusitis is back with vengeance and my face feels squashed by the infection. I pack up the tent and cycle to Aviemore, shop for food and book into the youth hostel there, a superb hostel with large windows around an extensive lounge. Sitting in there I watch as Red Squirrels come to peanut feeders. A relaxing afternoon and evening whilst feeling rough.

11.63 miles 563 feet elevation up 599 feet down

Tuesday 26th July Fresh SW

Sunny intervals

Having slept in the lounge to prevent me waking others in the dormitory with my snoring, I enjoy the antics of the squirrels. I am looking for Wood Warblers this morning and I set off into the woods.

Late afternoon, after having spent the day searching but not finding the target bird, difficult to find at this time of year as they don't sing, I have enjoyed watching lots of Willow Warblers, titmice and the occasional Spotted Flycatcher. The woods, mostly Silver Birch has been beautiful and I have a bag full of Chantrelle fungi for dinner.

3.21 miles 1143 feet elevation up and down

Wednesday 27th July Light SW

Sunny

After a visit to a pharmacy for medicine to alleviate the sinuses, I cycle to Insh Marshes and enter the RSPB offices in the village. On the way I stop to watch a Pipistrelle bat that unusually is out hunting. It is speedily hunting insects near to a large house and some teenage kids have seen me from an upstairs window. I ignore their lame attempts at distracting me and pretend that I have not seen their full moon!

I enter the RSPB offices and the greeting is wonderful. Thanks Karen, Karen and Kat! Sunshine girls.

I spend the afternoon walking around the nearest woodland section of the extensive reserve, the highlight being the sixteen Scotch Argus butterflies I see. These are the first I have seen this year. The view across the marshes towards the hills is magnificent.

12.27 miles   810 feet elevation up   788 feet down

Thursday 28th July   The RSPB Fun Day

I cycle to the Heritage Centre in Newtonmore for what will be a fabulous day; marquees are up and lots of RSPB staff are ready to enthral the many visitors that are sure to turn up at this superb place on such a sunny day.

I get my face painted, a bumblebee decorates my cheek. After talking with Brad about his job with the RSPB and his passion for finding about his grandfather's role in World War One, I explore the large site.

With Stephanie and Lexy I make a woollie creature for the bike. Further on Michael and a RSPB staff member have a tray of creatures from their pond dipping. Black houses, perfectly reconstructed show the life of Scots long ago.

The day is fabulous, the children excited by so many differ activities and the RSPB staff so energetic and . . fun!

Too soon it is late afternoon and time to pack up. A final activity to see, worm charming with Sarah. Sarah exemplifies the RSPB staff, constant smile with the sunshine personality and oodles of energy and enthusiasm.

An evening is spent at Kat, the organiser's, nearby house. A splendid relax with great food on a terrace and views over to the Cairngorm Mountains. Their beautiful house with a large garden has chickens and Kat's girls tell me about them all as they sit holding one each.

15.44 miles   745 feet elevation up and down

Friday 29th July

I need to get to Aberdeen but I am still feeling very rough. Mind you the weather is fine and the cycle to Nethy Bridge is pleasant enough. Lunch taken, I continue to Tomintoul. By now though I am feeling very ill and seeing a Youth Hostel I decide that maybe I should rest here for the night.

34.51 miles   2161 feet elevation up   1762 feet down

Saturday 30th July

Doctor's appointment kept and antibiotics and inhalers given. I go back to bed!

Sunday 31st July

Another day spent mostly in bed!

The target for July was ten so getting eleven is once again ahead of the game.

Statistics for July 2016 :

Green Year list	269 birds
Year ticks in July	11
Number of birds not seen in 2015	1
Mileage in July	535.72 miles
Total mileage for the year	4,446.72 miles
average mileage on days cycled	25.63 miles
elevation : up	30,783 feet
: down	30,330 feet

<u>Best Birds</u> : **Snow goose (!) and Capercaillie.**

8

AUGUST

One day this horror will end, of course, but with your help it will end a lot sooner and your grandchildren and those of the rotten criminals will thank you for it.

Chris Packham, talking about Grouse shooting and the destruction of Hen Harriers, ending the foreword in Mark Ian Avery's book – Conflict in The Uplands

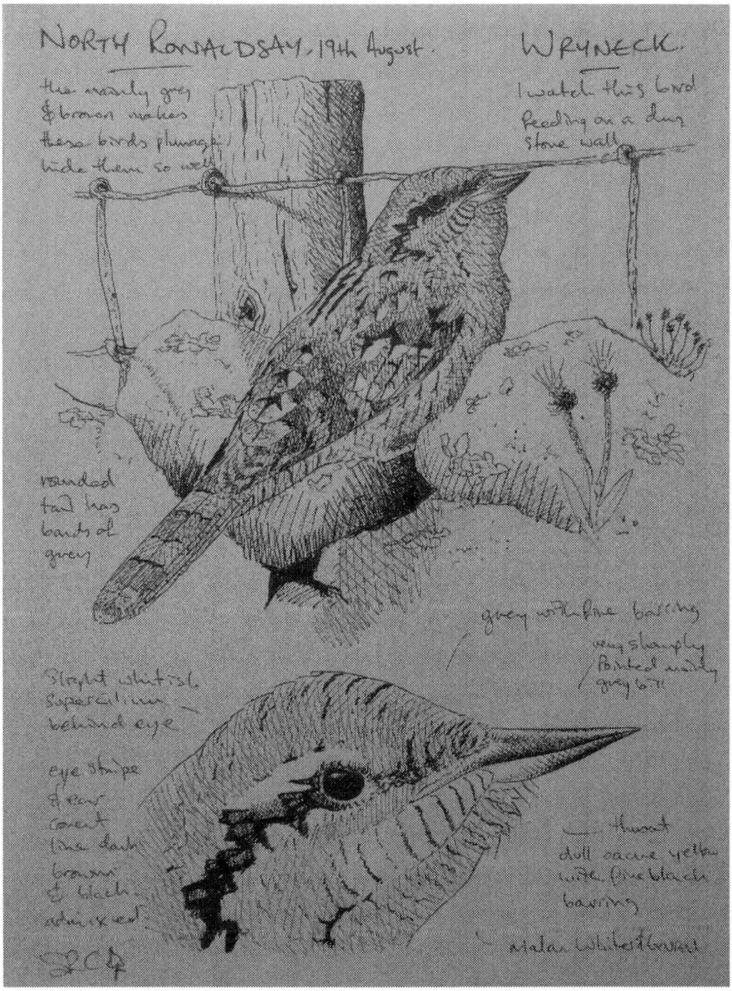

Monday 1st August **light SW**

Sunny intervals, warm

Hopefully I will see the American White-winged Scoter once I reach Aberdeen. News is that the mega is still there.

Today Ricky the Robin, the donation boxes on the bike, has been emptied and the money shared between the four charities I am supporting. When people do give money as I travel I try to write their names on my notebook and so . . .

Ricky the Robin emptying time. Many thanks to Yvonne, Jocyln (Smugglers Youth Hostel), Duncan and Tricia, Jasper, Donna, Susan, John, Clare & Eleanor, Ryan & Vicky, Henry, Jules, Moira & Ron, Jane & Lynda.

Some of the donations recently have been of things, like cereal bars, given to me. My attitude is that if someone gives me something then that is in my opinion, a donation.

By the way, I am paying for every aspect of my trip. No one gives me any money to do this. Just thought I would say as some people do ask.

The ride is a pleasant one today, mostly, with more gently and long downhill slopes than steep uphill climbs. An exception is when I have to push the bike up a steep section that approaches a large Ski resort. Red Grouse are numerous in the moors before the ski runs. Irony abounds as each ski lift is named after a bird of prey. There is absolutely no chance of seeing a Kestrel, a Merlin, a Peregrine or a Buzzard around here. Is it just thoughtlessness that has made the ski resort owners use such names. It seems like a sick joke as I push the bike up a steep incline. Grouse shooting moorland owners have all predators killed in order to maintain high numbers of grouse. To see a ski run named after Hen Harrier is particularly galling! All I have heard of this year concerning Hen Harriers is of satellite-tagged individuals either disappearing or being found dead. It is about time the Scottish parliament did something positive to stop this totally illegal travesty. Hen Harrier Day next week, an annual event to heighten awareness of just what evil is going on.

Ironically, a superb Osprey flies high over-head, heading north. Maybe here is a beautiful bird of prey safe from the hands of the worst of gamekeepers and grouse shooting land-owners; after all, they only eat fish. How sad, and actually despicable, that this is the case in too much of Scotland and England. I well remember although it was decades ago, a superb gamekeeper that protected a Montagu's Harriers nest and celebrated when the young birds flew for the first time. There are rotting crab apples amongst a basket of sweeter Granny Smiths.

The weather has been benign and the scenery lovely, with mostly very clear roads. The hills may not have been alive with the sound of music but my excited shrieks on some of the plunging downhill miles may have been heard throughout grouse shooting land.

A final thought . . . it's fabulous when a birding family gets in touch to tell of their birding. Thanks Jamie. Go for it Max and Oscar.

37.91 Miles 2491 feet elevation up 3134 feet down

Sunday 3rd August very light S

Sunny

After almost seven hours spent looking for the mega rare American White-winged Scoter at Murcar Golf Course, without a telescope, I return to Aberdeen Youth Hostel.

There had been plenty of ducks, thousands of them, but I couldn't find the special one. The most unusual sight was of a totally naked old man walking first south and then north along the beach. Now, fortunately, that is something you don't see every day!

Within half an hour of getting there, The Oracle - Phil Andrews phones. "Get back there!"

Twenty two minutes later I find that an Aberdeen birder named Paul is waiting for me just off the A90, along the road that leads down to the Golf Course. We swap valuable items. He has my bike and I have his Swarowski telescope. Good swap. Paul then leaves to go and play football, having already seen the American White-winged Scoter. I walk down to the road, declining his kind offer of a carbon lift, and cross the greens to the sand quarry that Paul had recommended I view from. Now with a top quality telescope to scan the large flocks I search but still cannot find the rare Yanky duck.

A phone call from another Aberdeen birder, Nick and an instruction to look south along the sand dune line. There is a wave from a very distant figure. Nick has the White-winged Scoter in front of him and so a trek down the beach is required. A very small seal cub is stranded on the beach, which is a bit worrying as I walk past it. It stirs as I do so but only by lifting its head a little. I hope a rest on the sand will recharge its batteries and it will be off back into the sea when the tide rises.

Nick's telescope immediately gives the lifer and year tick whilst he chats and gives a running commentary of the duck's movement among the massed Velvet and Common Scoter, Red-breasted Mergansers and Eider. **American White-winged Scoter** goes onto the year list, bird number **270**.

Thanks Nick and Paul … and many thanks to The Oracle, Phil Andrews for contacting Aberdeen birders and giving them my mobile number. The team work involved here to help me get the bird is both impressive and appreciated. Two wonderful birders that alleviated the problem of no telescope searching for a mega.

Paul returned at 8.31 p.m. a minute late (Monty Python fans will know what I mean). Items are swapped back and a chat and goodbye is followed by a cycle back to youth hostel to prepare for the night.

Lights on the bike, masses of fluorescence on my torso and a ride through Aberdeen City Centre to a lighthouse where Will and Mark, more Aberdeen birders, have arranged a Petrel ringing session. Eight birders sit comfortably on folding chairs, Midnight darkness, stars and satellites and the sound of Storm Petrel calls from two large speakers that will hopefully attract the same to the ringer's mist nets.

Will walks back from the large mist net with the first of three **Storm Petrels** in his hand. Bird number **271**. Ian and Penny were there as well, Paul and two birders who's names I didn't jot down.

After a couple of hours everything is packed up and we go to a small marshland area to try to listen for Spotted Crake. With no success I leave to cycle back to the youth hostel.

3.00 a.m. Back at the hostel and bed. I am feeling so good. It may be the lack of sleep that brings the euphoric feeling but more likely it is the feeling of the friendships that birding brings.

Ian and Penny, thank you. It was great to meet you Tuesday and last night. Ian I hope you got to see the American white-winged scoter.

Paul and Nick, thanks to you both. The combination of the both of you gave me not only a fabulous new bird for the year, the fore-mentioned White-winged Scoter, but also a lifer.

39.68 miles 1532 elevation feet up 1568 feet down

Wednesday 17th August

OK, guess which twit left his laptop charger at Insh Marshes RSPB Reserve? Thanks to the RSPB staff who posted it on for me. Brilliant of you and much appreciated. So, without a charger, I haven't been able to maintain the diary and so much has happened since those Aberdeen days.

I am now on North Ronaldsay, the most north-easterly of the Orkney Islands, staying in the hostel at the superb North Ronaldsay Bird Observatory.

I arrived on August the sixth. It seems so long now since that mill pond flat sea and clear blue sky, enjoyed whilst taking the ferry from Kirkwall.

Two days later, after having walked the west coastline on Sunday, and after having added **Sooty Shearwater** to the year list to take that to **272**, the sea at the northern end was a battering ram of the highest waves I have ever seen, creating a brown, cappuccino froth on the rocks in front of the seawatching hide. The hide was rocking as sixty mile an hour westerly winds whipped the sea into a frenzy.

No two days are the same here on this northern isle as the wind abated yet stayed from the west. I started to do census work with a superb Canadian girl, Larissa. Now the island is divided into six sections, A to F to facilitate a survey to be carried out of all the birds present on each day. The island is very flat with pasture for cows and many dry stone walls. Each sector has some sort of lake, except D. There are iris beds and crofters gardens. Crops are lacking with just one small area devoted to a small potato crop.

Then there is the coastline, rock with layered mud/sandstone and herds of the famous seaweed eating sheep, kept on the shore by an all-encompassing, tall dry stone wall. There is a rota of all the Bird Observatory staff so that they alternate which sections they cover.

Speaking of the staff, what a wonderful bunch of enthusiastic young people. George Gay and Samuel Perfect were here last year and it was great to see them again, both extremely knowledgeable and eager to find birds. With them are Erin and Bryony from Cheltenham, Larissa from Canada and Ellen. Gavin, the son of the Wardens Alison and Kevin, also surveys a sector. Gavin also carries out bird trapping duties with mist nets and Heligoland traps. All are talented, dedicated and fun-loving individuals who make a wonderful team.

Speaking of mist nets, I have to mention an early morning petrel trapping session with Erin, George and Gavin. Forty four Storm Petrels were caught and at 1:45 a.m. Erin shouted over to me, "Start to celebrate." She had just taken a Leaches Petrel out of the mist net. Bird number **273**.

Overall, it has been a week of seals, sheep and sea-watching, with most days being windy. Migration is yet to kick off yet yesterday showed signs that it may be just about to do so.

Whilst carrying out my survey of sector D one day I went to the front door of a croft to ask whether I could look in the three stone wall surrounded parts of a good-looking garden. The delightful lady, Lotti, said no problem and after a natter about how the island population is declining rapidly, I found three Willow Warblers in the fuchsia and sycamore.

So with winds from the south-east and more cloud and even rain forecast for the weekend, hopes are high that the year list will be added to soon. Target for August is ten of which I have four so far.

We have made a sweepstake of possibles at the Bird Observatory. Each participant picks two birds from a list of sixteen. The birds I hope to see by end of the month are:-

Great Shearwater
Pomarine Skua
Barred Warbler

White-rumped Sandpiper
Wryneck
Wood Warbler
Marsh Warbler
Citrine Wagtail
Sabine's Gull
Ortolan Bunting
Common Rosefinch
Buff-breasted Sandpiper
Icterine Warbler
Honey Buzzard
American Golden Plover
Booted Warbler

Dear reader, take a moment here to make your prediction over which bird species I see next during my stay on this magic isle. No peaking!

Saturday 20th August **fresh to strong E**

Rain AM, cloudy PM

Gavin, the Wardens' birthday boy son, rushes into the observatory and soon everyone is rushing into the ringing shed. He has trapped a juvenile Red-backed Shrike in one of the nearby Heligoland traps. Crowded into the small shed guests and staff admire the angry bird whilst I, after a quick view, quickly head off in the direction of the tall stone wall around the Observatory's fields. Gavin has seen a number of migrants sheltering from the rain and the gale along the sea wall and they included an Icterine Warbler; arguably the most important of the target birds for August. Gavin had texted me but I had stupidly not carried my mobile with me into the Obs, having left it on charge by my pillow!

I search the wall and am joined by Larissa, George and Gavin. Together we search as Willow Warblers, Pied Flycatchers and a Garden Warbler flit in front of us. No Icky, four of the birds end up in the Heligoland trap box and are taken to be processed.

What a wonderful start for Gavin's 19th birthday. There has obviously been a fall of migrants and who knows what else will turn up.

Larissa, the Canadian volunteer, has asked me to accompany her on census duties and together we set off for the expansive Section B. We walk and chat and pass Holland House before turning right towards a large area of irises and docks.

A phone call from Samuel Perfect. He has found an Icky and so I head off towards the potential Green Year tick. Within a couple of hundred yards Sam is phoning again, Gavin has found a Barred Warbler by the Post Office.

The location of Gavin's Barred Warbler is on my way to Samuel's Icterine Warbler and I meet up with Gavin first. For half an hour or so we search together but can't relocate the chunky warbler. I head off to the croft where Samuel had seen the Icterine; Samuel having left to carry on his census work. Reaching there I spend another half an hour watching a dense but small rectangle of willows and short sycamores but once again fail to see the special one. On returning to my bike I find that the gathered group of young bulls has chewed all of the laminated signs off the front of my bike. Gone is the RSPB – A Home for Nature, gone is the Marine Conservation Society and gone is the Stop Me and Buy One. They have eaten the lot, plastic, paper and all! At least they haven't eaten Albert the cuddly Albatross of the Birdlife International Albatross Campaign.

I rush back to Section B to try to find Larissa. I phone repeatedly but only receive 'leave a message' answers.

Eventually we do find each other. Larissa has found Garden Warbler and Pied Flycatcher whilst I was away. Larissa came to Britain with little knowledge of British birds but she has excellent field skills and sharp eyes. I cannot help but be very impressed with her attitude and ability.

We spilt up again in a short while as I head off for Brides Bay and Loch and she heads towards Stromness Point. This way we can cover more of Section B.

I meet two of the locals, Sheila and Ian, as they are persuading a group of black bullocks into a new pasture. I spend fifteen minutes or so talking to them about the island. Both born and bred on the island they say they would never consider leaving.

Two Whinchats are on fence posts along the road down to Brides and a Pied Flycatcher is the only migrant seen from a long walk along the seawall and beside the extensive iris beds at Bridesness Point.

Five Tufted Ducks are on Brides Loch and I wait here for Larissa, who I can see some way off searching around a ruined croft.

Together we circle the Loch, crashing through iris beds and tall grasses. At one point Larissa disappears and I am panicked thinking she has gone down in a muddy ditch. She has but luckily she has fallen horizontally into the mud which is only up to her knees.

Duck are flushed out, Shovelor, Teal and Mallard, waders too including two Green Sandpipers and a Ruff. A Reed Warbler is with a Sedge Warbler in the long grass; the former is a new bird for Larissa. We find the Whinchats and Larissa has yet another new bird for her growing British list.

Saturday 21st August **light NE**

Occasional fogs, mizzle

A **Barred Warbler** has been caught in the mist nets at Holland House and I cycle hard to get the bird onto the list. The first year bird even has faint flank barring as it is quickly and expertly processed, rung and released. I take a series of team photographs of the attendant volunteers and assistant wardens, everyone in a jovial mood, albeit tired. Three of them, George, Erin and Gavin haven't been to bed! The Barred Warbler is a regular scarcity that I know I will be seeing more in the field but at least this bird in the hand is securely onto my Green Year list.

From Holland House I decide to survey Section A and search along the dry stone walls that head towards Gretchen, a large pool not far from the Observatory.

A couple of visitors to the island, on approaching the hide at Gretchen, flush almost everything but once the three of us are settled inside waders soon start to return and what variety. Dunlin, Ringed Plover and Redshank, nine Black-tailed Godwits fly in and even better five Little Stints do likewise. These are topped by a Wood Sandpiper.

After Gretchen, two hours are spent searching Holland House gardens for migrants, a very tatty, ringed Chiff Chaff and a few Willow Warblers are seen.

The afternoon is spent surveying Section E with Larissa. The highlight is the time spent watching twelve species of wader at Westness. Four Little Stints, two Ruff, a Curlew Sandpiper and good numbers of other waders like Dunlin, Turnstone, Ringed Plover, Redshank, Curlew, Oystercatcher and Knot, all are feeding amongst seaweed and rocks in the large bay. Three Sanderling and none Golden Plover made the species count twelve.

Three Willow Warblers are in the nettles at the nearby ruined croft.

Heading along the beach north and searching the walls once more, a pied flycatcher is fly catching.

Back at Holland House, the ringers have packed up and sitting on a squat folding chair I watch a block of sycamores for an hour. The Barred Warbler with it's silver engagement ring is seen, a ringed Chiff, two Willow Warblers in better condition, a Blackbird, lots of House Sparrows and Linnets. A few Meadow Pipits pass overhead.

Late afternoon, Samuel has found a Greenish Warbler. Right at the far end of the island in the back garden of a croft in Section F, the bird is seen by all. Samuel is on a roll having found Wrynecks, Barred Warblers and Icterines and now Samuel has found a Greenish to add to his growing self-found list.

Sunday 22nd August

Early in the misty morning George Gay and I do the trap run, that is we see what birds are around the Heligoland traps around the Bird Observatory to catch and ring. It is a cool and foggy morning and a Lesser Whitethroat is caught at the first trap but an Acro eludes us by diving over the stone wall.

A Barred Warbler flies from out of cover at the next trap and flies hard across a field. One 'in the field', knew I would get one. Willow Warblers are taken with the Lesser Whitethroat to be rung.

I head off for the harbour to do survey work along the shore line. Eight Purple Sandpipers are the highlight, as confiding as ever once I sit down to watch them. A Redstart there is a new bird for my Year North Ronaldsay list.

Monday 23rd August   Happy Birthday Mum! Who loves you? Xxxxx

Ringing with the Three Musketeers again, Erin, Gavin and George, twenty eight birds involving twelve species caught including Pied Flycatchers, Swallows and a Wheatear.

This is at Holland House again with the twelve long mist nets set up mostly amongst the massed tall fuchsia bushes. Masses of bees buzz amongst the flowers.

Around the buildings behind the Laird's home a Black Redstart flits about as a sand martin flies with the Swallows.

I cycle around a few key locations, Ancum Willows being first. Here whilst talking with the ex-warden Pete Donnolly, who still lives on the island, a Whitethroat is amongst the iris flags and a Wryneck comes out onto the low stone wall nearby. It flies past us and lands on wires and even comes down onto the road nearby.

Later Lotti's garden has a Barred and a Willow Warbler in it. The Post Office garden has a Lesser Whitethroat.

Back at the Bird Observatory, Bryony points out two Red-backed Shrikes on the barbed wire fences.

In the afternoon it is Larrisa's turn to do the sea-watching session and together we sit in the sea-watching hide. A couple of Sooty Shearwaters pass west-bound and nine Manx Shearwaters. More exciting though is the appearance of five Risso's Dolphins. After getting Larissa onto them we phone the Bird Observatory and a full Land Rover arrives with the crew. Luckily everyone gets onto the dolphins albeit a bit distantly as they have drifted north west.

Continuing sea-watching alone another group of Risso's, six of them, come past. Three Storm Petrels do likewise and a summer plumaged Great

Northern Diver.

In the evening one of the Red-backed Shrikes enters a Heligoland trap and is rung to the delight of all of the visitors to the Obs. My evening is spent with two lovely Swiss ladies, one of whom is a contemporary dancer, who started dancing at The Mac Theatre in Birmingham, the city where I was born.

Tuesday 24th August

Up at 5:00 a.m. the fog is the thick and there is a light westerly. A Garden Warbler is caught at Holland and a Lesser Whitethroat is amongst the buildings. The Black Redstart is still around.

Larissa and I survey Section B once more. We do the first part together and see good numbers of Snipe, or snips as Larissa likes to call them, and Willow Warblers. We split up as last time; Larissa heads towards Stromness and I to Bride's.

The Golden Plover flock is close and numbers over a thousand yet no American or Pacific is hiding amongst them. A Fulmar has managed to get itself trapped in a ruined croft and I pick it up carefully, avoiding the spit out oil, and take it to the shore.

Wednesday 25th August

Bryony has found a possible Marsh Warbler at Bride's! Samuel, doing the survey with her, is convinced the Acro is a Marsh. I am at the sea-watching hide alone when the news comes in. I am there because George had a Cory's Shearwater pass earlier in the day. A speedy cycle run gets me to Bride's. With the crew assembled at the field where the possible rare warbler was last seen, a mist net is set up to try to catch it. At each attempt the bird misses the net by inches. The last attempt has the bird land seemingly at the bottom of the net but as Gavin rushes towards it the crafty bird appears behind the net and skips over the wall.

Beside the field is a huge area of iris flags and the bird flies off into the cover of these. Samuel is not giving up though and heads off in pursuit. Gavin, Erin and George remove their boots and follow. The fun that ensues is immense as the boys wade through thigh deep water in search of the bird. George even does a humpback whale breech impersonation into the deep waters of Ancum!

Eventually the search is called off and most people return to the Observatory with a question mark still hanging over the proper identification.

Samuel and I stay and for two hours search, find and get superb views of a **Marsh Warbler**. Bird number **276** goes onto the year list and is a great relief after what happened in May in Lincolnshire. You may remember that I found a Marsh Warbler, photographed it yet persuaded myself after a couple of hours that I was not sure that I was correct. My photographs mostly pointed to Marsh Warbler but I didn't count it. Now we have the bird and Sam is happy. He is phenomenal with his knowledge of birds and I stand in awe as he reels off the subtle ID features ad nausea.

Thursday 26th August

My plan had been to stay until the end of the month but the winds seem all wrong for further migrants (how wrong can one be!) and I decide to leave and head for Fair Isle via the Orkney mainland.

Samuel and I are out at 5:30 a.m. though hoping to refind the Marsh Warbler. My aim is to get better photographs, especially of the tertials and primaries.

We search but don't find it and after two hours return to the Observatory via Holland House garden.

Just time to shower, have breakfast and say the last goodbyes to everyone. A team hug ends in a mass tickle.

Onto the ferry, a phone call from George and as the boat heads off across the bay five distant figures wave. Tears and thanks.

North Ronaldsay is superb, the Bird Observatory, whether one uses the hostel or stays in the hotel-like Observatory itself, is likewise. The company is friendly and welcoming and the potential to find your own birds is high. Visit and you won't regret it.

The NRBO blog write up by George Gay later :-

On a sadder note, Gary Prescott the biking birder has moved on to Fair Isle for the next two months, it's been a privilege to learn from him for the last 3 weeks and the obs. staff will certainly miss having him around! We wish him all the best on his quest for 300 species and hopefully we'll have something good enough this autumn to draw him back!

Friday 26th August **Light SW**

Cloudy, calm and cool. Sun comes out late afternoon.

The ferry ride is reasonably smooth and the disembarkation likewise. Into the library in Kirkwall, the capital of the Orkney Isles, to check on a few internet things and then a cycle to Cottisgarth RSPB reserve. Here there is a fabulous visitors' centre overlooking the valley, with a remarkable resonance when one sings. I sing the evening away as the sun sets over the nearby moorland hills.

Saturday 27th August

A ride over the hills and down to Harray to meet with a dear friend, Alastair Forsyth, beside an Orkney loch. Alastair has no interest in LBJ's, little brown jobs. Not for him the thrill of a quick flash of dull brown, tawny brown, warm brown or buff. No tertials and primary projections for he to ponder over. No, Alastair prefers to look through a large flock of ducks and just maybe find the one with a slightly different head shape, a slightly different bill, a slight difference when in the eclipse plumage of summer. And thank goodness for that. Alastair has found an American duck, actually a **Ring-necked Drake** in eclipse. Eclipse meaning that nondescript plumage that many ducks take on during the Summer.

Bird number **277** goes onto the list. A male Hen Harrier drifts past, as does a Sparrowhawk and eight Ruff fly over the far shore of the loch.

Alan Beach, the local RSPB manager joins us. He asks me to say hello to David Parnaby, the Warden of the Fair Isle Bird Observatory, when I get there. That will be a pleasure.

The rest of the day is spent at Alastair's nearby house, with his wife Louise and one of their two daughters, Ellen. A lovely family of friends, we chat, observe what moths are within the moth trap from last night and look for hoverflies in their large garden. Alastair has a superb knowledge of both insect groups. The many moths in the trap include Northern Spinach, Snout, Square-spot and Rosy Rustic, Lesser Bordered Yellow Underwing, Dark Arches and any Large Yellow Underwings. There is also a new one for me, a Chevron and one that has Alastair exclaiming with delight, a Pink-barred Sallow.

They talk of their garden birds after a Hen Harrier flies overhead, especially of Louise's thrill at seeing a white phase Gyrfalcon on a fence post. Now that is an ambition bird for me. The closest I ever got to seeing one was when my second wife, Jane, our ten month old baby daughter, Rebecca and I were on our way down to Mousehole, Cornwall for a holiday. A superb male Gyrfalcon had set up residence in a quarry at Brixham, taking Jackdaws for a regular snack. We were on the way when Rebecca became ill with a fever. Sense dictated a doctor's visit. Still . . .

Louise Forsyth believes that crystals give protection to environments and she gives me a large whitish, heart-shaped crystal. This is for me to place in the ocean south of Fair Isle. The third one given, the other two are already in place; one protecting north Fair Isle, the other protecting the sea just south of Sumburgh Head, Shetland. I placed these thereon my previous Biking Birder trips; the former in 2010, the latter in 2015.

Ellen has a fascinating pet, a Bearded Dragon and holding him, well actually watching him climb my jumper, is thrilling. Ellen has a beautiful Orcadian accent, a sing-song lilt that is lacking in my throatal Brummie (Birmingham) monotone.

All too soon it is time to leave, the sun is setting and I need to get to the port in order to take the overnight ferry to Lerwick, Shetland.

Sunday 28th August

The ferry crosses a mill pond smooth sea and as the Shetland looms in the early morning, place names come and go along the east coast as the ship heads north towards Lerwick harbour; Sumburgh Head, Virkie, Channerwick, Mousa, I chat with an army veteran, Garry, who is here to help ex veterans with a project called **Military Veterans Agricultural Project.**

On arriving at Lerwick Harbour, only the Cooperative supermarket is open on this the Sabbath and my dire need of new shoes will have to wait until tomorrow to be sorted.

I book into the Lerwick Youth Hostel and meet two Swiss girls from Berne.

After walking through the deserted town in order to suss out a suitable shoe shop, I return to more mundane things with laundry duties at the hostel. The hostel is a large Edwardian house with shining wooden stairways and large, high ceilinged rooms. A group of young under twelve year olds from Orkney are here with their teachers and coaches for a football tournament against their local rivals, Shetland. Considering their age they are remarkably quiet. Graham is a native of North Ronaldsay, the island I have just left and we talk about the people of the island, the Tullochs and of the Observatory.

I receive a text from George Gay, the volunteer back at that Obs. *"just had an Icky Warbler. You should have stayed."*

An hour or so later, another message; a Sykes Warbler has been caught and ringed. Originally found by the ex-warden and announced as a Booted Warbler, the bird, on being netted, turned magically into a Syke's as measurements were taken. I am thrilled for everyone there. With an early morning Wood Warbler, that makes three birds that would have been new for my year list. I can only imaging the hilarity and excitement amongst the wonderful youngsters. They deserve such good fortune.

I watch an animation film, "Megamind", on Netflix and talk with an incredible German couple, Claudia and Michael, from a town in Bavaria. They are cycling tourists practising for a three year cycle together around the World that they will start next year. They are preparing a website, http://2like2.bike/ . I must keep in touch to see how this inspiring couple are getting on. Maybe we will meet up in Peru!

Evening, well 11:00 p.m. Facebook message arrives:-

North Ronaldsay Bird Observatory

Thanks Gary. Missing you already around the Obs.

Monday 29th August **fresh to strong SW**

Very sunny, in fact quite warm when sheltered from the wind

Happy birthday to my hero, my Dad! Love you. UTV!

New shoes are bought in Lerwick, Shetland! Now to get down to South Shetland where hopefully one or two of yesterday's rarities will still be around, especially the Booted and Icterine Warblers.

I count the roadkill victims along the way and sadly have a White Wagtail, the continental form of our Pied Wagtail, die in my hand as I pick it up, having just seen it just hit by a van. By the time I reach Cunningsbrough, there have been nine dead hedgehogs, four polecats of various colours from all yellow to all dark, two rabbits, a couple of gulls and the aforementioned wagtail. The hedgehogs and polecats reflect a problem population of these invading predators.

News from The Oracle, Phil Andrews, an Arctic Warbler is at Geosetter. The wind may be in my face but the tarmac is good and the news puts impetus into my pedalling feet. The places and views I have seen so often before during my visits to Shetland in the past, both Carbon and Green, I see again as I cycle south.

There is hardly a cloud in the sky and the strong sun is behind me as I search along the willows of the beck on arriving there. A warbler flits over from the adjacent crop field, famous for having a Thick-billed Warbler three years ago. It is a Willow Warbler. Further up the hill, as I cross a small bridge I see the Arctic Warbler and it dives into cover. It continues up the hill and eventually gives views when in a small valley with just a few less dense willows. It then flies uphill into the garden of a nearby house.

Roger Riddington arrives with another birder. Roger is the editor of the superb British Birds magazine and a brilliant and extremely intelligent birder. Together we circumnavigate the garden but can't find the Arctic. Roger goes to the head of the valley and heads downhill. I go downhill and search uphill.

The Arctic Warbler shows itself in a small willow to Roger and I hasten up to where he is. Three more birders arrive; Chris Dodds, the friendly Ranger from the Fair Isle Bird Observatory, Hugh Harrop, the very well-known bird photographer and author and Craig Nisbet from Noss. Soon, having seen the bird extremely well, most birders leave for pastures new leaving me and Hugh. He talks of the recent publishing of the bird identification book, *Britain's Birds: An Identification Guide to the Birds of Britain and Ireland*

He talks honestly about the few errors that are in it and of the ten years it took to collate all of the images. Having seen it in the bird observatory lounge at North Ronaldsay, in my opinion it is a magnificent book.

Arctic Warbler, bird number **278**.

The cycle ride to Quendale in the sunshine gives beautiful views of the Loch of Spiggie and the coastline, with its sandy beaches, sand dunes and prominent headlands. Searching the bushes around the watermill at Quendale doesn't give me yesterday's Icky Warbler, just three Willow Warblers.

Tuesday 30th August **very strong SW gales**

Cloudy with dampening mizzle

Cycling towards Grutness, South Shetland is only possible when going downhill and only then by leaning into the gale. The occasional larger vehicle, a lorry say or a transit van, has me almost fall off by the suck back from the wind. Uphill I struggle as I push hard and actually get blown over once as I fall onto the wet grass verge.

The barrier is down at Sumburgh Airport and the guard relates the reasons why he is on the island as we wait for a plane to come in. Years in the army, this Mancunian (from Manchester – red/United by the way) is bitter over the way life has dealt him jobs that apparently have a habit of failing him. Still he is a pleasant enough chap and a warm handshake sends me on my way over the runway once clearance is given. The plane having come in askance because of the side wind.

A visit of the Iron Age houses of Scatness is interesting. It is just a shame that the visitor's centre doesn't open until 10:15 a.m. It would have been lovely to be re-acquainted with the staff. I met them all back in 2010 when their help and friendship was greatly appreciated.

To Grutness and into the harbour waiting room with its heater and magazines. These include a couple of British Birds magazines and BBC Wildlife, as well as the RSPB's Nature's Home and various chat ones.

I don't expect the Good Shepherd to arrive for the crossing to Fair Isle, surely the wind is too strong. Yet arrive it does and the less said of the next three hours of my life the better. Hell, sheer hell with vomit and fear, two of us in the hold and both sick. One moment the cry comes from aloft "hold on!" The boat makes a sickening and sudden, almost vertical dive and crash, I am hurled along the back bench. An hour of filling sick bags and listening to music to try to take my mind away from the motion goes by. Maybe I fall asleep. I know I dream. Dream that I am on solid ground, traipsing the geos of Fair Isle.

Calmer waters, purgatory and then redemption and sanctuary, we arrive at North Haven, the harbour of the paradise that is Fair Isle, North Haven. Massive thanks to Neil Thompson, the Captain of the ship, a hug from Elena, a Fair Isle native and friend. A hug from Lee Gregory too. Actually I think he is shocked by the hug. I am just so happy to see him, a brilliant birder and friend. Rachel is there too, the kind young lady, who last year allowed me to camp on her croft's lawn for three weeks.

Lee points out a Long-tailed Duck on the nearby rocks, the first of hopefully many special Fair Isle birds. It is an earlier than usual arrival and has a wing depleted of flight feathers for some reason.

There is a Booted Warbler at Shirva and I cycle there past the magnificent building that is the Fair Isle Bird Observatory.

I search the small garden and, on not finding the rarity, turn around to find another friend perched on a stone up the grassy hill, Cath Mendez. Together we spot three people converging on the Meadow Burn downhill from where we are perched and head that way ourselves.

Booted Warbler, bird number **279**, goes onto the list but what a fast moving bird; one minute in front of us, the next half a field way. What a great bird to welcome me to Fair Isle.

Cath needs to get back to the Observatory where she is working as a volunteer and I go in search of birds. I walk around the east of the island and inquire about the availability of Springfield, a self-catering croft in the south. Fully booked up I head back north via Daa Water and Pund.

I arrive at the bird observatory just in time to see Lee holding a mist netted Barred Warbler.

The Bird Log at 9-ish, with its usual tolling bell and jugs of steaming hot chocolate for the guests, starts with highlights being 176 Wheatear, sixty three Willow Warblers, 106 White Wagtails, 180 Twite, 684 Meadow Pipits and singles each of Barred, Marsh and Booted Warblers and a Common Rosefinch.

Afterwards, the walk back to my abode for the month of September is under a Milky Way star-filled sky.

Wednesday 31st August **light to fresh SW**

Sunny AM showers PM

It is a glorious, very sunny and calm morning. I walk to watch the trap run but miss it as David Parnaby, the Observatory warden, drives past me.

My fault, I got up too late to catch David at the Observatory.

So to the North Haven and back along the road and dykes to the crofts Setter, Pund, Chalet and Barkland. Fascinating to see lines of Wheatears on the stone walls and Willow Warblers sometimes in pairs on angelica stems.

At Shirva an Acrocephalus Warbler sp. eludes me. Twice it flies fast over the thick vegetation and twice it dives straight into the same. I try sitting on a pile of uncomfortable stones on the other side of the garden but it offers no views. It seems to be of a rather too warm brown to be anything other than a Reed Warbler but I would like views that would confirm that.

To the shop for provisions, I meet Mati, the wonderful Venezuelan lady who is one of the crofters that makes original Fair Isle garments. She invites me to look at a book of indigenous tribes in the Amazon and I accept her kind offer of coffee at her croft half an hour later.

Years ago Mati and her then partner David cycled from London to Greece with a two year old toddler, Sebastian in a bicycle chair. Incredible.

A friend of Mati's, Kathryn, calls in with her two young children. Kathryn talks about being a library analyst on Anglesey a few years ago and of her love for the bird artist, Charles Tunnicliffe. She relates about how funds were raised to buy the Tunnicliffe artworks that were put on sale at Christie's auction house of London by the Tunnicliffe family upon his death. The successful purchase by the Anglesey Library brought the collection back to the island he loved.

I am here for more than friendly banter and memories though. I want to buy two garments; one for Dad, one for Mum. I look through the folders and choose a cardigan for Mum and a more traditional jumper for Dad. I have a problem. Purchase is not like that when one goes to a department store with machine-made racks of already measured items. Here all is bespoke and I need to get around a dozen measurements of both my parents. I want the garments to be a surprise! I need help and there is no one better at carrying out such a task without giving the game away than my sister, Donna. I text her and later send this email . . . .

Hiya Donna,

Hope retirement is suiting you! I know it is. Isn't life just great? How is everyone? How was France? Give my love to everyone.

Anyway I would love to be a fly on the wall when you try to get the measurements I need. Obviously don't let on what it is for. I know you will think up something and I know it will be hilarious.

Anyway . .

Please have a look at <u>www.mativentrillon.co.uk</u> for a measuring guide and have a look at the product variety. I have made a choice but if you have any advice I will take it *into account. You have the fashion knowledge and understand Mum and Dad more than me. Don't worry about the prices! I have that sorted. I have been saving up for something special.*

Mum … cardigan or jumper? If the latter, high or low neck, wide or narrow neck?

Measurements for Mum.....

1. *chest*
2. *hips*
3. *length – nape/neck to bottom*
4. *neck*
5. *armpit (not tight)*
6. *biceps with arm up (bent up at elbow)*
7. *fist measurement*
8. *armpit – palm start*
9. *top of collarbone to palm start*
10. *shoulders – front*
11. *shoulders – back.*

Dad ….

As above but consider what he would like; cardigan or jumper?

Thanks Sis. You're a star. I've been planning this for months. Mati is an incredible woman. She is from Venezuela and came here with her partner after he and she had cycled from London to Athens with a two year old toddler. Her croft is fabulous. You should see the views from the lounge and kitchen. I'll have to photograph it and show you. She is very arty and her garments are amongst the best. Last year Chanel 'stole' some by two of their representatives visiting and buying a few things. Then they returned to Chanel and they copied the garments! At least they apologised after an internet campaign showed them up for product theft.

The ferry ride over was sheer hell and I was very sick. Mind you, anything is worth it to be and I have so many good friends here. Read the blog and Facebook for details.

Love and thanks,

Gary xxx

Outside once more, Whinchat and Wheatear, Willow Warblers and waders, the way is slowly made towards the Obs. for the log call. A juvenile Rose-coloured Starling has been seen there, found by Cath Mendez.

Bird Log - Wheatear down to 126, Twite down to 145.

167 Rock Pipits. Now why does Fair Isle have 167 whereas North Ronaldsay, just twenty five miles away to the south west, have almost none?

No stars on the way back to my abode and the wind is strong in my face.

The Year List is **279**, twenty five more than this time last year. Importantly the list includes twenty five birds I didn't see last year.

August Monthly Statistics:-

Green Year list	279 birds
Year ticks seen in August	10
Bird species had, not seen in 2015	4
Mileage in August	395.82 miles
Total mileage for the year	5420.55 miles
Average mileage on days cycled/walked	15.55 miles
Elevation : up	13,649 feet
: down	14,328 feet

Best birds : ***White-winged Scoter, Leaches' Petrel, Wryneck, Barred, Marsh, Arctic and Booted Warbler, Ring-necked Duck.***

There are a number of amazing people who live on Fair Isle and produce a variety of garments. The future of the island's community depends on these small businesses thriving. To see more details please have a look at each of the following and make a purchase . . or two :-

The real Fair Isle knitwear, Local knitters and crafters:

EXCLUSIVELY FAIR ISLE
Elizabeth Riddiford
Schoolton, Fair Isle, Shetland ZE2 9JU
Tel: 01595 760 250
Email: [via website]
Website: www.exclusivelyfairisle.co.uk

FAIR ISLE MADE IN FAIR ISLE
Hollie Shaw & Catriona Thomson
Burkle, Fair Isle, Shetland ZE2 9JU
Tel: 01595 760 399
Email: shawderyk@btconnect.com
Website: https://www.facebook.com/hollie.shaw.3

FAIR ISLE KNITWEAR

Mati Ventrillon

Nedder Taft, Fair Isle, Shetland ZE2 9JU

Tel: 01595 760 255

Email: mativentrillon@mativentrillon.co.uk

Website: www.mativentrillon.co.uk

THE FAIR ISLE TEXTILE WORKSHOP

Kathy Coull

Ms Kathleen Coull, Upper Leogh, Fair Isle, Shetland ZE2 9JU

Tel: 01595 760 248

Email: kathy.coull@btinternet.com

Website: www.kathycoull.com & http://shetlandartsandcrafts.co.uk/members/the-fair-isle-textile-workshop/

TOMMY'S ART GALLERY

Tommy Hyndman

Auld Haa, Fair Isle, Shetland ZE2 9JU

Tel: 01595 760 349

Email:tommyartgallery@yahoo.com

Website: http://fair-isle.blogspot.co.uk/p/b-b.html

9

SEPTEMBER

"Fair Island" or possibly "Far off Isle" or Sheep Island."
The Norse form, *Frioaray*, literally means "calm, peaceful isle" or "Island of Tranquility."

Meaning of Fair Isle

Thursday 1st September **fresh to strong SW**

Cloudy and cool

A.D.I.P. - Another Day In Paradise

Early morning trap run with Lee Gregory, the trap run is when the warden or one of his assistants walks each of the Heligoland traps trying to catch birders to be rung with a small metal numbered ring and processed. Details measured and taken include primary feather length, the bird's weight and age. Today just a re-trapped Robin is caught.

A walk down to North Haven, three Arctic Terns are noisy and the long-staying Long-tailed Duck is busy diving. Interesting to watch how a Black Guillemot deals with a small flatfish that it has caught.

I spend a short time collecting the plastic bottles and such that were missed the day before on the beach at South Haven. One bottle has a language on it I don't recognise. Photographed, it is put into a rubbish skip in the harbour.

Back at the observatory yesterday's Rose-coloured Starling, found by Cath Mendez, puts in an appearance. The only other better bird I see is a Greenshank accompanied by a Dunlin flying over Pund later in the day. Now the lack of good birds could be because I have a wonderful time with Neil Thompson, the Captain of the ferry, The Good Shepherd IV. He has a new guitar to show off and plays U2, Floyd, Deep Purple, Steely Dan, Queen and Bad Company songs for a long while.

The evening's bird log details that the Booted Warbler is still present; as are sixty five Wheatear, seventeen Willow Warblers, singles each of Barred and Garden warblers, two Lesser Whitethroat and a Goldcrest. The latter is the five gram miracle termed by Lee, a bird weighing half a teaspoon of sugar that can fly over the North Sea and beyond. Meadow Pipit numbers are at 752.

The plastic bottle from the morning beach clean? Well the language turned out to be Haitian Creole, the bottle a chlorine-based water purification product. 7,000 kilometres in a direct line, the bottle being here is due to the hopefully here forever Gulf Stream.

Friday 2nd September **light to fresh SW**

Rain – AM, sunny PM.

A Barred Warbler is in the Observatory's garden and a Kestrel flies over nearby. The Goldcrest from yesterday is still down in the harbour area, as is the Long-tailed Duck. From the state of her wings, she isn't going anywhere fast.

The day is spent walking the south of the island, particularly around the crofts and South Lighthouse.

I have a task to perform that may save the ocean. Louise Forsyth of Orkney, who I visited last week, has given me a large, heart-shaped whitish crystal. This she believes has powers that will help the ocean. From an elevated position on a cliff at the southernmost tip of the island it is thrown into the surging waters.

Louise's website detailing her work in this is:-

http://crystalearthworks.net/about/profile/

Actually this is the third crystal that I have placed around Fair Isle. The first was back in 2010, thrown from the Good Shepherd IV into the waves north of Fair Isle. Last year the crystal flew from atop the high cliff at Sumburgh Head, South Shetland.

The evening log has the Wheatear count up at 227, a large increase on yesterday. Also up, yet less markedly are Willow Warbler at twenty three, whilst the number of Barred and Garden Warblers has doubled with two of each. Meadow Pipit numbers are rising fast, now at 822. How David, Lee and Ciaran count them is beyond me. Clouds of them in any field are extremely difficult to assess.

Maybe Louise's crystals do have magical powers for tonight there is the best Aurora Borealis I have ever seen. It is so good that a decision to walk all the way to the North Lighthouse in the dark seems the correct one. It is such a shame that my camera won't take a photograph that shows the curtain and flare against a green misty background.

Saturday 3rd September **light to fresh S**

Sunny start, sunny intervals later.

I love Fulmars. They are curious of anyone walking the cliffs and come close to watch you pass. They cuddle up in pairs or small groups on the cliffs and swirl en masse against any coastal aspect giving views of such magnificence that it takes one's breath away.

Today my walk takes me south once more, this time staying close to the cliffs and geos. Geos are rocky inlets in the high mound-like hills that have very steep inaccessible cliffs and some grassy slopes. Migrant birds have a habit of congregating near the top of such. Sometimes though it is worth sitting down and watching the cliffs themselves.

Starting at the top of Hill Dyke, a long high dry stone wall that bisects the western half of the island between the heather moorland of the north and the fertile fields of the crofting land to the south, a large female Peregrine causes some alarm to the other birds.

Down by the Raevas three Swifts are zooming about and in a field here are seven Ruff and ten Black-tailed Godwits.

Down at the South Lighthouse more waders are on the shore; Sanderling and Knot, Turnstone and Dunlin. Two Lapland Buntings are by the school.

The birders present, well that is Tony Vials from Northamptonshire, a birder who has been coming to the Fair Isle for many years and has many tales to tell, and I as well as the Observatory quartet, have been waiting for the south west wind to change. During the afternoon it does, the sun comes out to celebrate the famous south east wind. Tomorrow could be good.

Back in the Midlands, the land of my birth, the nature reserves have been having an all-dayer, that is a birdwatching competition where each reserve tries to beat each other over how many species they see in a twenty four hour period.

My all-dayer on Fair Isle gave me forty seven birds, a Barred Warbler late in the day being the last. The Fair Isle birding team; David, Lee and Ciaran's total is 68.

Sunday 4th September **very light E-NE**

Very warm and sunny, almost no cloud all day. Not typical Fair Isle weather!

Trap run with Lee again, and with quite a group of visitors too. The 'Merseyside' group have joined the run. There are more birds around today. On my cycle run to the Observatory before the trap run I had seen Willow Warblers and Wheatears along the dykes and walls. By the end of the six Heligoland trap run Lee has five birds in five bags; two Wheatear, two Meadow Pipits and a Reed Warbler.

The sun is a shining on a beautiful morning. A text, *Wood Warbler at South Raeva.* A fast cycle ride down the island, the bike thrown against the shop wall and a dash over a field. Wood Warbler on the list, bird number 280. Thanks Lee Gregory.

It might seem crazy to some birders that every Biking Birder year I struggle to get Wood Warbler on a Green Year list but they stop singing by the time I get to their breeding areas and once that happens they are so hard to find.

Walking back to collect the bike another text comes in, this one from the warden David Parnaby. *Phyllosc with a wing bar, South Naversgill.*

After collecting some nuts and raisins for my breakfast, I make my way to Hill Dyke and see David coming down the other side of the high dry stone wall. Thanking him for the text and then walking towards the west end of the wall, a large warbler lands on a nearby barbed wire fence. I shout to David, "Icky!" who turns to look. I have found an **Icterine Warbler**. Another new bird for the Green Year list. This is going to be a special day!

The rest of the day in glorious weather is spent exploring each and every geo from Gunnawark to Skinners Glig on the west coast of Fair Isle. Each geo has a small group of migrants; mostly Willow Warblers yet also Pied Flycatchers and the occasional different bird. Reaching South Naaversgill, or Tyneside just south of it, I sit down and remember the Red-flanked Bluetail of last year. There are three Willow Warblers down in the shadows. No there isn't. There are two. The other has a very faint wing bar; a Greenish Warbler and my third of this fabulous year.

The height of the cliffs is exhilarating and the views of roosting gannets massed on grassy slopes is enthralling. The views down high vertiginous cliffs is captivating and each geo has its own distinguishing features. One may have grassy parapets, another sheer rock face cliffs. Grey Geo has the latter and on the sun-facing cliff a Barred Warbler is sunbathing. Motionless the large warbler just perches on a small jutting out rock face. The next geo has a large bowl-like quality with Alum Bay like colours. It also has yet another Icterine Warbler hopping around the top. At one moment I pop my head over the cliff edge and find a Lesser Whitethroat sitting just below me.

To the top of the highest point on the island, Ward Hill, 217 metres high. Searching amongst the ruins of WW2 concrete no birds show themselves.

Down at the large radio mast, two noisy Arctic Skuas are resting and another Pied Flycatcher flits around.

To the Observatory eventually in the evening, the log details a remarkable day.

Green Year list – **281**. This is twenty six ahead of this time last year and I only reached the heights of 281 on 18th of November, 2015 with a Long-billed Dowitcher at Newbiggin Pools, Northumberland.

Monday 5th September **fresh to strong SW**

Cloudy

The day after the banquet and everything is quiet. I walk around the south of the fair Fair Isle. The Red-throated Diver is asleep as usual in area of the South Harbour and Tommy's Guest House, Da Haa has a Greenish Warbler in the garden.

Into the graveyard, I look at each headstone. The ages of the people interred here are mostly in the eighty years bracket and there is even one gentleman, James Anderson Stout, who lived to be 101.

The War memorial details the names of eight men who died in WW1 and one in WW2. Such a high figure for such a small island.

Utra has a single Dunlin probing its mud. Will an American wader drop in on the island soon? There are reports of Buff-breasted Sandpipers on North Ronaldsay. Send one here please.

A quiet day for me, with some time spent pensively atop cliff tops. I do, though, venture down a very steep incline to access a beach. The surge of the sea here is thunderous and the cliffs to the left of Malcolm's Head are huge. Plastic on the beach, long lengths of rope and a Lesser Black-backed Gull, a juvenile, that doesn't look as though it will sadly last much longer. It is being battered by the waves and every time it gets purchase on a rock it immediately gets washed off again.

The evening log at the Bird Observatory details ten species of warbler; thirty five Willow Warblers, four Garden warblers, three Lesser Whitethroat, two Chiff Chaffs and singles each of Icterine, Greenish and Booted Warblers, Blackcap and Whitethroat. Which species did I miss off my list? 135 Wheatears, a couple of Redstarts, nine Lapland Buntings and eleven Pied Flycatchers are also logged.

Tuesday 6th September **Fresh SW**

High cloud and sunny later.

Happy birthday Rebecca! Xx I love you very much.

A Spotted Flycatcher is around Pund first thing. Pund is my favourite starting point for a day's migrant search with its patches of nettles and dry stone walls.

On the trap rung with David Parnaby a new Robin is caught, as is a Meadow Pipit, three Rock Pipits and a Willow Warbler. Of great interest though is a Pied Flycatcher with a Norwegian ring on its leg. This is the first ever occurrence on Fair Isle of one from there.

I set off down to North and South Haven, ostensibly to clear these two beaches of plastic rubbish washed in on the tide. A bin liner full latter, I find a set of wings and the gruesomely bloody head of a Sanderling. There's a bird of prey around somewhere.

Beaches cleared I head for the south of the island again. Now by the Kirk a Lapwing has been seen by everyone else but me for the last week. Come log time in the evening it is always taunting me. Lapwing? One.

Today I have it walking amongst grassy tussocks that have been hiding it.

Down to Meadow Burn and the Booted Warbler is still there. The Raevas Geos have a single Redstart and Lower Stackhoul has a Lesser Whitethroat.

My daughter, Rebecca's birthday, yet I have to be happy enough that I can message her on Facebook. My mobile phone is dead and I have no other way to say . . . HAPPY BIRTHDAY ANGEL! Looking at the feral nature of the so-called Rock Doves here I may be able to send a message by carrier pigeon. Pure Rock Doves they are not.

Wednesday 7th September **calm with light SW**

High full cloud cover

A male Greenland Wheatear is caught on the trap run this morning. Great to see one in the hand, a favourite bird.

Lee Gregory shows me some of the detail to be seen on the dead Sanderling I found yesterday including the lack of a hind toe, a diagnostic feature of the bird.

I walk the cliffs away from the Observatory and via the Gully, where a Dunnock is hiding in the small patch of bushes, I head for east of the island and views over to Sheep Rock. The weather is benign and mild, a little soporific and I spend a long time sitting on cliff edges watching the activity of Rock Pipits and Fulmars on and around the steep cliffs and beaches.

Thursday 8th September **Fresh to very strong E**

Cool, thick fog mid-morning, heavy rain all afternoon. Clear skies and Milky Way to lead me 'home' around 10:30 p.m.

Up early, I set off before sunrise towards the south west of the island. There aren't many migrants but there are the usual good numbers of Bonxies. Maybe you know them better as Great Skuas but they are one of my favourite birds. I have a lot of favourite birds. Big, bulky and occasionally quite aggressive, the skuas come to investigate as I walk near to them. By North Raeva, a Flava Wagtail keeps going just over the next rise as I try and get good views of it.

I decide to seawatch at South Lighthouse but can't for when I arrive there fog descends and I can't even see the sea!

Walking back along the road towards the Observatory I take the small track to Setter, my friends Gordon and Perry Barnes' croft back in the Sixties and through to Hill Dyke. With the wind freshening I stay sheltered by the long, tall wall but sensibly think that searching the geos wouldn't be a safe activity.

Instead I make my way down Sukki Mire adjacent to the airstrip, and watch as a Greenshank gets chased by a Bonxie.

On reaching the Observatory boot room I am feeling that the morning has been OK; not one where rarities were everywhere but a nice solid morning's birding. Tony Vials soon changes my mood. "Ortolan Bunting!"

I had just divested my thick waterproofs and jumper. I put my coat back on and trudge to search the area where the scarce bunting was last seen. After two hours of squelching through wet grass and along broken stone dykes, still no Ortolan. I need this bird!

Tony and Cath Mendez join in the search. Tony hears it and points to some grass where he thinks it has dropped in. We circle it and tighten the circle. No Bunting. I head off towards the Gully trap. Three birds land on some rocks nearby. The first two are meadow pipits. The third has a large moustachial, a very distinct eye ring and a pink bill . . . **ORTOLAN**!!!

It pops behind the stones. The three of us go nearer and it flies over our heads calling, plopping down into the long grass some distance away.

Rain starts to pour and Lee Gregory arrives. We both want to find the bird for Cath Mendez to see. We go in search of it and find it. Turning to call Cath over, we can only see her departing along the stone wall back to the dry warmth of the Bird Observatory. Fair weather birder!

Lee and I laugh and enjoy reasonable views of this skulking flighty bunting.

Green Year list – **282**. This is twenty five ahead of this time last year. This day last year was my first birding day on Fair Isle in 2015, a day in which I saw a Citrine Wagtail and an Arctic Warbler. The latter was just before seeing a group of Orcas went past North Lighthouse. What a welcome!

Friday 9th September **Fresh SE-S**

Cool, high cloud, Ward Hill has low cloud over it. AM. Fog rolls in and leaves by Noon.

A Bonxie is watching me carefully as I approach the Gully. Maybe they aren't as aggressive at this time of year yet I still duck as it decides to torpedo me. There is something so attractively exciting about having such a big bird come zooming in at you at pace from a hundred metres away. They circle then fall until they are about a metre from the ground. Then the attack begins in earnest, only ending when they just avoid your head by turning at the last minute. No bonk this time from a Bonxie.

There has been heavy rain overnight and the Gully's waterfalls are somewhat larger than usual, cascades of dirty brown water that rushes down to the sea.

I walk the Parks area and explore each croft's gardens as I head south, Setter, Chalet and Barkland. Wheatear on posts and a Whinchat in Burkle are the most prominent birds.

Ward Hill has been covered with hill fog and this descends to cover the island with a thick blanket for a couple of hours.

In the afternoon I go into the island's museum and spend an hour or so going through photograph albums, finding photographs of my late friend Gordon Barnes and his wife Perry. I also read up on all of the Fair Isle men who died in the World Wars, whose memorial I saw in the graveyard.

On leaving the museum I bump into Lee Gregory, my dearest friend out of the assistant wardens and together we bird the south.

Sitting together on the bench at Schoolton, a Whinchat perches atop some twigs. It looks rather cold and pale and we call it a Siberian Whinchat; a sort of joke if one thinks of the plumage on a Siberian Stonechat.

Later today, Lee sends me a photograph of this bird on Facebook, calling it such and giving it a Latin name of *Saxicola prescottius*.

Lee is a brilliant birder and he soon spots an interesting Lesser Black-backed Gull, an *intermedius* sub-species. Its mantle is as black as the nearby Greater Black backed Gulls yet it is smaller and has yellow legs. My excuse at not having spotted it is that, to me, it is hidden behind a sheep. Pretty lame excuse. Lee is one of those seemingly instinctive birders whose speed on making a sighting is light years ahead of me. During the Biking Birder years it has been such a pleasure and privilege to bird with so many incredibly skilled birders. Lee is one and he reminds me of Howard Vaughan at Rainham Marshes RSPB reserve, Trevor Girling in Norfolk and Adam Archer in the Midlands. All are fine birders.

A Tree Pipit is on Tommy's garden wall at Da Haa.

The Red-throated Diver is in its usual position near to the beach.

Moving back up the island Lee goes off to the east, as I go back to the Kirk to collect my bike.

Earlier on I had met Nick Riddiford near there at Da Water. He told me that he had seen a Moorhen there with the young tufted duck. Returning now there is a Moorhen tucked into the grass adjacent to the open water. I can't make out much of it but from the black blob I can see I presume it to be an adult.

On the way back to the Fair Isle Bird Observatory Lee and I meet up again and walk together but only until Lee sees a Fulmar that has lost its way. A Fulmar shouldn't be walking down the middle of a Fair Isle road. Lee takes it back to the sea.

Saturday 10th September **Strong SW**

No cloud AM, sunny intervals PM

On this date last year Fair Isle had Yellow-browed Warblers and other such birding goodies. Today the island seems relatively bare of such. The early morning trap run catches five birds; three Rock Pipits, a Meadow Pipit and a Willow Warbler. What migrants await?

By end of day I have seen a reasonable number of Lapland Buntings, around fourteen, a couple of Swallows, three Golden Plover and not a lot else. The island has looked beautiful all day, though, with the sun shining, and it has been a pleasure to photograph crofts and landscapes.

Birds are going to come soon but we need the wind to change. A south-easterly would do nicely.

Late evening texts arrive from Trevor Girling. (22:38)

Hi mate. It's Trev Girling.

I reply. (23:10)

Thanks mate. Amazingly quiet here. BCNU.

Trevor. (23:12)

Just wait. Biggy coming your way by Tuesday. I have a feeling a Yellow Warbler.

Me. (23:12)

That'll do!

Sunday 11th September **light to fresh S**

Very sunny AM, deteriorating through the day to rain by early evening.

Still no new birds around my patch, Pund to start the day. There are four Lapland Buntings though by the road near Setter as I walk to the Observatory for breakfast. Three more Laplands are by the Plantation.

The Observatory garden has a Willow Warbler and twice its size, an Icterine Warbler.

The weather is fine and I decide to bird the bracken patches on the moorland north of the island's airstrip and head towards the geos from there.

Snipe come out of each bracken patch, four and three and Bonxies 'ork' and come close, sometimes too close for my comfort. Duck time again!

The geos look splendid in the sunshine, cuts into the cliffs with steep inclines and rocky ledges of various heights, depths and appearances. The trick I have been told and indeed read about with Bill Oddie's advice in one of his books, is to sit and wait. I do so at each geo in turn. An hour or so later, I have seen just a single Goldcrest. That was in Tyneside, a favourite geo. Today I don't recognise the geo coming from the north and am a little distracted. In fact, I feel rather lost and it's only with the help of Lee Gregory, who is doing the North census route, that I re-orientate myself.

Lee leaves for lunch and I head down a geo following a sheep track deep down into the geo, South Gunnerwark. There is a metal rope attached to rocks to provide some security that leads the way down to a ledge where I stop and watch beaches to left and right with dreams of an American warbler.

Returning to the grasslands near to Pund I receive a text from The Oracle. *Rosefinch on Fair Isle?* I haven't been told of one so I phone Lee Gregory. He hasn't heard of one either yet apparently it is out there on Rare Bird Alert.

A few minutes later Lee phones me back. Cairan has seen a Common Rosefinch by the South Lighthouse. I head that way.

I search the crop at Skaden. I search the fenced off area at Muckle Uri geo but I can't find a Rosefinch. There are Twite and Meadow Pipits but that's all.

I head off to search all of the nearby croft gardens.

Later in the afternoon as rain starts to fall I walk to the Observatory and on reaching it meet Suzanne Parnaby who tells me that Ciaran has had the Rosefinch again. Only one thing for it, I get on my bike and cycle south in the rain and the wind.

I meet Ciaron just south of Shirva and he tells me that he only saw it fly over. I decide that my chances of finding it in the murk and rain are slim at most. I head off for my bed.

Monday 12th September **Very strong SE gale**

Very sunny

It has rained heavily overnight. Albert the Albatross on the front of my bike is sodden yet Oscar the Otter looks chipper. To the Obs for breakfast the gale propels me there at speed, indeed scary speed as I go downhill from Setter.

A Willow Warbler is on the grass near to the lounge window and yesterday's Icterine Warbler seems to have decided to stay another day.

I walk down to the harbour and clear the plastic bottles and a long piece of rope from the gale-battered beach. Five Arctic Terns are in the shelter of North Haven and it is delightful when I come around a large container by the wall of the harbour and come across two Goldcrests at my feet. Here come the migrants, these are the harbingers of things to come, lost waifs weighing less than an ice cream wafer each.

With spray coming over the cliffs of Buness I make my way to the Observatory for a day of music and emails.

Tuesday 13th September **Fresh SE-E**

Thick fog - AM

Whinchat and Willow Warbler at Chalet first thing with fog so thick one can't see more than fifty yards. The walk to North Haven has the fog acting as a quietening blanket with occasional bird calls being somewhat muted. On arrival there is a young Cormorant in the bay and a single each of Goldcrest and Willow Warbler in the harbour area shows migrants are arriving. Confirming that the Bird Observatory garden has a Pied Flycatcher and a Redstart.

Breakfast ends and Cath Mendez rushes into the lounge. "Lee has found a Little Bunting!" "Where?" No reply, Cath runs out through the lobby just in front of me and we both get out into the courtyard. Lee is there. The rare bunting is just around the back of the nearby garage. Lee and I creep forward and the bird suddenly flies past us calling. It unfortunately lands behind some pallets near to the garden but out of sight.

Then it flies behind the garden itself still giving no grounded views. I am in my socks and I remove them to follow the bird bare foot. The bird flies again, all the way down to the Haven. I follow it despite the stones on the path but here it disappears never to be seen again. Untickable views, I am not going to count that on the strength of flight views and a couple of 'tsit' calls.

Socks retrieved and boots on, a walk down the island sticking to the cliffs and geos, occasional Willow Warbler on rocky beaches, occasional over-flying Lapland Buntings.

Nick Riddiford has a few moths in his fridge from last night's moth trap including a very large and spectacular Convolvulous Hawkmoth and a micro species that I can't spell properly, Acteris effractcena; well that's what it sounded like!

Outside and birding once more, a dozen Lapland Buntings fly over Da Water, as does a very high Grey Heron and a Curlew.

Thick fog descends once more and Lee and Cairan have had a very mobile Citrine Wagtail. I hear that it is at Da Water. Then it is at Kennaby. I search both areas but cannot find it.

I decide to sit and wait at Da Water and meet Sue, wife of Kenny and we chat for a long while. Sue, a woman with a lovely sunshine personality, tells me that she found a bird new for Britain in their garden, a Brown-headed Cowbird. I later found out that she phoned the Bird Observatory to say that she had a bird in the garden that looked like a brown headed Starling with a Hawfinch-like bill. That's Fair Isle. Well done Sue! I would have loved to have been on the island that day to see her face when she found out just how special her find was.

Down to the south once more I search the crofts and field, ditches and beaches.

A text......

possible Lanceolated Warbler – Field Ditch.

Ten minutes later the bird is seen sitting out in the open with tail cocked. Lanceolated Warbler should not be behaving like this! It stays there for a few minutes before diving into a shallow ditch. Now that is more like it. From here Cairan, the finder, Lee Gregory, Cath Mendez and I watch as it crawls amongst the grass not too far in front of us. A real MEGA, **Lanceolated Warbler** and it's on the list. Brilliant.

A group of people we are told are about to arrive on the Good Shepherd, an RSPB group from Aberdeen. What a baptism to arrive on the vomit bucket, be taken by minibus to see as their first bird on Fair Isle, a Lanceolated Warbler. The bird must realise how special it is as it stays in one spot in the grass for fifteen minutes or so so that even telescopes can be used to see all details. What an absolute cracker.

Happy with the Lancy, well over the Moon with the Lancy, I bird Pund and Setter.

No red flag flying from a Land Rover to tell of another rare bird, gone are the days of when the news of a rarity was announced by such means, instead another text . .

possible Citrine Wagtail Da Water.

Cairan has found another rare bird. He is on a roll and for the extraordinary effort he puts in every day he deserves it.

With Lee, Cairan and Deryk Shaw, the ex-warden who still crofts on Fair Isle with his wife and three children, we all venture out over the marshy Da Water bog. The Citrine is seen briefly amongst tall grassy tussocks but is it a Citrine. Maybe it is an Eastern Yellow Wagtail. No, **Citrine Wagtail** it is and so bird numbers **283** and **284** are secured; a double Year tick day. Things are going well and are going to get even better! One can feel it in one's birding bones.

Wednesday 14th September **light N**

High cloud at 6:00 a.m. but turns foggy later.

The morning Heligoland Trap run catches a couple of Blackcaps and a Whitethroat.

I head off for the north, once more following the cliff edges and geos. Past the incredible structure of the Guillemot monitoring hide. It looks a Health & Safety disaster, a small Heath Robinson affair of planks nailed together into the shape of a cuboid hide but it has been in position on it's precarious ledge for longer than some of the crofts! Inside the four fish drawn in Biro that I had laughed at last year are fading and will soon be gone. Going from the top there are superbly accurate depictions of three local fish; Whiting, Sandeel, Sprat and . . . Nemo!

It is such a shame to see these works of art fading away but I have a photograph to remind me that some people sitting in bird hides have, not only artistic abilities but also a great sense of humour. Stay child-like.

Bracken in Wirvie Burn is thicker than I have seen anywhere on the island and a single Willow Warbler is here following the stream.

Fog descends and visibility goes down to a hundred yards or so. Some duck are on Golden Water, three Wigeon and a female Gadwall. The latter is a rare bird on Fair Isle.

The North Lighthouse is hazily seen but only just as I approach in the thick fog. Staying there for an hour or so though and going to the large foghorn area, the fog rolls away to the west leaving blue, cloudless skies to the east and a bank of rolling fog to the west. Beautiful light changes with Gannets, Fulmars and Bonxies gliding past close enough to almost touch. With the clearing away of the fog Sumburgh Head can be seen on the horizon twenty five miles or so to the north.

Past the Gannet colony on the Stacks of Scroo, I descend towards Dronger. A text.....

Rosefinch in the enclosure at Muckle Uri.

It couldn't be any further away from where I am and still be on Fair Isle but I need it for the Year list so I jog/walk back to the Bird Observatory and get my bike. Down the island with the now fresh north wind behind me, I reach the South Lighthouse and just put my bike against the wall when another text comes in, this one in Capital letters.....

SHORT-TOED LARK *Water Towers.*

Back on the bike I cycle now into the wind and arrive at the Water Towers half way back up the island where Lee Gregory has found the bird. It, together with a Skylark flies off as soon as I arrive. Just like the Little Bunting of yesterday, it calls as it passes but flies off into the distance. Lee and I search the heather along Hill Dyke. We search the fields to the south and beside Setter but no good. Maybe it has gone back to the water tower.

It hasn't and Lee leaves for his belated lunch.

I cycle around to Setter and search the Parks area first. No good. At Setter the sheep must think that Ian, Setter's owner, has come out as all of the sheep for some distance come running up to me. Surrounded by them, some even allow patting and head stroking. They disturb a Skylark. With it another bird, smaller, takes off and both head back to the water tower.

I head back and after photographing a very tame yet shy Lapland Bunting, the **Short-toed Lark** is indeed back at the shed-like water tower. UTB . . Under The Belt and a very good bird to get on the Year list, bird number **285**. The list is growing rapidly towards the magic 300.

An attempt is scheduled for 4:30 p.m. to try and see whether a large Snipe seen at Da Water is actually a Great Snipe. A line of birders go through the area but only two Common Snipe come out.

I head for Lower Stoneybreak, Neil Thompson's garden, as the Common Rosefinch was seen in the garden there. I think I see a Locustella but it turns out to be a complete mess up as two garden warblers come out of the rose bushes where I thought the possibly rare bird had gone. Then the Rosefinch suddenly dives into some red current bushes in the corner of Neil's garden. I can't see it, well actually I did see it fly in. I see it fly out again and it heads off down the hill to the nearby shop.

I can't find it at the shop and return to have a chat with Neil. We talk about the Black-browed Albatross seen from the Good Shepherd boat that Neil is the Captain of back in the Summer. Neil's face, when describing the moment and his actions to get views of the bird as it circle the boat, is delightful, full of impish fun. Cairan is standing by us and he says simply, "Gary, Rosefinch."

Common Rosefinch onto the year list, bird number **286**; the bird is sitting on a rose stem low to the ground about ten yards away. Not the most inspiring of birds it is though another expected Year tick and so greatly appreciated.

Thursday 15th September **Fresh E**

Very thick fog all morning to hill fog and mist with drizzle in the afternoon with some the sun breaking through the haze on occasions.

Birds are difficult to see, visibility is down to fifty yards at best and the best place to see newly in migrant birds is in the Bird Observatory garden.

Walking off southwards I reach Setter. Text comes in . . .

YB Warbler Gully

Thanks Lee. I get there as Lee and Chris Dodds try to persuade the bird to come out of the small area of bushes at the bottom of the gully and enter the nearby Gully Heligoland trap. It doesn't. They leave and I stay, sit down and watch. A Garden Warbler is in some bracken beneath me down the slope and then out comes the sprightly little bird, eye stripes, wing bars, white underparts and green uppers. All in all a superbly lovely little bird and a miraculous one too having come from Siberia. Not that much bigger than a Goldcrest it is incredible that such a tiny bird can get here having travelled so far. Last year was a record year for them on Fair Isle with seventy eight having been seen in one fantastic day. Indeed I saw 111 (Nelson!) whilst I was on Fair Isle.

So **Yellow-browed Warbler** UTB; five new birds for the Green Year list in three magnificent days. Now at **287** I am only three away from beating my own UK Green Year list record, thirteen away from reaching my first major target of the magic 300 and eighteen away from beating Ponc Feliu Latorre for the European Green record.

I need to increase my Karma with nature as it has been so good to me over the last few days. With two large bin liners, the beach at the end of the gully takes two hours to be cleared of the plastic rubbish that has arrived there from the sea. Polystyrene, one-use plastic bottles and fishing equipment, ropes and pieces of an old tyre; one bottle has a label saying that it originated from Singapore, Malaysia. It hasn't floated here, one may imagine a cargo ship from there passing and a bottle being thrown into the sea from it.

The bin liners are pulled up the steep cliff where a bird's leg is found with a Fair Isle ring on it. The ring is given to David Parnaby, the Observatory warden. It is from a local Starling. The bin liners I carry to the Harbour and put in the skip.

The people one meets makes travel endlessly fascinating. Melia and Rick are from Alaska originally though now they work at Aberdeen University. Rick is an archaeologist working on recently uncovered Eskimo site in the Arctic, uncovered due to the excessive ice melt. Global warming in action.

Melia works in the Aberdeen University Museum and she tells me that they have just uncovered a box covered in thick dust from under a stairway. Upon opening it she found bird skins with labels on each detailing where they were shot and by whom, John James Audubon!

Micel and Sue from Coventry have arrived on Fair Isle in a small airplane piloted by Micel. It soon becomes apparent sitting with them that Mike has a very similar sense of humour to me. We love the same films; Blazing Saddles, Young Frankenstein and the like. We like the same cartoonists; Gary Larson soon has us all laughing as we share which of the World's best ever environmental minded cartoonist cartoons we love, like and remember. How do snakes say goodbye? Smoking cows and dingo farms. (Look up Gary Larson on google images and you'll find which cartoons are referenced here.)

They also point out a spoof TV series produced in Australia for the Sydney Olympics. The 'Prime Minister's' apology to the indigenous aboriginal tribes is wonderful.

https://www.youtube.com/watch?v=Dh0MNIFezME

Mike and Sue also talk about flying and how they have flown around Europe and Australia. What a life! They show a video to capture the feeling.

https://www.youtube.com/watch?v=7mxmFCw-Dig

Friday 16th September **Light SE**

Thick fog and heavy rain AM, clearing to sunny intervals with mist over hills PM.

A relaxing morning watching the rain, a wander to the airport to watch Mike and Sue leave but they don't. The front wheel on the small plane has a puncture and they aren't going anywhere until that is repaired.

The Short-toed Lark is still by the water tanks. Otherwise there are common migrants around in small numbers; Whinchat, Garden, Reed and Willow Warblers as well as a Yellow-browed, Blackcap, Lesser Whitethroat and a couple of Spotted Flycatchers, thirty five Lapland Bunting and the Ortolan. Still a highlight are four Brent Geese, a very rare bird on Fair Isle.

Saturday 17th September **Fresh S**

Cloudy cool

Nick Riddiford thinks he has seen a Bluethroat at Shirva but he isn't sure. He phones the Observatory and Susannah, the warden, David's wife sees me near to the Gully and tells me the news. Shirva soon after, wait and search. No Bluethroat. A couple from Wakefield arrive to search with me, Maureen and Keith are fresh in, keen birders and eager to see a good bird. Suddenly it pops up from an area I had searched. It must have been behind a pallet leaning against a dry stone wall. Anyway it hops up onto a five-bar gate and then onto the wall. Stunning bird and in no way diminished by having no blue and red gorget.

Bluethroat. Bird number **288**; only one behind the British Green Year list record.

Text message from Erin Taylor who is at North Ronaldsay Bird Oberↄvatory . . (10:53 a.m.)

Hi Gary. It's Erin and I'm writing to convince you of the three reasons why you should come to North Ron on the 21st of October. 1. It's the harvest dance and we're all excited and as you left before the last dance some of us (Larissa) feel like you owe them a dance.

2. You've been on Fair Isle for ages. Wouldn't a change of scenery for the weekend be nice.

3. We miss you! I think you should take these valid pints into consideration. Mucho love from the sexiest Bird Obs in the UK. xxx

Lovely to hear from one of next year's Champions of The Flyway Green Birding Team and it is so tempting to say yes to all at the Bird Obs there, after all my time there in August was the happiest time of this year but the focus of the year is the birds and Fair Isle may be the place that gives me a better chance to add to the Green year list.

I reply (11:11 p.m.)

After what I've heard about the North Ronaldsay love shack I think you all need a Grandad figure! It has been good to hear of the developments on there. Coming back? . . . Maybe. Really wonderful to hear from you.

Love Shack? Well Larissa and Samuel had got together whilst I was on the island and since leaving, two other pairings had occurred; Erin was now in love with Gavin, the warden Alison and her husband Kevin's son, and vice versa. Also George, who had so obviously wanted to pair up with Kevin and Alison's daughter, Heather, had done just that. Within the claustrophobic confines of a small Orcadian island choice may be a little limited but I couldn't think of any more perfect combinations. Eight young people within a confined space and now three couples.

Samuel and Larissa were so perfect together, their personalities matched so completely. Both being very energetic, intense and passionate as well as being extremely talented birders; their getting together had happened whilst I was on the island earlier. I couldn't be more pleased for them both. One may be from Canada but love will find a way.

George had been talking in private to me of his desire to get together with Heather whilst in the lounge back in August. What a beautiful couple they make; George being confident and fun to be around whilst Heather is rather shy and Frith-like. Heather though showed her true personality when playing her violin with her father, Kevin accompanying on guitar one evening in the bird observatory's lounge. What a splendid couple they make.

Finally there is Erin and Gavin. Erin is bubbly, quick to smile and laugh and a very enthusiastic bird ringer. Gavin is a young Gabriel Oak of a remote Scottish island, another pair well suited.

I text Erin once more with the news of the Bluethroat together with the bird list number of 288.

Erin's reply. (11:40 a.m.)

I'm sure I don't know what you mean, sir! We need a pro birder to look up to who keeps up birding in all weathers! Yaaaayyy for the Bluethroat. You're so close! How about we strike up a deal? If you hot 300 before the 15th of October, you come to the dance? X

My day is mostly spent exploring the south of the island with an interruption at 4 p.m. when everyone staying at the Bird Observatory tries to flush out a very hard to see Great Snipe. No one sees it. I find a Reed Warbler on a barbed wire fence. To see an Acro' so close out in the open and so tame is incredible. I sit on a nearby stile and watch it search for food in the short grass near to my feet.

I then spend some time sitting on a high cliff at North Raeva watching as text messages tell of Warwickshire Cricket Club (You Bears!) thrash Surrey in the One Day final at Lords. Brilliant.

On the way to the Observatory for the evening, with the light fading, I meet a couple I remember from last year at Chalet. Karen and Ray from Nottingham have returned for another week in Paradise and are staying at the self-catering croft, Springfield. Ray climbs over the stile at the back of the superb Chalet garden and flushes a barred warbler. The bird circles the garden, a large silver warbler, before diving straight into the roses never to be seen again. My seventh Barred Warbler of the Autumn so far.

Sunday 18th September **Light to Fresh S/SE**

Sunny intervals with high cloud.

Morning starts with a Lesser Whitethroat, a Willow Warbler and a Song Thrush around my 'patch' at Pund.

A Barred Warbler is at the Observatory in the garden.

Wanting to explore the north of the island upon reaching Wirvie Burn a text arrives from Lee Gregory.

Possible Great Snipe at Da Water.

Two minutes later another text from Lee. . . . .

GREAT SNIPE. Confirmed with a photo.

I rush down to an area of marsh just south of the Kirk where Lee has seen the bird go down. After waiting for all birders from the Observatory to get there, an organised flush begins and despite extensively searching three fields there is no sign of the rare bird. Once again it has eluded everyone.

Everyone leaves for lunch at the Obs except me. I have few boiled eggs and a banana. What more do I need?

I zig zag the area just searched and have the occasional Common Snipe and a single jack come zig-zagging out. No Great Snipe.

After a couple of hours of doing this, and just after a female Sparrowhawk has glided past low over the ground, Lee arrives back and tells me that he will help in the search in an hour or so, after he has finished his census.

Another hour of zig-zagging the area alone, I leave my coat and sweatshirt by Kennaby as the sun comes out. Along Kennaby's dry stone wall I search, along the barbed wire fence to the potato crop.

I lift my binoculars as Rock Doves come out from amongst the spud plants. Suddenly a Snipe, a big one, grunts and flies straight and low before turning to go in front of a group of four people on the nearby road. I scream 'The Snipe!' to them.

The bird disappears over a ridge and is gone.

Great snipe – bird number **289**.

I phone Lee. I am practically screaming and laughing down the phone to him, "I've got the Snipe! I've got the Snipe!"

An hour or so later, calmer but searching for more views of the bird another text from Lee.

RED-THROATED PIPIT near .Da Haa

I receive a call . . . Phil Andrews, The Oracle....

"There's a red-throated pipit." I reply, *"I know! I'm running for it!"*

A phone call from Lee . .

"Red-throated pipit." I reply, (!) *"I'm just coming past Deryk's"*

Five minutes later, standing with a group of birders, Catherine, David and Howard, the rare pipit is on the grass about thirty yards away. **Red-throated Pipit**, Bird number **290** and a new British Green Year List record.

A chat with the famous Tommy Hyndeman of Da Haa Guest House. Tommy is a friendly American and his garden list, 280, is the envy of many a birder. Indeed the dead tree in the corner of the garden has had eighty bird species in it including Citril Finch, Brown-headed Cowbird, Blackpoll Warbler, Siberian Rubythroat . . . to name but a few.

http://fair-isle.blogspot.co.uk/p/b-b.html

Monday 19th September **light SW**

One rain shower then a glorious day, blue skies and warm.

A gibbous Moon is still quite high to the west as I walk towards Da Water and a group of sixteen Pink-footed Geese fly high heading south.

The aim is for another organised flush by all at the Bird Observatory in order to try and see the Great Snipe.

The attempt ends with all fields where the bird has been seen walked through and with rain falling. A rainbow heralded the arrival of the shower.

Clouds depart and leave just blue sky; indeed hardly a cloud is seen for the rest of the day.

Warmed by the sun at my back I explore the geos and burns to the north, rest and have lunch at the fog horn by the North Lighthouse and see a couple of Puffins and a Razorbill from here with countless Gannets and Fulmars passing and the occasional Bonxie.

A Woodcock is in the bracken of Wirvie Burn and my first Chaffinch of the Autumn on Fair Isle passes me as I look down a high cliff.

Risso's Dolphins complete a beautiful day as a group of them cavort in the tide rip off South Buness.

A Facebook message from Kerry and Dominik Reynolds:-

Congratulations Gary Brian Prescott. One record down, more to go. So keep going!!! Good luck. Xx

Tuesday 20th September **light to fresh S/SE**

Sunny intervals, warm when sun out. Great visibility.

Last night's pleasures didn't finish with the views of the Risso's Dolphins. There was a superb gibbous Moon to light my way home.

Morning starts with a Little Bunting found at The Parks. I rush there as fast as possible but only see a shape disappear into the oat crop. With other birders I wait. A Yellow-browed Warbler is more obliging.

Two birders decide to walk the side of the crop and a small bird comes out and disappears to the north. I feel sure this is the Little Bunting and pursue the bird as it flies over The Parks.

Down at the plantation I meet five lovely ladies from New Mexico, USA. (Thanks Ann for the note and good wishes from the New Mexico Audubon Society. Thanks to the rest of you too, but, I'm sorry, I forgot to record your names. Senior moment!)

One of the birders at the Observatory comes up to me and says that the Little Bunting never left the oats and so I return and find it without too much trouble.

Little Bunting, Green Bird number **291**, the Green Year list record keeps on growing. Nine to go for the magic 300, surely this is the year.

Back to the Observatory, there is a Yellow-browed Warbler in the garden. Down to the three closest beaches to here, plastic is collected, about half a bin liner full and skipped. There is a dead Gannet and also a dead Razorbill on South Haven Beach, both in good condition, sadly.

With no news of any birds that would be new to the Year list, I head off for the geos of the west coast, my favourite area. Over the moorland heading west, Bonxies mob and Snipe zig zag; around a hundred of the former and a dozen latter.

Starting at Tyneside there are two Yellow-Browed Warblers here and a Goldcrest. A Song Thrush is at South Naaversgill and the sun is shining. I decide to photograph each geo in such wonderful light.

North Naaversgill is noisy; loud, echoing bangs coming from deep down this large geo. Moving around its cliff top rim, the famous bolt hole is filling and ejecting a large jet of seawater. As each wave comes in from the ocean, water fills an unseen cavern and pressure builds. Just like a geyser the pressure builds until the air inside the cave expels the seawater in a fifty foot explosion of spray. The pulse of energy surges through the enclosed water of the geo and washes over all close by rocks as the whole process repeats itself again and again. There needs to be a high tide for this to occur but the noise and spectacle make the trek over the hills well worth the effort.

There's a Yellow-browed here too. There seems to be a fall of these wonderful Siberian warblers going on.

Moving on next to Copper and Grey Geos, the views are stupendous. Up to Guidicam and Gannets mass on ledges and outcrops; three Yellow-broweds Warbler are here and one each of Goldcrest and Willow Warbler. On the way up a House Martin is circling around and a single Carrion Crow goes south.

The views from here over towards Orkney are extremely clear. I can easily make out the lighthouse on North Ronaldsay with my naked eye. Through binoculars the Laird's house, Holland can be seen and further round even Westray and Hoy.

Up to Skinner's geo, no less than five Yellow-browed Warblers in a small area with a Pied Flycatcher for company. Amazing.

Final section before heading back to the Observatory is around the mast with its W2 buildings. Another Pied Flycatcher is here.

Over a hundred Bonxies are in the air as I make my way downhill.

The evening has a superb talk by the Fair Isle Ranger, Chris Dodds detailing his time at Chatham Islands off New Zealand. The quality of the talks at the Fair Isle Bird Observatory is superb and Chris' talk is just that. Fascinating, it includes how the Black Robin was saved from extinction when there were only five left in the World to its present population of around 200. Still in danger due to being precariously positioned on only two islands.

Log at 9 p.m. Fifty four Yellow-browed Warblers on the island, the third highest day total ever. Last year's record total of seventy eight still leads the way.

Wednesday 21st September **strong S/SE**

Sunny intervals, some hill fog at times, short light shower.

A **Red-breasted Flycatcher** has been trapped at Gully. Brought back to the Bird Observatory, it goes onto the Green Year list once it has been processed, rung and released. Bird number **292**.

I know I must be on Fair Isle as a Lapland Bunting lands on the road in front of me as I cycle.

Lee Gregory has seen a Spotted Crake at Da Water first thing and I decide to head south and bird the geos of the south west and the crofts and ditches.

Yellow-browed Warbler and female Blackcap on the cliff at Steeness as I hold onto a fence and the strong wind is at my back.

Five Yellow-browed Warblers are in the reeds of Meadow Burn with a Willow Warbler, a couple of the former are very vocal, calling repeatedly.

Single Yellow-broweds are at both Upper and Lower Lough crofts and another is beside the road just north of here. The next one I see is at Burkle where two male Blackcaps accompany it.

Otherwise the birding is of the expected birds and despite a text arriving stating a very tame Lanceolated Warbler is near to the Bird Observatory, my aim is to try for the Spotted Crake.

Cleaning a window in the Kirk, positioning a chair to lean on, I watch Da water for three hours until the light is too poor to see anything as night falls. No Spotted Crake, the highlight is a Moorhen!

After the evening log I pay my Lifer dues to the Bird Observatory for the Great Snipe. The idea is that one gives a donation to the observatory for a lifer on a scale that increases the amount of cash the higher your life list is. Money into the pot. Money well spent.

Thursday 22nd September **fresh to light SE**

Rain – AM, sunny - PM

A morning of heavy rain gives way to an afternoon of sunshine and calm. Before the sunshine arrives, though, a Common Rosefinch shows well in the Fair Isle Bird Observatory garden.

South Haven beach has plastic bottles, large and small, on it, as well as dead adult and first year Gannets. I remove the former from the beach and place all in a skip.

Back at the Observatory garden a couple of Yellow-browed Warblers are on view, as well as Blackcap and Lesser Whitethroats.

More warblers are at the plantation; Yellow-browed Warbler, Willow Warbler and a Chiff Chaff.

Even more are at the small enclosed reedbed of Meadow Burn; four Yellow-browed, a Reed, a Willow and a Lesser Whitethroat. A nice selection.

With bin liner in hand I make my way down a precipitous slope, down to the beach of Steensi Geo. A full bin liner hardly makes a dent in the mass of plastic found here.

Along the coast north of here, Lee Gregory has found a Red-breasted Flycatcher. I find it down below on the stones of the beach and point it out to the Ribble Bird Tour group. It's flashing white tail patches show up well at distance.

Back on the road I take the road towards Shirva and have a Bluethroat with a blue necklace for company. It walks just in front of me and flies to a nearby fence.

An email from Mark Barrett, fundraising officer for the RSPB in The Midlands:-

Hello Gary,

I hope that all is well with you and that you are keeping well. Congratulations on surpassing the British Green Year record; I have been reading the blog this morning and great to see your continued success on your quest to seeing 300 species! Looks like you are very much on your way to surpassing that which is incredible; some fantastic images on the blog and Facebook too which are great to see.

Keep up the fantastic work and as ever thank you for your continued support, it is hugely appreciated.

Kind regards and many thanks,

Mark

Friday 23rd September **Fresh to Strong SW**

Very sunny

A Yellow-browed Warbler is still in the plantation and the Short-toed Lark is still by the water tanks. The Little Bunting at Field though is a new bird. It hasn't got a bird louse attached to it's right eye unlike the previous one!

A stomp through the Da Water marsh gives me a flying Moorhen but no Crake.

Then a dash. Humpback Whale off the west coast. I can see people climbing one of the Raevas and Tommy Hyndeman is already up there with a telescope. Seen from the South Lighthouse heading north, unfortunately the whale doesn't come around Malcolm's Head and the group of hopefuls dwindles until eventually I am alone on the edge of the cliff. A very small baby rabbit comes out almost at my feet. He keeps looking around at me and quickly disappears down a hole only to reappear at another hole not too far away. I sit still and manage to stroke it! Cute little thing.

Back on the road there is a Whinchat that lacks a tail. I call him Winny. My first linnet since arriving on Fair Isle is at Chalet as I pass.

Saturday 24th September **Strong SE**

Heavy rain nearly all day.

Soaked on the way to the Observatory, soaked on the way back home. I spend the day preparing to give a talk about Green Birding and rehearsing a new version of Morecambe & Wise's Bring Me Sunshine song with Sarah.

A break in the rain but not in the gale, gives me an opportunity to collect the plastic from the South Haven beach and also get up Buness.

In the evening I give my World famous Biking Birder talk. Sarah joins me on stage for the finale. Each member of the audience receives a songsheet.

Bring Me Sunshine – Fair Isle style :-

Bring us Sunshine
Eastern winds
Bring us birdies
Most with wings

In this world where we live
there should be more happiness
so much joy birds they give
there'll be Yankee birds tomorrow

We'll be happy
Full of tears
Celebrating
lots of beers!

Let our arms be as warm
as the Sun from up above
Bring us birds
Bring us sunshine
Bring us Love...

One can never tell how a talk goes down with an audience but some seem to really enjoy it.

Monday 26th September **Fresh S**

Sunny with occasional hazy cloud cover

Up to the radio mast, Snow Bunting and a Devil's Coach Horse Beetle found and onward up to the summit of Ward Hill. The sun is shining and the views are fabulous; some of the best scenery anywhere in Britain is at my disposal. Shetland is clear, the sea is silky smooth, reflectively blue. Very few birders come this way and I have it all to myself.

The views may be magnificent but the birds are missing. There are a few Meadow Pipits and the occasional Wheatear but gone are the numbers of migrants that adorned each geo last week. A single Redstart in the immense Grey Geo is the only migrant within the ones I search.

Naaversgill's water spout is active again but with nowhere near the intensity displayed before. There are a number of heavily pregnant seals on the rocks here looking ready to pop.

News of a Crake species in Meadow Burn, I head that way, call in the shop for some food and see yet another Yellow-browed Warbler in the Burn.

More news, a Great Snipe has been found by Deryk Shaw, the ex-warden for the Observatory. Everyone gathers and in a case of deja vu, the next hour is spent with lines of birders marching through fields and marshes but no sign of the rare bird. A different rare bird shows itself suddenly but briefly, taking off from birders' feet, it flies before disappearing just as fast into thick vegetation, a Lanceolated Warbler. After another hour it is caught in a mist net and everyone who wants to gets an eyeful of this wonderful rare Sibe. This is the third Lanceolated in the last two weeks!

Whilst searching for this bird a Crake flew behind most people. I saw it but only really in dark silhouette against the sun. A short-billed Crake most definitely, I couldn't though put my hand on my heart and say that I have now seen a Spotted Crake, though those who had better views than I say it was one.

I stay almost until dark trying to see or hear it to no avail. A year tick eludes me. Another year tick eluded me earlier today as well; a Long-tailed Skua was photographed earlier crossing the island by Long Dyke and reported at the Bird Log.

Tuesday 27th September **Very strong SW-W**

Heavy rain

Rain falls and the wind doth blow! A male Siskin and a couple of Yellow-browed Warblers are seen from the Fair Isle Bird Observatory windows before breakfast. Breakfast. Is there any breakfast as vast as the breakfast at the Fair isle Bird Observatory? Porridge or cereal to start, a full Scottish with seconds as available, fruit and coffee or tea, not forgetting rounds of thick toast with jam or marmalade. I am not staying at the Obs but I must say I do enjoy the breakfasts. Then there is the camaraderie of early mornings spent with birders. Thanks Susannah for suggesting I take my breakfasts with such wonderful company. Being a Biking Birder is an extremely lonely thing at times and these times are so very special.

Just occasionally, the rain stops and there are even quick glimpses of clearing skies. During one of these, I brave the gale and collect the plastic from the nearest beach. Once again the bottles on the beach include water bottles, one use only, which are from Pembrokeshire. Now in my imagination I cannot see how over a dozen of the same small water bottles, from the same company, can get to the same beach on Fair Isle by any other means than by having been dumped from a passing ship. The labels are too fresh. A cruise liner that sells this product? Most likely.

It all reminds me of what I saw being dumped into the Nile from the hotel ships at Luxor. Sitting watching the birds, Pied Kingfishers, terns and egrets, a gentleman brings out the bin liners full of waste and just tips them over the side, creating a slick of plastic floating downstream. If you ever go to Luxor you will see masses of plastic waste coating the river banks. Obviously this isn't just happening in Luxor but sadly everywhere.

A Redstart is on the chain mail wall of the harbour.

Rain . . . back to the Observatory.

Another clearing moment … I search the nearby geos and try to get further than the gully. The wind is brutal, though, and rain starts again.

By late afternoon I have decided to go home early; going back in the dark in this weather would be dangerous. Even so the rain stings my cheeks and hands and my waterproof trousers don't quite live up to their name.

Wednesday 28th September

Wind fades to nought then returns with a vengeance! W to SE and back to SW gales. Dry in the morning, heavy rain from 3:00 p.m.

The night has been noisy, sleep intermittent but Lee is doing the morning Heligoland trap run and therefore I am out early to catch up with

Lee and the others. Sunrise, a day full of promise.

Wheatears are more prominent today as I walk along the road north. Wheatears are already prominent in various ringing bags too.

At the Plantation trap there are a good number of Starlings caught; many already have a combination of a Natural History metal ring and a variety of colour rings on their legs. Lee and Nina, another trained ringer, log down the details from each starling so adorned and let each go. Starlings with naked legs are bagged up.

I spot a Barred Warbler that wasn't playing the game when Lee went through the bushes to persuade the birds to go into the collecting box. Lee soon has it caught though.

Back to the Bird Observatory and down to the harbour. Yesterday's Little Bunting, a bird I missed, is very tame and I sit on the grass and let it approach me.

The Redstart is still on the harbour wall and a couple of Yellow-browed Warblers are still in the Bird Observatory garden. What a great start to a day.

Things get better. Sitting opposite Andrew at breakfast, he asks me for a prediction, a bird that will turn up today. "Paddyfield Warbler," I say.

Panic in the observatory . . .

Paddyfield Warbler … Walli Burn!

All birders are taken in the minibus. I cycle there, the ride exhilaratingly downhill, a real adrenaline rush, to find two birders are walking the irises there, the rest are lined up on the nearby bank waiting for the pale Acro to show itself.

It does and dives into another iris bed. Eventually the bird decides to try a wire fence. It sits on the lowest wire, I kiss it, lick it, tick it … metaphorically. A LIFER and a Green Year tick, the **Paddyfield Warbler** doesn't want to be seen and dives once more into the irises.

Leaving it to its seclusion I head towards the South Lighthouse and seawatch for an hour or so. Three Kittwakes head north, a Purple Sandpiper and a Grey Plover are closer. Otherwise it is the usual mass of Gannets and Fulmars.

Sad to see a seal with a mass of blue plastic fishing netting around its neck.

Maybe I feel guilty but I collect another bag full of plastic yet hardly make a dent on how much is on the beaches here. PLEASE don't buy one-use plastic bottles.

Privilege to meet Horace replete with bird badges. We chatted for a while about his travels to the Faroes and Iceland. His real name is Wilfred Horace Smith. I didn't tell him he looks like Gromit to me. He thinks he is a bear! Who am I on about? Well a visiting lady comes up to me to ask me what I have seen and she has with her one of the best cuddly toys I have ever seen,

Horace. He is better attired than I am!
Crofts and dykes, ditches and fields; Yellow-broweds, Willow Warblers, a Common Rosefinch and some Lapland Buntings found.
The best thing today though has been watching scane after scane of Pink-footed Geese flying overhead. Some going straight on south whilst others circle the island, making the census counters job near impossible.
A good bird in Fair Isle context was a Pintail seen at Da Water earlier. Overall a really enjoyable day.

Thursday 29th September **Gale Force W to NW**

Heavy rain

Special Birding Days with The Birding Clams

The weather outside is brutal; sixty to seventy mph gales and heavy rain so I turn to a book to while away the morning hours. It brings back memories of years of birding with friends and it all started when I started a birdwatching club at a Secondary School in Wolverhampton.

The book I read is Birds New To Britain, 1980 – 2004. In it I read the details of the finding of the first Lesser Scaup for the Western Palearctic, back in 1987 at Chasewater, Staffordshire. Mentioned in the book are two ex-students of mine, Jason John Oliver and Alex Barter. The former is a carbon twitcher still going strong. The latter sadly died over ten years ago. Bart, very affectionately known as The Bear, was a phenomenal birder and all round brilliant bloke.

The description of the finding of the Lesser Scaup has the boys brought over by a local birder. Incredible to have two of my students present when such a special bird is found.

At that time, Jason and Alex, together with another ex-student, Richard Southall and I were a formidable birding team.

For a few years in the 1980s they, with their teacher, me, birded around the UK. As they grew into lads and then men, the friendship grew and now they and the birding students that followed have a bond beyond mere words.

We haven't always been called The Birding Clams, a name for our little group that came into being about five years ago. Back in 1984, I ran a Young Ornithologists Club (YOC), the RSPB's children's club at a Secondary School. A group of three Secondary-aged lads; Jason Oliver, Alex 'The Bear' Barter and Richard 'Dicks-out' Southall, all members of the school club, were in the back of a yellow Nissan Cherry with their teacher, me. Destination, the famous Olive-backed Pipit that had found a back garden in Bracknell to its liking.

A first trip for what was to become regular weekend overnight twitches by a number of Council Estate students from Coppice High School, Ashmore Park, Wolverhampton.

The trip was memorable for the four involved. The rare Pipit was seen easily enough but the other two scarce bird targets that day caused just a few problems. The Ferruginous Duck at some gravel pits south of Uxbridge wasn't seen. Victorian bottles were found though and a couple of carrier bags full of them were taken home. The area was pock marked with pits where London collectors had dug into the Victorian rubbish tip to find bottles rarer than the ones discarded by them but picked up by us. The Fudge Duck, to give it its colloquial name, turned out to have been hiding under branches overgrowing the gravel pit margins. Unknown to us at the time, all we had was a handwritten list of possible birds with the name of the site; no specific details of which tree, bush or lake to look on. Pagers and Smartphones have made things so much easier these days.

Smew at Wrasbury was written down on our list. Little did we know that Wrasbury was more than just an immense curved reservoir with a very high bank around which ran a perimeter road.

Workers had waved to us as we drove through gates they were painting. Workers had disappeared when we returned to those gates an hour later having not seen any Smew. The wet paint gates were locked.

Two hours later police arrived to deal with a group of lads who were trying to lift a different gate off its hinges so that an escape could be made.

Two hours later an old man arrived on a push bike with a key to open those gates.

The Smew, it turned out weren't on the reservoir but on some gravel pits a mile or so away!

My wife, Jane, had begged me early that morning not to go. She said that she felt that something bad was going to happen. Being locked in Wrasbury Reservoir for four hours watching ducks and the planes taking off from the nearby Heathrow may just have been what she foretold.

Actually, all this happened three years after a more successful birding weekend with J.J. Holian, Bill Low, myself and another Coppice student, Steven Turner, better known as Smoothie.

A weekend in Norfolk, with the four of us sleeping in the car, gave us Pallas' warblers, Richard's Pipits and various lesser scarce birds.

Those same three lads from the Wrasbury disaster day; Jase, Sout' and Bart, were in the car, March 1985, as we careered extremely excitedly, down the hill at Cuckmere Haven, East Sussex. A Little Crake had practically allowed birders to stroke it. We arrived the day after it was last seen. To make matters worse, later that same day I managed to flush a Red-breasted Goose not once but twice and both times before Jase had managed to see it. Rumours that one of the lads had a tattoo of the goose on his forearm in order to grip off Jase are surely found-less; too cruel a jest.

1989 Two months, two 'Firsts'.

My yellow Nissan Cherry car had a leaking radiator. A first for Britain was at Charlton Poll, Billingham, Teeside. Eggs and large bottles of water got the lads to the, hate to say it, most boring 'First' ever seen. The Double-crested Cormorant arrived at the pool at the allotted time. "Be there at 7:45a.m." we were told. In it flew at 7:45a.m. It landed on the water, caught a large fish, swallowed it and then stood on a pontoon for the next hour. There are only so many plumage and bare part details to take in and so, after that scintillating hour, we were off to more exciting birding at Bamburgh Castle to the north.

Chalk and cheese, Ying and Yang; how different a first for Europe bird only a few weeks later. Thousands trying to see a Golden-winged Warbler. It took us seven hours of searching around a housing estate near Maidstone, Kent before one of the present Coppice Twitchers, Ian Crutchley, found it on some pyracantha surrounding a town house.

Two Coppice Twitchers thought they had Twitched Their Last.

A new and wonderful girlfriend for the teacher and an American Vireo, Red-eyed, to go and see. Diane had already rescued the team from the disaster of having an old Escort blow up on the A2. Diane had even taken the team; the teacher, Ian Crutchley and Steve Allcott, onward to see the target bird of the day; the Marsh Sandpiper at Elmley.

The Vireo though was to bring terror into the proceedings. Who but Diane would, whilst driving at a naughty speed down the A30 through Devon, swerve off without thought or reason up the slip road. In fact, the reason for such erratic driving was never given and two trembling lads on the back seats will recall with horror the moment of screeching brakes and impending doom. The Vireo was secured later after a different driver had negotiated the narrow lanes around and to Cot Valley, Cornwall.

Clam Days Return

A new name for the group, not CTC but a name with fun and movement; now known as the T.I.T.S, each rare bird was greeted by a small dance from the lads. The Terpsichorean Inspired Twitcher Society racked up the list in 2005 as each tried to complete a Big Year and see 300 bird species.

The ex-Coppice students, Ian Crutchley and Steve Allcott, now into their late thirties managed it. Their ex-teacher didn't. He had spent too long watching the 2005 Ashes series, the best ever cricket test match series, to get the extra birds that would have lifted his respectable 292 to the magic 300. Mind you, he was with his son, Josh, at Edgbaston when Kasprovic gloved the ball to Jones off Harmison.

Clams Today

Nowadays, the glory of the Coppice High School Twitchers Club, now known as The Birding Clams, meets up every year on Shetland. The first week of October sees the group assemble and bird. The exploits of the C.L.A.M.S, the Clear Lunacy & Madness Club, can be seen on Facebook. There is a group page called just that, The Birding Clams.

The Clams have even enjoyed birding in France!

Some members have stayed faithful since that long off time back in 1984. Others are new and some didn't even go to the same school or have that teacher. Yet the group is strong is, the fun is still there and the most important thing, after the birds that is, is the deep friendship and camaraderie of the group.

Just a few memories of days past that while away a foul weather day on Fair Isle.

Friday 30th September **Gale Force W to NW easing**

Squally showers

Another day, when taking shelter is a better option, starts with a bin liner, worn over my clothes as I negotiate the gale, flying off me and heading at speed towards Norway!

September Monthly Statistics:-

Green Year list	293 birds
Year ticks seen in September	14
Bird species had, not seen in 2015	4
Mileage in September	310.21 miles
Total mileage for the year	5730.76 miles
Average mileage on days cycled/walked	10.34 miles
Elevation : up	22,830 feet
: down	22,830 feet

Best birds **: Icterine, Lanceolated, Yellow-browed and Paddyfield Warblers, Ortolan and Little Buntings, Common Rosefinch, Short-toed Lark, Citrine Wagtail, Bluethroat, Great Snipe, Red-throated**

Pipit and Red-breasted Flycatcher

September on Fair Isle summary

Green Year list now on 293 having had fifteen new birds whilst being on the Fair Isle, fourteen of them during September. I had a Booted Warbler on arrival at the end of August, so let's start with that wonderful bird.

BOOTED WARBLER *Iduna caligata* *30th August 2016*

Seen in the small reedbed that makes up Meadow Burn, a small, very pale warbler that showed well on the wires that surround the area. Booted Warbler comes from Central Russia and Asia.

There were a lot of migrants around on my arrival day; sixty three Willow Warblers, 176 Wheatear, 106 White Wagtails as well as a couple of Barred Warblers,and singles of Marsh Warbler and Common Rosefinch. Welcome to Fair Isle. A.D.I.P. ….. a day in Paradise.

My second Rose-coloured Starling, *Pastor roseus* was found by Cath Mendez at the Bird Observatory, coming down to feed on apples put out by Lee Gregory for just that possibility. A juvenile bird, pale and obvious, rosy is a vagrant from Central Europe.

Into September. The target was for fifteen year ticks and a spreadsheet was prepared months ago detailing the year tick bird species seen on Fair Isle during this month for the last 11 years. A percentage probability is mentioned after each of the following year ticks seen in brackets.

WOOD WARBLER *Phylloscopus sibilatrix* *4th September 2016*

One would have expected me to have added this bird to the year list whilst on the UK mainland but no, I wasn't near any of the declining breeding birds' areas during those crucial times before mid-June when they go quiet. One turning up on Fair Isle was a bonus not too unexpected. Sitting on a barbed wire fence with the occasional jump down onto the grass to catch an insect, a beautiful, bright warbler with white underparts, yellow throat and green back. (45.5% chance of occurrence in September)

ICTERINE WARBLER *Hippolais icterina* *4th September 2016*

David Parnaby, the Fair Isle Bird Observatory warden, had found a

Greenish Warbler, Phylloscopus trochiloides, in Tyneside Geo. I saw him walking on the other side of the long, tall dry stone wall called Hill Dyke and thanked him for the text message telling me of that bird. As I turned away a large Hippo' warbler landed on the barbed wire fence about thirty yards away. I immediately shouted to David, "Icky."

Another hoped to see warbler went onto the list; an obvious Hippolais, large and stronger than similar Phylloscs. After walking to the Greenish Warbler, I carried on exploring the geos, high cliffed areas of coast that provide shelter and food for many fresh in migrant birds. At Grey Geo, one of my favourites with a fast eroding cliff line and colourful rock and mud sections, another Icterine Warbler was foraging in short grass. Classed as a rare vagrant to the UK from the continent. (45.5% chance of occurrence in September)

Good numbers of migrants today, I found not only the couple of Icterines but also a sunbathing Barred Warbler on the cliff at Copper Geo. 4 Swifts were swirling just west of Ward Hill and the Greenish Warbler was my third of the year.

ORTOLAN BUNTING *Emberiza hortulana 8th September 2016*

Not an easy one to find, the bird hid in thick grass in the marshy area just above the Gully trap area. Eye ring and moustachial easy to see once it allowed good views. Another vagrant from Europe. (45.5% chance of occurrence in September)

LANCEOLATED WARBLER *Locustella lanceolata 13th September 2016*

Great to see one in the field, the bird was at first seen sitting in the open on short grass where it stayed for a few minutes before diving into some longer grass in a nearby ditch. Even in there it could be seen occasionally crawling between the grass blades. The very rare warbler eventually flew to an area of thicker grass but just sat in between grass tussocks in full view! A small, streaky warbler; they always look to me as though they have been squeezed from behind to give a front heavy appearance. A true Sibe goes onto the year list, another I saw in the marshy area of Kirki Mire later in the month. That bird was found when everyone was searching for a Great Snipe! (54.5% chance of occurrence in September)

CITRINE WAGTAIL *Motacilla citreola 13th September 2016*

A Citrine Wagtail had everyone searching around the island but couldn't be pinned down to one area. In the evening though a different bird was found by Cairan Hatsall, one of the two assistant wardens at Da Water. A good day for Cairan, this bird was added to the Lanceolated Cairan had found earlier. The lancy was the first one that Cairan had found.

The Citrine, not a showy bird, kept amongst the tall grass tussocks of Da Water, only showing itself briefly on the mud. Vagrant from Asia, obvious wing bars with pale around the cheek. (72.7% chance of occurrence in September)

SHORT-TOED LARK *Calendrella brachydactyla 14th September 2016*

Lee Gregory found this bird and despite it flying some way off when I arrived, I found it an hour or so later by Setter, the croft of my late, dear friend, Gordon Barnes. It flew with a Skylark back to the original place where Lee had found it and is still there today; sixteen days, a long-staying and welcome scarce migrant. Smaller, greyer and paler than Skylarks, an obvious bird with white underparts and streaky uppers. A vagrant from Southern Europe. (36.4% chance of occurrence in September)

COMMON ROSEFINCH *Erythrina erythrina 14th September 2016*

Seen at last in Neil Thompson's garden, Lower Stoneybrek, a finch with pale wingbars noted deep down amongst some roses. I have since seen two more rosefinches; one at the Bird Observatory perched high in the garden and another one I found perched on some wooden pallets near to the Fair Isle School. A scarce but regular vagrant from NE Europe. (100% chance of occurrence in September)

As well as the above, a lot of Lapland Buntings were on the island today with seventy four recorded.

YELLOW-BROWED WARBLER *Phylloscopus inornatus 15th September '16*

It would be a very strange year if one wasn't to see a Yellow-browed Warbler on Fair Isle in September. Gone are those days of the 1980s when one scratched around St Mary's on The Isles of Scilly looking for one or two. Here one has dozens and the first one for the year list was found by Lee Gregory in the Gully. A smashing tiny warbler with wingbars and eyestripes. More of them seem to be coming to Britain from their Siberian breeding area and one can only hope that they are finding a way to their wintering grounds. (100% chance of occurrence in September). Since that vanguard bird I have seen forty eight more on the fair isle!

BLUETHROAT *Luscinia svecica 17th September 2016*

Nick Riddiford, an ex- warden of Fair Isle Bird Observatory, thought that he had seen one at Shirva. Indeed he had for I found it there a short while later. A rare migrant from Europe I have since seen another that was at first running down the road in front of me as I cycled along. (90.9% chance of occurrence in September)

GREAT SNIPE *Gallinago media 18th September 2016*

Now was this one a hard one to find!? Lee Gregory, who else? found this in Da Water and after seeing it fly three times eventually thought he had it at a spot where everyone could get onto it. Birders assembled, a walk towards the bird's location gave no views and a continued search of the area did likewise. All went to lunch leaving me to search the marshes for over two hours, in two metre lines from one end of each marsh to the other. Only when I reached the end of a tatty (potato) crop did the Great Snipe suddenly emerge and how. Calling roughly it flew off over towards Kennaby where I subtly called to two birders. Did I heck! I screamed "THE snipe!" With larger size and darker belly noted as well as the call, Great Snipe not only goes onto the Year list but also my life list.

This bird has given everyone trouble since it's original finding. The whole process of found by one, searched for by many but not seen, was repeated over a week later when Deryk Shaw, another ex-warden of the Observatory found it in the field south of where I had found it previously. It may still be out there. (9.1% chance of occurrence in September)

RED-THROATED PIPIT *Anthus cervinus 18th September 2016*

Lee Gregory looked a bit vacant as we talked about the Great Snipe and where it might have disappeared to. He was thinking about a strange pipit he had just seen by the American Tommy Hyndeman's Guest house, Da Haa. Luckily Lee realised that it was a Red-throated Pipit and so another great year tick went down onto paper.

A grey looking pipit with obvious braces, the first time I have seen one whilst Biking Birding. Rare vagrant from Scandinavia. (27.3% chance of occurrence in September)

LITTLE BUNTING *Emberiza pusilla 20th September 2016*

In an oat crop this smashing little bird came out to sit as many birds do on a wire fence. This bird had a louse by it's right eye and so could be told from the next one seen at nearby Field a few days later. (81.8% chance of occurrence in September) I have now seen three Little Buntings; the last one a very tame bird near to the Bird Observatory.

RED-BREASTED FLYCATCHER *Ficedula parva 21st September 2016*

It never seems right to tick a bird in the hand, the first Red-breasted Flycatcher for the year was caught in the Heligoland trap at the Gully.

Much better was watching one fly catching on the rocks far below on the beach at Hjukni Geo. This bird's white sides to it's tail made it easy to see as it flew from rock to rock in search of flies. An Eastern European vagrant. (63.6% chance of occurrence in September)

A week goes by then . . .

PADDYFIELD WARBLER *Acrocephalus agricola 28th September 2016*

Over breakfast a birder, Andrew sitting opposite asked for a prediction for the day."Paddyfield would be nice," I said.

Paddyfield Warbler in Walli Burn, another LIFER for me. A cracking small and very pale acro', it flew around birders like a small moth, fluttering between iris beds.

So a month on Fair Isle, maybe another month to enjoy as well. What will October bring? Barnacle Geese and Olive-backed Pipits are 100% birds but then again, with an average of nine year ticks over the last ten years there will be some surprises. Male Siberian Rubythroat?

The book mentioned in the quote for the chapter, by Gordon Barnes, An Unforgettable Challenge, is available from the Fair Isle Bird Observatory at £5.00 plus postage and packing. The story of Gordon's time on Fair Isle as both assistant warden at the Observatory and as a crofter, the book is a wonderful insight into the hard life trying to make a living on a small and exposed island between Orkney and Shetland. Please do buy a copy. You would not regret doing so and you will be helping the World famous Bird Observatory. 3-star full board Accommodation is also available at the Fair Isle Bird Observatory : http://www.fairislebirdobs.co.uk/accommodation.html

Accommodation on Fair Isle is also available at :

***The South Lighthouse* :**

http://www.southlightfairisle.co.uk/index.asp **and**

***Auld Haa Guesthouse* : http://fair-isle.blogspot.co.uk/p/b-b.html**

September extra ...

A film came out in 1996, Fly Away Home, where a father and daughter plot involved microlight aircraft and a flock of imprinted Canada Geese. Redemption for a broken relationship between the two, the story is rather loosely based on the real life story of Bill Lishman and his original journey taking Canada Geese on their autumn migration south. The film made this into a journey taken by Bill and his daughter and received much critical acclaim. A tear inducing family film well worth a watch, especially as the fictitious daughter arrives just in time to save a wetland in North Carolina, USA from destruction and father and daughter reunite.

This September, a real life motorised paraglider journey began following the journey of Sacha Dench. Called The Flight of The Swans, Sacha will follow the route taken by Bewick Swans from their breeding grounds in Arctic Russia, starting at the Pechora Delta, (now where have I heard that name before?) to the UK. Taking ten weeks to fly the 7,500 kilometres, crossing eleven countries, Sacha will hopefully raise thousands of pounds for their conservation. Imagine the thrill and the privilege of flying with such graceful and beautiful families of swans. What an experience!

10

OCTOBER

The most effective way to save the threatened and decimated natural world is to cause people to fall in love with it again, with its beauty and its reality.

Sir Peter Scott

Saturday 1st October **very light N-NE**

Sunny for the most part with one shower around 1:30 p.m.

Sunshine, calm conditions and a flat sea, I decide to seawatch off Buness. A Slavonian Grebe is close in at North Haven as I walk past and a single Knot is huddled together with Sanderling and Turnstone on the disused jetty to be found there. On the furthest piece of Buness, on a seat-shaped rock, I watch the sea and all is well. The gentle swell gives a soundscape of serenity as waves gently cover rocky outcrops and fall away leaving cascades of white water. Hours pass.

Fulmars are passing, as always in good numbers and Gannets too. This makes it easy to spot any bird with different flight, with a different jizz as birders would say.

A Guillemot tazzes past, straight, direct and fast. A Grey Plover calls as it flies past in the opposite direction. A first year Kittiwake is going the same way and I naughtily think that my photograph of it could be photoshopped into a Sabine's Gull. How long before the first birding cheat tries to do such a thing? Has it happened already? Memories of the Caspian Gadwall.....

To see what that was all about click on the following link.

http://www.birdguides.com/webzine/article.asp?a=1303

You won't regret it. Flying Penguins, breeding Great Auks etc. Flying Penguins? Try this link to see what I mean about faking it.

https://www.youtube.com/watch?v=9dfWzp7rYR4

Two hours of soporific enjoyment, hoping for Orcas but reflecting on nature, goes by and it starts to drizzle. No problem, it adds to the atmosphere. Drizzle turns to not forecast rain. I head for the Bird Observatory and a coffee.

Plastic trawler net is on the beach. A large yellow fertilizer bag is on the beach. A large plastic bottle is on the beach. In the rain I collect them. At the skip I am told that I can't put the plastic waste I find in there any more. There is no room in the skip after the bin liners from the crofts and the Bird Observatory have filled it. "Get a box of matches and burn it."

It is not the fault of the crofter who tells me this. Cut backs means that there are now fewer waste skips brought to and from the island. I need to email some people. I won't stop collecting the obscene plastic waste that is found on every beach here. It arrives on every tide. The seal with a plastic neck-cutting necklace of fishing net deserves better than I walk past it all and do nothing.

A Yellow-browed Warbler is in the garden and two Redpolls. They look lesser to me but I don't get good views in the heavy pouring rain.

After a light lunch, an apple, the rain having stopped, I walk up to the radio mast and on to the geos of the west coast. From Skinner's to Tyneside, my favourite part of Fair Isle, I walk, sit for prolonged periods and enjoy the stunning scenery. There are almost no migrant birds; plenty of Fulmars and Gannets as expected. The only unusual bird is a Snow Bunting at Guidicam.

A text tells of a Humpback Whale moving not too far away over in Orkney. The whale, first seen off Sanday, has been seen off North Ronaldsay and I am hoping that it turns east. I am hoping that the wonderful young people of North Ronaldsay Bird Observatory are watching it. The conditions are perfect for whale watching. I can see the lighthouses on the Orkney Isle. I can see Foula to the north. The horizon is crisp and clear and the sea flat calm.

The sun starts to go down and so I head back for the observatory. Maybe tomorrow for the Humpback. Maybe tomorrow for some new migrant birds. Well the wind is north east, could be good.

Sunday 2nd October **very light E**

Sunny and amazingly clear with views of all surrounding islands.

Sunshine, calm conditions and a flat sea, I was here yesterday yet today feels different. Maybe the Blackcap, Willow Warbler and Lesser Whitethroat in the nettles at Pund show that birds have arrived.

A Bluethroat at Chalet, good bird, and two Redstarts on the fence by the fire station as I cycle down the island. There are birds!

I walk down to the Raevas and bird the geos. The view between the rocky headlands over to Foula, forty miles or so to the north, is as clear as I have ever seen it. One can make out buildings and rocky crevices.

Text from Susannah Parnaby at the Observatory:

Raddes Warbler between Burkle and Meadow Burn

Pedalling downhill a group of birders are standing around the cabbage patch at Quoy. They are looking for the Raddes. It hasn't been seen for half an hour or so. Very mobile is the news; that means the bird is flying around the island and could by now be anywhere.

Going over into the field at Meadow Burn, a Redwing is behind Nick Riddiford's garden at Schoolton. On his back fence is a Blackcap and a Lesser Whitethroat. I am about to search the reedy ditch that runs through the field when I spot two small warblers coming down the fence towards me. One is a Yellow-browed; the other isn't.

"Arctic Warbler," I shout. A brief view of a Chiff-shaped warbler with a good supercilium and just the hint of a wingbar. It and the Yellow-browed Warbler almost immediately fly off over towards Burkle to the south.

Birders search but to no avail. The Arctic Warbler is behaving just like the Radde's, both extremely flighty and mobile.

People are running and beckoning, the **Radde's Warbler** has been found again at Lower Stoneybreck. Once there I see it in flight disappearing towards Upper Stoneybrek. More views of it there, it goes from tall plant stems to hide behind a rusting metal container but it moves on towards the school. I finally get really good views when it lands on a wooden playground bridge and then on the surrounding fence of the school's playground. Not there for long though, it flies off towards the shop.

Bird number 294 and a good one to get, Radde's is another Siberian bird added to the list.

Another text from Susannah:

Chris has had a Blyth's Reed Warbler at the Obs.

I cycle there as fast as possible to find that the bird is down by the sheds at North Haven. The bird, an Acrocephalus, is following a short dry stone wall and it jumps on top of this giving a good view. It plays a game with myself and another birder as it keeps on disappearing behind the sheds only to come out the other side. Then it decides that it has had enough peekaboo and goes up the hill.

Half an hour later it is back around the sheds and more birders have gathered. The **Blyth's Reed Warbler** goes onto the beach and hides amongst the large stones. Then it comes back around the sheds and off up the hill again.

Bird number 295, things are getting better. How much better?

Text from Lee Gregory in capital letters:

BLUETAIL, Dog Geo.

Once having found that Dog Geo is on the south side of Malcolm's Head, I cycle to Lower Leogh and run across. Only Steve Arlow is there with his large camera and the very rare Siberian bird, a **Red-flanked Bluetail** is seen well fly catching in the shadows of the deep geo. The setting couldn't be better as both Steve and I lay down on the cliff edge and watch as the bluetail flits from rock to rock, fly to fly.

Bird number 296. Phew.

Walking back to Lower Leogh there are Yellow-browed Warblers everywhere; on the fences in the fields and in the roses at the croft. More are by the roadside at Meadow Burn.

Just before Shirva I think that Cairan has just waved to me. He has found something . . and how. **Pechora Pipit**!

Soon a long line of hopeful birders are assembled along a dry stone wall looking over an area of long grass at Shirva. Cairan walks through it but no

Pechora comes out. People disperse to search and the bird is soon found, on the short grass of the lawn at Shirva. I get it as it walks beneath some gas cylinders. It flies and lands to walk along the bottom of a dry stone wall. It flies again but only into a courtyard at North Shirva. It flies but into a window and goes off calling sharply around the building.

Bird number 297. Incredible.

Cath Mendez wants to see the Red-flanked Bluetail and knowing that the geo is a hard one to locate, I walk with her back to the bird. It is still flying around and after watching it some more I leave Cath to the bird in order to search the geos to the north. Steensi Geo has two Yellow-broweds and a Lesser Whitethroat. Linni geo has another Yellow-browed and a Blackcap. South Raeva has another two Yellow-broweds!

Back to the bike, left at Shirva, I head back for the Observatory, wanting to get better views of the Blyth's Reed Warbler. I get to Lower Stoneybrek and see a very pale, silver Whitethroat, another Yellow-browed, a Lesser Whitethroat and a Red-breasted Flycatcher.

Someone is running down the road. "Lanceolated at Shirva."

Once there, Steve Arlow, who is obviously having an incredible day bird-finding wise, has found the lancy and has it staked out in a tall grass clump. He, I and a few other birders, who have got there quickly, wait for Susannah to bring the minibus full of birders. The crowd assembled, Steve gently and slowly walks towards the bird. Out it comes and circles in front of everyone before disappearing into the long grass again. The bird comes out again on the next walk towards it by Steve and I decide to wait just up the road from the crowd.

How jammy can I be today? The lancy comes out and lands almost at my feet, the other side of a small gate.

Happy with my third Lanceolated Warbler of the year I head back to the Bird Observatory and carry on down to South Haven beach to sit with Steve Arlow and reflect on the day. There are three yellow-broweds fly catching on the washed up seaweed. Another one is even on the exposed Laminaria bed.

Text from Trevor Girling. (15:39)

Hope ur getting to these new birds today. 300 looming near.

I answer. (15:40)

Four year ticks today: Pechora, RF Bluetail, Raddes, Blyth's Reed. 297.

Trevor. (15:57)

Good man. Sounds amazing. Will have to go one year.

I send the following. (15:59)

Not a bad day. Add Arctic Warbler, Bluethroat, 20 or so Yellow-broweds, Whinchats, Wheatears, Redstart. Stunning t-shirt weather.

Just to finish the day the Blyth's Reed Warbler lands nearby giving great views. The Slavonian Grebe is still in North Haven.

Finally a 5 gram miracle, as Lee Gregory calls them, a Goldcrest, is in North Haven on the wire-netting around the harbour. Exhausted.

Now for the bird log!

Bird log highlights : - Five S*lavonian Grebe, one Merlin, one Peregrine, one Water Rail, twenty two Jack Snipe, twenty nine Goldcrest, one Short-toed Lark, nineteen Swallow , one Arctic Warbler, seventy two Yellow-browed Warbler (five away from a new Fair Isle record), [sixteen Yellow-broweds were rung], nineteen Chiff Chaff (of which seven were 'tristis'.), nine Willow Warbler, twenty Blackcap, five Garden Warbler, three Barred Warbler, thirteen Lesser Whitethroat , one Whitethroat, one Lanceolated Warbler, one Blyth's Reed Warbler, one Radde's Warbler (Fair Isle's 8th), 133 Redwing, two Bluethroat, one Redstart, six Whinchat, thirty nine Wheatear, four Red-breasted Flycatcher, three Pied Flycatcher, one Stonechat, one Pechora Pipit, one Red-throated Pipit, sixteen Goldfinch ,213 Twite, two Linnet, two Lesser Redpoll, one Little Bunting and a Red-flanked Bluetail (Fair Isle's thirteenth)*

If you have read all of that, well done. What a Super Sunday!

Monday 3rd October **Fresh to strong ESE**

Sunny, cool.

Sunshine starts the day after The Day but it is much cooler due to the fresh wind. It is in the right direction though so who knows, there may be good birds arriving. Like yesterday? Like Super Sunday? One can only hope but a day like yesterday is really a once in a lifetime event, or so it feels. Magic.

A Slavonian Grebe is close in at North Haven again. The Blyth's Reed Warbler is showing from the Bird Observatory garden before breakfast and a Common Rosefinch has been caught in a mist net. Measured and ringed, it is soon released.

Yesterday's list of rares is still on the Bird Observatory noticeboard daring everyone to find better birds today.

Down the island it is immediately clear that there has been a huge clear out of migrant birds. I don't see my first Phyllosc' for a couple of hours.

Jack Snipe, Curlews, Pipits, Fulmars, Gannets, Pink-footed Geese, Wigeon; the day goes by and although I see a group of birders gather to look at the Lanceolated Warbler, now to be found in the garden at Midway, I don't join them. I continue to search.

A text from Erin Taylor at the North Ronaldsay Bird Observatory. (11:01 a.m.)

So Gary I can't help but notice that you're dangerously close to 300 and it's only the 3rd!!! X

I respond (11:03a.m.)

Three to go. What a day yesterday. Would I swap it all for a Humpback? Nah!!!

The calm waters surrounding North Ronaldsay had been graced with one of nature's most fascinating and inspiring of creatures, a Humpback Whale, the previous day. How I would love to have seen one as close as all at the bird observatory had but this year is about one thing, getting the best Green Year list possible.

I text Erin once more. (11:07 a.m.)

BTW love to the best birding crew in crew in Britain! X

Erin replies. (11:13 a.m.)

Haha. I'll give them your love! But we've changed. We're now the best whaling crew in Britain! X

To which I send. (11:14 a.m.)

Wailing?

Erin. (11:20 a.m.)

Both.

To the shop in the afternoon for food, I go to the Kirk afterwards to read and have lunch. There is a library in the Kirk and it is a peaceful place to sit and read, recuperate and contemplate. Adam Gilchrist's autobiography is interesting in his honesty over his problems with depression. So many international cricketers have suffered with depression, too many. There is a collection of National Geographic magazines. A large photograph of a large eyed, young Indian girl staring at the camera is hauntingly beautiful and I leave it open at that page for me to see every time I come into the Kirk. I want that girl's face to remind me every day that I need to be more empathetic, more concerned and more proactive in the politics of the systems that cause poverty. Maybe this is a reaction to the stupidity of the Referendum vote. My rage over what happened continues to grow.

I look into her eyes.

After lunch I am walking the bike up the hill by the school when a bird comes out of the long grass. I think it looks good. I watch where it dives down into the grass and head that way. It doesn't flush until I almost tread on it and it flies like a bullet and into a ditch. What is it? A thrush? That size but behaving like this. Must check. I carefully walk the ditch and up it flies again heading away from me at speed to dive into a ditch once again. It looks like a thrush but which one?

I phone Lee Gregory who I can see a few hundred yards away near North Shirva. Lee is a great friend and he, with Cath Mendez, come over. Meanwhile I have been praying to my Guardian Angels that it is a good bird.

The three of us move over to the last place I saw the bird and out comes a . . .

Red-flanked Browntail! (work it out ...)

Oh well, always call out a bird you're not sure of. I have never seen a Redwing, for that's what it was, behave in such a way. Weird.

The three comrades walk back towards the Bird Obs. and laugh. One day it will be a mega but not today.

Tuesday 4th October **strong ESE**

Sunny, cool.

Barnacle Geese are coming over the island, flocks of them. I miss them from my tent. I miss them as I cycle to the Bird Observatory. I miss them whilst having breakfast!

A text, *Olive-backed Pipit, Field Ditch.*

I am there quick enough but it is clear the bird is nowhere on view. Birders are standing around or searching the fields. It has flown and in the strong wind the rare Sibe pipit could be anywhere. I search the fields, starting in those west of Chalet.

No pipit found by the time I get to Hjukni Geo via Gilly Burn, just a few Redwings and a Whinchat.

Chaffinch in the geo and a Chiff Chaff that trembles it's tail every time it stays put on the cliff. A Redshank stays by a pool long enough for me to photograph it before it does what Redshank normally do, noisily buzzes off.

Lee Gregory comes past on his census walk and points out three **Barnacle Geese** coming our way. "Year tick!" I say. "You must have had them before these," he laughs. Well hundreds had flown over the island already. No matter, **bird number 298** onto the year list, two to go.

I walk along thinking of my favourite children's TV series from when I was child, "Thunderbirds". Two birds to go, which would be Virgil. Thunderbird 2 was always my favourite craft and that take off! Down the chute, how come Virgil didn't slide out when it turned around? Collapsing palm trees, smoke and off. Great days.

What do old people say? They don't make them like that any more.

Virgil, now there's a train of thought. The Aeneid and an Odyssey, a quest if you will. A fulfilment of which mine may be only two birds away.

I decide that today I will explore the cliffs and geos from Hjukni Geo north. Each geo has migrants sheltering from the wind; thrushes, which most are Redwings but there are also Fieldfare, Blackbirds and Song Thrushes. A single male Ring Ouzel is at Guidicum.

A flock of Barnacles, twenty five of them, fly over, with three Wigeon, on their way seemingly to North Ronaldsay.

Goldcrests number around twenty and there are a couple of Yellow-browed Warblers and Chiff Chaffs. A male Blackcap is amazing in its tenacity of clinging to the rock near the base of an immense cliff of Gunnawark. Here I have clung to the metal rope and gone down the cliff to perch on a ledge far below the cliff tops. From here I can see the beach and watch the seals in the surf. The first of the new born seal cubs is on the beach asleep.

Back to the cliff tops I continue north. Two butterflies are flying, both Red Admirals and the water cannon is banging away in North Naaversgill. A regularly spaced jet of water that shoots skywards from a small cave as described before but maybe not as intense as last time.

The magnificence of the cliffs is as breath-taking as ever and with the sunshine making a deep contrast within the depths of each geo to the sunlit cliffs, the views are stupendous.

The day goes by quickly but by the time I reach Ward Hill I am beat and grateful that the way is downhill to the Bird Observatory.

October Target Birds

Once again I have a spreadsheet made up of the possible Year tick birds that have occurred on Fair Isle in the last eleven years as detailed in their wonderful annual reports.

Each bird has a percentage probability and the average number of year tick birds for October is 8.9. Let's make my target nine then, optimistic but I have already had five!

Radde's Warbler
Blyth's Reed Warbler
Red-flanked Bluetail
Pechora Pipit and
Barnacle Goose.

So what's left? Let's start with the birds I saw last October here on Fair Isle plus there percentage chance:-

Olive-backed Pipit (72.7% up to 100% in the last five years)

Well one was seen on the island today so hopefully that will be re-found tomorrow.

Siberian Rubythroat (36.4% but up to 60% in the last five years)

A high chance then of seeing one and I may be greedy but I wish for a male, unlike last year's hard to see female.

OK, now for the other birds that I didn't see on fair Isle last year but they have been here as follows:-

(81.8% chance)

Little Auk

(54.4% chance)

Waxwing, Iceland Gull (increases to 100% chance for the last five years)

(45.5% chance)

Arctic Redpoll [Snowball please, hornemanni.]

(36.4%)

Pallas' Grasshopper Warbler and White's Thrush

[What a pair these two would make!]

(27.3%)

Buff-breasted Sandpiper [it would be nice to have a Yank]

Black-throated Thrush [aah, memories of one nearly in my garden in Redditch in the '90s]

(18.2%)

Blyth's Pipit, White-rumped Sandpiper, Bean Goose, Siberian Stonechat, Grey-cheeked Thrush, Rustic Bunting, Sabine's Gull and finally . . .

(9.1%) - fantasy time.....

River Warbler, Red-eyed Vireo, Blackpoll Warbler, Honey Buzzard, King Eider, Thrush Nightingale, Pallas' Warbler, Siberian Thrush, Pine Bunting, Subalpine Warbler,

(since split but no details of which in report)

Hume's Yellow-browed Warbler

Right, there you have it. My Green Year list at the moment stands at **298** and I am hoping for four more birds over the next few weeks here on Fair Isle. The winds are south-easterly for the next ten days at least and the wind is set to calm down. Sunshine also for the next ten days, what a time to be on Fair Isle with the weather set fair. Those winds by the way originate from beyond Finland. What will they bring?

Wednesday 5th October **strong SE**

Sunny, cool

Gentle wandering around the island, feeling tired after yesterday's exploration of the cliffs and geos. Barnacle Geese are gathering at the most southern tip of the island, Skadan. Around 300 of them are there awaiting a signal from one of them for them all to lift into the air and head south.

A large grey US Air Force plane circles the island and heads south itself. Unusual to see here.

A Little Bunting is at the base of a dry stone wall near to the thistle patch by North Shirva. A male Blackcap is sheltering from the cool breeze in amongst the stones.

The Pechora Pipit has been found again and so the late afternoon is spent at Hjunki Geo watching this rare bird. I video it as it finds a worm. Unfortunately for the Pechora, a Meadow Pipit comes in and steals it.

Thursday 6th October **Fresh SE-E easing**

Very sunny day

Sheep Day. A day when all the sheep north of Hill Dyke are gathered together and the lambs sorted out for the crofters. A time when all the islanders and most Bird Observatory staff and a few birders, such as myself, Andrew and John, join forces to corral the sheep into a pen down the hill from Setter.

How naïve are Andrew and I when, once the sheep are collected from Buness and The Parks area opposite Sheep Rock, we think that the work is done. Not so, there is Ward Hill and the geos to be searched. The sheep there need to be collected also and brought down to the pens. I walk, run, jump and chase with Jimmy by my side. Jimmy, who is married to Florrie, is an original crofter whose father, Jimmy was a crofter before him. It is a privilege to be able to call Jimmy and Florrie friends and a privilege to gather the sheep with him. His sheep dog is superb and his obedience is perfect. Still a few sheep escape from the main group and Jimmy goes off around Tyneside to collect them.

It is hard work and the sweat over a huge smile on Cairan's face as the sheep eventually are penned, says it all. By now the fresh cooling breeze of early morning has eased to a light breeze and with strong sunshine all coats can be dispensed with.

Woodcock were disturbed from the heather moorland by all of this activity. I see two myself, large, chunky low-flying birds. Also nine Grey Herons are flying over Buness, occasionally cronking as they fly south.

Work done, time to go birding. An Olive-backed Pipit is rumoured so I head off south hoping to find one of the two new birds I need to reach 300. After three hours of searching I haven't seen the rare pipit, and actually miss both a Pechora and a Red-throated. I do find two Little Buntings though and it always nice to see Lapland Buntings and Bramblings close to. There is also a small flock of redpolls and at least two of them are pale **Mealy Redpolls**. Not countable on European lists being lumped with Lesser Redpoll over there, Mealy is a separate species on the BOU (British Ornithological Union) list and so I go onto 299 birds for the year. To continue the Thunderbirds thought from the other day, this leaves only Scott. How that name has kept cropping up during my life. Scott, Sir Peter Scott and the influence his letter had on me when I was a young boy. The desire to travel and love nature taken from reading Sir Peter's many books and the love of his art, his paintings especially of wildfowl that adorned our home in Swanage. One to go.

Walking back towards the Bird Observatory with the sun almost set, Susannah Parnaby stops in the van to tell me that a Red-flanked Bluetail has been seen at the far end of Hill Dyke in Gannawark Geo. It is a long walk but I make it up there. More amazingly though is the fact that a birder in a wheelchair is up there thanks to his friends. The strength of such friendship is the most wonderful and impressive thing of the evening and the fact that the Bluetail is missed by all is neither here nor there. Friends.

The walk to the Observatory is in the dark with a crescent Moon setting in the south. There isn't a cloud in the sky. The walk back 'home' later is going to be spectacular with the Milky way leading the way.

Friday 7th October **Fresh SE**

very sunny and warm.

The morning I search around the crofts, fields and dykes watching small, common migrants. Bramblings and Lapland Buntings are in the thistles at North Shirva.

An Olive-backed Pipit is found at Dronger, about as far up the north west as you can get. I get up there yet I am not too disappointed when I don't find the rare Siberian bird. The view is amazing with the epic coastline of geos and high cliffs stretching to the south. Somehow it all reminds me of the Formentor Peninsula on Majorca. Here the series of promontories are grass-covered. The consecutive pattern of high peak followed by deep gully brings back the image I remember from a sunrise time walk by the lighthouse, at the northernmost point of the Mediterranean isle many years ago.

Gannets are still in pairs on the cliffs and there are migrant birds up here too; Goldcrests, Wheatear, Meadow Pipits with Jack and Common Snipe. A Merlin chases a pipit along the cliff edge nearby.

At the observatory in the evening I find out that the Olive-backed Pipit has moved to Leerness making that area tomorrow's destination.

Saturday 8th October light to fresh SE

Very sunny all day

The Sun is shining gloriously as I walk along Hill Dyke, t-shirt weather with a need of sun tan lotion. Migrants are in every geo, Siberian Chiff Chaffs, Goldcrests, Redwings, Song Thrushes, Blackbirds and Robins.

There are butterflies too, a couple of Red Admirals and a Painted Lady. A Silver Y moth continues the Lepidoptera list.

Reaching North Naaversgill I spot Lee Gregory coming towards me near to Grey Geo. He turns around the other way, not to avoid me, he has seen a bird of interest. I make my way over to where he is. He lifts his camera. He starts to send a text and as he turns around he finds that I am running towards him. He points and says what I suspected, **"Olive-backed Pipit."** I look and see the bird for a few seconds before it takes off and flies over the immense space that is Grey Geo.

Bird number 300.

300!

The dream is accomplished. 300 birds in a calendar year, 2016. The Big Green Big Year for the UK is now heading into extreme uncharted territory and the 300 is mine to keep forever. The first British cyclist to reach 300 in the UK.

The Quest for 300 achieved. It's too much and I well up with a few tears. Handshakes and a hug from Lee. I am over the Moon with the fact that the most special birding friend on Fair Isle is here at this moment.

300. I have done it.

Lee is doing North as his day's census route and heads off south to continue his work, having already searched along the north coast. I stay, wanting to have more views of the pipit that is my 300th bird species for 2016, in case you hadn't realised it. The fact that the bird is an Olive-backed Pipit is not lost on me. It has a historic connection being the bird that started my life of twitching with a fantastic group of teenage lads from Wolverhampton. Back in 1984 I was a Secondary school teacher, Coppice High School, Ashmore Park, Wednesfield. There I started a YOC (Young Ornithologist's Club) and three members of the club came with me one weekend day to see an Olive-backed Pipit in Bracknell, Berkshire. We saw that bird and it is forever a source of delight that one of those boys, Jason Oliver, is now an extremely brilliant birder and very close friend; a leader of The Birding Clams. The Clams contain other great birders from those long off YOC days; Steve Allcott, Tony Barter and Ian Crutchley amongst others. The circle is complete, fate has made the first bird from then my 300th of 2016.

I text Erin Taylor at North Ronaldsay Bird Observatory. (1:22 p.m.)

300 OBP

Her speedy reply is ecstatic and persistent. (1:23 p.m.)

YAAAAAASSSSSSSSS WILL YOU BE ATTENDING THE DANCE? I'll understand if you feel the need to go for the European record instead! Congrats. You're awesome. We'll drink in your honour tonight. X

I send a simple text.(1:26 p.m.)

If Chris Mills is still with you please tell him. I would just love to come back. You lot are the highlight of the year.

Erin (1:31 p.m.)

We've told everyone! Ha ha well we'd love it too. We might even get you a few more birds. I had Hawfinch, Firecrest and Red-breasted Fly in the nets this morning. X

I search but can't find the pipit and as it is lunch time I sit on top of a high cliff to eat some fruit and watch whatever birds pass.

There is a bird far below on the beach at the base of Leerness Geo, at the end of Grey Geo. It is a Flycatcher. I look through my binoculars and my heart starts to race. It has a long white patch on the primary patch! Could it really be a Collared. I try to photograph the bird but it is constantly flitting around and staying in the shadows. Photographs once achieved with my Canon SX50 are inconclusive but I feel someone should come and have a look. I am just not sure. A Collared Flycatcher would be a mega, a Pied Flycatcher would be just another bird.

I get a signal as I climb the hill and I phone Lee hoping that he is close but he is at Hjunki, a long way south.

I walk back up and over the hills and see Will, a superb birder from Aberdeen. He is walking the stream and once I catch up with him I show him photographs. Pied is his verdict.

Nick Riddiford is the next birder I meet, Collared he says!

I go down to Lower Stonebrek. Two of the three birders there are unsure, the other says Pied.

I try to stop a van rushing past us with Cairan and David Parnaby inside but they don't stop. Half an hour or so later David is passing and he stops. Non-committal, he just asks where I saw it and says that Chris Dodds is up there.

Back at the Observatory later I show the photograph to Cairan. Collared he says.

There was no way I could get any closer to get any better photographs and I can only hope that the bird is there in the morning. No one else has seen it.

Party time, Elena has brought in a bottle of champagne to help celebrate the 300 with friends. Wonderful friends to share a very special and emotional moment.

300.

Done it!

Lee Gregory Facebooks his census details for the day:-

8th Oct 2016. North Census in beautiful blue skies and easterly breeze. The highlight for me was the juvenile Glaucous Gull which flew low overhead at the Wirvie Burn.
Census counts; 171 Meadow Pipit, 25 Rock Pipit, 3 Wheatear, 8 Skylark, 88 Twite, 13 Snipe, Jack Snipe, 8 Redshank, 7 Ringed Plover, 9 Turnstone, Chaffinch, 52 Goldcrest, 12 Robin, 87 Redwing, 84 Song Thrush, 19 Blackbird, 3 Woodcock, OLIVE-BACKED PIPIT, Fieldfare, 2 White Wagtail, Lapland Bunting, 2 late Garden Warbler, 11 Brambling, Redpoll sp. over, 7 Yellow-browed Warbler, 9 Chiffchaff, Siberian Chiffchaff, 3 Swallow, Kestrel, Short-eared Owl, Cormorant, 3 Snow Bunting, 5 Teal, Red-breasted Merganser and Knot. 2 Red Admiral and Painted Lady were enjoying the sunshine too.
Congratulations to Gary 300 Prescott for reaching his goal with the Olive-backed Pipit - it was great to experience the occasion - well done mate now for the European Record!

Sunday 9th October **Almost no wind**

Very warm and sunny

A Peregrine is flying along the Hill Dyke stone wall as I climb towards the geos to search for yesterday's Flycatcher. There's hardly a cloud and hardly a breath of wind. The sun is rising and the shadows are leaving the geos and cliffs.

A couple of hours I spend looking down at the Grey Geo but no Flycatcher is there. My chance for a really good bird dissipates.

I walk up Guidicom and around to Skinner's Geo. There are migrants, Goldcrests of course and a couple of Yellow-browed Warblers. Chiff Chaffs all seem to be of the nominate race.

The sea is amazingly flat, not a ripple and so blue! This is October and once again I need sun tan lotion.

I walk past the radio mast and around to view the sound between Shetland and Fair Isle. My hope is that Cetacean or two will show themselves. They don't but this doesn't detract from the stunningly magnificent scenery and views.

Houses can clearly seen on Shetland around Toab and Quendale. The lighthouse stands proudly atop Sumburgh Head, an RSPB reserve.

I explore the island after breakfast at the Bird Observatory. Birds become secondary to the main motivation of enjoying a warm Autumn day.

Silver Y moths are in the shop garden and migrant birds are still chasing flies. A perfect day.

Birds are obviously though still a focus. Little Buntings in the thistles at North Shirva with Reed Buntings, Twite and Bramblings. All look fabulous in the perfect light.

Even the Pechora Pipit gives views at Lower Stoneybrek.

In the late evening I head up Buness to watch the darkness fall and the Moon rise. Such clarity and beauty. Unmatched.

Maria Jesus Navarro Blaya, the wonderful woman in charge of the Chaskwasi-Manu project in The Manu, Peru sends a message via Facebook:-

Congratulations, Gary Brian Prescott, I am happy for you!

Monday 10th October

Sunrise is incredible. The sky is ablaze with colour from horizon to horizon. I can only remember a couple of sunrises as good as this before in my life and I sit n a small brick wall by Pund to take in the splendour.

Text from Trevor Girling (6.23)

A belated huge congratulations mate. Sorry it's late but I've been doing a bit of ringing here. Birding too.

I text back. (6.26)

Thanks Trevor. Just hoping the accentor is still there today. Earliest boat is tomorrow morning. Hope things are good with you.

I am on the trap round with lee and Nina. The sun breaches the horizon as if a distant nuclear explosion.

On the way back with a few bird bags full I spot a large splash half way out over the sea to the horizon. It has got to be a whale.

It breaches, once, twice then blows water six feet high as it breaths, a Minke or a Humpback I am not sure. Lee says Minke. It tail flukes and is gone.

After breakfast there is only one topic of conversation. How can we get to the Shetland mainland fast? A first for Britain bird, a Siberian Accentor has been found and all birders on the isle want to get there to see it.

The Birding Clams had it last night and whilst I was on Buness I had talked to them as they watched the bird on the phone. The fact that I could see the hill on which the mega rare bird was residing as I talked to the lads only increased to the tension.

Hard moments of decision making, I determine that I need to see it Green, well as Green as I can be whilst still using fossil fuels. The boat is greener than the plane. Hence I will take the Good Shepherd boat and not fly to it. The Good Shepherd will be leaving tomorrow, the plane goes today. Tough decision but necessary.

I watch the minibus leave with birders leave for the airport. I see them all return half an hour later. The plane has broken down!

Lots of justifiable anger in the lounge, how can such a vital service for Fair Isle be with a plane that breaks down?

I am desperate for Lee Gregory to see it. He deserves to see it and I say that if the only way for Lee to see the bird is by a plane charter then I would pay my bit and help make up the numbers. Cath Mendez phones a company but no plane is available. The frustrated anger rises.

At this time the news is that the plane might be fixed in two days time. Birders are booked onto the Good Shepherd including myself (thanks Susannah).

I have appointments; one to visit Jim and Florrie, two original crofters in the south of the island, and another with Mati over the purchase for Mum and Dad of two Fair Isle garments.

The former aren't in and I spend a few hours chatting with Mati about love and hearing Mati's young daughter playing the keyboard. She will be a superstar at this rate as she composes her own pieces. Not bad for an eight year old.

I get back to the Bird Obs to find the plane has gone after all. The time it left, 5:15 p.m. will mean that the birders who left will get ten minutes or so of decent light once they reach the bird. That is enough and I am chuffed to see that Lee has gone. Will that the accentor stays for me tomorrow. A clear star-filled sky with a large Gibbous Moon doesn't bode well.

On walking back to my rustic abode, with dreams of a CMF mega, The International Space Station flying over is spectacular, as are a number of shooting stars.

Tuesday 11th October **light SE**

Sunny intervals.

The Good Shepherd leaves on time and I am on deck with Ellen, the Fair Isle nurse, who is on her way to Romania, and Marc, a Belgian photographer, author and journalist. The sea is relatively calm but still the Good Shepherd rolls from side to side, occasionally throwing me about. I cling on to the rails. Sailing on this boat always seems to double time and the slow crossing takes it's usual age. The views of the distant Shetland islands are clear and Foula can be seen to the North West.

Sunrise, a Japanese flag of sunbeams, beautifully covers the eastern sky. Guillemots pass in groups of three, a single Razorbill and a single Sooty Shearwater. A couple of large trawlers do likewise.

Past Sumburgh Head and around into Grutness Harbour, I already know the news, the Siberian Accentor has gone.

Lee Gregory is at the quayside awaiting his return trip to Fair Isle. He saw the Accentor last night and shows me photographs of the First for Britain bird. I am thrilled for him. Lee deserves this bird. It is sure to bring his mojo back!

My mojo is disappearing fast. I find that a gear cable has rusted through leaving me with a single gear. Oh well, my mother, bless her little positive socks, always says that troubles come in threes so I look forward to the third. The bird, the gears and . . . ?

Boddam, well just before it, has a field to the east with waders and in with a single Ruff, a few Redshank and Curlew and a number of Golden Plover and Lapwing, is an American wader, a **Buff-breasted Sandpiper.** Bird number **301** goes down onto the list. At least that went well.

I head off for Quendale to have a walk. I don't feel like a long cycle to

Bressay despite the fact there is a mega rare bird there. Frankly I am tired out. I was late getting to bed last night and early getting up this morning to take down the tent, pack and get the boat. I need a rest.

Wednesday 12th October **light SE**

Sunny intervals

Around to Quendale again, I meet Jules, a Midland Birder, the one who was onto a recent photograph of The Birding Clams celebrating the Siberian Accentor. A natter and good luck wishes both ways, I head off along the valley and search the quarry and iris beds. I don't stop at the head of the valley but continue up the slope over the heather moorland to the top of Fitful Head to the radar station. I have a vain hope that the Siberian Accentor has relocated to this hill.

It hasn't and a text to say that there is a Pallid Harrier down the bottom of the hill has me careering down the hillside.

That's gone too.

A Little Bunting down the valley doesn't tempt me. Fair Isle withdrawal symptoms. I need my mojo back.

Facebook has a message posted by Jim Royer of California:-

Gary's Green Year of birding is going great - 300 species in the UK! He is now out to beat the European record. And raising money for charities along the way! Congrats Gary!

Jim collates Green Birding records, be they year lists, day, lists or big sits, from around the world. They can all be seen on his website http://greenbirdingworld.blogspot.co.uk/

Thursday 13th October **fresh SE**

Cloudy

I head back towards Quendale. A text from The Oracle.....

Black-faced Bunting still at Gunnista, Bressay.

I turn around and pack the bike. OK, Let's go for the bunting!

I reach the harbour in Lerwick at one o'clock and take the quick ferry across to Bressay. Gunnista doesn't take long to reach and the search begins for the elusive and mobile rare bird. There are derelict croft buildings and barns, each with bits of garden or weeds, piles of manure in a field and a pampas grass garden some way down a grassy slope. All are searched and a male Redstart, a Robin and couple each of Goldcrest and Rock Pipit reward me for my efforts.

A local farmer comes up to me on a quad bike. "It was in the turnip field this morning," he tells me.

How many times should one go around a large turnip field before saying enough is enough. I try five times clockwise, then five times anti-clockwise trying to change my luck. There are birds; Twite, House Sparrows, Skylarks and a single Brambling. Also there are a couple of rather tame Chiff Chaffs and a Wren. No Black-faced Bunting.

Getting dark and cloudy with the wind strengthening, I put up my tent. I will get it tomorrow.

Evening text from The Oracle. (21:39)

Your phone's turned off. Personally I would suggest u get to Bressay as early as possible and give the bunting another go. Nowt else to go for. Pallid has not been seen but I suspect still in the area. Also possible Taiga Flycatcher near Hillwell. Personally I would stay in until at least Monday as the eye of the weather front coming through is concentrated in Shetland and make decision during Monday whether to stay, go to FI or come off. At present birds back on the mainland are Bean Geese then Baird's Sand in Northumbria. Will send u updates on mainland position. Sibe acc at Spurn today.

Friday 14th October **very strong SE**

Occasional bits of rain, cold

Somehow the tent managed to collapse on me overnight as a gale blew. Not surprisingly it led to some interrupted sleep.

Awake early, I go around the turnip field again, same birds, few more pigeons, and around the manure heaps, the graveyard and the farm buildings. Same Redstart and Robin are present.

Two birders arrive, Neil from Holt, Norfolk and John from Holbeach. John sums up the situation succinctly. "What a hell hole!"

Together we search all of the areas already mentioned. No luck.

At 11:00 a.m. they go off to fetch another birder, Dan Poignton. The legendary bird-finder arrives. Dan will find the bird.

John, Neil and I are by the turnip field. A call on John's phone, Dan has found the rare bunting.

Unknown to we three there is a cabbage patch about 200 yards from the turnip patch. The Black-faced Bunting is in there. It flies out and amazingly lands on a five bar gate and just sits there for minutes on end. Telescope views show a bunting with a black face.

Phew! Hours of hell in wind and rain and the bird is now secured onto the Green Year list, **Black-faced Bunting**, bird number **302.** This is a very rare British bird, just six seen ever. I saw the first at Pennington near Wigan, Greater Manchester back in 1994 with a few of the Birding Clams. On that occasion I was so excited over seeing the bird that I left an expensive Barbour coat there draped over a barbed wire fence.

With this one we all want more views of the bird and continue to search for it for the next two hours. At no time though does it settle, it just keeps going on a circular tour of it's favourite places. One distraction on the bunting chase is provided by the most confiding Jack Snipe that just lays down in a ditch thinking we can't see it as we stand ten feet from it. It's prostrate form with two very clear mantle braces is comical, with it stretched out as flat as it can get with its beak on the ground in front of it. What a moment to have left my camera in the tent.

Time to go, I pack the tent in the gale and head back to Lerwick. I am just pushing my injured bike up a steep hill out of the town when I receive a text in capitals from The Oracle....

PIED WHEATEAR, SCATNESS.

The Oracle, Phil Andrews, even phones me.

"Have you got the message?"

"Yes, that's why I am pushing the bike up this hill!"

The wind is punishing and I get as far as Cunningsborough where I camp for the night.

At about one in the morning I am disturbed by some lads making a right racket in a car. Their empty Coca Cola bottles and chip papers are there in the morning. They live hard these Shetland teenagers.

Saturday 15th October **fresh to very strong SE**

Cloudy to rain

The Pied Wheatear is still present in the morning so I must get to Scatness as soon as possible. First though I need water. With the amount of effort that is needed to cycle a one gear bike twenty five miles, I am using up my water quicker than usual and I didn't have any left before retiring last night. The toilet block at Cunningsborough saves the day. Yes, the bike's gear system is causing problems with my short, fat, hairy legs go around speedily with little reward.

I reach Boddam to buy some food, having been tooted at by passing birders on my way. Then it's down to Scatness and a feeling of confidence that the rare wheatear is going to be still there. A friend, the brilliant birder Hugh Harrop is on the other side of a dry stone wall by the beach.

"Come on Gary. It's still here."

Pied Wheatear, bird number **303** and what superb looking bird. I lie down to watch it as it quickly goes from rock to rock chasing sand flies. A Common Wheatear comes too close and it's Pied cousin soon sees it off. Wheatears are one of my favourite bird groups and this bird is a definite highlight of the year; the first rare Wheatear I have seen whilst Biking Birding.

The bird flies off along the beach and I follow it. Hugh comes and joins me and I congratulate him on he and Judd finding the recent First for Britain, the Siberian Accentor. To hear the story of that bird's finding from the man himself is a humbling and humorous privilege. No expletives used in his account. He couldn't have been excited enough.

Hugh tells me that Roger Riddington, the British Birds magazine editor, had a Siberian Stonechat briefly this morning and I text him for directions. From Roger's reply I spend the afternoon searching the thistle beds and sand dunes around Toab and Quendale. No sign of the rare Stonechat, I am surprised to be almost slapped in the face by a very brave Red Admiral butterfly. A Goldcrest is by my feet quietly feeding as I video it, always a special birding moment to be graced by the presence of a 'five gram miracle.'

On the way down to the sand dunes I meet a mother with son, Anna and Lucian, who have just been clearing the beach of some plastic. These wonderful people deserve a Blue Peter badge at the very least but I have left all of my bird badges in my panniers hidden at Scatness. I take one off my coat, give it to them and say that they have really given me a great boost by their action. They continue towards Toab and I go around the sand dunes.

No sign of the Stonechat, I go back to where I have left my bike. Some farm workers are having a laugh taking turns riding a bike with a badly buckled back wheel.

I find my own less damaged vehicle only to find that Anna and Lucian have left an expensive bar of chocolate in the margarine tub I use for the bird badges I have attached to the front bag. Wonderful kindness, that will be a donation to the charities.

Later in the evening another great birding friend, Trevor Girling of Norfolk, phones to ask how things are going. He has been concerned at my lack of internet presence lately and the long chat is very greatly appreciated. Brilliant to hear from him. The world of birding brings wonderful friendships.

Sunday 16th October **strong to gale force SE**

Heavy rain AM

It is very early morning and a gale is blowing outside. Heavy rain is forecast so, feeling a little stir crazy, I text The Oracle with birding lyrics inspired by some of my favourite comedy music from the distant past.......

Hello Mudder
Hello Fadder
Here I am at Grutness Harbour
Here on Shetland
Gale is blowing
And the rain falls hard so nowhere I'll be going.

It seems ages
I've been stuck here
Bike is broken
Weather I fear
No boat coming
From the Fair Isle
I'll just wait and sing some songs sometimes puerile.

Take me home
Oh Mudder, Fadder
I'll not roam.
Won't go no farther
Can't one see that cycling's hurting me
And I have sardines for my tea.

Take me home
Oh, Mudder, Fadder
Hear my tome
My plea, my ardour.
I will stay inside and lock the door
And be as bored as once before.

Wait a minute,
It's stopped raining.
Sun is shining, wind abating.
Birds are singing,
Gee that's better
Mudder, Fadder kindly disregard this letter!

Then there's the old folk music classic . . .

Oh I'm going to the Fairest isle
I go there every Autumn
I'll search for birds

From dawn to dusk
And cry when I don't find them

And then a silly song with a wink to Charlie Drake, My Boomerang Won't Come Back .....

On the distant isle of Shetland
just a few days ago.
A first for Britain bird had left the hill
To where we do not know

I've got a lot of trouble Hugh
On account of a birding lack
Now tell me what's your trouble Gaz

The Accentor won't come back

The Accentor won't come back?

The Accentor won't come back
The Accentor won't come back
I've walked the hill all over that place
searched in stingers right into my face.
But of the Sibe there's just no trace
The Accentor won't come back

The Pied Wheatear was good
Yeah yeah
The bunting was too
Yeah, yeah
but the Accentor is better than both of those two
The Accentor won't come back

They banished him off to Fair Isle
Great birds for him to see
He had to list some new birds soon
The champion then he'd be

This is nice innit?
Getting banished at my time of life.
What a way to spend an evening.
Sitting by a geo on the edge of a cliff with some bins in my hand.
I shall very likely get pushed off!

Baaaaaaa

aaarhahhhh

Geroutofit
Nasty woolly animal

Think I'll make a nice cup of tea,

bonk, bonk, bonk, bonk.

Good gracious. There's goes a nice great skua.
Must have a practice with my binoculars.
Look at him as he flies past,
Now slowly to my eyes and . . .

If you look at me I'll bonk you right on your head.
Ak ak ak ak

Ain't it marvellous?
An island covered in Bonxies and I have to choose that one.

For three long hours he sat there
or slept 'til it was four
Then an old, old man in a Sunderland shirt
Told him not to snore

'Now I'm the Fair Isle warden boy
They call me Sunderland Jack
Now tell me what's your trouble boy

The Accentor won't come back!

The Accentor won't come back?

The Accentor won't come back
The Accentor won't come back
I've walked the hill all over that place
searched in stingers right into my face.
But of the Sibe there's just no trace
The Accentor won't come back

Don't worry Prez
I know the bird
It's here
To you I'll show it.
If you want to see the Accentor
then lift your bins
It's there
you know it?

Oh yeah.
Never thought of that
Doddy will be pleased.
(giggle)
Must have a go.
Excuse me.
Now slowly up and .. look.

Oh my Gawd
It's just a Dunnock

Can you find a Sibe Accentor?

Don't talk to me about a Sibe Accentor Gaz
You owe me for showing you the Dunnock
I learnt you to use your binoculars.
First thing first.

Yeah I know that
but I think that on this occasion ……

(fade and end)

I do so hope you will try to sing these songs!

The rain still pours outside, the gale still blows and sea froth is flying past la fenetre. One last song........ (sung to the tune of Peter Sellers, Any Old Iron)

Oh, Any new birds?
Any new birds?
Any new birds on Fair Isle?
It looks neat
a new bird is a treat

It would be special and would get me off my seat
I'm dressed in style
Haven't washed for a while
With my father's old green shirt on.
No I wouldn't give you tuppence for an old Moorhen
Let's find birds
Some new birds

Just a week or two ago
on 2 and 99
Dave found an Olive Pip
I thought that would be fine
So next day I popped along
to see the Sibe I hoped
Saw Lee Gregory
Using his 'scope.
I rushed along
Pushed him out the way
Thought I saw the pipit
and I began to pray
I rushed around and saw the bird
300 on the list
A lot of birders followed me
*They thought that I was ****ed.*

Oh, any new birds?
Any new birds?
Any new birds on Fair Isle?
It looks neat
a new bird is a treat
It would be special and would get me off my seat.
dressed in style
Haven't washed for a while
With my father's old green shirt on.
No I wouldn't give you tuppence for an old Moorhen
Let's find birds
Some new birds

And now Cairan would like to give you a Hoopoe
Go on Cairan

I would like to continue this birding list that you've just heard with my Hoopoe impersonation. Thank you.

Hoo hoo poo

hoo hoo poo

Oh temperamental ain't he!

WAIT A MINUTE......... a phone call from, coincidentally, The Oracle......note, a phone call . . . not a text. This means a **very** good bird.

Isabelline Wheatear, Near the Loch of Spiggie.

Forget the fact that a strong gale is blowing and it is raining hard, forget the song, it is another very rare Wheatear. I need it.

The wind blows me there, well almost. It blows me along until I reach the northern shore of the large loch. Then it is a case of head down into the wind and push until I get to the road junction where the rare bird has been seen.

I arrive. Six other birders are there. "It is in my 'scope," says one.

Isabelline Wheatear, bird number **304**. A small looking, very wet Wheatear, with a rather dull overall appearance with a rusty peach colour on the breast, except for feathers that are displaced by the water from the rain and terrain. Long black legs, creamy throat with a black bill and eyes, pale underparts. I need to see the tail pattern.

The bird keeps walking around the edge of this manured field. Photographers go closer. The bird flies briefly.

Job done, I can relax and two of the birders, Marco from London and Peter from the Cairngorms; the latter I met on last year's trip as I searched his area for Ptarmigan successfully, chat and take a few photographs of a bedraggled but very happy me. Great pair.

Roger Riddington, the British Birds magazine editor arrives and congratulates me on reaching 300. He even pats me on my back!

Time to search elsewhere, I head off into the wind finding a flock of around fifty Barnacle Geese down by the polluted loch. No fishing or bathing (!) here, too polluted. How sad. No actually, how appalling!

Back onto the main road towards Sumburgh I have to push up hills to make any headway into the wind. Near to the top of one a bus driver, Dougie, stops to ask if I would like a lift. I thank him for his kindness and tell him that I cannot accept the offer. Just before that another Dougie had stopped his car to tell me that he was following my progress and was a Facebook friend, Dougie Preston. Brief encounters such as these really keep me going. Wonderful people.

Waders on the beach at Virkie are the usual candidates; Redshank, Sanderling, Dunlin and Turnstone.

Down and around Scatness, thrushes, mostly Redwings. Also Blackcaps, Blackbirds and Chiff Chaffs.

Into the Sumburgh Hotel and a cup of coffee given free. I must be looking bad. A tad tired I am grateful for it. That will be a donation and I note that down in my notebook. In fact I need to collate the donations from the last couple of days. There's money for the chocolate bar found on the bike, money for this coffee, a donation from a couple, who say they saw me on BBC Springwatch last year, named Margaret and Martin from Cambridge, Paul Sclater and Michael.

An evening in the bar of the hotel before retiring to my 'abode' is great with bloke-ish company of locals and workers from Glasgow mixed together sharing banter. One of them, Neil, offers a drink but as I have only £2.09 I can't accept the offer as I wouldn't be able to reciprocate. The problem is with my bank. They are unable to transfer money from my savings to my current over the phone. Apologies are given by the customer service staff and even advice sought from advisers but to no avail.

Tea later is sandwich spread and Marmite on bread.... yummy! I love it.

Monday 17th October **strong to gale force SE**

Dry and cloudy

Up Sumburgh Head, after searching the Grutness Garden and quarries along the road to the former first. In the first quarry I find a Barred Warbler and text Phil, The Oracle to place news of the bird on RBA (Rare Bird Alert)

Dan Poignton turns up and the warbler flies out between us. "Oh, you've found the Barred then." He had found it sometime before, unknown to me.

Robins and Thrushes are on the dry stone walls and in the fields; birds are moving.

Getting up to the RSPB Lighthouse, after stopping to photograph Darth Vader of course, is extremely difficult due to the gale. Snow flake sea suds are flying in a tempest past me as I struggle to get up the steep climb. Past the fibre glass orca, I eventually get to the top and view down the right hand geo. Three Bramblings are feeding in the shelter afforded down there with a few Goldcrests and Blackcaps. More of the same, with Robins, Thrushes and Blackbirds, are in the revamped Lighthouse garden. A lot of money has been spent on the area and the lighthouse buildings and despite everything being closed due to the lateness of the season, it is amazing to stand on platforms looking over to Scatness Bay and beyond.

Nowadays there are even self-catering apartments and in one of them are three very attractive young ladies, Jill, Andrea and Catherine. Their first time here and with no car, they ask about what is local and of interest and I tell them of Shetland's best Viking spot, Harlshof and a couple more archaeological sires including Old Scatness. Selfies are taken.

I knock on the window of the RSPB office and meet Helen again, a superb RSPB staff member. Great to be re-acquainted.

Outside again, I meet Martin, who works at monitoring seabirds and the effects of the local oil industry. Martin gives a donation and tells me about how any oil found on bird carcases can be identified to the country and even the field of origin.

A text from The Oracle,

White's Thrush at Spiggie Hotel.

An hour or so later I am there to find that the inimitable Dan Poignton has found the bird, that it has flown off and everyone is searching for it.

Dan heads off across the valley to Scousborouh and I go to the garden where it was originally seen. I knock on the door of the house belonging to the garden's owner and give the owner, a lovely lady called Jemyna, a chocolate bar and say thank you for letting birders search around. Jemyna chats, OK and so do I, about birds, the history of the area, especially the history of the hotel and her own family history. She tells me that her interest is in finding out more about this and that she has managed to go back to the 1850s. Jemyna remembers meeting my late best friend, Gordon Barnes when he used to stay there in the 1960s and I tell her that when I return to Fair Isle I will buy Gordon's book and post it to her.

Off in search of the White's again, I find Yellow-browed Warblers and other common migrants. A Moorhen is my most unusual find as it scampers into a tunnel it has made beneath a huge pile of manure when it spots me.

Meeting up with Dan again, with the White's no-where to be found, I complain.

"You find a White's Thrush, I find a Moorhen!" It was ever thus.

I may have said it before but Dan Poignton is a phenomenal young birder, one of the best bird finders in Britain. Tireless and immense,I can only stand and admire his strength and skills, knowledge and drive.

Cycling/pushing towards the main road, a large car stops and out pops Logan, the young birder I had met a couple of times on Fair Isle. He was hoping to see the White's Thrush. He is with an ex-South African, Paula. Paula empties her purse of coins into my collection boxes and gives me a small cuddly owl to join in the company of heroes on the bike. "Call him Spiggie," I am instructed.

Logan has something to show me, a sadly dead Northern form of the long-tailed Tit. With its pure white head it is wonderful to hold one but oh, for a live one; a real ambition bird. Logan will become a superb birder one day. With Paul Harvey's old binoculars around his neck, a South Shetland megastar birder, he can't go wrong. Living on Fair Isle and Shetland, to be in the presence of extremely talented and famous birders such as Paul Harvey, Roger Riddington, Steve Minton, Nick Diamond etc. on South Shetland as well as the superb Fair Isle Bird Observatory team of David Parnaby, Cairan, Chris and Lee, and the ex-wardens who still live on the island, Nick and Deryk, how can he go wrong? Reach for the stars Logan.

In the Sumburgh Hotel again for the evening, my teaching pension has been paid into my current account and for the first time for over a week I can have a meal; haddock and chips followed by a magnificent hunk of cheesecake.

Late in the evening as I go to leave, the lads ask why am I doing all of this and on hearing "for charity" they insist I come back whence I return from Fair Isle.

Fair Isle. I return tomorrow, if the gale abates, the seas calm down and the Good Shepherd sails. There are three new birds for my year list on Fair Isle. Coincidentally I need three new birds for the European record, 307.

Bean Goose, Siberian Stonechat and Pine Bunting are all available. I just need them to stay one more night, hopefully.

Will I get there and will I get the birds? You will have to wait for tomorrow's instalment. BCNU.

Tuesday 18th October **very light SW**

Very sunny

I am up very early, too early for daylight and I spend the dawn going outside to marvel at the speed in which weather can change on Shetland. Yesterday's gale has gone and the Moon is shining in a clear sky. Has the Moon taken away the birds I need? That won't matter if the Good Shepherd doesn't come. I worry over the state of the sea between Fair Isle and here. Will it be able to get here?

I wash the windows and mop the floor of the place where I have slept for the last three nights. Breakfast is simple and light; just enough to settle my stomach for the gut churning boat ride and not too much.

9:30 a.m. the Good Shepherd comes into view around the headland. I will get to Fair isle today.

Noon, we set off. My plan for avoiding the usual sea sickness is to stay on deck, hold on to the rails for dear life and sing/whistle Rock music the whole way.

Joe Jackson, Juzzie Smith, Pink Floyd; it seems to be working and I even record my dreadful tones in order to concentrate on that instead of the deeply rocking boat. Rock on Prezza!

At times it amazes me that the boat doesn't capsize as the large swell barrels us one way and another.

Deryk Shaw comes out and asks me whether I am suspicious. The boat's Captain is, whistling is not allowed. Whistle up a storm.

It is so hard not to whistle to the guitar parts but tapping the rail as a form of air guitar keeps my mouth shut.

Emerson, Lake and Palmer's Pirates song with full orchestra seems appropriate somehow. "Who'll drink a toast with me, to the Devil and the deep blue sea?"

Three hours. Fair Isle reached. Never has a harbour looked so wonderful. No sickness and I am off the boat fast.

Rachel, Florrie, Joe and Mati greet me with smiles and comments. Another lady on the quay I have never met before, Margo does likewise. We talk about singing as I tell her my about my new, successful anti-seasickness strategy. On hearing that I saw a TV programme about Ella Fitzgerald the previous evening, this wonderful Young at Hear lady starts to sing an Ella classic and what fabulous voice! I tell her and her husband Bill that she must be recorded.

Right, mid-afternoon, three bird species to find but where are they?

I push the heavily laden bike up the hill past the Bird Observatory. A shout from the balcony of the same and there is Lee Gregory with his usual massive smile and next to him . . . Jumbo! Two fantastic friends to give me instructions quickly. Jumbo, who's real name is Clive, together with his birding bud, Gary are from Essex and we have met up on Fair Isle a couple of times before. Two brilliant blokes and birders, it is really fabulous to see them here again. Shame that the usual Essex trio has a missing member; where's Peter?

Bean Goose, field by Upper Stoneybrek. Getting there, I find no geese so I carry on along the road down to Lower Stoneybrek. A small flock of geese are here. Two White-fronted Geese, a Fair Isle tick for me, a single Barnacle Goose, some Greylags and a few Pink-foots and ......

Bean Geese! Bird number **305**, two to go.

Photographs quickly taken, text sent to Lee and I am off for South harbour where a very rare form of the Siberian Stonechat is on the beach, Stejneger's, or so it is thought to be.

"*Piece of cake,*" texts Lee. *I'll meet you at Quoy for the Pine Bunting in about 30 minutes.*

I get down to South Harbour and find a large log seat next to a beach as per the instructions given. No Stonechat. I search the low cliffs and rocks around there and the graveyard. No Stonechat. Piece of cake? It must be me. I need to calm down, relax and think.

Another birder comes, meeting me beside the Puffin National Trust for Scotland hostel. David, a birder I had met and got on with before leaving the island for the Siberian Accentor dip, is looking for Purple Sandpipers but he quickly tells me I have the wrong beach. There is another smaller log bench on the one over there. Looking in the direction he is pointing I can see the superb bird photographer, Steve Arlow, sitting near to that bench aiming his large camera at a bird on the beach in front of him. As I cycle off I hear David shout for joy; Purple Sandpiper goes onto his Fair Isle year list.

Bike left by the style, I run over to where Steve is photographing a mega rare bird for Fair Isle, a Blue Tit!

A little further away along the beach is .....

Siberian Stonechat, the thinking amongst the birders is that this may be a Stejneger's. Looks good either way.

Bird number **306**, I am now level with Ponc Feliu Latorre. One to beat the magnificent Spanish Green Birder. Thanks Steve!

Quoy. Another birder is there, Shaun from Poole in Dorset. No sign of any buntings, the first year pine bunting has been seen with Yellowhammers. Lee arrives and a bird flies in to land on a bit of vegetation next to the netted enclosure in Stuart Thompson's vegetable garden.

I look at the bird. I photograph the bird. I know what it is but I quietly say to Lee, "is that it?"

"Yes."

Pine Bunting, bird number **307.**

Ladies and gentlemen, behold ....

the NEW EUROPEAN GREEN BIRDING CHAMPION!

Gary Prescott aka The Biking Birder has done it.

Chris Mills
Simon Woolley,
Nick Moran,
Ponc Feliu Latorre!

Ponc has been beaten. Spain has been beaten.

The British flag can be raised. "Bring the urn home."

The bird flies away. I turn once more to Lee and say, " Can I?" A simple nod.

Yeeeeeeaaaaaaahhhhhhhhhh!!!!!!!!! I've done it! I've done it!
I've only gone and done it!

Tears and dancing, screams and dervish runs, hugs and high fives, handshakes and huge smiles.

:) :) :) :) :) :) :) :) :) :) :) :) :) :)

Wednesday 19th October **very light NE**

Very sunny

My morning starts with joining Lee Gregory on the early morning trap run; a walk around all of the active Heligoland traps with the intention of catching and ringing migrants. Early! It is practically still dark and yet Lee soon catches a superb Hawfinch in the Gully trap. What a bill!

A text from Adam Archer, a comrade from the Midlands. (9:43 a.m.)

Hi Gaz. It's Arch. Just wanted to congratulate you n that fantastic achievement. You're superhuman pal. Take care.

My response. (9:45 a.m.)

Thanks Adam. That means a lot. Enjoy Nadia . . . . Congratulations and see you next year.

Adam has recently got married to an RSPB employee, Nadia. Now I heard of Nadia from quite a few RSPB men when cycling my first Biking Birder adventure in 2010. "You must meet Nadia." They would say as I approached Old Moor RSPB reserve. Nadia wasn't there when I arrived and has since moved on to Middleton Lakes and here she is marrying one of my best birding pals. Honeymoon in Costa Rica, birding and romance, the perfect combination to start married life.

Adam (9:57 a.m.)

When are you back in the Midlands pal? We'll all meet up and treat you to a curry.

Biking Birder replies. (9:58 a.m.)

December. Depends on the birds. An evening of Clam entertainment. You're on!

I need to improve my accommodation and spend the rest of the morning doing just that, sweeping and cleaning.

After lunch the intention is to ensure that each of yesterday's year tick birds, the Bean Goose, Stejneger's Stonechat and Pine Bunting, are seen well and on a day where I haven't used carbon transport. I am very well aware that I have used ferries this year. Britain has a number of incredible islands and many are extremely good for vagrant birds, the absolute best of which is undoubtedly Fair Isle. Other than by pedalo my only way of accessing the riches to be had is by ferry and I have never pretended that this is anything other than the use of carbon whilst on a so-called Green Big Year. On Jim Royer's Green Birding website there is a large 'F' in brackets after my name denoting this.

So down to South Haven I go and spend a couple of hours first watching Deryk Shaw and his son, Ythan trying to mist net the special Stonechat so that a small DNA sample can be obtained for analysis. This bird may look like a Stejneger's but may not be. A DNA sample should prove it one way or the other.

After they give up, the bird being very adept at avoiding the net, I have the bird all to myself and sit on the rocks to enjoy such a fabulous bird, a bird with such a perky personality.

It repeatedly hops up about a foot or so to catch flies and perches on rocks close by. Occasionally it is chased by a Rock Pipit and disappears over a rocky promontory over to the next beach. It always returns though to the beach where I am sitting after just a couple of minutes.

One fascinating aspect of its plumage is how the colour of the rump changes according to the light. Sometimes appearing rather dull when the sun is hidden by a small cloud; the weather by the way is warm and very sunny and I sit with the worry of getting sunburnt on the side of my face, and then the rump is a rich, warm orange when the sun is out. A delightful, fascinating bird, which Lee Gregory tells me is exactly the same as the 'Portland bird.'

There are other birds amongst the rocks and stranded seaweed and some come very close to me indeed as I lie prone on the lowest rocks leaning against a grassy bank. Turnstones turn the seaweed, Rock Pipits and Starlings catch flies and the rarest bird on Fair Isle at this time is doing the same, a Blue Tit.

Meeting a few birders along the road by Quoy, I find out that there has been a Waxwing at the Bird Observatory. I neeeeeeed it! I phone Lee Gregory and he tells me that he has just caught a first year male Waxwing in the Plantation Heligoland trap and is on his way to the Observatory to process the magnificent bird.

Cycling hard up the island, I catch up with Lee by the Double Dyke trap and together we walk and chat. He is as close to me as a friend as my brother and talking with him is always a real pleasure. I am desperate to see what is in his bag; the Waxwing inside is still and relaxed and probably wondering how on earth it got in this pickle.

At the Observatory I wait outside the back door by the ringing room and await the arrival of the bird.

Lee and Cairan come out and there it is being gently held in Lee's hands. Photographs, admiring smiles and comments, the bird is passed to Cairan to release. Yet the bird doesn't want to go. It just sits on his hand. Minutes go by then eventually with a short squeak he flies, the Waxwing that is, into the nearby garden bushes. WOW! Or maybe ... WAB! What a bird!

Oh yeah, almost forgot ...

Waxwing, bird number **308.**

Facebook has the following posted by my daughter, Rebecca:-

My Dad is now even better than your Dad. My Dad just got the EUROPEAN GREEN BIRDING RECORD Y'ALL!

Thursday 20th October **very light E**

Very sunny

Orion, the Hunter is below a large Gibbous Moon as I stroll around the island. I have had a very poor night trying to sleep and having only snatches with dream-filled nightmares. It is only 5:00 a.m. and it is still, cool and awe-inspiring. South Lighthouse has it's beam rotating and spreading the intermittent beam across the dark landscape. The distant North Ronaldsay Lighthouse is doing the same. I walk around for over an hour as dawn starts to spread some pale orange light through thin clouds along the horizon to the east.

Text from Howard Vaughan of Rainham RSPB reserve comes in at 6:02 a.m.

It's Howard! Well done buddy. Going to be owing you some money come New Year.

Now this text is in response to my asking who had sent a text a few days earlier, where I hadn't known the sender due to the phone in the water incident. That text turned out to have been sent by Howard.

Congratulations! Clams have just told me.

My reply yesterday . . .

Thanks .... Who are you please? LOL :)
My response to Howard's 6:02 a.m. Text . . . (6:08 a.m.)

Morning!!! Brilliant to hear from you. Seems ages since that cold, frosty day at Rainham but still fresh in my mind is the fun and privilege of that day's birding with you because of your sunshine personality and your phenomenal birding skills. Thanks Howard. That day will always be a highlight.

Howard Vaughan – (8:18 a.m.)

My pleasure. Keep on rolling.

Howard Vaughan – (8:19 a.m.)

I presume you are back on Fair Isle?

Me again.- (8:59 a.m.)

Indeed. Until next Tuesday.

Howard Vaughan – (9:55 a.m.)

Still time.

Little did Howard know how true those words would prove. I return to my bike and with the light growing as the sunrise approaches, I start to search for my binoculars and camera. I left them somewhere last night and am not sure where! I put my earphones in to listen to Juzzie Smith, Good Vibrations and search for my equipment in my usual places.

On reaching the Bird Observatory and finding my stuff in the boot room, there is panic all around me. David Parnaby shouts, "possible Eastern Olivaceous Warbler at Chalet!"

David gets the minibus and goes around the island picking up birders and they head off to see the rare bird.

I cycle to Chalet. Steve Arlow has found yet another great rare bird but states that it is an Icterine Warbler, not an Olivaceous. It comes out onto the fence and everyone agrees with him. A very rare bird in October. Nice one Steve.

After ten minute or so everyone has gone and I have the bird to myself. Deryk Shaw and Micky arrive from Burkle to have a look. Micky is on the way to the airport for the first plane back to Shetland. His next port of call is Unst, the northern most island of The Shetlands. Another birder strolls past, Angus and another, Shaun. I tell Shaun of a Long-eared Owl that I have been told about at the ringing hut by the Plantation and he walkie talkie's the message to others.

I cycle there and there can't be many birds as easy to see. It is sitting at the base of a post beside the dry stone wall. It stares at me with large orange eyes as I sit down to watch and enjoy.

Shaun is coming from the Setter direction after I, seeing him approaching, have waved to him that the bird is by me. He can't see it from where he is due to a bank obscuring his view.

Just as he gets to me and just as I am about to point out the bird, I get two strange text messages:

First text . . .Howard Vaughan (10:57 a.m.)

go go go go>>>>

What does that mean?

Another text arrives in quick succession . . . .Steve Nuttall (10:57 a.m.)

Hope you enjoy your Sibe Accentor as much as me. The pain of missing the Shetland bird will make you appreciate it that much more

In growing panic I text Steve back …. (10:58 a.m.)

What Siberian Accentor?

Me to Shaun " I think there's a Siberian Accentor on the island!"

Another text from Steve Nuttall (10:58 a.m.)

One mega for fair isle on pager now

A third birder kindly sends a text . . . Trevor Girling (10:59 a.m.)

Sibe acc troila geo fair isle. Go get it.

"There's a Sibe acc at Troila! Run!" I scream to Shaun.

We're off and it is going to be tough running there. Having been on the fabulous Fair Isle for seven weeks I know where Troila is. Up towards the airport runway we run, across Burrashield Marsh we trudge and run through the water. Up the steep banks, gullies and hills that lead to Troila Geo we scramble, trot and walk. Woodcock are flushed but the only thing that slows us down are our exploding lungs. This is extremely painful but there's a Siberian Accentor up there. We need to get there as fast as possible.

Yet another text from Steve Nuttall (11:02)

it's at Troila Geo

Surfbird's highest British year list carbon twitcher at this time is the fourth text to arrive . . . Gareth Hughes (11:12 a.m.)

I hope you are still on Fair Isle Mr P!

Very soon yet another one arrives text from one of Norfolk's most well known birders . . . . . Penny Clarke (11:15 a.m.)

Get that Siberian accentor!!!! Just come on RBA for Fair Isle at Troila Geo!!! Best wishes Penny

Sixth text . . . . Phil 'The Oracle' Andrews

Sib acc????

Cairan is there. "It was here but went over the ridge. Lee is over there looking for it." Cairan points towards Tyneside, a long way off and hopes of seeing the bird dim somewhat.

Troila is a huge slope of scree and grass with a large rocky ridge half way down which prevents a view down to the beach. If it is down there this is not going to be easy. We all search frantically. Robins, wrens . . . .

Cairan thinks he has the bird.

"See the slab half way down, behind there!"

I can see a shuffling shape and, forgetting to change the ISO setting for the darkness of the geo, take a photograph of it. I show it to Cairan. "That's it!"

I phone Lee. "It's over here back in Troila."

Over the next two hours the bird climbs the banking ever closer and twenty or so birders get eye-popping views of a stunning, ever moving Accentor; a shuffling, feeding Dunnock with a badger's head. All the Bird Observatory staff are here sitting together on precarious ledges and the huge smiles denotes the wonder and excitement of Lee's find. Yes, Lee Gregory found it! The cherry on the icing on the rich fruit cake, Lee, my dearest of friends, found it.

Deryk Shaw and Nick Riddiford are here. Tommy Hyndeman with his son, Henry and all the birders staying at the obs are all here.

Some birders from the Aberdeen RSPB group have just got off the plane. Not a bad first bird to see on Fair Isle. One up on their Aberdeen RSPB comrades who's first bird was a Lanceolated Warbler.

Even Micky is here. He was just about to get on the same plane when the news broke!

A Who's Who of present day Fair Isle birders assemble along the geo edge. The happiest couple though are Lee Gregory and Cath Mendez, huge Cheshire cat smiles on their faces as they cuddle on the cliff edge.

I start to text those wonderful friends who informed me of the bird's presence.

Got it!!!

Trevor Girling responds (12:30 p.m.)

You beauty. Get in.

I text The Birding Clams, Jason Oliver first. (12:36 p.m.)

Siberian Accentor utb

Jason replies . . . (13:58 p.m.)

Brilliant mate, they are superb birds

The bird eventually comes up to the birders' perch. It even sits on a tripod!

There is not only an intense pleasure in seeing a mega rarity, especially after dipping on the first for Britain one on Shetland last week, but add to that the delight in seeing everyone enjoying the occasion and the fact that my best friend on the island found it.

It dow ger any berra than this our kid!!!!!

No bird is officially on my Green Year list, or even my British life list come to that, until I phone and tell Mum and Dad. They may never understand the thrill, the desire and the commitment but they can enjoy hearing their oldest son ecstatic. That done, I go down and photograph and watch the long-eared owl. For some strange reason I have it all to myself.

A late text Chris Craig (22.56)

I had everything crossed when I saw the message!!!

Friday 21st October **very light SE**

Sunny and warm

I have been to Fair Isle on three occasions including this visit. My first time was back in 2010 whilst on my first cycling-birding adventure. That was for a week when I stayed at the South Lighthouse with the brilliant proprietor, Dave..

Last year I came for almost five weeks with a gap of a couple of weeks when I returned to Shetland in order to see friends from The Midlands, The Birding Clams (Clear Lunacy & Madness Society) and visit the RSPB nature reserves on the islands, that is Fetlar, Yell, Spiggie and Sumburgh Head, Mousa. Ramna Stacks I had to view over the sea from the Mainland and Yell. I also saw some excellent birds. The birds included Eastern Subalpine Warbler, Olive-backed Pipit and American Golden Plover.

Last autumn was also the last time I was to see one of the most inspirational and incredible birders, Martin Garner. I will always the huge hug he gave me at a car park in Lerwick. Martin, as all birders who had the privilege of knowing him know, will be hugely missed. God speed, Martin.

This year's visit is coming to its conclusion. The weather forecast for the next ten days tells me that there is an 'escape window' on Tuesday next when the wind is a light south-easterly. This compares to the following Tuesday when a strong north-westerly will make my suffering horrible sea sickness more likely. The Good Shepherd is my only option yet how I would love to fly away!

I have been here since the penultimate day of August with a break of a week when I dipped on the First for Britain, Siberian Accentor; a bird that Fair Isle gave to me yesterday. Thanks Lee Gregory!

In all that time of being on this paradisical island I didn't realise that there was a Village Hall! Sure I had seen the biggest building on the Island, apart from the World famous Fair Isle Bird Observatory but I just thought it was a gymnasium for the Primary school children. It is attached to that and part of the school complex.

This morning I need the loo. Desperately.

I know that there is a toilet next to the 'gym.' On going to it I don't see the toilet to the right, a toilet that I have seen every time I have used the left hand toilets. There is a door. It is open. With a curious streak I peak inside and go through it after going through two glass doors between the entrance and the open door. There are two people in there setting up a cinema and an animation is showing as they check sound levels and connections. The presumed gymnasium has been transformed into a Village Hall and a cinema for an event, I am told, for the next evening.

What I had always thought of as another toilet to the right is just the reflection of the left hand toilet in the glass doors!

Yet wait, there's more.

There are more toilets; one set for Ladies and another for men. Using the latter I find hot water! Luxury.

By the Mens there is another open door leading to another room. It is open and inside I can see a Pool table!

There is not just a Village Hall but also a Social room with a pool table and two dart boards. I'm flabbergasted.

How fantastic it would be to see the room used as a meeting place for birders and islanders? Maybe a dart's night with teams of each; a pool tournament. Who knows? Next year perhaps.

A couple, Trudi and Len are walking down the road towards the Kirk and they stop me to show a photograph of a redpoll species. On the photograph the rump looks very white but that could be due to the image quality from using a bridge camera. I remember how it was difficult to ascertain the flycatcher in Grey Geo species a couple of weeks ago because of flare.

I find the redpolls where they say and settle down to try to get good views of one that is obviously paler than the other Mealies and lesser Redpolls.

There seems to be a conspiracy against me today for every time I try to get a look at the pale bird, a vehicle goes past disturbing them all and sending them away to Da Water.

They always soon return, bless them, but the final straw is when Florrie, a lady who has been on Fair Isle with her husband Jimmie for all of her life, drives past. Jokingly I throw my arms up in desperation and we both laugh as she passes. Jimmie and Florrie are two of my favourite people on the island. Always happy, it is a privilege to think of them as friends.

Eventually I get the view I want and with bill too large, streaking on a pale rump and overall shape I put the bird down as a pale mealy. Interesting bird though.

The weather is unbelievable for October, very warm and very sunny.

Another couple are looking at some nearby Lapand Buntings. Bernard and Carole from Cambridge have a now famous tripod. They own the tripod I mentioned, the one that the Siberian Accentor, still the talk of the island amongst the birders, actually sat on. I joke that they should sell the tripod immediately. It would raise enough funds for them to come back to Fair Isle next year!

Facebook has a photograph and comment posted on it by Lee Gregory:-

Gary breaking the European Green Year list with 307 species with Pine Bunting at Quoy - well done Gary a well earned record!

Saturday 22nd October **Very light SE-E**

Sunny, warm

Down to Fair Isle's wonderful shop for a few provisions and a chat with Fiona, a Director of The Fair Isle Bird Observatory. As a focal place for islanders to meet it has no equal and a few of them are inside the shop when I enter. Their friendliness towards strangers, such as I, and towards each other is inspiring.

A reported Great Grey Shrike is down by the Kirk but I don't get a good view of it as it is directly in line with the bright sun sitting on a fence.

In the field immediately west of Lower Stoneybrek there feeds my favourite flock of birds on Fair Isle at the moment. There may be a Pine Bunting, a new one from the other day, at Parks. There is still the Siberian Stonechat on South Harbour beach yet the small flock of grey geese that have been here for a few days holds my attention the most. Where else but Fair Isle would one have five species of geese together and less than fifty yards away. Yes they watch you as you watch them, the sentinels aware of you and of their role as protectors of the flock. Yet I can sit and watch, photograph and video each species; Bean Geese, Greenland Whitefronts, Greylags and Pink-footed Geese with the lone Barnacle Goose.

I sit and remember the flocks of hundreds of European White-fronted Geese that used to frequent the WWT (Wildfowl & Wetland Trust) reserve and headquarters at Slimbridge, Gloucestershire. From the high vantage point afforded over the Dumbles from Holden Tower, one would, back in the 1970s and 80s, looking for maybe a stray Pink-footed Goose, Bean or with real luck, a Lesser White-fronted Goose, usually a first year bird. Nowadays at Slimbridge there is a feral flock of Barnacle Geese and Greylags, Canadas and the occasional stray but there isn't the wintering European White-fronted Goose flock at Slimbridge these days. They have decided to stay over in The Netherlands.

At this range each feature that denotes each species is easy to view. The Bean Geese having a small band of orange on their bills that have just a slight bulge along the baseline. Pink-feets have shorter necks; obvious when they stand next to a Bean Goose.

I want to look at the redpolls again and head in that direction pushing my bike along the marshy path beside Buini Mere.

I walk up the hill along the road by the school when a small bunting starts to fly towards me. It is small too for as it lands just the other side of the barbed wire fence in the grass just a few feet away I see that it is a spanking Little Bunting. That's Fair Isle, they come to you.

The evening is spent in the company of many islanders and Bird Observatory staff at the newly found by me Village hall. A couple from Shetland Mainland have brought over a selection of superb films. For two hours all present are treated to locally made films showing a wide variety of aspects of life on Shetland. The mini film festival starts with a well constructed and powerful film about the problem of depression amongst men. With humour and a huge nod to the islands' Viking heritage, Ragnar, shows the relationship between father and son, friends and landscape. It hits home without being maudlin and the end shows a possible light at the end of the tunnel.

There followed eight short films with a wide variety of styles. Sometimes I couldn't understand the strong Gaelic brogue but then again, if I 'spake wid me owen axunt,' would they understand me? No matter, the detail and content was plain to see despite language-differences.

From a mackerel fisherman of old to the avant garde of a man who couldn't put his jacket on, comic Dance, Dance heroes to The Curse of the Wereduck cartoon, all films were excellent in their own way and thoroughly enjoyable.

One memorable scene was when a toddler is tied to a rope just like a sheep would be, to allow 'tha wee laddie' to wonder safely in the fields. No cruelty here just fun and love and a child enjoying the intensity of his parents' affection.

No intermission meant cramp in the backside but one couldn't look away from the last film; a forty-five minute feature about the history of the island of Havera until the departure of its last inhabitants in the early 1920s.

Coffee and biscuit at the end, I had been sitting with the most sunshine personality on the island Dave of South Lighthouse. Dave's whole manner is one of excited geniality and to spend time with him is a pleasure that lifts spirits. His sunbeams are infectious.

How wonderful to sit with Britain's most remote community and know the names of each person present. The wonder of Fair Isle is its people.

Sunday 23rd October **very light NE-E**

bit more cloud, still mainly sunny though, cooler

I feel like being a bit of a lister today and make myself a target of fifty bird species. Pink-footed Goose and Hooded Crow are on the list whilst I lie in my sleeping bag at 5:00 a.m. They penk and caw.

It is still dark at that time yet I decide to get up and have a walk, sleep being very hard to come by at the moment as my asthma is playing up a bit. Fresh, cool air will do it good and I walk down the island with Orion ahead of me again.

Silhouetted on Da Water's pool are a number of duck and by the light of the Moon I can see Lapwings, five of them.

Sunrise around 7:30 a.m. and Lapland Buntings are in the field by the Kirk. Two Grey Heron cronk their way south, flying high and a Black-headed Gull that sadly doesn't look too well is sitting in a marshy area.

The day list is on twenty five by the time I reach Springfield. Here, after seeing Chaffinch and Brambling together, I change my mind. I was going to take the short route along the iris bed stream to the Haa but I think I will go around the Moeness cliffs instead.

Finding a sheep dug seat on a finger of rock jutting out into a geo, I sit and watch. A seal is fast asleep, kettling in the calm sea at the base of the cliff where I am sitting. He is 'solid gone man!' I film and photograph him, watching him for around twenty minutes with all thought of the day list dispelled. How often can one's sleeping companion be a sleeping seal? I feel like having a speed nap myself.

He, I think of the seal as a male but it might be a she, wakes up and sees me watching from above. Unperturbed and probably with an 'it's Sunday, I'll have a lie in' attitude, the seal carries on sleeping.

Leaving him to his dreams of fish and kelp, I walk around the cliffs and marvel at what I can see. The early morning sun makes for superb, magnificent even scenery. The South Lighthouse stands out in its whiteness against the greens, greys and blues. The Skerries are being washed over by a gentle swell. There are large and deep caves to be seen along the cliff bottom that I would love to explore but have no way of reaching.

A Chiff Chaff is on a cliff top making ready for the immense fly south, the thrill of witnessing migration. Eider drakes are head tossing and making the Frankie Howard "Ooo" calls in display to the attendant female Eider. A stunningly white full adult male long-tailed drake flies past. Two Purple Sandpipers are feeding in their usual habitat and I start daydreaming again as I approach South Harbour.

News of yet another Siberian Accentor for Britain and Fair Isle comes in. This one has been found by David Parnaby, Fair Isle Bird Observatory up near the North Lighthouse. Only five miles away yet I choose to carry one exploring the south. I am thrilled for David. He deserves to find this mega and hot on the heels of Lee Gregory's different Siberian Accentor too; a sixth and a seventh for Britain in this incredible, totally unprecedented Autumn for the species.

Siberian Accentor, never before seen in Britain. Now there have been seven, no eight. One has just been found on Unst. And as for Europe, the last time I heard there had been over 120!

I walk along above South Harbour beach but to be honest I don't give it the once over grilling I should and don't see the special Stonechat. Instead I sit and marvel at the Chiff Chaffs on the seaweed.

More Chaffinch and Brambling at Utra, nine Wood Pigeons are in the field there. The geese here include eight White-fronts, six Greylags and two Bean Geese.

Just below Shirva I meet the teenage ram pair who are engaged in a bout of head banging. A short charge then head down . . . bonk. They are bonkers too but come to my call for a scratch of their oily fleeces.

Around fifteen Bramblings, surely one of many people's favourite finches, are in amongst the thistles at North Shirva. A male stands out amongst the first year and female birds. Not as gaudy as a male Bullfinch maybe, Bramblings to me have a charm all of their own and the variety of orange tones is a delight to see.

I take another good look at the mixed geese flock and head for the Parks oat field to look at the new Pine Bunting.

Now here I must say how I feel about getting the new European Green Year list record back on the 18th.

Yes, as you may have seen from the photograph, I was more than thrilled to bits to see the three birds I needed for the record on that day. Yet I was unhappy over seeing them on a day when I had used carbon transport, namely the boat, The Good Shepherd.

I feel that a purer 'Green' record is when the birds are seen on a day when no carbon transport is used. With that in mind since that wonderful day I had endeavoured to see each of the species involved on carbon-free days. Bean Geese were easy and what a thrill to think I wouldn't have to search around the west of Falkirk area in November for beanies. Last year it took all of a snowy day to find them. Of course, as usual, I enjoy the search and adventure, the challenge and the elation of finding them but having some fifty yards away, ... I'll go for that in my dotage of being a sixty year old.

The possible Stejneger's or Siberian stonechat I watched for a couple of hours absorbing its jizz (behaviour) and plumage. A subtle bird, I hear both pooh and a feather have been sent off for DNA analysis to ascertain the race.

So with two of the three covered I make my way to the third, the Pine Bunting.

I search each croft garden on the way there, say hello to the 'lads', rams in pairs in fields on the way and walk the edge of the oat field. Two birds come out. The first of the two is bright yellow. Yellowhammer onto the day list. The other is a paler bird with quite well head markings; Pine Bunting goes officially onto the Green year list and Ponc in Barcelona can now be informed of a new record. I wonder how he'll take it.

Great views of this Pine Bunting, a more interestingly marked bird than the Quoy bird.

There's a Waxwing been seen at the Bird Observatory. On the way there I stop for a chat with a birder, Andrew. His eyes suddenly expand. He has seen a cracking male Black Redstart on the wall behind him. Gorgeous bird. Thanks Andrew.

Waxwing onto the day list.

Down to The Havens, Goldcrest and Wheatear put down in the notebook.

Heading back to my little abode a flock of Golden Plover fly around Setter, bird number fifty three for the day.

Monday 24th October **Fresh E**

Cloudy with showers

The weather forecast for the next ten days tells me that tomorrow is the only day that I can be assured the Good Shepherd will sail. Wind tomorrow will be light to fresh south-west compared to a strong north easterly next Tuesday; the boat is now on its once weekly Winter timetable.

Also the wind for the next few days will also be south westerly so that will be from almost behind me as I cycle towards Lerwick, the capital of Shetland.

It would be reckless to risk staying until next week. The thing that would keep me on Fair Isle is the friendship of Lee Gregory and Cath Mendez.

I need to pack. I need to say goodbye to some wonderful people who it is a real privilege to know. I head for Florrie and Jim's croft in the south of the island and chat with them whilst enjoying my first coffee for days. The view from their kitchen is amazing; a vista of sea and land with green and blue, white spray and mist. Paintings on the wall would be superfluous, their view changes all the time. Both Jim and Florrie have friendly, full smiled personalities and they tell me tales of birdwatchers from decades ago who weren't as well behaved or as conversant as today's birders. There is also a fear that some aspects of what makes Fair Isle so very special; the openness, the lack of any sort of crime and the wonderful sense of community in, may be lost in the future. All must work together, crofters, Bird Observatory staff and visiting guests to the island, to ensure that that never happens. Communities like Fair Isles, are extremely rare and therefore so very precious. A jade jewel of such splendour, a place to visit and marvel at the magnificence of person and landscape.

Birding on the way back north, I watch the geese flock again. Goodbye and thanks to Fiona and Robert at the shop and a donation given to the November the Fifth firework fund.

Up from there to Lower Stoneybrek, Neil is back and I am so glad to see him! Neil is now retired as Captain of The Good Shepherd so I won't be able to say goodbye from the quay at Grutness, Shetland tomorrow.

As Neil closes his door after saying we'll see each other again next year, a Northern Bullfinch flies along the roadside and lands in the field nearby. This magnificent, large mass of pink topped by a black cap bird hops around in the grass, behaviour very unlike any I have seen display by British Bullfinches.

The afternoon is spent with a broom kindly lent to me by yet another crofter, Rachel. I sweep out my abode and brush the wooden walls. My aim is to make it shine before I finish.

Three hours later, having packed and cleaned, I go down to Lower Stoneybrek and leave a donation to the Island Development fund. I always do so and it is a duty to do so. The island has been so good to me during my extended stay.

Tuesday 25th October **Strong S-SW**

Occasional Showers

Early morning singing session to take my mind off the ever-rocking Good Shepherd as she sails away from Fair Isle, starts the day. Goodbye to Lee Gregory at the Quay. I will miss this wonderful birder and friend.

The sea swell is I suppose normal yet enough to cause some white knuckle moments as I cling on and sing.

A single Little Auk passes the boat but I can't count it on the year list; carbon transport involved. A Sooty Shearwater does likewise and I wake Nina, a volunteer from the Fair Isle Bird Observatory who is heading home and sleeping in a corner of the deck. I am sure she would like to see such a great bird.

Grutness, goodbye to Shaun, Deryk, Kenny and Ian and many thanks. A great crossing, it is always such an adventure and with me a complete lottery over whether I will chuck up or not.

This time I hadn't.

I feel tired and sleep for a few hours! The day goes by with me oblivious to the harbour activities, asleep in the harbour waiting room and when I wake up the quay is empty, The Good Shepherd has left to return to Paradise.

My evening is spent in great company. Into the superb Sumburgh Hotel for a meal, my first cider is a gift from the proprietor, hence a donation to the charities.

Wednesday 26th October Strong to very strong gale force SW

Occasional Heavy Showers, sunny intervals and rainbows

Three aims to the day; one to get to Lerwick as soon as possible to find a tick, those being the Coue's Arctic Redpolls there. Then get the repairs required for my bike done and finally get the ferry to Kirkwall, Orkney.

Heavy rain and a strong south-westerly, which is mostly coming from behind me, makes for a reasonable cycle despite the lack of gears. Oh for that moment when, with bike fixed, I ride with a full set of gears again.

The views along the main road north alternate between moody magnificence when showers hit and brilliant beauty when the sun shines brightly.

A proper Shetland downpour when I reach Lerwick, I take shelter at a bus stop and chat with a lovely old couple, who wave when they get onto their bus eventually.

The rain slows and I find the cemetery where a flock of Redpolls has Lessers, Mealies and two Coue's.

Half an hour later, **Coue's Arctic Redpoll** goes onto the year list, **310** – the crossbar goes higher.

Into Lerwick town centre and in through the entrance of the fantastic Shetland Community Bike Project. Incredibly to me they manage to repair all of the things required, gears, cables, front and back brakes, front tyre and inners. All completed in time for me to get to the ferry to Kirkwall, Orkney. The salty air of Fair Isle doesn't do metal much good.

Maybe having a meal before getting on the boat wasn't such a good idea. I see it all a couple of hours later as the end of a film, watched deep down in the ferry's bowels, Finding Dory, is approaching and the ship is rocking violently in the large swell south of Sumburgh Head.

I lie down between seats in the ship's cinema and try to sleep.

The horror!

The night is the worst I have ever experienced on a ferry, a punishment for me being on it, I suppose. Huge waves must be crashing over the boat as loud bangs serenade one's attempted lullabies. The immense dives into the waves' troughs are followed by steep climbs that has one slide on the cinema floor carpet. Sleep is impossible. Much more of this and I may call upon God to save us all!

Saturday 29th October **Light to fresh SW**

Low cloud, drizzle, mild 10C

So, after two days of resting in the company of very good friends, Alastair and Louise Forsyth and their children, Ellen and Molly; not forgetting Molly's boyfriend Liam, Sid the bearded dragon, who is stunningly beautiful and finally mentioning Cora their dog, I get to the harbour in Kirkwall. Whilst loading the bike, Steve the travelling cyclist I first met in The Lake District six years ago, is here once again. We chat until the ferry that will take me back to North Ronaldsay arrives.

A huge thank to The Forsyth's. I never ask for assistance or accommodation but Alastair is always there to offer both whenever I arrive on Orkney. They are such a lovely family and being in their company is always a sheer delight.

Alastair and I had attended a superb talk the previous evening by Julian Branscombe in Kirkwall. His topic had been the Orkney Vole and what a fascinating history that has. The hall, connected to St Magnus' Cathedral, was full with Natural History-minded enthusiasts and the question and answer session after the excellent talk was one of the longest of such I have ever seen. Great evening.

Julian, tall and resplendent with a incredible pair of across the cheek moustachial stripes, which birders and RAF aficionados would appreciate, was witty and quick and he must be commended for the research he has carried out on the voles. A very extensive study with a possible conclusion that the vole population started when Neolithic Man brought the voles to Orkney in clay pots. This could have been a food item or a creature of religious significance or maybe even just a docile pet. However they got here, this species of vole is found nowhere else in Britain.

As I mentioned before I first met Julian back on my first Biking Birder ride in 2010, when he put me up for the night after meeting me whilst birding the Deerness area of Orkney. Our next meeting was on Papa Westray, one Orkney's Northern Isles. Julian had found a first for Britain, a Chestnut Bunting, and despite taking four days to get from Fair Isle, I arrived late one misty afternoon to see that bird crawl around the birders' present feet. I stayed with the mega until dark and it wasn't there the next day. The soles of my shoes were checked for feathers!

Onto the ferry and a two and a half hour crossing ahead, heading for North Ronaldsay, mostly in benign waters. The exception being the final hour of the crossing where the boat takes the eastern route around Sanday. Here there is something of a swell but not too severe. Despite misgivings brought up by The Oracle over my returning to North Ronaldsay, I feel confident that some of the seabirds I need, Little Auk for instance and

Pomarine Skua, will turn up and save me a cycle to the East England coastline. Also and more likely this is the stronger reason for my return, I want to be part of the Bird Observatory community again. I have a proposal to make to the youngsters over a project for next year. I hope that they will be open to the suggestion!

The birds I see, whilst carrying on my latest stop seasickness routine of singing, include eight Long-tailed Ducks, nine Eider, a few Tysties (Black Guillemots) and three Great Northern Divers.

Onto North Ronaldsay, I cycle the short distance to the, I know I always say it, superb North Ronaldsay Bird Observatory and, whilst placing my bike against their hostel wall, I hear what I instantly recognise as Erin's laugh.

On turning around I see the giggling pair of Erin and George, volunteers at the Observatory, holding sparklers! Their two small sparklers, both attached to sticks as Erin is scared of the sparks, soon fizzle out but our laughter doesn't. Hugs and smiles. What a 'home-coming!'

Into the Observatory, so great to be back, and a large Milky Way cheesecake is presented to me as a trophy for the new Green Birding crown. Larissa, the brilliant Canadian birder, has remembered that Milky Ways are my favourite sort of chocolate bar. Well I'll devour that later when all of the staff are back from their census work. Sorry we'll devour that!

I go to the hostel to sort my gear. I just sit down in the kitchen when George Gay rushes in.

"Northern Harrier out here now!"

We rush out but it has moved on. Oh well, at least it is still on the island, a mega to be seen.

George and I then cycle to the far end of the island to seawatch. Over a two hour watch, some of which I do alone whilst George surveys 'F', we see the following:

<u>A) In half an hour census/seawatch count</u>

68 Gannet, 202 Fulmar, 43 Kittiwake

<u>B) in the two hours</u>

3 Great Northern Divers, 2 Bonxies (Great Skuas), 1 Manx Shearwater, 27 Sooty Shearwaters, 1 Long-tailed Duck
and 2 Risso's Dolphin. George saw five!

An evening of sheer enjoyment with Observatory staff, laughter and cheesecake being the winning combination. Bird log at nine o'clock reveals that there are some special birds to see; Hoopoe and Green-winged Teal are present. Tomorrow will be good. Good to be back!

An email warms the cockles of my heart. Such generosity is wonderful and I am so thrilled and grateful:-

Hi there

This is Graham. We met at Titchwell and I offered you £100 for achieving 300 birds. I gift aided the RSPB £100 last week. I also offered and extra £50 if you make it to 310 thus properly beating the European record.

Anyway Congratulations on your success.

All the best,

Graham

I placed this onto my personal Facebook page and The Biking Birder – Quest for 300 Facebook page after finding a thread on Birdforum :

Wow. I have just been onto my thread on Birdforum, bravely maintained by the wonderful 'Oracle', Phil Andrews, and seen such fabulous comments of congratulations.

Here is a selection of them appertaining to the 300 and the European green Birding Record . . . .

Phil Andrews Saturday 8th October

Gary reached his next landmark today with his 300th species (BOU) of his Green Year list - an Olive-backed Pipit (still on Fair Isle)

Brosnabirder

Congratulations and well done.

Stuartvine

Great job

Dantheman

:)

WACCOE

Well done

Paul Higson

Yowser !!

Nutcracker

Nice !

Spoonbill finder

Well done mate. Hope Shetland will bring you nearer to your next target.

Jasperpatch

Congratulations! Great news.

A few days passed, never to be forgotten by me . . . . and then.......

Phil Andrews 18th October

And now for some good news - the Good Shepherd did sail with Gary on it. Three potential ticks on Fair Isle today.

Flurry of ticks on Fair Isle this afternoon with the addition of Bean Goose (BOU #305, AERC #303) and Siberian Stonechat (BOU #306, AERC #304).

Almost there!!! Just one more bird . . .

THE RECORD IS GARY'S
He has just broken the European Green Birding Record with Pine Bunting on Fair Isle (BOU #307, more importantly AERC #305).
Paul Higson
Absolutely brilliant.
Saluki
Fantastic! Well done Gary!
Stuart Reeves
Agreed! I can't help but feel that this is a greater achievement than the world and ABA records being pursued at the moment because of the sheer stamina and commitment required.
David Ball
I'd second that.
Farnboro John
Superb achievement! Well done Gary!
Andrew Whitehouse
Brilliant achievement! I guess there might well be quite a few more species to follow too.
Jasperpatch
Congratulations! So very very well deserved. Hope there is more bubbly available tonight!
Edenwatcher
Amazing achievement. Many congrats to Gary. Onwards and upwards!
WACCOE
Nice one
Spoonbill Finder
Absolutely magnificent!
Phil Andrews
Clearly I am biased but I couldn't agree more Stuart. Not only the endurance and physical effort of pursuing this all year but also the minimal financial outlay. Gary has been funding this year purely from his pension; indeed when he has been offered free food / accommodation he has insisted contributing an equivalent value to charity.
Wheatearlp
.. and also he's done this for two consecutive years! Amazing stamina & commitment IMO, so more than pleased Gary has finally achieved his goal.

Gary Biking Birder Prescott 28th October 2016

Can I take this opportunity to say a massive thank you to all of you on these pages for the immense support I have received from you? Your comments of support and congratulations have been so important to me. I especially want to thank Phil Andrews, The Oracle.
Just over two months to go, I would love to raise the bar to around 320.

Thank you so much everyone.   Gary xx

Sunday 30th October **Light SW**

Low cloud, mild 10C

After hearing about yesterday's number of passing Pomarine Skuas and Sooty Shearwaters at the bird log, I am up early to go seawatching off the northern end of the island.

Porridge and banana chips for breakfast, Samuel Perfect suddenly pokes his head around the kitchen door and we are off.

Immediately the male **Northern Harrier** is in front of us flying around Gretchen. **Bird number 311 BOU** (British Ornithological Union) but only **308** on the **AERC**. Northern Harrier is not a separate species to the Europeans. One day it will be I am sure.

Eight Bean Geese are in a field to the right by the World War memorial. Pink Feets are to the left and then a large flock of Greylags by the Ancum Willows. Here we stop to look over Ancum Loch and see fifty four Whooper Swans, and singles of Goldeneye and Greater Scaup.

To the seawatching hide, we start to properly seawatch at 8:30 a.m.

Almost immediately the first Sooty Shearwaters fly past mid-range to distant; all are heading north west coming from the east. Sam gets on a Great Northern Diver and I have a **Little Auk** quite close. **Bird number 312 BOU**.

More Sooties, usually singly but occasionally in threes and fours pass and then a flurry of **Pomarine Skuas**. **Bird number 313,** three year ticks already today and after only thirty minutes or so of seawatching.

9:10 a.m.

Me : Manx going left, close. No it isn't! Sam you need to get on this!!!!!

The bird is joined by a Sooty Shearwater, both going left, that is to the north west.

Samuel : FEA'S PETREL!!!!

The bird takes maybe three minutes or so before it is gone, heading north west. Screaming, laughing and general disbelief, a legendary Fea's Petrel has just passed us, more than an ambition bird, a pure dream of a bird.

More screaming, more expletives, hugs and high fives and a complete lack of any further serious sea bird counting due to shaking, laughing, cheering, all accompanied by a few tears.

Phone calls made, texts sent :

Texts are sent to friends to celebrate the sighting (10:40 a.m.)

Four year ticks this morning. Northern Harrier, Little Auk, Pomarine Skua and a FEA's PETREL!!!

Response from Penny Clarke (10:42 a.m.)

My goodness! You're on a roll!!! Congratulations!!!!
From Trevor Girling (10:49 a.m.)

Bloody hell! . . . . nice.

From Steve Nuttall (11:07 a.m.)

That is tremendous Pal. So pleased for you. You've got to put that record out of sight!

Chaotic celebrations follow, interspersed with bouts of goosebumps, nervous laughing and a slow realisation over what had just happened. I have two videos. The first from an attempt at getting the bird itself. The second is of the phone call back to the Observatory. Have I managed to get the bird. I can't see it on the camera screen. We will have to wait and see what can be seen once it is downloaded to a laptop.

Sam is drawing sketches of the bird. Plumage and jizz details are discussed and notes made.

We settle down at last to carry on birding. Vegan Dutch fruit cake is shared and clinked together as one would with champagne. Cheers Sam!

At Noon we total up :-

114 Sooty Shearwaters, two Manx Shearwaters, ten Pomarine Skuas, nine Bonxies (Great Skua), three Little Auk, seven Great Northern Diver, three Red-throated Diver, twelve Long-tailed Duck, six Wigeon and four Lapwing.

We have also seen a few cetaceans; two or three minke whales and single Risso's dolphin and harbour porpoise.

One o'clock we start to make our happy way back towards the North Ronaldsay Bird Observatory. A ring-tail Hen Harrier passes. It's happy banter all the way.

A text comes from Paul Higson.

Interestingly, a Fea's Petrel flew north past the north east of Shetland – Lamba Ness, Unst at about Noon.

Surely not our bird. It would need to be supersonic. Two bird theory, how fast can a petrel fly?

In 2014 a Fea's went along the East coast. It was reported from headland to observatory, birding spot to pier, promenade to cliff top. I wonder if anyone has worked out that bird's speed? I remember seeing a chart in the superb seawatching hide at Whitburn last year that showed times of the bird passing each place. It would be interesting to see the times and work out speed accordingly.

A quick look over Ancum, a few more Whooper Swans are on there compared to this morning. Birds are moving.

A look around Holland and down towards the Observatory. Sam receives a phone call from Larissa. We turn around and cycle fast towards Hooking. Larissa has found a Glossy Ibis.

Half an hour later we all have the bird in view. It flies from Hooking Loch to the beach and back again before disappearing to the north.

Our evening is spent celebrating birds and friendships, and a Fea's!

Monday 31st October **Light SW**

Low cloud, some rain, mild 10C

Up early for another seawatching session with Samuel Perfect. I am awake at five partly due to a frightening scene in a dream - nightmare where Wayne Rooney and I are on the way to The Olympics in a lorry, as you do! We never got there . . . I woke up trembling.

Rain is falling and has been for most of the night. Breakfast for champions is porridge with banana chips and honey and my travel mix of nuts and dried fruit is made up today in two bags; one for me and the other for Samuel. He deserves it being such a fantastic young man. Seeing Samuel with his Canadian girlfriend, Larissa is lovely. Both are superb birders, Larissa found the Glossy Ibis yesterday, the latest in a string of good finds. Considering she is new to the UK, how she has developed into such a good birder is a credit to her. She is always the one in last when doing census and I remember having a nine hour census day when we did census area B together back in August.

Gosh, it is so good to be back on North Ronaldsay! Great to be part of the team and part of the 'family,'

There was great excitement at the log call last night, not only over the Northern Harrier, Hoopoe, Green-winged Teal, Bean Geese, Glossy Ibis and what Samuel and I saw on the seawatch (FEA'S!) but also because last thing, at the mist netting thrush roost session, a bat was flying around Holland. Now this is a very rare event in late October but the hope is that George Gay's photographs will lead to an identification.

Due to it now being what I call British Wintertime, that is the clocks have gone forward, it is now light at seven, just. How can one top yesterday's seawatch. Answer to that is one probably can't so maybe today Samuel and I will concentrate on counting the birds! The seawatch yesterday had no counts for Fulmar, Gannet, Auks, Kittiwakes . . . . oops!

Samuel and I are at the seawatching hide by 8:30 a.m. as yesterday. The change of wind direction and the freshening of it, gives different conditions to yesterday and after deciding on making fifteen minute counts of all bird species that pass, we settle down to the task.

Sooty Shearwaters are passing, heading north west, as are good numbers of Fulmar, Gannet, Kittiwake and various Auks.

Every fifteen minutes we collate the counts and note 'specials'. We count the Divers, Skuas and a number of Sooty Shearwaters, Gannets, Fulmars and Kittiwakes; Auks of five species too.

Samuel leaves at 10:30 a.m. for census work, leaving me to continue to count the main three; Gannet, Fulmar and Kittiwakes, whilst noting all other species.

By Noon there is the following seawatch list :-

536 Fulmar, 555 Gannet, 109 Kittiwake, one pale phase Pomarine Skua, one pale phase adult Arctic Skua too. One Great Skua, one Skua sp. fifty three Guillemot, thirteen Razorbill, ten Puffin, eight Black Guillemot, five Little Auk, thirty two Sooty Shearwater, five Long-tailed Duck, one Teal,

one Greylag, twenty one Whooper Swan, six Great Northern Diver, seven Red-throated Diver, five Common Gull, five Great Black Backed Gull, two Cormorant, three Shag, three Purple Sandpiper, one female Goldeneye.

The pale phase adult Pomarine Skua was a particular delight, passing close in and showing extensive spoons. Two of the Great Northern Divers were in Summer plumage still.

Returning to the Bird Observatory, I see Samuel counting wildfowl at Ancum. All of yesterday's Whooper Swans have gone; just singles of Pintail and Greater Scaup amongst the Shovelor, Mallard and Wigeon.

An evening of Halloween entertainment followed Log. Fabulous time with everyone dressed up in a blistering array of evil-looking costumes. Dunking apples is fun even though the bowl is too shallow for anyone to get seriously soaked. There is a new nickname from Larissa for me, Crusty The Clown!

October Monthly Statistics:-

Green Year list	314 birds
Year ticks seen in October	21
Bird species had, not seen in 2015	11
Mileage in October	335.06 miles
Total mileage for the year	6065.82 miles
average mileage on days cycled	11.55 miles
elevation : up	23,906 feet
: down	23,848 feet

***<u>Best Birds</u>* :** **Blyth's Reed and Radde's Warblers, Red-flanked Bluetail, Pechora and Olive-backed Pipits, Barnacle and Bean Goose, Mealy and Coue's Arctic Redpolls, Buff-breasted Sandpiper, Black-faced and Pine Buntings, Pied and Isabelline Wheatears, Waxwing, Siberian (Stejneger's?) Stonechat, Northern harrier, Little Auk, Pomarine Skua and Fea's Petrel.**

Accommodation, both self-catering hostel and bed & breakfast, full board is available at the wonderful North Ronaldsay Bird Observatory : **<u>http://www.nrbo.co.uk/Accommodation.htm</u>**

Something truly exceptional and totally unprecedented happened this autumn. Phenomenal can be the only word that describes the almost daily arrival of not only the scarce and the rare but also the mega-rare and even the CMF, as Bill Oddie called them rather naughtily in his Little Black Bird Book.

Birders way back in the prehistoric days, before rare bird news became available to the twitching masses via telephone birdlines, pagers, mobiles and internet, that is pre-eighties, may have dreamt of seeing a Pallas' Warbler. The ambition Sibe, replete with stripes and squared off yellow rump, would delight one with a quick hover as it took minute insect life from a delicate twig in the canopy. The prefect warbler it may have been called at the time but from mega rare status, they started for some unknown reason to arrive in the UK in larger numbers and was relegated to rare status. Yet it remains a highlight bird of one's birding day and year if seen.

Birders moved on to another mega for their bird finding dreams, the magnificent Siberian Rubythroat. A perfect chat with extreme rarity status, sporting a stunning scarlet throat bordered on each side with black then white, a Siberian Rubythroat is still described as the ultimate Sibe. Yet it has become more common, especially for those prepared to make their birding way to Shetland.

The Birding Clams will never forget their first male Siberian Rubythroat. In 2014, whilst searching for a Little Bunting way north of Lerwick on their last day of the annual Shetland birding adventure, two other birders came running down the road screaming, "Siberian Rubythroat Levenwick!" Inevitably and incredibly, the inimitable Dan Poignton had found a male, they blurted out. The Pagers siren alarmed MEGA and the people carrier filled with all BCs, including myself, Captain Clam and Jason Oliver sped the vehicle south. In the blink of an eye, one had to keep one's eyes shut through sheer terror brought on by the driving and fear of a dip, we arrived to find car parking spaces along the small lane rarer than a Yellow-browed. Park we eventually did and all joined the throng trying to see the bird, which did it's best not to be seen by staying deep in the cover a small garden provided. Large and thick Hebe and Fuchsia bushes meant that any views were brief and the speed that it would move to stay out of view was impressive and frustrating. I found my way somehow at the front of the crowd, up against a small wire fence with a view of a very small grassy area and a gap between some close by bushes. The main path up from the road to the small bungalow was maybe five metres in front of me. This had a small wall on it's far side from me and a white stone. For an hour or so I saw my first Siberian Rubythroat as it sped from one bush to another, only for it to disappear in the thick undergrowth. Kneeling down against the fence, with three Heatherlea ladies to my left and a crush of birders behind me, the incredible bird suddenly sat atop the small white stone and stared at me! My Anglo-Saxon utterance at this was admonished by the ladies but understood by all, a true CMF – Cosmic Mind Fucker. I moved around to the road to enable birders behind me to get a better view themselves. From my tarmac position I could see right up the path and watch as occasionally the Rubythroat would cross it one way and return minutes later. I was engrossed so much in watching this special bird that a tap on my shoulder seemed like a major intrusion upon my private viewing spot. I turned to find an attractive young girl who asked, " can I get up my path." It turned out that here was the owner of the bungalow, the magic bushes and garden. I recognised her accent and asked where she came from for here was a fellow Brummie speaking not an expected Shetlander. "Oh, I come from Stourbridge," she stated. Stourbridge, the town of my favourite childhood years, she was here to find peace and quiet and to complete her degree studies in a house bought for her by Mum and Dad. A crowd of hundreds of desperate yet quiet birders must have come as somewhat of a shock.

All Clams having seen it; hugs, high fives and relief induced hilarity and congratulations sealed the group's birding bonds. A mega rare and dazzlingly beautiful bird had been shared and seen.

A new ambition bird had to be found to fill one's dreams for a first and none better than a masked badger face Dunnock, the Siberian Accentor. Siberian Accentors leave their Siberian breeding grounds in early September and head south, usually, towards their wintering grounds in China and Korea. Never before seen in Britain, there had only been thirty two records in Europe ever. 2016 changed all that. Lee Gregory's bird on Fair Isle was Britain's sixth in this astonishing year. David Parnaby's was Britain's eighth. The first ever for Britain, in a quarry high atop the moorland-like Mossy Hill in South Shetland, had been found by Judd Hunt only eleven days before the Fair Isle first! The second ever for the UK had been at Spurn and had been seen by an estimated 4,000 birders during it's week long stay. By the 24th of October nine had been found in Britain whilst Europe had had a fantastic 153! 2016, the year of the Siberian Accentor, t-shirts commemorating the avian event became a must have birding fashion accessory.

Yet the Siberian Accentor was at the summit of a mountain of Siberian rares seen during October. Yellow-broweds had arrived on the east coat of Britain in unheard of, and seemingly ever growing numbers. Indeed Flamborough had had 139 in one incredible day in September when reports of passing Sabine's Gulls and Long-tailed Skuas were ignored so that all Yellow-broweds were counted. So many were there that observers couldn't cover all areas and so how many there really were remains conjecture. Maybe a hundred more were missed along the dykes!

The month may have started with a first for Britain from a different direction, an Eastern Kingbird from across the Atlantic, with other crossing 'The Pond' birds being seen in the UK such as Rose-breasted Grosbeak, White-throated Sparrow and a Sora but Siberia was the starting place for so many of the wonderful rare birds arriving seemingly every day. Being on Fair Isle, my own list of Sibe birds started on Super Sunday with the Pechora Pipit being the star bird. Away from the Fair Isle the list of birds arriving from an anticyclone covered Siberia, with a superbly directed jetstream of easterlies, included Black-throated, Dusky and White's Thrushes while a wonderful friend, Howard Vaughan and his friends, found a Siberian Thrush on Unst. Brown Shrikes, Stejneger's Stonechats, Black-faced Bunting, Two-barred Greenish, Eastern Yellow Wagtails, Pine Buntings and Eastern-crowned Warbler all appeared over the month. A record number of seven Isabelline Wheatears around the country must have been associated with this weather pattern.

Such an incredible autumn may never occur again but birders who saw any of the listed birds will never forget it.

11

NOVEMBER

The wonder of the world
The shapes of things,
These I saw.
The beauty and the power,
Their colours, lights and shades,
Look ye also while life lasts.

'BB'

Tuesday 1st November **Strong W** **Very high seas**

Sunny intervals, one very quick light shower, cool

After the last two days seawatching, after a very late bedtime the previous night due to Halloween fun and with a very strong North west to west gale blowing, I decide to have a rest morning.

A video of the passing dot, I mean Fea's Petrel is downloaded onto Youtube. That takes over three hours for a twenty second or so video! Such is the state of outer Orcadian Island broadband.

Just two months to go before I hang up my cycling boots and relax into my dotage. You think?

October on Fair Isle and North Ronaldsay was so special. I could never have dreamt that October would bring such birding riches, culminating in that incredible moment of having a Fea's Petrel whilst seawatching with Samuel Perfect in the seawatching hide on North Ronaldsay, Orkney.

The list keeps growing in such delightfully unexpected ways. There are birds to head for once I leave North Ronaldsay next Friday, weather permitting. Will the garish Western Purple Swamphen be the final bird or will an Iceland Gull be at Bartley Reservoir or Chasewater in The Midlands around the end of the year? Whatever happens one can always say that predictions are a difficult thing to make in birding. Some mega birds might just turn up. Birding is a constant parade of wonderful and exciting surprises.

Two months is a long time and it would be nice to add another six birds to the year list. Will Ponc go for it next year? Will anyone ever beat MY record? I hope so. If anyone tries they will have my full support and congratulations if they beat it. A Green Birding Year is hard, very hard; a barrage of physical and mental challenges to overcome. The rewards though, are immense.

Out eventually after lunch, I head for the harbour quay with the intention of looking along the seaward side of the high sheep-proofing dry stone wall. This wall goes around the island keeping the World famous seaweed-eating sheep on the seaweed located side of the wall. There is a large flock of these sheep doing just that, eating seaweed. Adds to the flavour, I have been told.

The gale is strong, whipping up the sea so much that there are areas of white or chocolate coloured foam amongst the rippled rocks. Purple Sandpipers are on the calmer, sheltered side of rocks whilst shags ride the waves.

The usual disappointing amount of plastic is to be found, mostly large, clear plastic bottles and carrying them soon proves to be a problem without a bag. One hard plastic ring has come from Bergen, Norway. I wonder whether 'Rosendahl' would like it back?

To Gretchen, after admiring the rolling coasters and the crashing waves, into the battered hide and with seven teal viewed I have my second Green-winged Teal of the year. The windswept pool has over a hundred Wigeon, thirty nine Teal and six Mallards, a Curlew, four Redshank and three Common Gulls.

Back to the Bird Observatory, I see that the bags of plastic I collected from the beaches back in August are still behind the shed. What should one do with so much plastic waste when one is on a remote island far away from any recycling facilities? Leave it there in the forlorn hope that one day it will be taken to a recycling plant or burn it. I will leave it for the former. It isn't going anywhere.

My evening is spent in dialogue on Facebook with many birders over the Fea's Petrel Samuel Perfect and I saw a couple of days ago. The video of the bird on Youtube is the cause of the light-hearted debate:-

The video, entitled :

Fea's Petrel Moment, (HONEST!!!) North Ronaldsay October 30th 2016 Biking Birder

has the following accompanying text:-

9:10am. Having already seen Northern Harrier, a male, Little Auks, Pomarine Skuas and Sooty Shearwaters, Gary Biking Birder Prescott called.... Manx left...... No it isn't...... Sam (Perfect), you need to see this..... FEA'S PETREL!!!!!!! I realise that the video lacks immensely but it captures the moment. What we presume to be the same bird went past Unst, Shetland around two and a quarter hours later. A truly fabulous, heart-stopping moment.

Meanwhile my Facebook entry starts with an introduction:

Downloading a video takes over three hours here. Broadband it isn't. Anyway, here is part one of the passing Fea's Petrel video. Spot the Sooty Shearwater with Fea's Petrel shortly afterwards!

https://www.youtube.com/watch?v=Fr_MzOa7Nfc&feature=youtu.be

The comments that this amazing piece of North Ronaldsay avian history brings forth start with one from the famous birder, Paul French, chairman of the British Birds Rarities Committee (BBRC):

Paul French : *Errrr.... Great commentary, but is there a bird?*

And continues thus:-

Jason John Oliver : *Untickable views Gaz LOL :)*

Me : Luckily our eyes and Swarowski telescopes gave incredible views. Samuel Perfect's drawing immediately after it had disappeared north. (see below using link:)

https://www.facebook.com/photo.php?fbid=1183089505070524&set=p.1183089505070524&type=3&theater

Jason John Oliver : *I was only joking mate. no question on you're find ! A big congratulations to you both !!*

Jason John Oliver : *I've looked a few time's off my phone and can't see it mate.*

Nigel Scott : *I can see birds flying but can't ID them so I'll take your word for it!*

Mark Thomas : *Its clearly there, sooty goes through then it follows, sheers up at one point (with accompanying 'ahh' comments) black underwings and white belly clearly on view ! Well done mate, zoom function next time please !*

Jason John Oliver : *What? ?? Clearly there LOL*

Me : *I can't see how you can all miss it! Attach your computer to a large flat screen TV. Turn the lights off and enjoy crippling views!*

Philip Risdale : *Make sure video is playing in 720p or higher in settings.*

Paul French : *Tried on phone, tablet and laptop. Nothing doing. Seawatching records from Buckton about to receive close scrutiny...*

The above is a reference to Mark Thomas's patch!

Juan Brown : *Can we have some directions please?*

Paul French : *It's about 70 miles SW of you*

Paul French : *Be good if this video was part of the submission though, I'm sure it's just the crap compression that's making it so bad, if you send the full video file to the BBRC secretary it'll probably be fine. And will make a great addition to a submission.*

Mark Thomas : *Screen grab below at 19 secs in - clear as day !*

https://www.facebook.com/photo.php?fbid=10154735703799525&set=p.10154735703799525&type=3&theater

Paul French : *Still nope!*

Tim Jones : *comes into shot at 7 secs in top left side and is on view till 21 secs! Right side even.*

Mark Thomas : *Gary Brian Prescott make mine a pint.*

Jason John Oliver : *I'll have to look on my laptop*

Me : *Fantastic to read through all the comments from such respected and eminent gentlemen! Downloading the video where even the sea isn't seen!!! A Canon SX50 is not up to the job.*

Niall Keogh : *(another screen grab showing the dot, I mean bird arrowed in red)*

https://www.facebook.com/photo.php?fbid=10154507539436183&set=p.10154507539436183&type=3&theater

Matthew Capper : *If you change the settings on YouTube to the highest quality and then pause and drag the video frame by frame you should be able to pick it up. (another screen grab)*

https://www.facebook.com/photo.php?fbid=10154639844136449&set=p.10154639844136449&type=3&theater

Lee Geoffrey Richard Evans : *I have now reviewed this video ten times and still can't see a single bird fly by - very frustrating*

Me : *Come on Lee! Sooty first then the Fea's......*

Tim Jones : *Join the club! Awesome stuff (Tim has a link for video on Youtube of a Fea's Petrel at Spurn)*

https://youtu.be/ynsuFdGZTrk

Me : *This is brilliant!!! Thanks Tim. BCNU*

Tina M. Lindsay : *That rocks!!!*

Ian Dillon : *Lost count of how many times I've watched this but I FINALLY got a glimpse of the bird. Outstanding effort*

Janet Hankin : *I think you are hallucinating, Gary! Not a whiff of a bird to be seen by the time your video arrives in Wales. Something to do with the broadband, I'm sure...*

Mike Wheeler : *I guess they left this one on the cutting room floor when they were putting together Planet Earth 2. Think I'd stick to the day job Gary!*

Wednesday 2nd November　　Strong NW　　High seas

Sunny intervals, heavy showers. Lots of rainbows!

Another early start seawatch from the hide at the north-west end of the island. Samuel Perfect and I see six Little Auks during four hour seawatch. Also 113 Sooty Shearwater, one Manx Shearwater, six Long-tailed Duck, 233 Fulmar, 131 Kittiwake, ninety five Gannet, four Red-throated Divers, one Great Northern Diver, twenty eight Guillemot, two Razorbill, one Puffin, six Black Guillemot, ninety seven auk sp.
Twenty one Snow Buntings fly in from far out at sea and head quickly inland. Great to see Passerine migration in action as well as the seabirds. Heavy showers briskly pass, their coming forewarned by beautiful rainbows, including a few doubles. The Sun is low in the sky here in November, making each rainbow tower high overhead.
A restful afternoon before a meal and then a meeting of a newly formed Green Birding Group. Plans and requirements listed and discussed for a future event.
An email arrives stating the RBA (Rare Bird Alert) weekly round- up of the rare birds seen during the week. On opening it and scrolling down we find the Fea's Petrel we saw a couple of days ago listed and detailed.
Also they have placed our Youtube moment of the sighting onto the page!

Thursday 3rd November　　Light S-SE

Sunny intervals at first, heavy showers later.

Yet another early start seawatch from the hide at the north-west end of the island. Samuel and I enjoy them so much and the variety of birds passing each time holds the promise of yet another very special bird.

The clarity of the air, as we cycle the four miles from Observatory to hide, is superb and Fair Isle is a series of dark, rocky lumps on the horizon.

We follow the same routine as of the last couple of seawatches; that is we block four x fifteen minute counts to make a first hour total of all passing bird species and then free seawatch for the next three hours, listing the 'better' birds.

Our total for the first hour then goes like this:-

3,383 Fulmar, seven Blue Fulmar, 213 Gannet, 251 Kittiwake, 212 Auk sp, thirty two Guillemot, five Little Auk, one Black Guillemot, twenty six Sooty Shearwater, one Manx Shearwater, seven Long-tailed Duck, two Red-throated Diver, two Great Northern Diver, five Greylag, six Pomarine Skua, six Mallard and one Purple Sandpiper.

There is a temptation to continue to count the Fulmars as such high numbers are passing. We don't because there are so many other distracting bird species to watch. The number of Blue Fulmars and Sooty Shearwaters is relatively high and the skuas are passing again.

Then there's Fair Isle. Today the island is mirage-like and bits keep disappearing in the haze. Sheep Rock is almost a constant, except when a heavy shower hits the island from the south. Yet Malcolm's Head is suddenly not there. The geos of the west coast and Ward Hill are usually clear and just occasionally features can be seen on the cliffs.

I am watching for passing seabirds, using Sheep Rock as a reference marker, when a few intermittent tall splashes occur just to the south of it. I alert Samuel and we both watch as a very distant whale species breeches repeatedly. Too far away to discern what species it actually is, most likely a Humpback, we do see it clear the water on a few occasions. Frustratingly that is the last we see of it and also frustratingly we can't alert the other volunteers at the Bird Observatory as the mobile signal is out of action. Two hundred yards from a couple of huge radio masts and no signal!

We count for a further three hour. Our count gives us :-

Twenty seven Blue Fulmar, eight Little Auk, six Puffin, two Black Guillemot, eighty seven Sooty Shearwater, three Manx Shearwater, six Long-tailed Duck, one Goldeneye, two Red-throated Diver, one Great Northern Diver, five Pomarine Skua, six Great Skua, three Skua sp. eight Mallard, four Wigeon, two Teal.

It is disappointing to find out later in the day that if we had continued to count the Fulmar then we may have beaten the day count record for the island. Counting Fulmar with one passing every second for a whole day, well personally I would have lost the will to live! A team of birders to share the load would have sufficed.

Sunday 6th November **Very strong N – easing to strong later**

Heavy showers AM, cold 7C

The day starts with a message from Nepal on Facebook. Mike Grundeman is asking how things are going. Attached is a superb photograph of The Himalayas that reminds me I haven't been in high mountain regions for a couple of years. The Cairngorms and The Highlands of Scotland are incredibly beautiful but not as high as the mountain chains I love' the Pyrenees, the Alps, The Tatra Mountains and the Andes.

Out early again, cycling into the gale and showers with Samuel Perfect to go and seawatch from the hide on the north-west coast of North Ronaldsay.

The last two days had been tough weather wise and although this morning is no different one can only go so long before raising one's binoculars.

Only minutes pass once we have set up and I shout . . .

"White-billed Diver! White-billed Diver heading north."

The diver is very close to the shore and flying straight past us. Flying just above the waves prevents it from being lost in troughs of the waves and swell. Both of us have great views of such a rare bird.

Maybe we are tired but we don't display the same ebullience we had with the Fea's Petrel a week ago. Instead we carefully go through the features we both saw and it is handshakes and congratulations.

White-billed Diver, bird number **315 BOU**.

Texts are sent and I phone Mum and Dad with the news of yet another Green year tick.

Back to the seawatch, Sooty Shearwaters are passing but in fewer numbers than recently. Erin and George arrive from the Bird Observatory and together the four of us seawatch for an hour or so.

Soon after they have left, George phones to say he has something avian to show us. Their Land Rover is parked about one hundred yards away and Erin is sitting with a juvenile Gannet on her lap. They take it back to the Observatory for assessment, processing and ringing before releasing it from the harbour.

I start a one hour count. The final figures for that hour are as follows:-

1,208 Fulmar, eighty six Gannet, fifty Kittiwake, thirty six Auk sp, fifteen Guillemot, two Little Auk, two Tystie – Black Guillemot, twelve Sooty Shearwater, one Cormorant, sixteen Great black backed Gull, forty five Common gull, seven Herring Gull, one Curlew, one Purple Sandpiper and three Long-tailed Duck.

Totals for the three and a half hour seawatch :-

twenty seven Sooty Shearwater, one White-billed Diver, one Great Northern Diver, three Red-throated Diver and three Little Auk.

12:30 p.m. Samuel and I start to cycle back towards the Observatory. We stop to look over a large pool; two pairs of Gadwall, one pair of Shovelor and a pair of Red-breasted Mergansers on here with twenty six Bar-tailed Godwits on the side.

Around twenty Snipe are sheltering behind a tall dry stone wall and a little further we come across the Bar-tailed Godwits again in a field.

A relaxing afternoon, I read about the race over in the US, not for the Presidency but for the Carbon Birding Big Year. Always fascinating, 2016 is no different and the ABA (American Birding Association) Blog details the four front runners.

http://blog.aba.org/2016/11/aba-area-big-year-update-8-weeks-to-go.html

Monday 7th November **Light N**

Cloudy, cold 5C

A calmer day, wind-wise, George and I run out of the Bird Observatory lounge when the Northern Harrier passes.

Later a walk down to the beach at Nouster, a group of Common Seals are on the rocks nearby and I crawl on some grass to get close views.

Down to the harbour, a single Kittiwake and a couple of Fulmars are sitting on its end.

Back to the Bird Observatory, a female Hen Harrier passes nearby.

A belated Bonfire Night after dark is fun, with fireworks provided by Alison and Kevin, the wardens of the Bird Observatory. A somewhat prehistoric feel ensues as a line of figures is silhouetted against a large and fierce bonfire. It is so wonderful to be on this island sharing such moments with such true friends.

Tuesday 8th November **Very strong SE-E**

Sunny intervals and heavy hail showers, cold 5C (wind chill makes it feel 1C)

The wind is back with a vengeance and from a different direction as of late, south-easterly. Samuel Perfect and I make our way to the north-west end of North Ronaldsay yet again for a morning's seawatching. A face-stinging rain shower has both of us sheltering behind a dry stone wall but it soon passes in the gale.

Most passing birds are hurtling past but a long way out. Immediately apparent is the number of Auks; hundreds of them, Guillemots and Razorbills, maybe Puffins but too far out to discern species. We take turns in counting them for half an hour each. The one hour count is 1411!

Otherwise, bird-wise there are just a few Sooty Shearwaters and Red-throated Divers, three of each, two Great Northern Divers and fair numbers of Gannets and Fulmars, all zooming past in fewer numbers than of late.

Leaving the shelter of the trembling, rocking bird hide, Samuel and I go to look out over The Skerries to search through the gulls hunkering down on the rocks. Great Black Backed and Herring Gulls only, we turn our faces back into the wind. Two Whooper Swans have recently arrived and move from a small pool to the larger Bewan Loch.

Remembrance Poppies are available at the airport waiting room. I feel better for having one for Remembrance Day, this Friday.

Friday 11th November **Fresh to Very strong SE-E**

Sunny intervals, Heavy rain in the evening, cold 7C

The ferry timetable on the Orkney Ferries website states the ferry to Kirkwall will leave North Ronaldsay at 11:00 a.m. I feel relaxed as I pack the bike and clean the hostel. It is time for me to start the long cycle south. Time to go home.

Everything is done. The kitchen, bedroom and bathroom are all clean and the bike is as heavy as ever with the four panniers full, the tent and sleeping bag beneath The Lads and Ophelia the Orca. I come out of the hostel. Where's the ferry? I saw it in the harbour ten minutes ago.

It has gone!

The time is 10:20 a.m. and it has gone.

I rush around to see that it is half way across the bay heading towards Papa Westray. I am stuck on North Ronaldsay!

I rush into the Bird Observatory and check with Larissa and Samuel on the internet.

11:00 a.m. - that's what Orkney Ferries website states. No notice of any changes on the company's home page. Two weeks ago the Friday ferry here was postponed until Saturday due to the weather. That was displayed on the home page. No such changes displayed this time.

Not too happily, actually I am rather cross (!), I phone the main office. The first lady who answers soon passes me on to another colleague. The next one does the same. The next one asks for my telephone number and says that she will ring back after consulting someone else.

By now it is ten to 11 and thinking that I will be here for another week on North Ronaldsay, I go with Larissa and Samuel to the World War Memorial about a mile away to pay respects; Remembrance Day, 11th of the 11th at 11.

Larissa reads a poem out by John McCrae after which, we observe the two minutes silence.

In Flanders fields the poppies blow
Between the crosses, row on row,
That mark our place; and in the sky
The larks, still bravely singing, fly
Scarce heard amid the guns below.
We are the Dead. Short days ago

We lived, felt dawn, saw sunset glow,
Loved and were loved, and now we lie
In Flanders fields.
Take up our quarrel with the foe:
To you from failing hands we throw
The torch; be yours to hold it high.
If ye break faith with us who die
We shall not sleep, though poppies grow
In Flanders fields.

A phone call from Orkney Ferries. They are sending the ferry back to fetch me. I can't believe it!

Twenty minutes later after a mad dash back to the Observatory to collect everything, I am on the ferry waving goodbye to Alison, Kevin, Larissa and Samuel as they stand on the harbour quay. Kirkwall here I come.

Thank you Orkney Ferries. I hope you will put my suggestion on your home page in capitals:-

IF YOU SEE THE BOAT IN THE HARBOUR, GET ON IT!

Sunday 13th November **Fresh SW**

Cloudy morning and heavy rain in the afternoon.

Cricket delays me. England may beat India in the First Test match. Wicket after wicket is falling.

It is a draw. Very creditable for England though.

Large, tall beech trees arch over the road with a variety of colours of Autumn leaves. These are the first such trees I have seen for over three months. No such trees on the Northern Isles. Well not along any roads that I have cycled down.

A Great Tit on a roadside fence post. The first Great Tit seen in over three months too. No Great Tits on the Northern Isles too. I remember that a Blue Tit on Fair Isle, seen back in October, was a extremely rare bird there.

Back to the reality of the Mainland, the plan for the day is to cycle just twenty two miles from Stonehaven to Montrose. The weather forecast is for heavy rain from 4:00 p.m. It arrives early and added to that the wind in my face, all is conspiring to making the going rather tough.

My body has to get used to cycling distance again. A different group of muscles are needed compared to the ones used for birding the islands. The last three months spent mostly birding, mostly walking around the ditches and dykes, cliffs and geos of Fair Isle and North Ronaldsay, have been superb but now I need to cycle many miles every day. I need to get south.

In a beautiful Bed & Breakfast, The Hermitage in Montrose; one where I stayed last year too, I find a friend request on Facebook from my wonderful nephew Tim. Friendship accepted, I message Tim to say hello. He replies asking whether I have broken the European record. I go to Jim Royer's superb Green Birding Record blog to show Tim and am surprised to find that the banner photograph at the top of the page is me! Thumbs up Pressa.

I send a message of thanks to Jim. Here is his reply:-

You've really done well this year! And you've been a great ambassador for green birding. Congratulations. I've enjoyed following your year. Good luck for the rest of the year!

Thanks Jim and Tim.

22.11 miles 1077 feet elevation up 1065 feet down

Having internet access in the evening I email Orkney Ferries:-

Dear All at Orkney Ferries,

My name is Gary Prescott and today you were amazing in bringing the ferry back to North Ronaldsay to collect me.

I just wanted to say a massive thank you to you all and please, in some way, let visitors to the Northern Isles that the ferry might not leave at the scheduled time on the website! The islanders I talked to said that they knew the ferry might leave as soon as cargo is sorted but a visitor, such as myself, using the website, didn't know that this thing happens frequently.

So THANK YOU! I am extremely grateful to you all.

Now for the long cycle south. Worcestershire by Christmas and then the end of the two year cycle ride around Britain.

Thank you again,
Yours faithfully,
Gary Prescott

Monday 14th November Fresh SW

Mild and mostly sunny, a lovely day. 14C

Scanes of Pink-footed Geese fly overhead as I pass Montrose Basin, an large inland estuarine habitat. No time to stop at the superb Visitor's Centre sadly. I need to push on.

Push it is as I climb a hill towards Arbroath. The wind at the top is in my face yet again and becoming rather tiresome. I need a strategy to stop what I call the demons from dominating my thoughts. At times like this, when every day is a long cycle ride, negative thoughts take over the eternal conversation inside my head. Incidents from my past turn up vividly, especially those involving my late wife, Karen. Why the sad or bad ones? Recent political events take over. Disappointment and disgust. Climate Change, thoughts of the people who deny it is happening.

I pass some large wind turbines.

Happy thoughts required. After over twenty two months on the road I know what to do. I choose a holiday destination from the past, Disneyland Paris. One replete with wonderful moments, as a family of husband and wife with four children we went there a lot.

In my mind I can see ever attraction, every pathway, even every toilet! I choose a circular route, clockwise.

I start with arrivals. The first time there with my own two children, Rebecca and Joshua. I had driven to Paris from Wolverhampton, taking an overnight ferry and they being so young at the time, seven and five years old, had no idea they were near Disneyland. Their faces as we came up to the archway entrance brought tears to my eyes then. The memory of that moment makes me laugh out loud and tear up again. I remember how poor I was at the time, 1993 and how when my second wife divorced me, I promised my children that one day I would take them to Disneyland. Well we may have had to camp instead of enjoy the expensive luxury of Disneyland Hotels but we had made it there.

Another memory, Joshua with a twig and a short length of fishing line, a hook and a worm, caught a trout! Delicious addition to a meal shared with a family in the tent next to ours.

Another arrival a few years later, once more the children having no idea where they were. This time though with four children. I had met and married my late wife, Karen and she had two children, Claire and Sarah, from her first marriage. Whilst staying at my brother Paul's house in Brittany, Karen and I took the four children to 'the beach', or so they were told. Leaving very early in the morning, with four children sleeping in the back of the car, their ages now so perfect at ten, nine, eight and seven, I drove to Paris. Only when Rebecca and Claire, the two oldest, noticed Disneyland signs on the motorway about ten miles before the famed destination, did the penny drop. Their faces captured in a photograph, comes into my mind to dispel all the negatives.

That's better, happy moments. Cycle on Pressa!

Through Arbroath and a wonderful cycle path is adjacent to the busy dual carriageway practically all the way to Dundee. It has great tarmac and the almost flat landscape means that the cycling is reasonably easy despite the wind.

31.41 miles 1131 feet elevation up 1104 feet down

An email from The Oracle:-

Hiya mate,

Based on a conservative 25 miles a day my suggested route / timeline is as follows:
Tues 15th to Fri 18th - 105 miles - Dundee to Beith
Sat 19th - tick Hooded Merg
Sun 20th to Wed 30th - 280 miles - Beith to Alkborough
Thurs 1st to Fri 2nd - tick Swamphen
Sat 3rd to Sun 4th - 39 miles - Alkborough to Tetney
Mon 5th to Tues 6th - tick Pallid Harrier
Wed 7th to Mon 12th - 141 miles - Tetney to Romsley

So you will have a week to ten days to play with if any other targets appear.

An email from Orkney Ferries responds to mine sent to them yesterday:-

Gary,

Good luck with the rest of your trip. We have discussed the website timetable today for a resolution.

Regards

Fraser Murray, Ferry Services Manager, Orkney Ferries Ltd

Tuesday 15th November Fresh SW

Mostly sunny, another lovely day. 10C

Across the long Tay Bridge from Dundee with its central cycle path and along roads that take me west along the southern coast of the Tay Estuary. Autumn colours come to the fore, vivid reds and oranges.

I pass a group of Eastern Europeans who are working hard covering a huge area of a brassica crop with mesh. They wave, I wave back. They shout "good morning;" and ask how I am doing. "Fantastic!" I shout back.

Hills and quiet country lanes, Pheasants and signs asking for cars to slow down. The local farmer doesn't want his Pheasants hurt by cars. No, not when he can shoot them himself or be paid by bird murderers who enjoy blasting easy targets out of the air. Daft thoughts go through my head. Why don't they shoot sheep as in a Tom Sharpe novel? They are just the same sort of easy target as Pheasants except maybe they don't fly! It all angers me so much. Some people get immense pleasure out of shooting lions, elephants, giraffes. Some people!

I hate the vileness and hypocrisy of it all and cycle on.

Today's landscape is far more hilly than of late, which means more get off and push moments.

Through Newburgh and over to Auchtermuchty, in both places I stop awhile to peruse the World War Memorials. More slaughter, as evidenced by the names, some of them repeated on plaques. To the glory of God, King and Country; each memorial gives a variety of responses to this basic idea of why the brave boys were killed. Last year I observed the two minutes of silence at 11:00 a.m. on the eleventh day of the eleventh month here at Auchtermuchty.

I have dozens of photographs of War Memorials around Britain. I have collated them over the last two years. I must make a Facebook group page on the subject. The memorials never cease to dismay me as the massed names demonstrate the devastation caused to each community and family visited. Lambs to the slaughter.

My Granddad Prescott, My Dad's Dad, was there at the Somme and so many other battle sites during the conflict. Wounded three times, he survived, physically.

Negative thoughts.

I need my latest strategy to move onto new, happier thoughts. Disneyland yesterday, how about birds whilst cycling today. I try to think of special birds chronologically but my memory won't allow such disciplined order. I want to think of the rarest birds I have seen this year yet my mind immediately goes to a Black Redstart that came and sat by me at the lookout over The Severn Bridge whilst I was eating a tin of mackerel back in 2010.

The strange, washed out but very beautiful Stonechat seen with Howard Vaughan at Rainham Marshes RSPB reserve pops into my head next.

The Syke's Warbler at Channerwick, Shetland, now that is more like it; a real mega rare bird.

Tomorrow I will try to remember the special birds from last year's New British Green Record list.

34.87 miles 1981 feel elevation up 1699 feet down

Wednesday 16th November Fresh to strong SW

Cold with a few heavy showers.

A strong breeze in the face greets me as I turn from Kinross High Street around to the west, onto the road to Falkirk. It is a cold wind and the road is a busy one with lots of large lorries passing. Rain showers make the going even more uncomfortable.

Thoughts whilst on the road, birds from last year's Biking Birder sojourn, there is only one that really stands out. A Siberian Rubythroat that I saw on fair Isle? No. The Chestnut Bunting on Papa Westray, surely that must be the most remembered bird. Memorable in so many ways it may have been, not the least over how I got to the island but no. The bird that springs to mind as I cycle ever onwards I saw after cycling fifty six miles in order to see it, the Citril Finch at Holkham, Norfolk.

Eventually over the old Kincardine Bridge and into Falkirk. I need a rest. The weather forecast for tomorrow is vile. My eyes are bloodshot and after five days cycling into the prevailing wind, I am going to have a day off.

26.11 miles 718 feet elevation up 967 feet down

Friday 18th November Light SW

Cold and sunny

I await news on the Hooded Merganser. Hooded Merganser? Well, one has been either at Lochwinnoch RSPB Reserve or at water courses nearby for some time and I really would like to see it. Unfortunately though I am feeling somewhat down and the thought of another hundred miles into the SW wind is not encouraging.

With no news by 10:30 a.m. I decide that I need to move on and head off towards Edinburgh. It is wonderful to be cycling with a light breeze behind me and with the sun shining. Snow tops the hill north of the Forth and everything feels good; better than things have felt since leaving Orkney. My spirits rise.

Through Bouness and the first push of the day up a hill, a text from George Gay is quickly followed by one from The Oracle, Phil Andrews:

It's back!

A decision to make. Do I turn around and go for it? It would be a particularly good bird to get and the only one that I have seen whilst on a Biking Birder adventure has been the so-called 'plastic' one at Radipole, Weymouth.

I text Phil: *Forget it. I am half way to Edinburgh.*

I know that for the first time in a week I am feeling OK, just. I say just because I know I am very close to the edge both physically and mentally. I am constantly tired and my head is feeling very tense. There is the thought that soon I will see my family again. My daughter, Rebecca lives in Newcastle, 160 miles away and I am heading that way.

There have been times in my life when things thrown at me have caused stress problems and my decision to continue towards Edinburgh relaxes me. The tension in my scalp, which has on occasions caused so much heat that I have had to sit wearing a packet of frozen peas on my head, hasn't been so extreme recently but it has been there.

The ride from Bouness is beautiful with views along the Firth of Forth and a relatively easy road. I am surprised when I reach Queensferry and I spend some time photographing the three fascinating bridges from the small quay. To the east is the rusty red rail bridge. To the west the old suspension bridge and beyond that the almost completed new road bridge. The huge, totally different bridges to cross The Firth. Wonderful engineering feats to look at and wonder.

Cycle paths, convoluted and with confusing signposts that have distance to city centre numbers that would provide physics students with motion parallax problems; 7 miles, 5 miles, 6 miles, 7 miles. I have cycled two miles but I am still seven miles from the City Centre. This becomes funny and looking at all the signs one has the feeling that the people who put them up were having a laugh at cyclists' expense.

Great to be in a hostel in Edinburgh; in fact it is called The Hostel. Adam, the manager couldn't have been nicer or more helpful and Helen, also behind the reception counter, is a biologist with experience of butterfly surveying in Mexico. Both are wonderful characters and a pleasure to meet.

As are the French couple from Nice. With all emails, Facebook names and blogs are swapped for possible future meetings in Peru.

28.17 miles 1659 feet elevation up 1562 feet down

Saturday 19th November Light W

Cold and sunny

Pancakes for breakfast set me up nicely for a day's cycling. Birding opportunities will be lacking as I head along the east coast towards Dunbar. Seeing a group of Goosanders on a river in Musselborough is wonderful. The beautiful ducks are so close.

Turning a corner at the end of the road adjacent to the river I come across knitted red poppies attached to steel railings in front of a church, hundreds of them.

It is so different to cycle with a breeze, no matter how light, behind me. I eat up the miles with just the occasional stop to admire the view along the Firth.

30.70 miles 1024 feet elevation up 1148 feet down

Sunday 20th November **Light to fresh NW**

Cold, icy and sunny

Feeling so much better than of late I go down to reception to pay for the night's stay at The Royal Mackintosh Hotel, Dunbar. Imagine how my improving mood is even further enhanced by the receptionist, Lesley, saying that the hotel would like to donate the cost of my stay to the charities I am supporting. £55 to be shared by Chaskawasi-Manu, the RSPB, Asthma UK and the WWT. I am so grateful for this wonderful gesture.

Cycling today will involve using the Sustrans cycle routes numbers 76 and 1. These will keep me off the busy A1. I can't believe that in 2010 I cycled from North Berwick to Newcastle along the A1and A19. Obviously I survived but I have no intention of tempting the fates again.

The cycle path, sometimes grassy, sometimes with frozen mud, goes past a cement works and a nuclear power station, Torness. Across the dreaded road and along to a beautiful river valley with autumn colours on the large beech trees. I stop to photograph the scene and hear Waxwings calling. Actually I am thrilled to hear them as I had thought my hearing must be going when on Fair Isle. A Waxwing had flown over me by the gully Heligoland trap and I hadn't heard the call whilst other birders had. The ones I find by call in a few trees nearby, over twenty of them, prove that my ears are not too aged, yet. I cannot get a decent photograph of them though, as they are atop the trees in poor silhouetted light. I stop a car from driving past too quickly and spooking the birds. I explain to the driver why I had begged him to go slowly. He is interested in seeing them for himself and pulls over, climbs out and enjoys the view of these gorgeous birds. A walker, Jonathan, asks what I am looking at and I lend him my binoculars to have a look. He is delighted and even gives a donation he is so thankful that I pointed out the superb birds to him.

The road takes a serious dip down to sea level and, after cycling through a ford, the push uphill lasts for miles. I reach the top. Looking back to the north I can see the nuclear power station with the immense Bass Rock behind it. One day I must get a boat out to visit the famous Gannet colony.

At last I can cycle again, passing large wind turbines before a downward stretch to Eyemouth. From here I have no choice, I have to cycle along the A1. This part of the road takes me to the border between Scotland and England. Crossing the border line, I feel sorry to leave Scotland. Of the four countries that make up the United Kingdom, Scotland is the most beautiful and the people are so friendly and interesting.

Through the town of Berwick Upon Tweed, crossing the river by the old stone bridge and onto the A1 once more. I eventually find tonight's already booked bed and breakfast after missing it and having a two mile detour. A strenuous day due to the hills, nevertheless an enjoyable day due to the wonderful start with the hotel donation, the views and the people met.

38.21 miles 2349 feet elevation up 2326 feet down

Monday 21st November Light to very strong NE – E (50mph)

Cold, very icy morning, cloudy and showers before very heavy rain

The owner of the Island View Inn, Chiswick is an ex-squaddie, who left the Marines after being injured by a land mine whilst on tour. I listen about his time in the forces over breakfast, taking the meal slow as there is thick frost outside. I don't want to set off before some of it has melted. I have no intention of cycling down the A1 with ice on the roads.

I take the country lanes and find the Sustrans Cycle Route 1. Now I know what to expect as I cycled this way north back in July. I know that really there isn't a cycle path, just a muddy field with cows and a narrow strip of frozen mud along low sand dunes. Avoiding large cow pats I push the bike for a few miles, stopping to photograph a Stonechat and a pale hybrid goose amongst a large flock of Pink-footed Geese and Greylags.

A gravel path that is cyclable has a dyke alongside it. A Little Egret flies out of and a Kingfisher darts down the middle; both are birds I haven't seen for months and are great to see.

Two young people are sampling the water from a larger water course further along the path. Working for the Environment Agency, they are checking for nitrate levels in the water. Too high they say and with the number of cows, sheep and other crop levels around the area it is easy to see why.

Carrying on along I am stopped by a lady out walking a small, friendly dog. "Are you The Biking Birder?" She asks. Hence I meet Julie, out celebrating her birthday no less. Julie tells me that Ian, her husband will be disappointed to not having met me as he is a birder. She also says that we have met before, back in January at Dart's Farm on The Exe Estuary. It is such a cheer me up moment. Happy birthday Julie and thanks.

The route takes me past Budle Bay where there are a number of duck and gulls to see. Then over a hill before a downward plunge into Bamburgh. Maybe my favourite castle view from the village, Bamburgh Castle, looms large in front of me and a quickly passing shower with hail no way diminishes the magnificent scene.

Through Seahouses with The Inner Farnes beyond a white-capped seascape; the wind has been strengthening throughout the day and is now very strong. Coming from my left side, from the east, the going gets very tough.

Fifteen miles to go to my abode for the night I cycle hard and after drinking a whole litre of pure orange juice I find that it all becomes a bit easier!

Rain starts to fall heavily but finding a cycle path for the last three mile stretch from the Alnmouth turn to Warkworth means I can cycle safely in the dark and the rain. Reaching The Sun Hotel I may be soaked but I am so happy. Over forty miles ... Go Gary!

41.14 miles 1355 feet elevation up 1415 feet down

Wednesday 23rd November Light NW

Mild and sunny

I thank Zoe at The Sun Hotel with a present bought for her off eBay, a Batman rubber duck. Zoe has given me a fabulous welcome back to the hotel, a hotel I stayed in at the beginning of July this year and as she has a collection of over 500 different rubber ducks what better way to say thank you than to buy her one she doesn't have? A great hotel and after a day of rest, wonderful breakfasts and friendly staff, I need to be back on the road today.

Outside the hotel the view of Warkworth Castle is superb.

The cycling this morning is beautifully easy. The road is mostly flat and there is almost no wind. The first twelve miles go quickly enough and I spot a cycle path off to the right. Along it I meet a lady out with her son and two dogs for a walk. She has just been out to Peru and describes her experience of going to Machu Picchu as I walk along with them.

The path comes out next to a car park and a fenced off colliery sort of place. I head out towards the main road and am stopped by Mandy, a friendly guard at the entrance to the museum. She explains that this was a working colliery and is now a museum. As Red Squirrels and titmice come to a peanut feeder nearby, I decide that I can spare an hour to explore.

Glad that I do for after storing the bike away in a site office, I go into an art gallery displaying artwork by The Pitman Painters. Coal miners from many decades ago used art as a release from the stresses of their daily work. On the walls there are dozens of large paintings, mostly in oils depicting scenes of either the mines or of the miners' home life. A Primary school class of children are on the floor doing an art lesson on perspective using one of the paintings.

The Woodthorn website :

http://www.experiencewoodhorn.com/the-pitman-painters/

https://en.wikipedia.org/wiki/Ashington_Group

I look around the old colliery buildings and then, with the hour up, I leave to continue my way towards Newcastle. The way from Ashington becomes complex and many times I get lost and things aren't helped by the position locator on the maps app. on my mobile being half a mile out!

The first twelve miles take me around an hour. The next twenty takes three hours.

Through Newcastle Centre, a man crossing the road in front of me stops me and asks what I am doing. Daniel works at Newcastle Hospital and he deposits a donation into one of my collection boxes. Thank you Daniel.

Pushing the bike down the main shopping High Street, a six year old boy shouts "wow" at the lads and lasses on my bike. His laughing face is a delight.

Over the Tyne and uphill into Gateshead, I find my daughter, Rebecca's and her partner, Les' apartment. A couple of days to catch up ahead.

33.18 miles 1155 feet elevation up 1111 feet down

Thursday 24th November Light SE

Mild and sunny again, clouding over in the afternoon.

Rebecca and I walk into Newcastle Centre by going over the High Level bridge. There are hundreds of padlocks attached to wire mesh, tokens of love put their by lovers. It reminds me of the paper notes declaring undying love, stuck on the wall of Juliet's house in Verona, Casa di Guilleta, with chewing gum.

Past the castle and the cathedral and past a particularly ugly statue of Queen Victoria.

Down to view the Vampire Rabbit! Along to the Laing Art Gallery and then a return to Gateshead. We call in on an art café about to open this evening. On the walls are extremely colourful pieces depicting actual bird species of various sizes yet with most wearing trainers!

My daughter, Rebecca talks with the café owner Pam while I talk with the artist, Bob (Bobzilla). Bob does workshops for schools and has commissions for large pieces of street art and sculptures.

Friday 25th November

Still staying with my daughter, Rebecca and her brilliant partner, Les in Newcastle. A few days rest I feel is well deserved and gives a chance to consider next year.

My flight back to Peru in 2017 is already booked for April 12th so that's done. Returning to The Manu National Park, to the children and staff of the wonderful Chaskawasi-Manu Project is going to be very emotional and special. A three month stay this time which will include a visit to a dear family of friends in Lima first; Mani, Katia and the boys.

The Champions of The Flyway event in Eilat, Israel will take up the last week of March 2017. Back when I was on North Ronaldsay I asked the young staff members there if they would like to take part in the event. You may remember that earlier in the year, as I attended the Norfolk Bird Fair, I was asked to create a Green Birding team for the event. Well, over the following months I got to thinking about it and realised that as a statement for the future of birding, having a team of very enthusiastic youngsters, those who will be most affected by the Climate Change effects that are already occurring, would be perfect. The team? Myself, Erin Taylor, George Gay and Samuel Perfect; an old Biking Birder with three incredible and young birders from the North Ronaldsay Bird Observatory. The excitement is palpable now. Have a look at the video that the links takes you to.

https://www.youtube.com/watch?v=jIrHupa19RY

I am spending the morning researching the butterflies of The Amazon.

http://www.amazonian-butterflies.net/

and finding out more about the Stratford Upon Avon Butterfly Farm, Europe's biggest. I have already emailed the latter over working there as a volunteer in January and am really looking forward to that. Wandering through their photographs on their Facebook page shows how many species they have and working in such an environment with other wonderful staff members, who have a passion for butterflies, is going to be a thrill. In the time between the New Year and going to Eilat with The Spokefolks in March, there is so much to do.

Time to enjoy the company of friends and family again.

http://www.worcswildlifetrust.co.uk/reserves/upton-warren

Friends to get together with again after two years of cycling away from them. So I will be birding at Upton Warren in Worcestershire again. I will also be going birding with The Birding Clams, the three close friends; Jason Oliver, Steve Allcott and Tony Barter.

Upton Warren is a Worcestershire Wildlife Trust reserve near to Bromsgrove. With a variety of habitats, such as freshwater pools, reedbeds and even a briny saltmarsh area, the bird list is superb. Avocets breed there and the rare birds that have occurred there are many. The best thing about the reserve is the fabulous people who bird there, keen and knowledgeable birders and great friends. The Birdforum webpage gives one some idea of the Upton Warren community.

http://www.birdforum.net/showthread.php?t=8097&page=1301

The Birding Clams is a group of Birders most of whom are ex-students of Coppice High School in Wolverhampton. Back in the 1980s a certain teacher started a bird watching group, an extra-curricular club, and from those long off days there are lads who still passionately bird.

https://www.facebook.com/groups/492704280806443/

OK, time to go for a walk and explore Newcastle Upon Tyne again.

Sunday 27th November **Almost no wind**

Drizzle, cool, 4C

On the road again in the afternoon after four lovely rest days with my daughter, Rebecca and her partner Les in Newcastle.

Yesterday Rebecca and I went to Tynemouth Market, which takes over some of the platforms in the station. Stall after stall with the usual variety of home business ware with arty-crafty things and more usual market stall stuff, books and DVDs. Great to see that there are no stalls of mass produced, cheap clothing that seems to have taken over markets in every town these days. It is so enjoyable going around and being part of the 'usual things people do' world again.

A stall has framed Amazonian insects amongst the mass of bric-a-brac. Shame for such fantastically beautiful creatures to be harvested for such display.

One stall has feathers framed, each delicate feather has a superbly detailed painting on it, birds, mammals on others even a bumble bee! The artist, Imogen Clarke, chats for a moment and gives me a business card; Dusty Souls Art. Imogen describes herself on the card as a portrait artist and she certainly has talent.

www.dustysoulsart.com

Moving on, there's a stall where two excited young people are taking bookings for what they say is a Live Escape game, Pirate Escape – Whitley Bay. I am attracted to the stall by a large, metal scarlet macaw.

www.PirateEscapeRooms.co.uk

Sounds fun.

One stall has Balinese artefacts and I think about how easy it is to get such creations from all over the world these days.

Leaving the market Rebecca and I walk to the seafront where people are enjoying the Winter sunshine and lack of wind.

The evening is spent sitting on an expansive settee with a takeaway, watching a favourite film, Inception. Perfect.

Thrilled to meet Les' parents, Carol and Lance, this morning; a sign of commitment in Rebecca's and Les' relationship. All one wants for one's daughter is happiness and it seems so obvious that Rebecca and Les are very happy together. An hour or so spent talking with a couple who radiate sunshine; another pair made for each other.

Packed and ready to be on the road again, I set off. The road through Gateshead and Chester Le Street has a cycle path either as part of the road or as a separate entity that keeps me safe from the busy traffic. If only this was the case everywhere. If it was then there would be so many more cyclists and fewer car drivers.

Past Durham Hospital a cloud of Bramblings fly from the leaf litter below some tall beech trees.

Into Durham after a steep downhill dive and then a push up the eastern side of the cathedral city to find tonight's Bed & Breakfast, Gilesgate Moor Hotel, a public house, a cheap and cheerful place with a bed one simply sinks into. Into it I sink, bushed! Smashing.

16.91 miles 958 elevation feet up 764 feet down

Monday 28th November Almost no wind

Sunny, cool, 4C, very light drizzle for ten minutes - lovely rainbow.

What a difference a week and a rest makes as I feel confident about cycling fifty miles today. Good old Durham has got more cycle paths so I can listen to music on the Ipod and sing the miles away.

Not a lot happens along the way south and the riding is reasonably easy. Birds are few and far between with Corvids and Winter Thrushes to the fore.

Past Darlington's football ground, the road heads south then west and over the attractive River Tees. Views over fields have The Pennines, seen distantly to the west and The Yorkshire Moors to the east. The lightest drizzle brings forth a high rainbow as the sun sets.

Over fifty miles cycled today. Mission accomplished.

52.39 miles 1444 elevation feet up 1646 feet down

Tuesday 29th November Almost no wind again

Sunny, cold, 1C maximum. Very deep overnight frost, early fog.

Thick freezing fog has left the trees white and I await the Sun's thawing of the hoar frost before setting off for York. Breakfast at The Vale of York guest house in Thirsk is ample and the waitress, Rosie kindly gives a donation to the charities I am supporting. Her cat Bob is present during the meal. Poor Bob! Run over twice, Bob is lucky to be alive and has no tail and a crunched in face as souvenirs for his narrow escapes. I wonder how many of his nine lives he has left? It can't be many.

The cycle to York is as easy as yesterday's was to Thirsk; easier really, fewer miles. York Youth Hostel is soon reached and an afternoon of relaxation is spent listening to good Rock music; Free, Rory Gallagher and Blind Faith.

I meet an Australian woman in the hostel's kitchen, Ros. She has been travelling for a few years and she shows me a heart-warming video of her daughter and Aboriginal son-in-law receiving an award for being the best Western Australian small business. The video tells of how he overcame racial discouragement, especially from one of his teachers who told him that he would come to nothing. Tears as Ros' daughter relates this to the award audience. As usual, great people met when in a youth hostel.

24.30 miles 462 elevation feet up 515 feet down

Wednesday 30th November

So the end of another month, number twenty three on the Biking Birder tour 2015-6 and the beginning of day 700! With 6,500 miles cycled this year so far, I am going to enjoy another day off and explore York. I have only had one new bird for the year list this month; the White-billed Diver off North Ronaldsay. There is another bird available about fifty miles away, Pallid Harrier near Spurn and that will be the direction I will take tomorrow. York Minster and the Jorvik museum, I haven't been to them since the children were small.

Now there has been a lack of birds in my life recently. Winter thrushes and Bramblings occasionally whilst cycling and a few Treecreepers from the window of the youth hostel dormitory yesterday, isn't a large amount of birds but needs must. I need to get the distance covered.

When cycling one of my strategies to keep the negative voice at bay is to consider a route to bird when I return to Peru in April next year.

Let's dream together ……………

Lima, San Isidro Park and the pier at Miraflores: *Long-tailed Mockingbird, Saffron Finches, Vermilion Flycatchers, Amazilian Hummingbird, House Wren and the ubiquitous Rufous-collared Sparrow. Neotropic Cormorant, Inca Terns, Peruvian Booby and Pelican, Franklin's Gulls and Blackish Oystercatcher*

A ride down to Los Pantanos de Villa : *Black Vulture. Great Grebe, Multi-coloured Rush Tyrant, Peruvian Meadowlark, Peruvian Thick-knee. Burrowing Owl and Pied-billed Grebe*

Tambo Colorado Hostel, Pisco, Peru.

Back in 2014 I visited this hostel quite a few times. The best visit though was for my daughter, Rebecca's birthday . . . . Flight over the Nasca lines with Happy Birthday sung by Japanese tourists. Later a party back at the hostel afterwards.

So with the lovely Silvia Vilchez to organise our taxis and boats . .

Paracas National Park: *Surf Cincloides (endemic), Grey-headed Gull, Chilean Flamingo, Least Sandpiper, Peruvian Tern. Turkey Vulture, Kelp Gull and Royal Tern*

Pisco Beach : *Wilson's Phalarope, Striated Heron, Snowy Egret, Great Egret, Cinnamon Teal, Gray Gull and Black-crowned Night Heron*

Ballestos Islands : *Red-legged Cormorant, Humboldt Penguin and Inca Tern . . . birds by the half million!*

I have heard today from a great friend, The Birding Clam previously mentioned, Jason John Oliver. He has phoned to say that he is going to accompany me when I return to Peru next year for a couple of weeks birding! Jason hasn't been to Peru before. It is going to be a superb start to my three month stay there.

November Monthly Statistics:-

Green Year list	315 birds
Year ticks seen in November	1
Bird species had, not seen in 2015	1
Mileage in November	478.88 miles
Total mileage for the year	6544.7 miles
average mileage on days cycled	19.95 miles
elevation : up	18,132 feet
: down	18,135 feet

Best Bird *:* **White-billed Diver**

12

DECEMBER

The Dodo used to walk around
And Take the sun and air.
The sun yet warms his native ground
The Dodo is not there!

The Bad Child's Book of Beasts, verses by H. Belloc, illustrations by B.T.B.

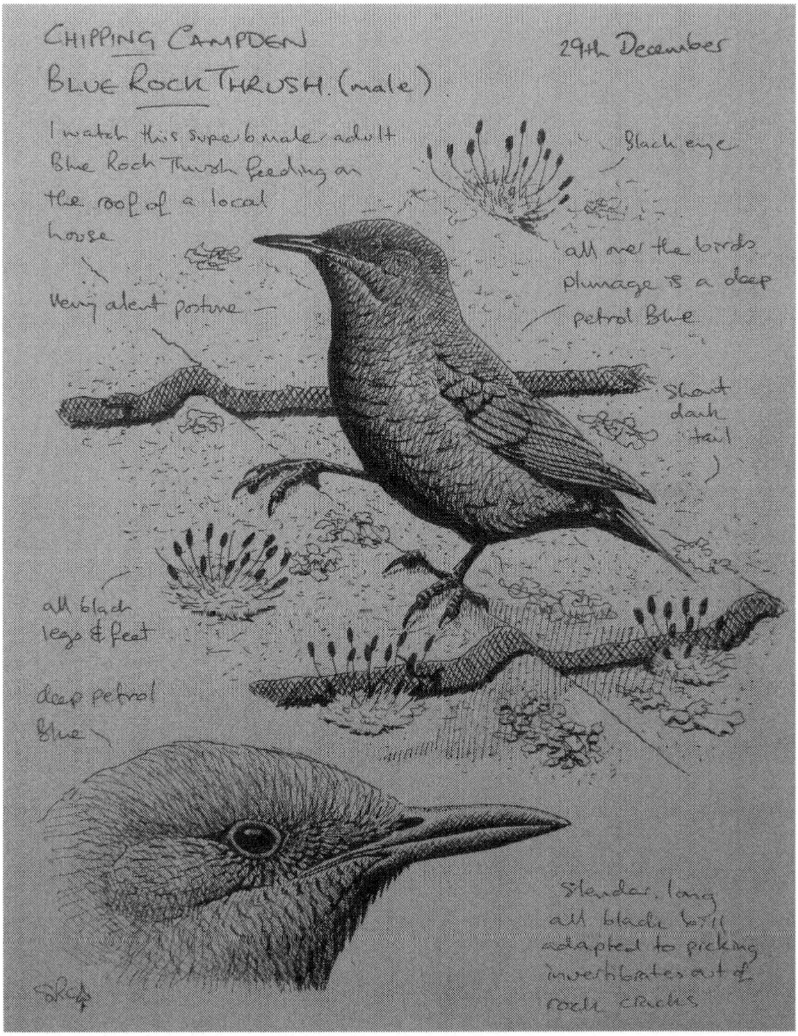

Green Birding, a BIGBY, A Big Green Big Year, is one where a birder aims to see all of his or her birds without the use of hydrocarbons, fossil fuels.

Is it a sport? My Dad, if he could keep his eyes open, would watch sport 24/7. He doesn't think that anyone looking for birds is taking part in a sport. I disagree. The physical challenge of a year's cycling-birding in all weathers is considerable. The mental aspect brings stresses comparable to any sport. One may not be as far away from another person as, say a round the World sailor but the cycling road is very lonely at times. Statistical considerations, immense and don't forget the little thing of knowing what you're looking at. Records to beat, personal goals to achieve, yes I think all things considered that Green Birding is a sport.

Let's look at the achievements of the main Green Birding Celebrities.

First up there is the amazing Dorian Anderson. Dorian Anderson has the BIGBY (Big Green Big Year list) World Record at 618 different bird species. In 2014 Dorian cycled around the USA beating the previous record by around 300, almost doubling it!

Dorian's incredible blog is linked below:-

http://bikingforbirds.blogspot.co.uk/

I love to dip into it at random and read of his exploits. Exciting Green Birding and all the more inspiring when one knows that Dorian did all of his birding by his own physical efforts instead of just pressing a gas pedal.

Ponc Feliu Latorre had the European Green Birding crown until this year. Ponc saw 304 bird species in his native Spain in 2013. He still has the purest European Green Birding crown though! On Jim Royer's webpage, Ponc is still above me with the highest accolade in Green Birding beside his name, a 'G'. My record, despite being a few birds of Ponc, has the less creditable 'F'. I have no problem with this. I used some ferries to get to the remote islands I love so much.

All this makes me wonder what will happen when electric bikes become more popular? At the moment they are charged from the electricity mains. How will Green Birding's ethos be viewed when such fantastic bikes are powered by solar power and other renewable energy sources?

So, time for my own Green Birding trumpet to be blown. Having spent 35 months cycling, the end of the third year Biking Birding is approaching. Let's look at each year starting with 2010.

The main aim for 2010, other than to survive it as the Winter weather in the UK was the worst seen since 1963, was to visit every RSPB (Royal Society for the Protection of Birds) and WWT (Wildfowl & Wetland Trust) nature reserve. Over 200 nature reserves were to be visited in a year. The route I had mapped back in 2005 as an idea to help me keep my sanity during a time of tremendous personal stress. Diversion from desire conflicted with love and safety.

The weather in 2010 was truly atrocious at both ends of the year and really I didn't have the money to do the year comfortably. I camped or slept rough most of the year. I remember vividly one night of extreme cold sleeping in a church porch in Essex, wriggling most of the night to try to stay warm. I lay in my sleeping bag still dressed with multi-layers of clothing, including a Ghostbusters like decorator's outfit and thermals; the sleeping bag stretched out upon bristly door mats to prevent contact with the clod, stone floor.

Sardines and doughnuts were parts of my usual daily diet being so cheap. Waiting for supermarkets to reduce some food items at the end of the day kept me going; that and a determination to not only visit all of the reserves but also beat the UK Green Year list record then held by Chris Mills of Norfolk.

I achieved my aim of every RSPB nature reserve on an icy day in December in Bedfordshire when a group of RSPB staff cycled with me the last few miles to the HQ, Sandy. I went over the finish line with a flat front tyre!

That day ended with ten inches of snow falling in an hour and me having to push the bike to Bedford. The following day I cycled back to my parent's home in Warwick. Fifty five miles cycled that day along snow-covered, slushy roads, four punctures endured. I had no money that year for such luxuries as a new tyre let alone inner tubes!

I ended the year on 253, a new record. Looking back later I removed sooty shearwater. I considered the bird I thought I saw to have not been well enough seen to be fully certain of the identification. That brought me back to 252.

Then the British Birds Rarities Committee report into the rare birds of 2010 decided that the red-breasted goose that I had seen in Devon at Exminster Marshes RSPB reserve was an escape. I was now level with Chris on 251.

2010 was a wonderful tour of the whole of the United Kingdom. England, Wales, Northern Ireland and Scotland, I visited them all, criss-crossing to remote areas, visiting ancient monuments, cathedrals and museums, schools and colleges along the way. I had a whale of a time meeting so many fabulous people and seeing how diverse a country the UK is.

I collected money for charity, for the RSPB, the WWT and also for Asthma UK; the latter due to my own asthma.

Back then I didn't consider the fact that the list might be an European record. That was until one day when I was sitting looking at a Western

Sandpiper at Cley. Sitting next to me in Daulkes hide were two Belgians who had come over to see the mega rare American wader from Brussels. They recognised me as The Biking Birder and told me that their friend, Laurent Raty was trying to beat my European record. News to me that birders from Belgian knew me, I never did hear whether Laurent beat my, and Chris' total of 251.

In 2014 though I heard about Ponc Feliu Latorre. A Spaniard had not only beaten 251, he had gone past 300! I had to beat that! I started to plan for 2015.

2015. I wanted to be the first British birder to get past 300. Yet again, I wanted to visit every RSPB and WWT nature reserve and yes, I really wanted to beat Ponc. England versus Spain, The Armada, Trafalgar, The Spanish Inquisition, Barcelona having the best football team. Bring it on!

A similar route to 2010 was mapped out, except for May being spent in East Anglia. I had missed several easy birds in 2010 by not going over there. If I was to get close to 300 I needed to see turtle dove, stone curlew, nightingale and hobby.

Even by June in 2015 I realised that the 300 target would not be achieved but I kept going. The hope of a phenomenally good Autumn in the Northern Isles and the desire to visit all of those fantastic nature reserves kept me pedalling.

I ended up on 290. Creditable but not 300. I slept in a bird hide on New Year's Eve and carried on.

Now I have seen 300 and I have beaten Ponc. My total BOU (British Ornithological Union) is 315. AERC, the European listing authority has me on 312 at the moment; Hooded Crow, Mealy Redpoll and Northern Harrier aren't treated as separate species on this, the official European bird list.

I am still collecting money through donations for the three charities previously mentioned; Asthma UK, the RSPB and WWT. Also I am collecting money for the incredible rainforest children of Chaskawasi-Manu in Peru. These wonderful children who leave their homes from deep in the Manu rainforest, to stay with volunteers and staff at the Chaskawasi centre, in order to access the local school and get an education. Their desire is to help protect their rainforest and I had the privilege of meeting these children in 2014. I will be returning there next year. A truly wonderful project that deserves mine and hopefully your support.

Many thanks to all who have done so.

31 days to go. Will Ponc have a go at beating the new record next year as he said he would? Will another Green Birder have a go themselves? I sincerely hope so.

Friday 2nd December **Almost no wind**

Sunny AM, rain all afternoon. Mild, 6C

Happy Birthday Karen.

Time to get back on the road after a couple of days exploring York. The weather is fine, well at for at least the morning and the route for the first twenty miles is flat and straight, once I get out of York anyway.

What have I been up to the last two days? Well, other than relaxing in the superb York Youth Hostel, I have walked along the River Ouse into the city each day in order to access either York Minster or the Jorvik Museum.

Strangely my Biking Birding year of 2016 is beginning to feel like that of 2010. Back then not only did I visit every RSPB and WWT nature reserve but I also visited around forty cathedrals around the UK, not York Minster though.

Having paid the necessary entry fee to get into this huge church, the magnificent medieval stained glass windows take up my time. It is fascinating to look at the variety of expressions and styles in the depicted faces and wonder what stories each window tells.

The memorials of metal or stone attached to the walls tell stories of their own. A grave adorned with figures gives moral guidance with a sting in the tale. More stained glass take up more time and the best yet, The East Window, replete with stories from The Book of Revelations. The huge North Window is dark, grey and oppressive.

The Jorvik Museum is closed. Clues as to why I had seen along the way into the city; high debris mark on fences around riverside trees and thick silt on riverside steps and paths show that floods have passed this way recently and more extensively last Christmas. The entrance to the museum is guarded by a large Viking man and and his lady. Dressed as in those long gone days, they tell me about the Boxing Day floods and of how the famous Viking exhibition ride, replete with faecal smells and artefacts, is now being refurbished following the damage done by the water.

A temporary, smaller exhibition is available just a few yards away so I head there. Artefacts in cabinets and display boards detail the original finds, the extensive archaeological dig and the history of Jorvik – York. There are Viking people to meet once more and talk to; Benedict, Rachel, Adam and 'Bork.' Only of the last do I remember the Viking character name. All surround the fantastic centrepiece of a reconstructed Viking boat.

Adam has a loom to show. Benedict has actual Viking artefacts to talk about and allows one to hold; a metal knife, a leather shoe, ladies size 4. He also has a Viking game that looks like a cross similar to chess. Benedict explains the rules, complex and interesting.

Bork has the same game and lots of Viking clothes for one to try on.

And so to today and a comfortable ride to Beverley. No wind and quite a few cycle paths alongside the main road keeps me safe. The road is flat until just past Market Weighton where a long hill takes me over a chalk escarpment. The only stop is to photograph a perfect but sadly dead Tawny Owl. Such a beautiful animal with no apparent damage from the impact with the vehicle that killed it.

Into Beverley and the Minster, another church to visit. The carvings in the choir and along the walls attract attention here.

32.59 miles 924 elevation feet up 950 feet down

Saturday 3rd December Almost no wind

Sunny, AM. Hazy sunny intervals PM. Mild, 6C

Flat landscape again and a lack of wind make the cycle from Beverley to Welwick easy enough. Through eastern Hull and along the main road, I leave my panniers at a bed and breakfast just before Patrington. Reaching Welwick Saltmarsh Nature Reserve beside the Humber Estuary, there is a group of birders looking over the grasslands. The reported Pallid Harrier had been seen just before Noon. I stand and wait and chat.

In the three hours that follow there are few birds but those seen include many birds of prey; Merlin, Kestrel, Sparrowhawk, Buzzard and both Hen and Marsh Harriers. There are even a few Short-eared Owls quartering the marsh.

Light is starting to fade when I make the mistake of going for a stroll to warm up my frozen feet. I only walk a hundred yards or so but when I return to the birder group, they are all celebrating the Pallid Harrier having flown past! Some birders start to leave happy in their distant views.

Ten minutes later a ring-tailed Harrier flies towards us. **Pallid Harrier** UTB! Bird number **316**.

It flies over fields in a large circular route before appearing in front of us over the saltmarsh again.

Brilliant. Another great bird goes onto the Green Year list. Will this bird be the last addition to the list? Will it be the final fabulous bird in this fabulous year?

One sad note, I lose my cycling gloves. Battered, full of holes but they have been with me since January 1st last year. Treasured but gone.

32.42 miles 524 elevation feet up 550 feet down

Sunday 4th December **Light E-SE**

Mostly sunny, cold as sun went down, 4C to 2C

I cycle to and through Hull and up and over the Humber Bridge. Not a lot happens except one exciting moment when a male Sparrowhawk almost hits me as it comes from behind a hedgerow beside the road!

38.31 miles **928 elevation feet up** **625 feet down**

Monday 5th December

A day off! I stay in a superb farmhouse bed and breakfast room and sort out emails and organise some projects for next year. A really lazy day! Fabulous and boy, did my back and joints deserve the rest!

Tuesday 6th December **No apparent wind**

Very thick fog and very cold, 2C

An early morning Text from The Oracle, hinting at the Dusky Thrush near Chesterfield (8:17)

Where did u stop? As nice as it would be to see u today the bird has allegedly been there for two weeks so don't kill urself getting there!

I reply. (8:21)

I won't. Did you see the programmes about Fair Isle? Programme 2 has lancy and bluetail and a famous Biking Birder. LOL.

Oracle texts.(8:25)

No mate. Will try to find it on Iplayer. Uv dodged the question as to where u are again! Famous or infamous?

There have been moments when I have wanted to strangle the devil on my shoulder that nags me over getting to the next bird. Tat may sound ungrateful when I am talking about The Oracle. Phil has been with me all of the way and his support and information has been vital. He does push me though and, yes I know I need it but sometimes I just want to whine "leave me alone!"

To which I text. (8:26)

I wonder why? Thick fog and ice again.

Phil phones and, against my inner desire, I answer, after which I text. (8:55)

Good to hear you .. makes me feel close to home.

I cycle to Retford taking as much care as possible due to the tricky weather combination of frozen roads and thick fog. A stop in Kirton in Lyndsey to admire the World war memorial and read of the local RAF heroes. https://en.wikipedia.org/wiki/RAF_Kirton_in_Lindsey

Tough going it may be but it is fabulous when a motorist comes alongside me as I cycle, well careering down a steep hill. He opens his window and laughingly says that I am going forty miles per hour. I doubt that but laugh at his cheek.

38.91 miles 1085 elevation feet up 1099 feet down

Wednesday 7th December Fresh SW

Very mild, 12C

Reaching Chesterfield, the town with the crooked spire atop the town's main church, today's cycling was different to the last few days in that there was wind in the face and steep hills to contend with.

Twenty four days to go and a new life starting at the end of those. It is going to be interesting but first the little matter of seeing the Dusky Thrush.

25.33 miles 351 elevation feet up 1108 feet down

Thursday 8th December

A day sorting out my health! A few birders have been in touch to ask why I haven't rushed to the mega rare Dusky Thrush, only ten miles from where I am in Chesterfield. Well, now that all is sorted I can reveal that I needed to see a doctor. As I hope you all know, one of the four charities I support is the wonderful Asthma UK. As is usual when one supports a charity, it is often because of a close personal link. I have been asthmatic since being a young child. I cannot remember a time when I was anything but and memories of asthmatic attacks in my past come flooding back as I type. Paris, when I was twelve years old on an exchange programme and a doctor was called out in the middle of the night to help me. It was the week of Neil Armstrong's 'One small step for Man.'

I also remember driving a car around, also at night, with all the windows open to try to force air into me when in my twenties.

Anyway, recently, there has been a niggly tightness in my chest, not helped by a lack of Salbutamol. I ran out of my 'blue' inhaler a couple of weeks ago and so today a doctor's appointment at the superb medical centre here in Chesterfield to receive a brand new inhaler to keep me going.

Couldn't explain before; my loving Mum is watching my every move on the blog and Facebook and she, bless her, worries about her eldest. Little Miss Sunshine! Being from Birmingham I will always be her 'Bab' no matter that I am now sixty years old!

Sixty! Free prescriptions. Yes . . . . free medicine for the over sixties. Thank goodness for the NHS. Never did understand why asthmatics aren't exempt from prescription charges, as are so many other debilitating conditions. Oh well, I am getting old.

Tomorrow, hopefully, the Dusky Thrush will become bird number 317 on my year list; a list that is already replete with so many incredible birds thanks to one of the best Autumns for rare birds ever.

Friday 9th December **Light to fresh SW**

Mild, 12C, cloudy, some light drizzle but mostly dry.

There is a wonderful ninety four year old man next to me at the breakfast table this morning, John from Chatham, Kent and can he chat! John is fit and very conversational and it is a pleasure to listen to his stories about both his family and his life as an engineer so many years ago. John has caught two coaches from his home town to come up to see his sister, who is in a care home in Chesterfield. Gaynor, the proprietress of the excellent Acorns Guest House, tells me that John is a frequent visitor. John makes me feel as though maybe I am only two thirds of the way along my own life journey. What a fabulous inspiration.

An extremely rare thrush, a Dusky Thrush, from China has lost her way and is in a small village, Beeley, about ten miles from where I am as today's cycling is started. Will this incredible year ever stop throwing up such rarities. This must be the best year ever for rare birds and next year's Rare Bird Report in British Birds Magazine is going to be a must read. The year of the Siberian Accentor, the unprecedented number of this incredibly rare passerine that have been seen across Europe is over 250. So many other extremely rare birds, especially from the east, has made every birder's year so very special, so memorable.

With the road through the town negotiated, a turn onto a cycle path takes the bike alongside a large pool and into a small wood. My mood is extremely carefree today with songs and laughs and a stop to chat with a passing lady dog walker cheers her up. She says that she has been feeling extremely stressed recently and hearing singing and whistling from someone with such an unusual collection of friends on his bike has helped tremendously. Good deed done for the day, a collection of smiling people stop as a decorated Christmas Tree stops me a little way further.

The Chesterfield Nordic Walking Group are walking their way back into town; as lovely a group of people as one could ever meet. Laura seems to be their leader and she tells everyone the story of how a family started to decorate this evergreen tree in the wood and that it has become a local tradition ever since. It is gratifying to see how many decorations are on the tree and that no one vandalises it. With photographs taken and reasons exchanged it is time for goodbye and to carry on.

Through the village of Holymoorside, the hill to the west towards Beeley seems never ending; a rise of 600 feet in one and three quarter miles. At least the long push gives chances to watch winter Thrushes in the fields, hundreds of them with a lot of Starlings too.

More unusual is a fantastic male Hen Harrier that crosses the road in front of me before heading off southwards.

The quickest route to Beeley has a road blocked off for repairs. A car stops to offer advice, two young Chinese tourists, their English perfect, tell me that they think I will be able to get through.

The blocked off road descends towards the destination village and I am relieved when the two workers, sitting in their van having a cuppa, tell me that it is OK to cycle through.

Into the village, it is soon apparent that the Dusky Thrush is a very rare bird. There are birders everywhere. Around eighty of them are gathered by the broken down dry stone wall of the village orchard. Fruit on the floor beneath the old fruit trees is attracting Fieldfares and Blackbirds, Redwings are flying overhead but there is no sign of the Dusky. A couple of hours pass.

Suddenly birders are on the move. Some walk, some run. I do the latter. Up a short hill, through a courtyard, negotiate a fence and ditch and into a field where around a hundred birders are gathered watching a distant mega. **Dusky Thrush** goes onto the Green Year List, bird number **317**. A lovely couple, Malcolm and Lynn lend me their telescope to get great views of a really beautiful thrush. It is just a shame that my camera isn't good enough to take good photographs at this range.

Happy after watching the bird for an hour or so and having had chats with birders, I need to head off to get a bed for the night. The first attempt on finding a bed & breakfast has me cycling on. I am sorry but I cannot afford £148 for the night.

11.11 miles **1138 feet elevation up** **1070 feet down**

An evening email:-

Hi Gary

Thank you so much for your messages and fabulous pictures. It was great fun to meet you today. We are normally at Hardwick Hall on Fridays and changed our walk to visit our tree at the festival. The group and I are so glad we did we really enjoyed meeting you and learning about your adventures too.
All the best for 2017 and Happy Christmas to you and your Mum and Dad.
Laura x
PS I hope the inhaler keeps that asthma at bay - stay safe!
Laura Daniels - Nordic Walking Instructor
Chesterfieldnordicwalking.co.uk
07950 222988

Saturday 10th December **Light SW**

Light cloud, still mild, 12C

The cycle down the A6 seems easy. With the road heading mostly downhill in long stretches the going is pleasant and I cannot help but sing a repertoire of old comedy songs.

The Sun has got his hat on! It hasn't but who cares?
https://www.youtube.com/watch?v=GDIpkz6DOi8

When you're feeling down try positive thinking. Always do.
https://www.youtube.com/watch?v=ODTAATrM1Fs

When You're Smiling, The Whole World Smiles With You.
https://www.youtube.com/watch?v=-EclGYJ8TGk

I Know a fat Policeman . . . . . ?????
https://www.youtube.com/watch?v=hI1nPd7hezM

Through Matlock, along a widening river and into Belper; I suddenly spy Olaf! "There's Olaf!" I shout to shoppers on the High Street pavements.

Maybe giving away a secret but I meet Olaf/Kevin, who is advertising a nearby store but tells me that he wears the Olaf costume, the snowman from Disney's film Frozen if you hadn't realised, to help some local charities. Good man.

Cycling from Belper to Derby with new songs to sing.......

Bees that buzz; kids will pull dandelion fuzz.
https://www.youtube.com/watch?v=UFatVn1hP3o

Tale as old as time.....
https://www.youtube.com/watch?v=xDUhINW3SPs

Hakuna Matata
https://www.youtube.com/watch?v=nbY_aP-alkw

It might seem crazy what I'm 'bout to say . .
https://www.youtube.com/watch?v=ZbZSe6N_BXs

Needless to say my mood is carefree and . . . . . . HAPPY!

37.19 miles 1386 feet elevation up 1616 feet down

Sunday 11th December Light SW

Low, misty cloud, still mild, 12C

A day just cycling a few miles through Burton on Trent to Alrewas where the main problem was in finding my way with a lack of directional road signs and a dodgy signal on the mobile.

17.74 miles 586 feet elevation up 565 feet down

Monday 12th December Very light S

Rainy, mild 11C

Into Lichfield after a stay at one of the best Bed & Breakfast's of the year. Amber Guest House, Alrewas has even won awards for being so great and with such wonderful company in the shape of the lovely couple, Theresa and Barry, who chat for two hours or so, I enjoy a fabulous stay. Theresa and Barry are looking after the establishment while the actual proprietor is away. Great to be with two Brummies again!

A cycle in the rain into Lichfield and, after a lot of assistance by Tom, residing behind the entrance counter, over storing the bike and belongings inside the cathedral there. Thanks Tom. I explore. Masses of white paper angels hang from ceilings and a display of Christmas Trees in the aisles can be seen. Then into the Chapter House to peruse ancient artefacts.

In darkness and with rain falling I find my way along very busy main roads to tonight's accommodation.

11.11 miles 1138 feet elevation up 1070 feet down

Tuesday 13th December Light SW

Misty, mild and cloudy

A curious couple are at breakfast, psychics. The hour spent with them was an hour too long as they plied me with questions, received my sceptical responses and were completely off track when I offered them the small stone that has been worn around my neck for over ten years now. Complete con artists, sad to meet and my anger towards them was ill-disguised.

On the road again, I enter Walsall Arboretum remembering how this was the venue for the wonderful Walsall Illuminations when I was a child. It was such an adventure to myself, my brother and sister, Mum and Dad to go there when we kids were small. It involved multiple Birmingham buses, the ones with the sign 'No Spitting' on the walls, that seemed to take hours. I remember taking my two children, Rebecca and Joshua, there when they were small. Laser beams over the lake to the sound of Beverley Hills Cop theme music and the usual Blackpool Illumination-like attractions filled the park that evening.

Now the park has been refurbished and I hear that the Illuminations are no more; part of the council cuts. Most sad.

I reach Walsall centre and after admiring a small stone hippopotamus, various bare-breasted sculptures that adorn a municipal building and a plaque to commemorate the author of 'Three Men in A Boat,' Jerome K. Jerome; I read a sad memorial to a young twenty one year old soldier, John Henry Carless, who received the Victoria Cross. Just twenty one by two weeks, John was mortally wounded in the stomach but continued to man his gun station and assist other casualties until a new gun crew arrived. Another plaque beside the statue of John is to celebrate the laying of a stone by His Royal Highness, Prince Christian of Schleswig-Holstein in 1902.

The rest of this drizzly, cool December day is spent cycling through The Black Country reaching the lump that is Romsley Hill by late afternoon. One long last push and I am home. Well, here I am at my parent's home. Hugs, coffee and chat, the rest of the evening is a rest. I await news of birds.

26.53 miles 1458 feet elevation up 1055 feet down

Two weeks of feet up relaxation with Mum and Dad, I have deserved this and the only news of rare birds that would be additions to the Green Bird Year List are birds that are too far away to allow me time to cycle to and back in time for Christmas. Mum and Dad are in their mid-eighties and I want to have Christmas with them.

Days pass . . . Christmas with Mum and Dad. Wonderful.

Thursday 28th December **No wind**

Very cold, minus 3C, very sunny

It's amazing but the thought of a cycle ride to The Cotswold's seems miles away and daunting whereas earlier in the year the thought of cycling all the way to Land's End barely caused any consternation! Yet there is a Blue Rock Thrush in The Cotswold's, at Stow on The Wold and I need to see it. This is a bit of a controversial sighting, with some birders calling it plastic. Meaning an escape from someone's aviary, the bird hasn't helped itself by sleeping in a bucket and eating cake. Still it is on limestone buildings, similar to where they come from in the Mediterranean, and I have to take the chance that it will be accepted by the BBRC as a genuine bird.

Anyway the route today involves a lot of downhill sections along roads I know so well. What could go wrong?

Gears broken! I have two available and my legs whizz around like Billy Whizz and Roadrunner with little forward propulsion. I stick to the main roads, including dual carriageways through Redditch. I feel safer on these than I do the country lanes. Indeed as I pass over one such narrow country lane, near to where I lived in a campervan for nine year, I remember that one cyclist was killed here by a speeding car. It always seems ridiculous and downright disgusting that vehicles can go at the national speed limit along such narrow roadways. I have even seen small roads coming off large dual carriageways where the speed limit increases as one turns into the smaller lane!

Past Coughton Court I cycle, between Studley and Alcester in Warwickshire. A stately home with English Civil War history, how sad to see that the long Elm tree parade I remember from my childhood has gone.

By the time I reach my lodging for the night I am quite exhausted and chilled. The roads are icy and hoar frost covers the trees. I am too tired to eat and am soon sleeping.

A few text messages in the evening wake me up:-

Rob Williams (17:43)

Hi Gary. I hope you had a good ride today. Where did you get to and what are your planned timings for tomorrow? Best wishes, Rob.

I reply. (18:47)

Hi Rob. I am in Temple Grafton. Breakfast's at 7 and will be on the road asap. My bike is broken. Only one gear but should be there by noon at the latest. Hope the fog lifts. BCNU.

Rob Williams (18:51)

Hi Gary. Thanks for the updates. I will get up there mid morning and look for you en route to get some 'action' shots. Will text when I am in the area.

I reply (18:52)

Great. See you tomorrow.

Steve Nuttall (19:55 p.m.)

Are you still coming to Belvide tomorrow or going for the Blue Rock Thrush?

I reply... (19:57 p.m.)

Sorry mate, Blue Rock Thrush. Have you been for it? I will visit Belvide in the New Year.
Steve replies . . . (20:02 p.m.)

Don't blame you. Saw one on the Scillies. Blyth's Pipit as well? The latter comment refers to a Blyth's Pipit reported at Blagdon Lake, Somerset

My reply to that . . . (20:03 p.m.)

Not the Blyth's, not enough time.

Thursday 29th December **No wind**

Very cold, minus 3C, very sunny

An icy road and a clear sky, thick frost covering every twig, blade of grass and hedgerow, I cycle south towards The Cotswold's. There is a Blue Rock Thrush, maybe only the seventh ever to be seen in Britain and to finish the 2016 Biking Birder adventure with such a mega rare bird will be quite amazing.

It is so cold and the roads aren't too safe as ice patches are quite frequent. The sunrise is beautiful but soon the sun shining on the icy road is blinding. I have only two gears and along flat sections my legs are a blur! Beep beep.

I stop and try to get the gear system fixed. Probably corrosion has caused this but after twenty minutes of poking and adjusting I manage to get four gears.

Through Mickleton and onto the start of hill after hill as I reach The Cotswold's escarpment. Steep hills keep me pushing and the twenty two miles I need to cycle start to feel like fifty.

Stow on the Wold is eventually reached and I soon find the massed ranks of birders from near and far. There is a film camera filming me as I cycle up the lane. Rob Williams, a famous National Geographic and freelance film maker is going to film me today and I laugh as I realise that, despite feeling very self conscious, this is going to be fun. His ten year old son, Oliver, is the sound man holding the Dougal and what a joy it must be to work as Father and Son.

The Blue Rock Thrush isn't on view. It was last seen on nearby rooftops. Rob tells me of his Peru adventures. Rob spent ten years there and Oliver proudly says that he was born there. Rob spent a lot of time in Salvacion in the Manu, the village where the children's charity that I am supporting this year is located. As well as having a massive Peru Bird list of 1651, Rob is also famous on TV for having bought some rainforest with Charlie Hamilton Jones. It turns out I have been to the village where they did so and can see it all in my mind's eye.

http://video.nationalgeographic.com/video/ng-live/160523-nglive-james-rain-forest-part1

An hour passes and suddenly birders are moving away en masse. The thrush has been seen.

I cycle to the spot to hear that it has just flown away. Minutes later it is back and the **Blue Rock Thrush** goes onto the Green Birding list at **318**. This may be not be accepted, though, being a potential vagrant, as there is an undercurrent of birders who think that this bird is an escape. I will have to wait and see. In the meantime I can enjoy the company and the bird.

The most famous Carbon Twitcher in the UK, Lee G.R. Evans comes past. I stop him to say thanks for the encouragement he has given me over the last two years and Rob asks us to chat for a while as he films us. Carbon Twitcher meets Green Birder, both of us have the same focus, a love of birds.

Birders who either know me or know of my exploits come up and say hello, sometimes saying where we met during the year. One couple, Ethelyn and Richard from Northamptonshire, tell me that they remember meeting me at Loch Ruthven RSPB Reserve near Inverness back in 2010. A lovely couple and wonderful to meet again.

Maybe a little more affluent, the housing estate brings back memories of the chaos of trying to find a Golden-winged Warbler on a town housing estate in Maidstone, Kent back in 1989. Not such a crowd today but enough to show how rare this thrush actually is.

The great birding couple, Lee Gregory and Cath Mendez, turn up and the thrush comes very close. I can't wait to see the photographs that they both will have got.

Having given Rob's son,Oliver, one of The Lads from off the bike, Bruce the Snowman, I give another one away to another young ten year old birder, Bethany. Bethany is with her Mum and Dad,

Mum is a Villa fan, same as I. Bethany follows her Dad's team, Sheffield Wednesday. I give Bethany, appropriately, Spiggie the Owl from off my bike. After all the nickname of Sheffield Wednesday is The Owls.

Friday 30th December **very light SW**

Fog patches, mild, 6C

An early text from Rob Williams. (8:38)

Hi Gary. Hope you found a good place to stay. Thanks for your time today. I will be editing soon and will let you know how it looks. Congrats on the record. Best wishes, Rob.

A text message from Steve Nuttall, the main man at one of my old patches, Belvide Reservoir in Staffordshire.

Iceland Gull roosted at Belvide last night Pal. Do you need that for the year?(9:02)

Iceland Gull is a bird I indeed need. I saw half a one, if you remember, back in January at Mousehole, Cornwall.

I reply :

Yes but I can't get to you! I have to be at Upton Warren tomorrow. Ironically yesterday's Blue Rock Thrush might be seen as an escape whereas the Iceland would have been solid. BCNU. UTV! (9:53)

Steve responds (9:57 a.m.)

That's a shame. Would have loved your final tick of the year to be at the Golden

Pond.

To which I reply (9.58 a.m.)

Same here. An old patch still loved.

A simple aim today, to get to Redditch, the town of my teenage years in Worcestershire. The weather is slightly warmer than of late and the start has me heading towards Chipping Camden before the descent to the Vale of Evesham. Occasional fog patches cause me some concern as visibility goes down to tens of yards and cars approach from behind and in front, unseen but heard.

I cycle past the glider club I went to many years ago for my first lessons in the aviation art. Back in 1990, while I was searching for butterflies at a Worcestershire Wildlife Trust nature reserve adjacent to the River Avon, I saw a glider flying high overhead and determined to find from whence it came. Half an hour later I was up in one with a new friend, Hoppy. He was to train me this moustached, RAF caricature man and that moment of my first time swirling amongst cotton wool clouds, looking down on the river environ, is remembered.

Over the stone bridge at Bidford Upon Avon but no calendar view due to the fog. The view upstream of the Parish church overlooking the River Avon is a pastoral British scene of note, beautiful on a sunny Summer's day.

The road continues north, past Coughton Court, a noted National Trust property and one I used to cycle to back in my youth from my home a few miles away.

Through Studley and along to the new town area of Redditch, the road goes past warehouses built in the River Arrow valley built in the 1970s to provide employment for an influx of Birmingham people when Redditch was chosen as the location for an extensive new town. Redditch itself was mainly on top of the surrounding hills and ridges, it's main church, St Stephens, is on top of such surrounded by shopping malls these days.

A large lake, Arrow Valley Lake was dug around that time and I pass along it's western shore amazed at how high the trees are there now. I remember exploring the deep clay dug out forty seven years ago that destroyed my exploration area of fields, hedges and copses before water filled the deep depression creating the large lake there now. It became a place for the young to swim on warm, sunny days.

I cycle up Beoley Road in order to see the shop that my parents had back then. A Post Office that we moved to in 1967 is now an empty shell having recently been a failed pizza deliver shop. The whole area now looks squalid with litter and smashed fences, boarded up windows and broken glass. A sad sight, I move on to cycle past my old High School and so continue my nostalgic day. My memories of my school days aren't the happiest. I arrived there at the age of twelve from a Boy's Grammar School, King Edward's in Stourbridge and was soon badly bullied. I used to run away and get a bus back to Stourbridge in order to pretend that we still lived there. My main tormentors' names I remember well, even after so many years, Paul and Richard, and how they arranged some of the children of my form into a line by the door to hit me with rulers when I came in one day. Too many bad memories, I am glad to pass it quickly as the road goes downhill.

Down to Forge Mill and after going past the mill's large pool I stop to talk with some travellers camped by the main road with their beautifully painted, traditional caravans arranged around a smoking camp fire. The children are suspicious of me but the men chat and bring a Harris Hawk over that they have tethered beside a large horse.

A cup of over-sweetened coffee and a piece of almost burnt toast later, I continue towards the saddest location, the grave of my youngest brother, Chris. I was nineteen and Chris was only four when he was hit by a car and his grave says it so simply, 'a precious son.'

"Derby!"

Saturday 31st December **Light SW**

Cloudy, misty and cool, 6C

So here it is, New Year's Eve and the final day of the UK Biking Birder adventure. Today three years of cycling - birding, 2010, 2015 and 2016 come to a conclusion.

It is early morning, breakfast is in ten minutes and then it is the cycle to Worcestershire Wildlife Trust's flagship nature reserve, Upton Warren.

I buy a bottle of champagne bought to share the moment with friends. I also get cake on the way. To see friends at my favourite UK birding patch, one I have visited for many years, is going to be special.

The final cycle down to the Moors part of my favourite nature reserve is indeed wonderful. A group of friends have gathered by the car park and I am surrounded by friendly, smiling faces. There's the Upton Warren stalwarts, Mary and Tim, John, Mike, Andy, Peter, Phil and Gert. There's Sue and Dave Wilkes with their grandsons. Liz Bradbury has come from Warwick with her son, Jack and The Birding Clams, Jason, Steve and Tony. Of course The Oracle is here, Phil Andrews! I have so much to thank him for.

Some of them want a video of my arrival so I cycle back up the lane to repeat that moment. I almost run into a much taller than the last time I saw her Mary and her Dad, Tim.

Champagne and cake in the Arthur Jacobs hide after team photographs, I see that Liz has rabbit fingers behind her son's head! Typical of this most wonderful of Mums

Chat and birding, the day passes and people start to leave.

In the afternoon there is a chance that a final bird will be added to the Green Year list. An Iceland Gull came into the gull roost at Bartley Reservoir on the edge of Birmingham last night. Having only seen half a one this year, the front half, it would be great to see the other end.

I set off but fog envelopes me and the road becomes lethal as cars zoom by. I decide that half an Iceland will be enough and turn for my parents' home once more.

And so The Green Year Biking Birding list finishes on **318**. I have achieved the targets I set myself for the year. I am the first British birder to see over 300 different bird species in one year by cycling. I have beaten the European Green Year list record held by Ponc and by some margin.

My hope is that someone will beat this total by just visiting the UK mainland. That would then be the greenest of records. Will anyone else do what I have done? Who knows. It would be a thrill in my dotage to see a young whipper-snapper going for my record. Maybe they would do a blog. Maybe they would make video updates with video footage of each bird seen, each place visited and each person met. If anyone does set out on such an adventure I will be fascinated to meet them on its conclusion.

I am a tad tired and I go to bed early, safely back with Mum and Dad. See in the New Year? Well, I will try. Yet I cannot go to sleep before saying a massive thank you to everyone who has supported me, cheered me on, helped in some way, commented, posted, advised, shared moments or donated to one of the charities I have done all this for.

Today at Upton Warren Nature Reserve, the Worcestershire Wildlife trust flagship reserve, the amount of money raised for charity was an incredible £711. Thank you so much. It was a very emotional welcome home. Thank you. Xx

On Just Giving tonight there was another £195 donated. Thank you, thank you, thank you!

This is not the end of the Biking Birder, far from it. Next year's adventures will be online as usual with the aim of an attempt to beat Dorian Anderson's World record in 2018. I have a general route for that adventure but need to research it by going there for a few months next year in preparation. Needless to say it won't be in the UK or Europe. I need to beat 618 birds!

Until then, thanks for being with me. The support, friendship, kindness and laughter has been so vital to my life over the last twenty four months.

Love to you all.

Gary, The Biking Birder

December Monthly Statistics:-

Green Year list	318 birds
Year ticks seen in December	4
Bird species had, not seen in 2015	4
Mileage in December	391.01 miles
Total mileage for the year	6,975.33 miles
average mileage on days cycled	23.44 miles
elevation : up	16,879 feet
: down	16,886 feet

***Best Birds** : Pallid Harrier, Dusky and Blue Rock Thrush*

Biking Birder 2016 Big Green Big Year BOU list

British name	**Scientific name**	**Location (scarcities)**
Brent Goose	*Branta bernicla*	
Canada Goose	*Branta canadensis*	
Barnacle Goose	*Branta leucopsis*	
Snow Goose	*Anser caerulescens*	Coll, Hebrides
Greylag Goose	*Anser anser*	
Pink-footed Goose	*Anser brachyrhynchus*	
Tundra Bean Goose	*Anser serrirostris*	Fair Isle & North Ronaldsay
White-fronted Goose	*Anser albifrons*	
Mute Swan	*Cygnus olor*	
Bewick's Swan	*Cygnus columbianus*	
Whooper Swan	*Cygnus cygnus*	
Egyptian Goose	*Alopochen aegyptiaca*	
Shelduck	*Tadorna tadorna*	
Mandarin	*Aix galericulata*	Virginia Water, Surrey
Garganey	*Spatula querquedula*	
Shovelor	*Spatula clypeata*	
Gadwall	*Mareca strepera*	
Wigeon	*Mareca penelope*	
American Wigeon	*Mareca americana*	Bowling Green RSPB reserve
Mallard	*Anas platyrhynchos*	
Pintail	*Anas acuta*	
Teal	*Anas crecca*	
Green-winged Teal	*Anas carolinensis*	Seaford Wetlands, Devon & North Ronaldsay
Red-crested Pochard	*Netta rufina*	Titchwell RSPB reserve
Pochard	*Atytha ferina*	
Ferruginous Duck	*Aythya nyroca*	Blashford Lakes, Hants
Ring-necked Duck	*Aythya collaris*	Loch of Bosquoy, Orkney
Tufted Duck	*Aythya fuligula*	
Scaup	*Aythya marila*	
Lesser Scaup	*Aythya affinis*	Chew Valley Lake, Avon
Eider	*Somateria mollissima*	
Surf Scoter	*Melanitta perspicolla*	Filey, East Yorkshire
Velvet Scoter	*Melanitta fusca*	
White-winged Scoter	*Melanitta deglandi*	off Murcar Golf Course, Aberdeen
Common Scoter	*Melanitta nigra*	
Long-tailed Duck	*Clangula hyemalis*	
Goldeneye	*Bucephala clangula*	
Smew	*Mergellus albellus*	
Goosander	*Mergus merganser*	
Red-breasted Merganser	*Mergus serrator*	
Ruddy Duck	*Oxyura jamaicensis*	
Capercaillie	*Tetrao urogallus*	
Black Grouse	*Lyrurus tetrix*	
Ptarmigan	*Lagopus muta*	
Red Grouse	*Lagopus lagopus*	
Red-legged Partridge	*Alectoris rufa*	
Grey Partridge	*Perdix perdix*	
Quail	*Coturnix coturnix*	

Pheasant	*Phasianus colchicus*	
Golden Pheasant	*Chrysolophus pictus*	
Lady Amherst's Pheasant	*Chrysolophus amherstiae*	
Red-throated Diver	*Gavia stellata*	
Black-throated Diver	*Gavia arctica*	
Pacific Diver	*Gavia pacifica*	Marazion, Cornwall
Great Northern Diver	*Gavia immer*	
White-billed Diver	*Gavia adamsii*	North Ronaldsay, Orkney
Storm Petrel	*Hydrobates pelagicus*	North Ronaldsay, Orkney
Leach's Petrel	*Oceanodroma leucorhoa*	North Ronaldsay, Orkney
Fulmar	*Fulmaris glacialis*	
Sooty Shearwater	*Ardenna grisea*	North Ronaldsay, Orkney
Manx Shearwater	*Puffinux puffinus*	
Little Grebe	*Tachybaptus ruficollis*	
Red-necked Grebe	*Podiceps grisegena*	
Great-crested Grebe	*Podiceps cristatus*	
Slavonian Grebe	*Podiceps auritus*	
Black-necked Grebe	*Podiceps nigricollis*	
Glossy Ibis	*Plagadis falcinellus*	Shapwick, Somerset, Pett Levels, East Sussex and North Ronaldsay, Orkney
Spoonbill	*Platea leucorodia*	
Bittern	*Botaurus stellaris*	
Little Bittern	*Ixobrychus minutus*	Old Moor RSPB reserveYorks
Cattle Egret	*Bubulcus ibis*	Mudgley, Somerset
Grey Heron	*Ardea cinerea*	
Purple Heron	*Ardea purpurea*	Minsmere RSPB, Suffolk
Great White Egret	*Ardea alba*	
Little Egret	*Egretta garzetta*	
Gannet	*Morus bassanus*	
Shag	*Phalacrocorax aristotelis*	
Cormorant	*Phalacrocorax carbo*	
Osprey	*Pandion haliaetus*	
Golden Eagle	*Aquila chrysaetos*	Mull, Scotland
Marsh Harrier	*Circus aeruginosus*	
Hen Harrier	*Circus cyaneus*	
Northern Harrier	*Circus hudsonius*	North Ronaldsay, Orkney
Pallid Harrier	*Circus macrourus*	nr Welwick, Humberside
Montagu's Harrier	*Circus pygargus*	Norfolk
Red Kite	*Milvus milvus*	
White-tailed Eagle	*Haliaeetus albicilla*	Mull, Scotland
Rough-legged Buzzard	*Buteo lagopus*	Choseley Barns, Norfolk
Buzzard	*Buteo buteo*	
Water Rail	*Rallus aquaticus*	
Corncrake	*Crex crex*	Coll, Hebrides
Moorhen	*Gallinula chloropus*	
Coot	*Fulica atra*	
Crane	*Grus grus*	Ouse Washes RSPB, Cambs
Stone Curlew	*Burhinus oedicnemus*	Wheeting Heath Norfolk Wildlife Trust reserve
Oystercatcher	*Haematopus ostralegus*	
Black-winged Stilt	*Himantopus himantopus*	Cliffe Pools RSPB, Kent
Avocet	*Recurvirostra avosetta*	

Lapwing	*Vanellus vanellus*	
Golden Plover	*Pluvialis apricaria*	
Grey Plover	*Pluvialis squatarola*	
Ringed Plover	*Charadrius hiaticula*	
Little Ringed Plover	*Charadrius dubius*	
Dotterel	*Charadrius morinellus*	
Whimbrel	*Munenius phaeopus*	
Curlew	*Numenius arquata*	
Bar-tailed Godwit	*Limosa lapponica*	
Black-tailed Godwit	*Limosa limosa*	
Turnstone	*Arenaria interpres*	
Knot	*Calidris canutus*	
Ruff	*Calidris pugnax*	
Broad-billed Sandpiper	*Calidris falcinellus*	Frampton RSPB, Lincs
Curlew Sandpiper	*Calidris ferruginea*	
Temminck's Stint	*Calidris temminckii*	
Sanderling	*Calidris alba*	
Dunlin	*Calidris alpina*	
Purple Sandpiper	*Calidris maritima*	
Little Stint	*Calidris minuta*	
Buff-breasted Sandpiper	*Calidris subruficollis*	nr Dunrossness, Shetland
Long-billed Dowitcher	*Limnodromus scolopaceus*	Farlington Marsh, Hants
Woodcock	*Scolopax rusticola*	
Jack Snipe	*Lymnocryptes minimus*	
Great Snipe	*Gallinago media*	Fair Isle
Snipe	*Gallinago gallinago*	
Red-necked Phalarope	*Phalaropus lobatus*	Blacktofts Sands RSPB
Grey Phalarope	*Phalaropus fulicarius*	Slimbridge WWT, Glos
Common Sandpiper	*Actitis hypoleucos*	
Green Sandpiper	*Tringa ochropus*	
Redshank	*Tringa totanus*	
Wood Sandpiper	*Tringa glareola*	
Spotted Redshank	*Tringa erythropus*	
Greenshank	*Tringa nebularia*	
Greater Yellowlegs	*Tringa Melanoleuca*	Whippingham, IOW
Kittiwake	*Rissa tridactyla*	
Bonaparte's Gull	*Chroicocephalus philadelphia*	Wansbeck Estuary, Northumberland
Black-headed Gull	*Chroicocephalus ridibundus*	
Little Gull	*Hydrocoloeus minutus*	
Franklin's Gull	*Leucophaeus pipixcan*	Abberton Reservoir, Essex
Mediterranean Gull	*Ichthyaetus melanocephalus*	
Common Gull	*Larus canus*	
Ring-billed Gull	*Larus delawarensis*	Ennestrevan Farm, Cornwall
Great Black-backed Gull	*Larus marinus*	
Glaucous Gull	*Larus hyperboreus*	Marazion & Newlyn Harbour, Cornwall
Herring Gull	*Larus argentatus*	
Caspian Gull	*Larus cachinnans*	Blashford Lakes, Hants
Yellow-legged Gull	*Larus michahellis*	
Lesser Black-backed Gull	*Larus fuscus*	
Sandwich Tern	*Thalasseus sandvicensis*	
Little Tern	*Sternula albifrons*	

Roseate Tern	*Sterna dougallii*	opp. Coquet Island RSPB
Common Tern	*Sterna hirundo*	
Arctic Tern	*Sterna paradisaea*	
Black Tern	*Chlidonias niger*	Alton Water, Suffolk
White-winged Black Tern	*Chlidonias leucopterus*	Eldernell, Cambridgeshire
Great Skua	*Stercorarius skua*	
Pomarine Skua	*Stercocarius pomarinus*	North Ronaldsay, Orkney
Arctic Skua	*Stercorarius parasiticus*	
Little Auk	*Alle alle*	North Ronaldsay, Orkney
Common Guillemot	*Uria aalge*	
Razorbill	*Alca torda*	
Black Guillemot	*Cepphus grylle*	
Puffin	*Fratercula arctica*	
Rock Dove	*Columba livia*	
Stock Dove	*Columba oenas*	
Woodpigeon	*Columba palumbus*	
Turtle Dove	*Streptopelia turtur*	
Oriental Turtle Dove	*Streptopelia orientalis*	Otford, Kent
Collared Dove	*Streptopelia decaocto*	
Cuckoo	*Cuculus canorus*	
Barn Owl	*Tyto alba*	
Tawny Owl	*Strix aluco*	
Little Owl	*Athene noctua*	
Long-eared Owl	*Asio otus*	Saltholme RSPB & North Ronaldsay, Orkney
Short-eared Owl	*Asio flammeus*	
Nightjar	*Caprimulgus europaeus*	
Swift	*Apus apus*	
Kingfisher	*Alcedo atthis*	
Bee-eater	*Merops apiaster*	Spurn Point, Yorkshire
Hoopoe	*Upupa epops*	Wall Heath, Staffs & Holme, Norfolk
Wryneck	*Jynx torquilla*	North Ronaldsay, Orkney
Lesser Spotted Woodpecker	*Dryobates minor*	New Forest
Great Spotted Woodpecker	*Dendrocopos major*	
Green Woodpecker	*Picus viridis*	
Kestrel	*Falco tinnunculus*	
Merlin	*Falco columbarius*	
Hobby	*Falco subbuteo*	
Peregrine	*Falco peregrinus*	
Ring-necked Parakeet	*Psittacua krameri*	
Red-backed Shrike	*Lanius collurio*	
Great Grey Shrike	*Lanius excubitor*	
Goldon Oriole	*Oriolus oriolus*	
Jay	*Garrulus glandarius*	
Magpie	*Pica pica*	
Chough	*Pyrrhocorax pyyrhocorax*	
Jackdaw	*Coloeus monedula*	
Rook	*Corvus frugilegus*	
Carrion Crow	*Corvus corone*	
Hooded Crow	*Corvus cornix*	
Raven	*Corvus corax*	
Waxwing	*Bombycilla garrulus*	Fair Isle & Thorntonloch

Coal Tit	*Periparus ater*	
Crested Tit	*Lophophanes cristatus*	
Marsh Tit	*Poecile palustris*	
Willow Tit	*Poecile montanus*	
Blue Tit	*Cyanistes caeruleus*	
Great Tit	*Parus major*	
Penduline Tit	*Remiz pendulinus*	Titchfield Haven, Hants
Bearded Tit	*Panurus biarmicus*	
Woodlark	*Lullula arborea*	
Skylark	*Alauda arvensis*	
Short-toed Lark	*Calandrella brachydactyla*	
Sand Martin	*Riparia riparia*	
Swallow	*Hirundo rustica*	
House Martin	*Delichon urbicum*	
Cetti's Warbler	*Cettia cetti*	
Long-tailed Tit	*Aegithalos caudatus*	
Willow Warbler	*Phylloscopus trochilus*	
Chiffchaff	*Phylloscopus collybita*	
Iberian Chiffchaff	*Phylloscopus ibericus*	Margate, Kent
Wood Warbler	*Phylloscopus sibilatrix*	
Dusky Warbler	*Phylloscopus fuscatus*	Ham Wall RSPB, Somerset
Radde's Warbler	*Phylloscopus schwarzi*	Fair Isle
Yellow-browed Warbler	*Phylloscopus inornatus*	Fair Isle
Arctic Warbler	*Phylloscopus borealis*	Geosetter, Shetland & Fair Isle
Greenish Warbler	*Phylloscopus trochiloides*	Lowestoft, Suffolk; North Ronaldsay, Orkey & Fair Isle
Great Reed Warbler	*Acrocephalus arundinaceus*	Paxton Pits, Cambridgeshire
Sedge Warbler	*Acrocephalus schoenobaenus*	
Paddyfield Warbler	*Acrocephalus agricola*	Fair Isle
Blyth's Reed Warbler	*Acrocephalus dumetorum*	Fair Isle
Reed Warbler	*Acrocephalus scirpaceus*	Fair Isle
Marsh Warbler	*Acrocephalus palustris*	North Ronaldsay
Booted Warbler	*Iduna caligulata*	Fair Isle
Icterine Warbler	*Hippolais icterina*	Fair Isle
Grasshopper Warbler	*Locustella naevia*	
Savi's Warbler	*Locustella luscinioides*	Minsmere RSPB, Suffolk
Lanceolated Warbler	*Locustella lanceolata*	Fair Isle
Blackcap	*Sylvia atricapilla*	
Garden Warbler	*Sylvia borin*	
Barred Warbler	*Sylvia nisoria*	North Ronaldsay, Orkney & Fair Isle
Lesser Whitethroat	*Sylvia curruca*	
Whitethroat	*Sylvia communis*	
Dartford Warbler	*Sylvia undata*	
Firecrest	*Regulus ignicapilla*	Penzance & Stithians Reservoir, Cornwall
Goldcrest	*Regulus regulus*	
Wren	*Troglodytes troglodytes*	
Nuthatch	*Sitta europaea*	
Treecreeper	*Certhia familiaris*	
Rose-coloured Starling	*Pastor roseus*	Lizard, Cornwall & Fair Isle
Starling	*Sturnus vulgaris*	
Ring Ouzel	*Turdus torquatus*	

Blackbird	*Turdus merula*	
Dusky Thrush	*Turdus eunomus*	Beeley, Derbyshire
Fieldfare	*Turdus pilaris*	
Redwing	*Turdus iliacus*	
Song Thrush	*Turdus philomelos*	
Mistle Thrush	*Turdus viscivorus*	
Spotted Flycatcher	*Muscicapa striata*	
Robin	*Erithacus rubecula*	
Bluethroat	*Luscinia svecica*	Fair Isle
Nightingale	*Luscinia megarhynchos*	
Red-flanked Bluetail	*Tarsiger cyanurus*	Fair Isle
Pied Flycatcher	*Ficedula hypoleuca*	
Red-breasted Flycatcher	*Ficedula parva*	Fair Isle
Black Redstart	*Phoenicurus ochruros*	
Redstart	*Phoenicurus phoenicurus*	
Blue Rock Thrush	*Monticola solitarius*	Stow-On-The-Wold, Glos,
Whinchat	*Saxicola rubetra*	
Stonechat	*Saxicola rubicola*	
Siberian Stonechat	*Saxicola maurus*	Fair Isle
Wheatear	*Oenanthe oenanthe*	
Isabelline Wheatear	*Oenanthe isabellina*	nr Loch of Spiggie, Shetland
Pied Wheatear	*Oenanthe pleschanka*	Scatness, Shetland
Dipper	*Cinclus cinclus*	
House Sparrow	*Passer domesticus*	
Tree Sparrow	*Passer montanus*	
Siberian Accentor	*Prunella montanella*	Fair Isle
Dunnock	*Prunella modularis*	
Yellow Wagtail	*Motacilla flava*	
Citrine Wagtail	*Motacilla citreola*	Fair Isle
Grey Wagtail	*Motacilla cinerea*	
Pied Wagtail	*Motacilla alba*	
Richard's Pipit	*Anthus richardi*	North Landing, Flamborough
Meadow Pipit	*Anthus pratensis*	
Tree Pipit	*Anthus trivialis*	
Olive-backed Pipit	*Anthus hodgsonii*	Fair Isle
Pechora Pipit	*Anthus gustavi*	Fair Isle
Red-throated Pipit	*Anthus cervinus*	Fair Isle
Water Pipit	*Anthus spinoletta*	
Rock Pipit	*Anthus petrosus*	
Chaffinch	*Fringilla coelebs*	
Brambling	*Fringilla montifringilla*	
Hawfinch	*Coccothraustes coccothraustes*	New Forest & Fair Isle
Bullfinch	*Pyrrhula pyrrhula*	
Common Rosefinch	*Carpodacus erythrinus*	Fair Isle
Greenfinch	*Chloris chloris*	
Twite	*Linaria flavirostris*	
Linnet	*Linaria cannabinna*	
Common Redpoll	*Acanthis flammea*	
Lesser Redpoll	*Acanthus caberet*	
Arctic Redpoll	*Acanthus hornemanni*	
Crossbill	*Loxia curvirostra*	
Goldfinch	*Carduelis carduelis*	
Siskin	*Spinus spinus*	

Corn Bunting	*Emberiza calandra*	
Yellowhammer	Emberiza citrinella	
Pine Bunting	*Emberiza leucocephalus*	Fair Isle
Ortolan Bunting	*Emberiza hortulana*	Fair Isle
Cirl Bunting	*Emberiza cirlus*	
Little Bunting	*Emberiza pusilla*	Fair Isle
Black-faced Bunting	*Emberiza spodocephala*	Bressay, Shetland
Reed Bunting	*Emberiza schoeniclus*	
Lapland Bunting	*Calcarius lapponicus*	
Snow Bunting	*Plectrophenax nivalis*	

Birds revised – January 1st 2018 BOU :

Fea's/Zino's Petrel	*Pterodroma feae*	North Ronaldsay, Orkney
Hudsonian Whimbrel	*Numenius phaeopus*	Marazion, Cornwall

Both are now treated as sub-species.

Champions of The Flyways

March 2017

Annually, in late March, as part of the Eilat Birdwatching, the Champions of The Flyways event takes place. Champions of the Flyway, COTF, is a twenty four hour bird race, which raises money for bird conservation, led by the Israel Ornithological Center and Birdlife International. The COTF race takes place in the unparalleled migration hotspot of Eilat, Israel.

In such a troubled and complex part of the world, an event that brings together not just birders from around the globe but also Palestinians and Israelis, is vitally important. There are those who vehemently disagree with the event but I see it in the same vein as the incredible Peace Marches by thousands of Israeli and Palestinian women. Bring people together, not divide them.

The COTF is a wall and barrier breaker in many ways. It is a fund raising event that seeks to prevent the illegal killing of millions of birds along the Flyway. With no regard to political and other boundaries, the funds raised go to where they are needed most. It is a meeting point between birders from different countries and birding cultures. A major event that introduces birders and nature conservationists, from places and backgrounds that are in need of help and support, be that technical, financial or even just recognition, to other conservation and birding organizations that can give them a hand. It is friendly, family-like and it is open for all.

The Palestine Wildlife Society, Mahmiyat.ps, and Palestinian individual birders, not only chose to take part in this event year after year but do so within a joint Palestinian-Israeli team. This participation came naturally to them. Yes, Palestinians participate despite the occupation and all are looking forward to Palestinian independence but until then, all participating birders appreciate our help and friendship. All keep their passion for nature conservation higher than their political struggles and thoughts. Participation for Palestinians means global recognition in a Palestinian independent conservation effort and this brings all sorts of help from BirdLife partners, such as community renovated optics from the Netherlands. The equipment from other partners and all international connections bring many benefits that we Palestinians will most surely use whenever the need arises.

Noam Weiss, Director
International Birding and Research center, Eilat
Israeli Ornithological Center
Society for The Protection of Nature in Israel

A decision to participate in an event that brings people together, within a political polemic of long standing conflict, is not one that can be taken

lightly. Yet the cause is so vital in other ways to the political, humanitarian one. Twenty five million birds are slaughtered each year in the Mediterranean region and the tens of thousands of dollars raised each year by COTF and given to a different Birdlife International country promotes conservation with masses of people.
Jonathan Meyrav, one of the main organisers, is a phenomenal character. His drive, energy and passion is exemplary. His love of family, friends and nature is without doubt a major reason why birders come to COTF. Another is Yoav Periman, who states :

I first met Gary at 2016 Norfolk Birdfair. We had a good conversation in which I told him about COTF. Gary got hooked on the idea, and a year later – he has a team! It's a special team because it's one of the few green teams in the race – Gary and his young intrepid teammates from Orkney will cycle through the playing field of southern Israel.

Let the team members tell you their thoughts on the event and what transpired . . .

Erin Taylor

Champions of the Flyways taught me a lot. Not only did I see thirty one bird species on the first day that I had never seen before but I also discovered how angry I can get when hungry and hot! This event was not only a chance to visit a new, and having been, incredible country but also to go birding and be recognised on an international level. Being a young female birder in the UK, the kind of friendship, camaraderie and willingness to share ideas at COTF was perhaps not a novel experience but it was one that was unanticipated and greatly appreciated.

When we formed our team on North Ronaldsay, none of us really knew what to expect. We all wanted to see some new birds and new places. To be honest it seemed a bit mad to travel to a desert to cycle around an unknown landscape and compete with some of the best birders in the world. . . birders who were traveling with cars. One consolation we had was that we had a green message, one that we are all very proud of and want to share with the world.

George Gay

It was back in August 2016 on North Ronaldsay and Gary had returned to the island for the second year running to the delight of me and Samuel who had spent time with him the previous year.

With all of us behind Gary in the pursuit of his Biking Birder goal we all asked what next? A plan was hatched between me, Gary, Erin and Samuel that we should attend the Champions of the Flyway in Eilat, Israel and be the first International Green team. Having Gary head up the team was an honour. It's not every day the European Green Birding champion ask you to be on his team!

With all the hard work, planning and fund-raising done it was time to head to

Israel. Scouting was hard work, especially for me, Samuel and Erin. We never need to cycle more than four miles at a time on North Ronaldsay! By the time race day came we felt ready! We knew we could reach our pre-set goal of 100 birds!

The race was hard but we excelled even finding a couple of rarer species on race-day, the highlight of which was probably a Robin in Canada Park at 4 a.m!

Race day passed, we found 122 bird species and it was time for the ceremony. We weren't expecting anything so to be called up and given a trophy as Green Champions was unbelievable. The whole trip was a privilege. Being part of Gary's team, birding an amazing country with three close friends, seeing birds you look at in books and dream of; even meeting some of the birders that wrote those books. All were remarkable. I would say it was once in lifetime experience but we plan to defend our title next year and reliving the experience will be just as special a second time around. All that's left is to say Thank you to Gary for making it all possible!

Samuel Perfect

It was as I imagined the old days of birding to be like. The five of us were crammed into a flat which we turned into our base. The place had been turned into a campsite with food, clothes, and optics strewn everywhere and most importantly we were there for the birding and that made it excellent!

I find it fascinating hearing the old stories from when birds used to be commoner and listen to them with a good measure of jealousy. However, on this occasion it felt to me as though we were all given the opportunity to relive the past and see how awesome the birding scene used to be.

My early birding experiences have a rather humble beginning, starting with garden and farmland birds which I encountered around my home in Kent where I grew up as a child. Here, seeing Kestrel and a Sparrowhawk chasing and tackling a pigeon to the ground in my back garden fired up a lifelong admiration for birds. Nevertheless, a big grin of near disbelief crosses my face when I think of the places this simple hobby has led me and the people I have met along the way. So, when Gary Prescott, Rebecca Prescott, Erin Taylor, George Gay and I boarded a plane at Heathrow bound for Israel it became quite apparent how far we were willing to go for a bunch of feathers!

On arrival, we could hardly contain our excitement. Mountain Gazelles running off the airstrip as we came into land, Brown-necked Ravens circling above, Spotted Sandgrouse flew over as we taxied to a halt, and White-eyed Bulbuls perched in the palm trees above us as we walked into the airport terminal. In fact, our frantic pointing and peering around drew the attention of security, so much so that we were called aside to explain our antics. Only then did it hit us, we were standing in a country ravaged by war, we had to be more cautious what we did or said. Regardless, Gary ignored all the serious etiquette of airport security in Israel and explained at the top of his voice with an immense degree of pride our mission to participate in the Champions of the Flyway 2017. With heart rates risen somewhat we finally passed through customs and once again began our frantic pointing and calling "more White-spectacled Bulbuls!", "look, White Wagtail, a trip tick!"... We later came to realise how special the event was in its ability to peacefully draw together people from across the world, even those suffering conflict.

Throughout the following week we were treated to some world-class birding. From our flat balcony alone we experienced thousands of migrating Steppe Buzzards, and hundreds of eagles including Steppe, Booted and Short-toed. We were awoken by the calls of House Crows, and Laughing Doves, as well as the loud and lively hustle and bustle of city living.

It was our ambition to compete in the event by "green" birding methods only, so in the week leading up to the race and the during race itself we found ourselves exploring the "playing field" of southern Israel entirely by bike or foot. This proved to be immensely successful. Not only were we spending the entire day in the field, wasting no time sat in a car traveling between sites, but we also gained a greater appreciation of our surroundings. We familiarised ourselves with the endless supply of sights and sounds of the wildlife around us, including Bluethroats scuttling about in the crop fields, chancing upon stunning male Pallid Harriers, screeching to a halt to admire Little Green Bee-eaters, and Pied Kingfishers eking out a living beside the canal. Even indulging in some fruits growing beside the track, all of which could not have been as enjoyable from the back seat of a car.

The entire week was spent solely scouting Eilat and the immediate area by bike. We worked well together as a team, finding some quality species, taking some brilliant pictures and even getting a few opportunities to observe close up a few species in the hand (we felt like kids in a playground with something for everyone). Being on bikes also encouraged us to venture off-course, explore parts of the countryside ourselves and revel in our own personal highlights. However, a quick shout from any one of us and we'd all come running, as sharing the best birds with one another was the most rewarding experience. Gary was an immense inspiration and role model, striking up some brilliant friendships with other competitors, many of whom were renowned experts in their respective fields including field guide authors, conservationists, artists, event hosts and many more.

I would like to take the opportunity to thank Gary Prescott for his incredible support and enthusiasm, many awesome birding moments, moral guidance and the opportunity to see what futures can lie ahead of us. And finally, congratulations on achieving the British Green Birding Year record!!!

We won! What a surprise. Was it just coincidence that the carbon team of birders from Finland, the mighty and seemingly unbeatable Arctic Redpolls were sitting with us at the awards ceremony morning breakfast? They won the main title, Champions of The Flyways having seen an incredible and proudly received their golden trophy, so well deserved. Other teams won different categories; Guardians of The Flyways, the team that raised the most money and Knights of The Flyways, the team that did the most to promote the cause and birding.

Then Jonathan surprised everyone by announcing a new category trophy, a Green Birding trophy. I think we all sat there not expecting us to be the winners; after all Israeli and joint Israeli – Palestinian Green teams had taken part but suddenly the winners were announced and we were up on stage to receive the first ever COTF – Green Birding winners trophy. So proud of the three youngsters, the time on stage included speeches that brought tears to the eyes of those present. Yet a young, confident girl summed it up months later when the event video, now to be seen on Youtube, was premiered at Rutland's Birdfair in August of 2017. Erin spoke from her bike, sitting in the heat seconds after Kentish Plover had been added to our growing list and said . . .

" We've got a bit of a Green message I guess, trying to prove that you can do just as much birding through Green methods as you can through driving a car all over the place."

Erin's smile, laugh and obvious pleasure accentuates what we all feel. Green Birding is a wonderful way to enjoy birding.

Do not go gentle into that good night
Don't succumb to the peaceful release of death.
Old age should burn and rave at close of day;
Rage, rage against the dying of the light.